# How To Cope With COPE

# How To Cope With
# COPE

*The Political Operations of*
*Organized Labor*

BY

## TERRY CATCHPOLE

### ARLINGTON HOUSE

NEW ROCHELLE      NEW YORK

*For The Family*

# Acknowledgments

A number of very special individuals have earned the author's warmest gratitude for having helped this book along its detailed, tortuous and somewhat extended way. At Arlington House, the initial confidence and lasting faith in the project of publisher Neil McCaffrey, and the insights and care of editor Theodore Lit, were essential in the conception and execution of the book. The cooperation of many public officials and political aides has been appreciated in gathering research; particular gratitude in this area is also due those persons in organized labor, including COPE, who freely provided valuable information and materials, knowing all the while the nature of the project. Then came the indispensable assistance of my typists, especially Dawne Cina and Helen Souder, and for her typing and much, much more, there is Catherine. The final and deepest debt of gratitude goes to the three co-owners of *Human Events:* Publisher Bob Kephart, Editor Tom Winter and Capitol Hill Editor Allan Ryskind; their combined and individual encouragement, support and assistance made this book possible.

T.C.

# Contents

# How To Cope With COPE

# Dead Aim on 1968

NOTHING better characterizes the thoroughness and dedication with which the AFL-CIO Committee on Political Education applies itself to its task than the eight words occupying the cover of its bi-weekly publication, "Memo From COPE," in the first issue after the 1966 elections: "The Time To Start for '68 is *Now*."

These eight words clearly show that for COPE political action is not a once-every-two (or four)-year job, to be practiced only when a major election looms. Unlike most so-called "political action" organizations independent of the two parties, COPE's efforts comprise an all-day, year-round devotion to the basic goal of winning electoral victories for organized labor's friends.

COPE campaigns in city and municipal elections held on odd-years. COPE works as hard in off-year congressional campaigns as it does in presidential-year contests. When it is not campaigning somewhere, COPE is out registering voters, distributing propaganda, or plotting new political strategies. Labor's political machine is kept in tune through constant use.

Back in the odd-year of 1957, COPE's then director James McDevitt described this organizational diligence in these words:

"The folks on the sixth floor of the AFL-CIO building who constitute the staff of COPE are pretty friendly and cooperative people with generally jolly dispositions. About the only way you can get a frown from any of them is to say: 'What are you all so busy about? Isn't this an off-year?' It's like asking a frontline infantry soldier: 'Don't you know there's a war on?' "[1]

And this attitude is not limited to COPE's headquarters staff. Through repetitious propaganda constituting an almost daily call to arms, labor's political field troops are kept always at the ready, always working. "Keep in mind," COPE tells the rank-and-file in its *How To Win* handbook of practical politics, "that what you're beginning will take time and effort—a lot of both—because effective political education and action is a year-round job."

Such dedication to duty has resulted in what labor columnist Victor Riesel has called "the smoothest political machine in the land." Senator Barry Goldwater, who has faced labor opposition in all his campaigns, thinks COPE is "the best political organization I have seen."

Political observers holding similar views of COPE may have had some room for doubt following the 1966 congressional voting, and this brings up a second remarkable aspect of COPE's eight-word headline directive. The '66 elections had been a decisive defeat for organized labor, with its bloc of pro-labor congressmen being sizably reduced, yet here was COPE telling the rank-and-file to get to work for 1968 "now."

As COPE views political action, the only way to make progress is to leave the past behind and get to work on the future today. Its leaders viewed the '66 losses as only a temporary setback, and for them to think otherwise would be suicidal; after all, the elections represented COPE's first strikeout in six campaigns and its previous record of success is imposing. As Dodger fans used to say around Ebbets Field in Brooklyn, "Wait 'til next year; it'll be a new ballgame."

COPE's own comment on the election results was terse and to the point: "For liberals, the statistics of 1966 are appalling." As labor union leaders watched the congressional election returns trickle in on the evening of November 3, 1966, they did not like the picture forming before them. When their newspapers next morning confirmed the sweeping victories scored by conservatives and Republicans, they knew they didn't like it. They were, in fact, "appalled."

Labor's loss was decisive and extensive, stretching from the cold reaches of upstate New Hampshire, where freshman liberal Rep. J. Oliva Huot (D) lost to a conservative Republican, to the warm sunny clime of southern California, where freshman liberal Ken Dyal went down in defeat before a GOP conservative. Buried among the ruins of the Republican landslide were such long-time champions of the labor cause as Governor Edmund "Pat" Brown of California, Senator Paul Douglas of Illinois, and Michigan's senatorial candidate, G. Mennen "Soapy" Williams.

And at the same time these labor favorites were being rejected at the polls, such point-blank targets of labor campaigns as Carl Curtis of Nebraska, John Tower of Texas, Jack Miller of Iowa, John Ashbrook of Ohio and Joel Broyhill of Virginia were scoring easy victories with large pluralities.

Defeat after labor defeat rolled in on Election Eve, 1966, and the number of high-powered, pro-labor names among the victims was impressive. Far more significant were the "appalling statistics" COPE spoke of in its post-election "Memo," for these numbers represent the sheer losses suffered in terms of congressional power. Among the more "appalling":

* 152 out of the 333 candidates COPE had formally endorsed for the House of Representatives went down in defeat;
* 13 of the 22 Senate candidates backed by COPE were rejected by the voters;
* In the Senate, COPE lost two members—Douglas of Illinois and Maurine Neuberger of Oregon, who retired—who had COPE ratings of 100 per cent perfect "pro-labor," while another—Ross Bass of Tennessee, who was defeated in a primary—had an 83 per cent rating;
* In House contests, 36 incumbent representatives with a COPE rating of 75 per cent or higher were defeated, including nine members (Rivers, Alaska; Senner, Arizona; Dyal, California; Bandstra and Schmidhauser, Iowa; Mackie and Clevenger, Michigan; Huot, New Hampshire; McGrath, New Jersey) who had chalked up perfect ratings in the 89th Congress;
* 33 Representatives who had voted for repeal of Section 14(b) of Taft-Hartley, labor's Number One issue of the 89th Congress, were not returned to Congress;
* 30 of the 59 liberal incumbent House members running in so-called marginal districts, which COPE listed as "make-or-break" contests in the summer of 1966, were defeated;
* COPE lost such staunch friends as Representatives Bob Duncan (D-Ore.) and Teno Roncalio (D-Wyo.) when they tried to "step up" and run for the Senate; four other representatives with a perfect 100 per cent COPE stamp of approval did not even make it to the November elections, having either retired or lost in primaries.

Labor's most injurious—not to mention most "appalling"—setbacks occurred in races for the House of Representatives, where the labor bloc previously held a solid majority of 230 plus; for the 90th Congress, labor could count on no more than 190 "certain" votes. Large as these reversals may have been, the more dramatic blows to the labor political machine came in gubernatorial and senatorial races in the states of California, Michigan and Illinois. Here is where the big names fought it out in crucial, tight races, on which hung the prestige of both labor and its opponents.

California's Republican gubernatorial candidate, Ronald Reagan, was the closest thing there was to a Number One labor target in 1966. The effort against Reagan was concentrated, intense and well-heeled, representing an unprecedented united California labor campaign against a single candidate.

COPE's propaganda battery was trained on the handsome former actor almost from the moment he declared his candidacy, and it was a rare issue of the "Political Memo" which did not contain at least one barb thrown his way; one entire issue of the "Memo," in fact, was devoted to the purported tale of "How Reagan Rode Right-Wing Issues To Political Stardom." Labor's purse-strings were elasticized for Pat Brown's benefit; in the last days of the campaign, it is reported, national AFL-CIO hotlined $75,000 to Brown's faltering effort, and—in sum— unions contributed an estimated $1.5 million to the Brown bankroll.

From the upper councils of the AFL-CIO, president George Meany dispatched a top-level team of advisors, consisting of five federation vice-presidents, to California to help direct the Brown candidacy. And among Golden State unions, the usually warring Machinists, Teamsters and Longshoremen buried their differences temporarily and came out swinging in unison against the Reagan drive.

But, on election day, "Little David" Reagan smashed this imposing labor Goliath with a stunning victory of close to one million sunkissed votes.

Labor's diligent effort to re-elect long-time friend and champion Senator Paul Douglas in his fight against GOP liberal Charles Percy was remarkably like that waged in California's gubernatorial donnybrook: Meany named another blue-ribbon, four-man team of AFL-CIO vice-presidents to advise the Democrat-liberal candidate, and the federation threw $75,000 Douglas' way in the closing moments of his race. Also, the efforts of individual unions on behalf of the white-maned, hulking Douglas were considerable, with the United Auto Workers donating over $5,000 from its treasuries and running a full-page paean to the "Giant from Illinois" in the March 1966 issue of its publication, *Solidarity*.

With the labor forces arrayed against him—despite his own affirmed liberalism and pro-labor position—Chuck Percy won a sweeping victory, in the process cutting Douglas' plurality in the union stronghold of Chicago by 336,000 votes over the incumbent's margin in his last campaign in 1960.

If there was one single most stunning labor loss out of the avalanche of defeat, it came in the Michigan senatorial race, where G. Mennen "Soapy" Williams lost to the interim Republican incumbent, Robert Griffin—appointed by Governor George Romney to fill out the term of the late Pat McNamara—by 200,000 votes.

Michigan's Democratic Party has been ruled for two decades by organized labor, and "Soapy" Williams has always been the rulers' fair-haired knight in shining armor. Back in 1948, when the labor forces under the firm hands of Walter Reuther and Gus Scholle, heads of the UAW and state CIO respectively, solidified their control over the state

Democrats, they selected the liberal Williams as their gubernatorial candidate.

Williams took the statehouse from the GOP that year and went on to serve a full six terms in Lansing as the liberal-labor juggernaut increased in size, effectiveness and power, providing its gubernatorial frontman with larger-and-larger pluralities. In 1960 Williams stepped down to accept President Kennedy's appointment as assistant secretary of state for African affairs, a diplomatic plum which many political commentators thought was, at least in part, JFK's way of repaying labor for its dedicated effort on his behalf in the '60 campaign.

No sooner had Williams left, however, than the Republicans recaptured the Michigan statehouse behind former auto salesman George Romney, who won a repeat victory in 1964 and appeared headed for a landslide re-election in '66. To hold down the Romney tide and keep the GOP from sweeping in the Senate seat along the way, the Reuther-Scholle combine persuaded Williams to leave the Dark Continent and return to the Motor State to take the lead in creating the hoped-for labor renaissance.

It was a foregone conclusion that labor would be behind Williams all the way (a fact that led the ex-governor's primary opponent, Detroit Mayor Jerry Cavanagh, to ask, "Has the mighty labor movement which found its true greatness in this state fallen to so little measure that it must play with a stacked deck?"[2]), and when his opponent turned out to be former Representative Robert Griffin, labor's effort was even more intense. The hostility of Messrs. Scholle and Reuther to Senator Griffin was understandable, in view of the fact that when he was in the House, Griffin had had the audacity to co-sponsor a bill—the Landrum-Griffin Labor Management Act of 1959—which went so far as to police corruption and dishonesty in union affairs. With this in Griffin's background, labor prepared a vigorous campaign to win one more for "Soapy."

Rank-and-filers were reminded in union publications that "just about everyone in Michigan benefits today from laws first proposed, then fought bitterly hard for, and finally won by the man who served 12 years as a Democratic Governor . . ." Rather than tell the workingmen "Soapy" also left the state in virtual bankruptcy, the labor leaders boasted that "Soapy Williams is a giant of a public servant who'll be a giant of a senator."[3] Meanwhile GOP opponent Griffin was attacked by Williams as "anti-labor, anti-progress, anti-city and anti-people," his record was constantly distorted by the labor press (which smeared him as "Senator No") and he was the target of occasional physical abuse from emotional unionists.

And always there was the concentrated attack on the Landrum-Griffin

Act, with Williams and most of his labor bosses calling it simply "anti-labor," and Teamsters' chieftain Jimmy Hoffa (who also backed "Soapy") going a bit further and calling it "the worst piece of labor legislation ever passed in the United States." It was just this voluble assault on the law he helped write, however, that probably did the most to help Griffin win the race. All he did was point out the true meaning of the act, and how it protected the rank-and-file from corrupt officers; then, Griffin noted, not only did John F. Kennedy and Lyndon Johnson vote for the act in 1959, but so did Michigan's two supposedly pro-labor senators at the time (McNamara and Phil Hart) and most of the rest of the Senate—it had passed the upper body 95-2 and the House by an equally overwhelming 352-52.

With these items on the record, Williams was forced to admit that had he been a senator at the time he probably would have voted for Landrum-Griffin himself. When the Scholle-Reuther gaffe of trying to pin the whole campaign on this one bogus issue hit the light of day, and when the rank-and-filers realized the magnitude of the lies their supposed leaders had been feeding them, there was nothing that could salvage the floundering Williams campaign.

As the votes rolled in on election eve, Walter Reuther and Gus Scholle found they could not always push the button on the labor political machine and produce automated, neatly packaged victories. In sweeping the state, Senator Griffin racked up an estimated 43 percent of the union vote, carrying the top-heavy labor city of Flint and gaining an imposing 45 percent in the UAW stronghold of Wayne County (Detroit).

Michigan politicos offered sharp and acerbic assessments of labor's political activities of 1966, with Democratic deputy state attorney general Leon Cohan summing up the comments by observing, "The [Democratic] party and COPE organizations just don't get the troops out. Besides, their methods were archaic in this electronic age."[4]

In Michigan, as in other areas of the country and on a national level, the labor political forces had cause to reassess their strategy in view of the 1966 electoral results. They were to study hard the lessons these contests taught them and apply them to future campaigns. This in no way means, of course, that these studies will slow the preparations for the coming contests.

COPE led the charge into the 1968 battle with its war cry: "The Time To Start for '68 Is *Now*," and the political organizations in Michigan, as in every state and community, will follow this lead. After listing all those "appalling statistics" the '66 voting produced, COPE was able to wrap up its election summary by admonishing that "the key lesson, though, is that there can be no letup in politics, and that the 1968 elections started the day the 1966 elections ended. If that lesson has been learned well by liberal forces, we can look for a comeback next time."

There can be no doubt that even though the '66 outcome was a blow to labor, its political strategists found good reason to be optimistic, primarily since this was COPE's first meaningful defeat in ten years. What must have galled the COPE leaders the most about the disastrous election results was their coming on the heels of labor's most mighty campaign effort in some time: "We raised more money, put more workers into the field and made more contacts than ever," said COPE national director Al Barkan shortly after the '66 voting.[5]

COPE did its homework and laid its groundwork well in preparation for these elections, including the inauguration of such new projects as computerized checks on voter registration. Campaign bankrolls were funded by national COPE to the tune of close to $1 million, the propaganda mills worked overtime grinding out the stuff to convince wavering rank-and-filers, and truckloads of midnight oil were trundled to COPE headquarters in Washington. Yet, after the tumult and voting had died, the pro-labor forces in the House and Senate were drastically depleted. Why? Had the nation's mightiest political machine suddenly gone awry?

COPE director Barkan himself provided the best clue to the unusual 1966 elections and labor losses when he commented after the voting that "we just couldn't overcome factors beyond our control." And COPE had a number of factors that it simply in no way could control.

By 1966 the American electorate—from coast to coast—had had enough of liberal rule in Washington. After six years of the New Frontier and its Great Society offspring, the voters went to the polls intent on rejecting Administration "rubber stamp" candidates in favor of more conservative representatives. From organized labor's standpoint, the result was not a rejection of its candidates as *labor* candidates, but rather defeat in their role as promoters of LBJ's free-spending Great Society programs.

"I don't know of any place where labor was an issue in the election," said Barkan when asked for his observations on the voting. "I don't think the election swung on any labor issues at all." The main issue in the minds of the American electorate was slowing down the galloping Great Society, and when the voters become so fixed on one target of opposition no amount of propaganda and electioneering to the contrary can allay this fixation. In 1966 the voters wanted to throw out a lot of Great Society supporters and nothing COPE—or any other pro-Democrat organization, least of all the party itself—could do would change this feeling, despite COPE's considerable political skill.

This factor alone would have been enough to hinder COPE's usual effectiveness, but in 1966 labor had more than one "factor beyond our control" to contend with.

The utter inadequacy of the Democratic National Committee and the breakdown in the chain of Democratic command were well publicized before and after the '66 campaign; candidates complained of getting no assistance, state parties were locked in internal warfare, and the buck was passed regularly from the committee to the White House and back again. Though labor in several sections of the country has always *been* the Democratic Party, such chaos at party headquarters in Washington was bound to hurt its efforts. "We found ourselves working alone for the first time in many areas," said AFL-CIO head Meany after the elections.

Labor's propaganda efforts were hampered not only because they could not salvage popularity for the Great Society, but also in that they had no single "enemy" to use as a whipping boy. This was pinpointed by Meany as labor's primary problem in 1966, when he admitted "We had only one handicap this time: We didn't have Goldwater against us."[6]

What Meany meant, of course, was that in the '64 presidential contest labor dwelt almost singularly on the propaganda pitch that Republican nominee Goldwater in the White House would mean, among other things, probable destruction of all unions, not to mention the entire world; labor was one of the prime movers in the outright smear campaign to brand Senator Goldwater as a trigger-happy warmonger who would push the nuclear button the first chance he got. How well this ploy had worked is a measure of COPE's effectiveness. An indication of COPE's heavy reliance on such smear propaganda is that Meany thought it was the lack of an "enemy target" that made the difference in the '66 elections, and not the failure to develop solid issues.

Other factors which figured in the unique '66 congressional balloting included the so-called "white backlash," which both Meany and Barkan saw in rank-and-filers voting against candidates who supported such civil rights measures as open housing. There was also the continuing war in Vietnam, with laborers (as well as others with relatives losing their lives in Southeast Asia) voting against the party which not only escalated the war, but had mismanaged it magnificently.

This array of contributing elements of '66, together with the basic ingredient of voter antipathy to the Great Society, presents a virtually insurmountable wall of obstacles that all the Democrat-aligned groups together could not overcome. In the face of such difficulties, it may even be said that organized labor came out better than might have been imagined; after its initial defeat in six campaign battles, it still ended up with a House contingent of close to 190 sure votes and a still-solid Senate bloc of sixty.

Instead of comparing COPE's 1966 results with 1964, it might be more effective to match them with the previous congressional off-year elections in 1962, a year in which liberal candidates were supposed to have done rather well; in that campaign 190 COPE-backed candidates won House races, as compared to 1966's 182—a small difference. This was, in fact, the comparison used by COPE itself in the confidential analysis of the '66 elections it presented to the AFL-CIO executive council, where it argued that labor officials might have over-reacted to the 1966 results.

Another example used in the COPE report, showing that "the organization functioned better than ever," was that labor was the decisive factor in saving some congressional seats which could easily have been lost. Singled out were the victories of Reps. Don Irwin (D-Conn.), William Hathaway (D-Me.), James Hanley (D-N.Y.), and Joseph Vigorito (D-Pa.). In other cases, said COPE, its forces were instrumental in racking up a larger vote for a liberal candidate, even though he lost, than a liberal had ever received before in an off-year election in that District, mentioning Michigan's 2nd District and Illinois' 19th as examples.

Indeed, non-partisan analysis would show that labor could have done worse and that the factors causing whatever loss there was were not connected immediately (or even remotely in most cases) with organized labor's political machine. Every indication is that 1966 represented but a temporary setback to labor's political aspirations.

Fully aware of labor's comeback capabilities, members of the Congress were not about to go out on a limb and risk invoking labor's wrath by passing union-curbing legislation the moment the 90th Congress convened. No such "anti-labor" emotion was evident when the comparatively conservative Congress met in January, 1967, and there *was* evidence, in fact, that labor's voice was still harkened to. Columnists Evans and Novak reported early in the 90th Congress that the powerful chairman of the House Ways and Means Committee, Rep. Wilbur Mills, an Arkansas Democrat who could never be described as a labor sycophant, was awaiting labor's blessing before beginning committee work on LBJ's controversial tax-increase legislation.[7] Such is not the respect normally accorded a special interest group which supposedly has lost its political power.

One very good reason Rep. Mills and politicos all across the land were willing to grant deep respect to the labor political machine, no matter how badly COPE fared in '66, was the organization's long and impressive list of previous victories. This record of achievement offers the most convincing case for construing the '66 results as only a temporary setback.

COPE's string of electoral successes began scant months after the Committee on Political Education was formed in the confusion of the AFL-CIO merger in late 1955. In the presidential-year contests the following fall, the fledgling COPE saw labor increase its House bloc by one vote and Senate bloc by two, at the same time that Dwight D. Eisenhower was sweeping the country for the Republicans in his bid to remain in the White House.[8]

In 1958—three years after its formation—COPE scored one of the biggest victories on its record. As voter dissatisfaction with the Eisenhower Administration was on the rise, and a mild recession lowered buying power, labor's political machine was greatly responsible for the addition of eleven liberal pro-labor votes in the Senate and thirty in the House. These smashing victories gave labor its first congressional majority since New Deal days, and the infant COPE was beaming.

In the presidential year of 1960, with the nip-and-tuck Nixon-Kennedy dogfight at the top, labor lost some of its rich haul of 1958, with eleven House votes disappearing (however, this was still nineteen more than labor had in 1956). But, in the Senate, labor managed to pick up two new votes to add to its already-solid bloc of fifty-three.

Two years later, estimated pro-labor strength in the House of Representatives rose to 225 and 190 COPE-backed candidates were successful; in the Senate such candidates as Birch Bayh of Indiana and George McGovern of South Dakota won upset victories—thanks to labor money and manpower.

Doubtless 1964 is the banner year thus far in COPE's brief history. In that presidential contest, COPE was instrumental in spreading the fears about Senator Barry Goldwater which led to the overwhelming defeat of the GOP presidential candidate. By distorting the race for the White House, labor was able to produce a long string of liberal victories, as the fears created of Goldwater resulted in antipathy to the entire GOP ticket and subsequent defeat for Republicans everywhere. The labor achievements may have been of dubious (some might say despicable) quality, but their quantity was indisputable.

A few months before the '64 voting, COPE director Barkan had said one of the organization's goals was "a House of Representatives needing only 20-25 more liberals to break out of the horse latitudes and achieve a legislative record of greatness." When the votes were counted for the 435 House seats, 237 (out of 354) COPE-supported pro-labor candidates had gained admittance to Congress.

In the Senate contests, COPE aided heavily in knocking off three incumbent Republicans whom it considered "anti-labor" (Keating of

New York, Beall of Maryland, and Mechem of New Mexico), while losing only one of its own (interim Senator Pierre Salinger of California), for a net gain of two votes to add to its previous bloc of 60-plus.

As the liberal Democrat victories rolled in in November, 1964, a gleeful President Johnson took pen in hand and sent thanks to the man whose organization had so helped his party: "During the campaign the American labor movement gave us its full support," LBJ wrote AFL-CIO President George Meany. "Certainly no group worked harder for a Democratic victory. For that I am grateful. . . ."

After receiving the presidential epistle, Meany, like the proud father of a piano prodigy receiving congratulations from old family friends, said of the one who truly deserved the praise: "COPE this year did an outstanding job, the best job it has ever done."[9]

Just as Meany was proper in directing the plaudits to COPE, LBJ had every right to be "grateful" to organized labor. The congressional cushion provided him through COPE's effective work in '64, resulted in the passage of virtually every piece of Great Society legislation Johnson sent to Capitol Hill. Medicare, federal aid to education, a Department of Housing and Urban Development, rent subsidies, demonstration cities—all were supported by the AFL-CIO and voted through the 89th Congress by the COPE-elected representatives.

(The irony of this situation was that labor's own pet project for the 89th Congress—repeal of Section 14(b) of the Taft-Hartley law—was finally rejected. This provision of the 1947 law permits individual states to pass right-to-work statutes outlawing the union shop; the union shop is provided for in a collective agreement between management and labor whereby all the workers in the bargaining unit must join the union, after a specified period of employment, or else the employer must fire the workers. Under a state right-to-work law, such collective agreements are prohibited, and employees are genuinely free to join or not to join a union.

(Rather than indicate any loss of allegiance on the part of the COPE-backed congressmen, however, the defeat of repeal in the 89th Congress was more indicative of labor's larger problem of "complacency" and tendency to live—at times—in the past; repeal was an outdated issue which labor pushed too strenuously, with the result of alienating many of its "friends" on Capitol Hill. Repeal did breeze through the House with an 18-vote margin, but pro-labor forces could not break a Senate filibuster—no one ever accused labor of controlling the two-thirds Senate votes necessary for cloture—and the issue was dropped by the Democratic leadership.)

Confident of congressional respect and of its ability, proven in previous battles, COPE is going full steam toward the 1968 presidential elections. Leaving the bitter memories of the recent past behind them, COPE strategists will take the results of '66 in stride and use to their advantage any lessons learned from them; toward this end, the AFL-CIO executive council met in February, 1967, to analyze past elections and suggest improvements and refinements for the labor political machine.

The first result of this analysis was an exhaustive poll of AFL-CIO members, commissioned by COPE and conducted by the professional firm of John Kraft, Inc. The Kraft Poll "profiled" union members as to age, income, area of residence and other factors, and examined their attitudes on possible presidential candidates and a broad array of legislative issues.

The findings of the Kraft Poll, together with COPE's "long hard look" at its operation, produced some tangible results rather quickly. In response to the poll's showing that approximately 50 percent of union members live in the suburbs and the fact that labor-backed candidates had done poorly in suburban areas in 1966, COPE inaugurated—in summer, 1967—a program to win these voters (and their non-union neighbors) back to the labor fold. "A suburban COPE can be to the community what the grievance committee is to the workplace," said COPE in introducing its 10-point organizing campaign.

A poll finding that "nearly 50 percent" of the AFL-CIO's members were under 40 years old (and 25 percent under 30), and COPE's conclusion that it was failing to attract these youthful rank-and-filers into political action, prompted the committee to take two steps. The first was to establish "Teen COPE," a strategy designed to use union members' teenage offspring in registering voters, distributing propaganda and other nuts-'n'-bolts campaign work.

COPE also established an alliance with the United States Youth Council, an "umbrella" group representing several other organizations, such as the NAACP's youth division. Under this arrangement, the Youth Council will supply volunteer workers for an assortment of COPE activities, notably registering and "educating" voters in low-income areas. As with Teen COPE, the national committee hopes the enthusiasm of the youthful council volunteers will rub off on the younger AFL-CIO members.

Another positive step taken to repair the damage of 1966 has been to establish a better working relationship between the political forces of labor and the national Democratic Party. Reporting on the Democratic National Committee's post-election self-improvement exercises, the *Washington Post* noted on March 7, 1967, that "liaison has been re-established . . . with the leaders of organized labor's political arm, the AFL-CIO Committee On Political Education." Although there is still

some skepticism as to how much the Democrats' headquarters operations have improved, such a prompt and cohesive action indicated the
extent to which the Democratic National Committee and COPE are
mutually dependent in seeking political success.

On COPE's immediate agenda of preparatory steps for 1968 was
wholesale participation in the 1967 elections held in thousands of cities
and counties in every state. This odd-year project was started on a broad
scale in the '65 municipal elections, when COPE was active in approximately 1,000 cities of at least 10,000 population; the purpose of the
unique activity—aside from winning the elections—is to keep COPE's
army of volunteers "in shape" for the bigger battles to come.

In 1967 COPE again took part in thousands of local elections, including major contests in Philadelphia, Cleveland, Boston and Gary, Ind.
The net results were some surprising victories for labor-backed candidates and a big step forward on COPE's "comeback trail"; "whatever
the reasons," reported *Time* after the '67 balloting, "labor voted with a
cohesion unsurpassed since the Kennedy-Nixon election of 1960."[10]

In helping re-elect Mayor James Tate "organized labor mounted its
most massive campaign in Philadelphia history to keep the city hall in
Democratic hands."[11] Tate had been the underdog in both his primary
and general election races, but COPE's herculean effort (consisting of
money, manpower and organizing assistance) helped pull him through
both contests with a comfortable plurality.

In Cleveland and Gary the labor political forces aided mightily in the
victories of Carl Stokes and Richard Hatcher, the first Negroes ever
elected to govern major U.S. cities. In both instances COPE had opposed the final winner in his primary fight, sticking with the Democratic
organizations' candidates, but had swung to Stokes and Hatcher in the
general election.

The only significant defeats labor suffered in '67 were the Kentucky
gubernatorial contest, where COPE supported a lackluster Democratic
candidate, and the battle for control of New Jersey's state legislature. A
crucial issue in the Jersey campaign was a state law (fully backed by the
AFL-CIO) guaranteeing unemployment benefits to striking workers,
passed by the legislature which had gone Democratic in 1965 for the
first time in 50 years; New Jersey Republicans campaigned for repeal
of the law and regained control of the state senate and assembly.

These important statewide losses notwithstanding, the '67 elections
did conclusively demonstrate that COPE had retained its ability to
amass big city votes for its candidates; this lesson was not lost on
political observers who realized that the Democratic Party will be relying
on COPE to round up these same votes in 1968. And coincidental with
this success at the polls, COPE's 1967 odd-year election project re-

affirmed the value of keeping its campaign volunteers working, active and "in shape."

Another "special project" COPE streamlined for 1968 is its vaunted "Marginal District Project," a strategy begun in 1964 and one which has had remarkable success. Under this plan, COPE strategists select those congressional districts in which the incumbent won in 1966 with 55 percent or less of the total vote—a so-called marginal district—and give special attention to the contests in these areas. This emphasis includes extra financial assistance from national COPE and individual unions, and manpower assistance in the form of a field representative assigned to the District from COPE or some union.

(In 1966 COPE had only 50 percent success with its Marginal District Project, winning in 29 of the 59 contests placed in this category. But, this figure must be balanced by noting the 59 districts were all held by pro-labor incumbents, many of them the first Democrats or liberals elected to Congress in their areas since the Piltdown man lost a close one. Also to be considered is that in the project's inaugural year 1964, COPE won 61 out of 89 selected marginal districts—69 percent success.)

Overall, the COPE directors seek ceaselessly to improve and implement the strategies that have proved successful before, keeping its political apparatus—from the national headquarters down to the lowliest precinct—in good working order. To achieve the single-minded goal of electing public officials who agree with the AFL-CIO's legislative program, COPE has a full-time staff averaging 25 persons, a yearly salary budget approaching $400,000, and a well-ordered chain of command to run its political machine.

The COPE operation has its roots in the 14.3 million working men who belong to unions affiliated with the American Federation of Labor-Congress of Industrial Organizations. Each local union is supposed to have its own political education committee, with the political activities of all AFL-CIO unions in a given area coordinated by a local COPE branch organized on a city, county or congressional district basis, depending on geographical necessity and political convenience. These local COPEs are governed, in turn, by a state AFL-CIO Committee on Political Education which makes policy concerning matters pertaining to its state. Ruling the entire organization is the COPE national headquarters office located in the AFL-CIO building in Washington.

At the uppermost echelons, COPE's operations are watched over by the AFL-CIO's Executive Council—composed of the federation's president, secretary-treasurer and 27 vice presidents—and the Council president acts as the chairman of the political committee. Most strategy planning and day-to-day decisions, however, are left to COPE director Al Barkan and his staff.

In the COPE scheme of things, then, it is the grass-roots political committees, on the state and local levels, staffed with men appointed by the AFL-CIO councils in each area and paid from local union treasuries, which provide the vital manpower cogs. The Washington staff furnishes the money, material strategy, and experience to make the machine hum and purr. Still, other independent political organizations have recourse to as much money and expertise as COPE possesses, a factor emphasizing the importance of COPE's volunteer "foot soldiers" in the labor machine: this is the aspect separating COPE from all other political groups—the vast army it can put at the disposal of favored candidates.

The wide range of activities this formidable political organization practices covers the ground from ringing doorbells to actually running a candidate's race. Most of these activities are outlined in COPE's political action handbook, convincingly entitled *How To Win,* a publication professional politicians generally regard as the best of its type in print (Senator Goldwater once said that when he prepared for a campaign, "I just get out COPE's book on how to do it and use it."). In this 110-page manual, COPE lists four "main jobs . . . essential if we are to get union members and their families interested and active in politics":

* You must register union members, their relatives, and their friends who are of voting age.
* You must educate them on issues and candidates.
* You must get them to vote on Election Day.
* You must collect voluntary dollars for COPE to help elect liberal candidates.

Of these four primary tasks, the one receiving the most concentration is the registration of potential pro-labor voters. The purpose of the registration project is elementary: to see that every union member, his family and friends (others, who may not be unionists, living in working-class neighborhoods) are qualified to vote and have their names on the electoral rolls. An indication of the success of this campaign can be glimpsed in the statement made by Al Barkan before the 1964 elections that upwards of 70 percent of the 13.5 million men then in the AFL-CIO were registered to vote. When this figure (approximately 9.4 million) is added to the number of other members of a laborer's household also eligible to vote (wife, children, parents) and non-union residents of the workers' community, contacted by COPE, you arrive at an impressive total of voters whom one political organization has had a hand in registering.

To improve its voter registration efforts, COPE in 1968 plans to expand a project inaugurated on a limited experimental scale in 1966. This advance, possibly one of the most revolutionary political action operations in years, allows COPE to check the voter registration status of its members on data processing computers, rather than by the tedious process of examining registration rolls. COPE used the computers in only three areas in 1966, but the effort proved so successful it will definitely be expanded to eventually cover most major population centers.

The second item on COPE's list of four "main jobs," "educating" union members, is where the organization fulfills the "education" portion of its title and where it spends a great deal of money and time. No matter how effective COPE's registration project is, it would be useless if there was no way of making potential pro-labor voters actual pro-labor voters. To help fill the wide gulf between signing voters up and having them pull the right levers inside the ballot booth, COPE has the reams of propaganda it distributes with the intent of "educating" its members and their friends toward making the "right" choices when they vote.

Political propaganda is COPE's biggest—and most visible—enterprise. For starters, COPE publishes a bi-weekly, four-page sheet called the "Political Memo" for union member consumption, ladling out the liberal line in sizable portions. From this one regular publication (supplemented by the AFL-CIO publications, *AFL-CIO News* and *Federationist* magazine) COPE's propagandists move on to an array of brochures, pamphlets, research papers and assorted materials, all aimed at motivating the rank-and-file into backing its leaders' choice of candidates and issues.

The registration and propaganda duties may consume the most time and effort at COPE headquarters, but there are a number of other activities having their own importance and receiving a goodly share of attention. Generally categorized, these are:

* Educating the public at large. Through union publications and pro-labor newspapers, widespread distribution of propaganda, speakers and films, organized labor attempts to reach beyond its own membership to carry its "liberal" message to the public at large;

* Working within the community. In another tack in reaching the general public, union members are urged to become active in as many civic and community affairs as they can manage, in this way personally contacting members of their neighborhood who might otherwise be oblivious to labor's social-political goals;

* Working with other pressure groups. By joining in informal alliance with other liberal-oriented pressure groups and voting blocs (such as the National Farmers Union, Americans for Democratic Action, League of Women Voters, rural electric co-ops, civil rights groups), organized labor is able not only to spread its influence, but also to get more effective legislative action for its proposals;

* Working in party affairs. COPE members are individually active in the inner mechanics of the Democratic Party (oh, there might be a dozen or so in the GOP), with particular importance placed on taking part in the conventions where candidates for office and party officials are selected;

* Compiling voting records. At the end of each session of Congress, COPE's research department, with an assist from the AFL-CIO's Legislative Department, will select from ten to twelve votes taken during the session just ended, votes judged to indicate a congressman's position on organized labor. After compiling these roll call votes, COPE lists the position of representatives and senators on them, adding up the number of "right" and "wrong" votes and arriving at a figure which supposedly indicates a congressman's "pro-labor" position.

When it comes to the question of how this mighty COPE political machine is financed, a whole Pandora's box of wild charges, hidden spending, unreported expenditures and legal loopholding opens up. COPE is governed in its spending by the same Corrupt Practices Law regulating all federal political financing. The law says that national labor organizations cannot spend union dues money for political purposes, just as business corporations cannot give funds from their treasuries to a candidate or party. COPE must, then, raise the money it spends on political activities from voluntary contributors—the rank-and-file—and for this purpose it has a year-round dollar drive, the "Give a Buck to COPE" campaign.

The question of the degree of voluntariness connected with this project is only one dark corner in COPE's financial operations. Another comes with the definition of "educational"—as opposed to political— expenditures, which do not have to be reported to Congress, as does the political spending, and for which union money can be used. For example, a direct contribution by COPE to a specific candidate is most assuredly a political expense and has to be reported, but the funds spent on propaganda for the same candidate, or to pay a COPE worker on his staff, are not political, but "educational," as they have some remote connection with COPE's direct relations with its members.

Such confusion and ambiguity in the law are one reason COPE can elude reporting exactly what it spends and can, instead, report, as in 1966, that it spent but $906,165.53 (for contributions to candidates, funds given back to state COPEs, and incidentals) in a major campaign year. Actually, its spending could have gone as high as $25 million, considering the amount of propaganda issued, voting records distributed, field representatives at work and other items classified "educational." This additional funding was made available by individual unions, taken from the dues money workers (at least in union shop states) must pay in order to keep their chosen jobs.

The COPE bankroll is certainly an integral part of the labor political machine, but it is the manpower the organization can provide, and the activities this political army and the COPE staff participate in that ultimately have the most influence on the outcome of an election. These operations were impressively successful until the 1966 elections and, keeping in mind that it was not the labor machine itself which failed the liberal camp, they will be improved to an even greater degree of excellence for the 1968 contest.

The skill and potency of this machine, together with an indisputable winning way as evidenced by a mass of past victories and a slew of Republican electoral corpses, have given organized labor its position as the most politically powerful economic bloc in America. This position was achieved through developed expertise and diligent work, not divine providence or voter whim, and one election setback is not going to cause it to disappear. COPE will be in the thick of the '68 election battle, working as never before to reassert its campaign effectiveness and to show the skeptics that it is eminently qualified to fulfill labor's political role.

## CHAPTER TWO

# Labor's Political Role

IT may seem a simple matter to define the role organized labor plays in contemporary politics: it seeks to elect candidates who will vote to pass the legislation endorsed by labor. Undoubtedly true, but in application and when placed in the context of America's complex political system, labor's political role demands further examination and explanation.

This analysis is necessitated, to a great extent, by the problems organized labor as a whole is currently facing. As readers of the public press well know, in the mid-sixties labor, in the person of the AFL-CIO, has been assaulted from all sides and by persons of virtually all shades of opinion: conservatives say labor has too much "power," liberals denounce labor's "complacency" and "weakness." Ironically enough, both sides sometimes use the same evidence to support their divergent conclusions.

A close look will show that organized labor does indeed confront a multitude of problems, some serious, others more easily resolved. This situation and, equally important, the criticisms which have both revealed and helped create it, have direct bearing on the nature of labor's political role—the part it plays in helping to decide the future of the nation.

In the past one hundred years, the social and economic character of the blue-collar worker in the nation's urban areas has changed more than that of any other single segment of the population. In the late 1800's sweatshops were common in industrial plants—now studies are made of how workingmen may fill the increasing leisure time made available by paid vacations; a century ago labor leaders were workers themselves, organizing, striking, and walking the picket lines—now union executives tend toward the portly side, live in split-level suburbia, and see the rank-and-file only at conventions; and management, which

—under the firm hand of the "Captains of Industry"—used to look on labor organizers as something akin to lepers, now recognizes a labor bargainer as an equal, generally agrees to contract demands, and gives thanks that it was not hit by a crippling strike.

As the national economy grew and stabilized over the past one hundred years, organized labor saw to it that the workingmen got "their share" of the prosperity. When the radical Keynesian planners flooded the Roosevelt Administration in the 1930's and re-ordered the economy, the radicals in the labor movement hopped aboard the leftward freight and got unionism a ride to affluence and power. And following World War II, with the nation's industry reconverting to peacetime production, labor was able to make heavier demands than ever before and finally to solidify its position as an indisputable, undeniable economic force.

In the twenty-plus years that have elapsed since the war, changes have come over the character of organized labor itself, changes basically unrelated to the economic status of workingmen but which ultimately affect them most of all. In this span of time, organized labor—as now represented by the American Federation of Labor-Congress of Industrial Organizations (AFL-CIO)—has grown in power and complacency. With the spurt of success after 1945 and the arrival at a relatively secure position of influence and prestige, organized labor ceased being the great shining "crusade" which men had fought and died for in the 1930's. It lost its surging momentum and its position of power hardened: the unions and their federation secured their beachheads of influence and dug in, wielding their power to the utmost effect.

One of the first results of this action was a public outcry over labor's abuses of its power and its seeming immunity to prosecution when this power was flagrantly injurious. This power became manifest in a number of ways, both in the unions' ability to make inflationary contract demands from management and in the ability to make management suffer bitter consequences if it dared refuse the demands.

Today, if the leaders of one big union, say the United Auto Workers, give the word, they can tie up the entire automobile industry by bringing production to a standstill. Unions in New York City can silence all seven of that city's newspapers—as in 1963 and 1965—(not to mention that these strikes were directly responsible for the disappearance of four of these newspapers) or labor can strike the subway and bus systems in that same city and bring transportation to a halt—as in 1966.

Admittedly, these are bitter consequences for the public and for any management to have to face, but, unfortunately for organized labor, the unions may themselves ultimately suffer damaging penalties. The New York strikes, including the nine-day sanitationmen's strike in 1968, are the kind of union behavior that has prompted a voluble public cry for strong legislation to curb union power. Even before the strikes mentioned, an assistant editor for George Gallup's American Institute of Public Opinion was able to write (in 1963), "For the past 20 years many nationwide Gallup Polls have shown the public in favor of stricter regulation of unions by more than 2 to 1."[1]

Among the general public, growing union power has come under criticism from elements traditionally strong supporters of the labor movement. A 1963 survey conducted by the Chase Manhattan Bank among the nation's economists in colleges and universities—normally considered a liberal element—showed that 44 percent of these experts thought monopoly power of labor unions to be "a major economic problem" in this country. Secondly, over half of those polled—53 percent—replied that labor unions should be subject to the same type of anti-trust laws governing industry, a position organized labor thoroughly abhors.[2]

Final proof of the degree to which abuse of union power has rankled the American public is revealed when a pro-labor newspaper columnist such as Drew Pearson can write, ". . . in three decades labor has gained power that no one would have thought possible [thirty years ago] . . . and the big question today is whether labor is using its power wisely."[3]

But labor has thus far been able to roll with the punches coming from the critics of its "power," even when they originated with an old ally like Pearson. The charges of power have been around since the AFL was founded back in 1886, and in the intervening years only two major legislative measures—Taft-Hartley in 1947 and Landrum-Griffin in 1959—have been passed to restrict, albeit ineffectively, this power.

At the same time that the public has been reprimanding organized labor for its detrimental actions, leftist intellectuals and political activists have been using these same events as indicative, not of labor power, but of basic weakness. Labor has come to be so complacent with its economic and bargaining success, the argument went, that it is incapable of making anything approaching progress and is left with the power only for wreaking havoc and disrupting public life.

During the mid-1960's, labor observers from various vantage points were given a number of opportunities to reappraise (agonizingly so, or not) the status of organized labor. The consensus seemed to be that labor is impotent and weak, with decay imminent unless quick remedial action is taken. In addition to the strikes of 1965-66, there was the bitter war of words when labor refused to follow President Johnson's wage-price guidelines in 1966; then came the defeat of labor's pet legislative project for the 89th Congress—the repeal of the right-to-work proviso of Taft-Hartley—an action which in turn caused AFL-CIO president George Meany to make sounds indicating a split in the long-term labor-Democrat marriage; in November, 1966, labor—along with the rest of the liberal-Democrat coalition—lost heavily in the off-year congressional elections; and in early 1967 the policy differences between Meany and his most prominent Executive Council member, Walter Reuther, simmering below the surface for ten years, finally burst with gusto on the surface, with Reuther resigning from the Council and other AFL-CIO posts.

The pundits concerning themselves with labor matters had a field day with this sequence of events, and AFL-CIO leaders must have felt, at times, like permanent laboratory specimens under mighty micro-scopes. The *Wall Street Journal* succinctly summarized the hurricane of criticism the AFL-CIO underwent when it reported in 1967: "The liberal intellectual community and the opinion molders maintain that the trade union movement is stalled on dead center, failing to generate social ferment, out of touch with the rank and file, hidebound by aging leaders more interested in retaining their hard-won respectability than in daring to break new ground."[4]

There is every sign that the patriarchs of the federation have heard this criticism and are preparing to move. Many of the more liberal critics in the "intellectual community" have proposed Auto Workers boss Reuther as the perfect doctor to solve the AFL-CIO's ills, and certainly Walter himself has long entertained similar notions; but Meany has always been in firm control, and now that Reuther is on the outside, Meany is out to prove he can "rejuvenate" the federation with the same determination he used in keeping it together for ten years.

The final outcome of George Meany's rejuvenation efforts will ulti-mately involve every one of the AFL-CIO's 14.3 million rank-and-file members and each of the federation's activities, from collective bargain-ing to congressional lobbying. But, for all the criticism and hostile feel-ings which have come its way in the past couple of years, any losses organized labor has thus far suffered have been in those intangible areas having to do with "public opinion" and prestige. It has lost nothing at the bargaining tables, no labor-curbing legislation has been passed by Congress since 1959 and there has been no mass desertion of members.

Thus, while from a surface viewpoint—on the outside looking in—it may appear labor has had a pretty rough time of late, when it comes to chalking up items in the won-lost columns, there is very little that can be placed on the minus side. Certainly labor can still throw the nation into chaos with a strike if it likes; it can and does demand the fattest contracts it can get at negotiating sessions; and it can yet wield strong influence within the American community through its membership and power of numbers.

The basic day-to-day functions of the AFL-CIO structure—lobbying, bargaining, organizing, etc.—have remained unaltered through all the *sturm und drang* wrought by public-intellectual criticism. The success of these functions may at times be somewhat affected, but much less so than would be thought, simply because these functions are not carried out on a level where they could be subjected to the public spotlight and public reaction. Rather, the functions operate on the local level, whether in the carpeted conference room of an executive suite in Detroit, or on the dirt streets of a migrant labor camp in California, and here there is no sign of the labor complacency charged by leftist intellectuals.

Labor has built its structure well, and the AFL-CIO is so organized that any reappraisal which may be done at the uppermost level will leave its grassroots activities largely unaffected until some permanent change occurs. For this reason, Walter Reuther can have his open warfare with George Meany and still go into contract negotiations with the nation's largest auto manufacturers, confident that his union and most of the AFL-CIO leaders are—whatever their opinion of him vis-à-vis Meany —firmly behind his demands.

Likewise, that function of the AFL-CIO which probably affects the nation most vitally, its political operation, keeps going as an awesomely powerful machine even though this function may be the one *most* in the public spotlight and the one *most* influenced by any fluctuations in the "image" of organized labor.

Organized labor does not propose to give up its political function and start believing the charges of "decay" any more than it will cede its power in collective bargaining. Labor has fought hard to gain the powers it wields, and nowhere was this fight more prolonged or intense than in the battlefield of practical politics.

Although in its early years organized labor, led by Samuel Gompers and his American Federation of Labor, was not intended to act as a disciplined power bloc in American politics (not forgetting that the Democratic bias of Gompers and his lieutenants sometimes obscured this position), this approach changed with the establishment of the Congress of Industrial Organizations in 1936. The CIO was openly and blatantly an organization led by men committed to the radical left on the American political scale, elements—including socialists and Communists—who have always held that labor had a role to play as a political force; as long as the AFL dominated the labor scene this view was not allowed to prevail, but with the coming of the CIO, labor leaders began to use a mass organization of workingmen to gain political power.

Coupling themselves with the like-minded liberals in the New Deal Administration in a marriage of sublime convenience, the CIO in some instances ran the Democratic Party outright. The militant CIO leaders were not interested in purely labor legislation, the so-called "bread and butter" issues the AFL concentrated on exclusively, but were more concerned with broader social and economic programs which would move the country to the collectivist, welfarist Left. They saw no need in being—even nominally—bi-partisan, what with the Democrats eager for labor money, manpower and organizational talent, and willing in return to accept the counsel of CIO leaders and to advocate the legislation the labor federation desired.

Following the merger of the AFL and CIO in 1955, this CIO approach to politics—the use of the rank-and-file as an activist, well-disciplined power bloc and employment of the Democratic Party as a political vehicle—prevailed almost intact in the new COPE.

Led by such old CIO hands as Walter Reuther, the AFL-CIO set about, through its Committee on Political Education, to elect Presidents, senators, and representatives—invariably Democrats—who would pass on the legislation aimed at bringing about the collectivist-type state envisioned by the CIO leaders back in the 1930's. COPE grew in power and skill and in 1964 it aided substantially in electing the first solidly pro-labor Congress since the New Deal days—237 representatives and 63 senators. The day after the 1964 elections, organized labor was at its peak as a political force.

Two short years later, however, and the AFL-CIO found its political skills being called into question, along with the age of its Executive Council members. To many, the defeat of hundreds of labor-backed candidates in 1966 showed that the labor hierarchy had "lost touch" with the rank-and-file and was no longer rallying the workers to the banner of "progress."

What is needed for the federation to regain its political force, many critics argued, is for labor to recommit itself actively to so-called social progress, as did the CIO in the 1930's. Their criticisms are ideological and centered around the charge that labor is no longer a political force in either ideology *or* vote-getting. Typical of such opinions is that offered by Jack Newfield, a leading spokesman for the New Left:

". . . the AFL-CIO hierarchy is more hawk-like on Vietnam than the President, presides over bigoted locals, refused to endorse the 1963 March on Washington even after Cardinal Spellman offered his blessing, and it lent support to our Dominican intervention. The labor bureaucracy (one can hardly write the word 'movement') is so conservative it sees Walter Reuther as too radical to replace George Meany. If C. Wright Mills were alive today he would be writing against the Labor-Military-Industrial Complex."[5]

Besides Newfield's strident and doctrinaire bellowings conveniently overlooking the fact that the labor rank-and-file has moved to the *right* of the AFL-CIO hierarchy, as demonstrated in several 1966 elections which will be described later, his diatribe (one can hardly write the word "analysis") against the federation's leadership reveals the basic fallacy of this line of liberal criticism of organized labor.

If labor, as Newfield and his fellow critics of the Left say, no longer provides the "progressive ideas" it once did and is not actively committed to "social progress" as it was in the thirties, then it most certainly does support other organizations which fulfill these functions and public officials who will vote on legislation embodying liberal concepts. Labor may not have charged out of the foxholes of power it dug after World War II and led an assault for pure Leftism, but, in a very substantial way, primarily through a superb political machine, it has contributed immensely to all domestic liberal "progress" since 1945. This represents both a refutation of the criticism and a picture of the present nature of labor's political role.

Sometimes the blindness of this line of criticism can be embodied in a single individual, as in the person of the late Senator Robert F. Kennedy (D-N.Y.). In words that could have been written by his idolator Jack Newfield, Kennedy said to a dinner sponsored by the Americans for Democratic Action in 1967:

"Labor has been in the forefront of many a great battle. But youth looks with other eyes, and their view is very different: they think of labor as grown sleek and bureaucratic with power, sometimes frankly discriminatory, occasionally even corrupt and exploitative; a force not for change but for the status quo, unwilling or unable to organize new groups of members, indifferent to the men who once worked the coal mines of Appalachia, a latecomer to the struggles of the grape pickers of California or the farm laborers of the Mississippi Delta."[6]

Kennedy went on to admit this picture might tend to be a bit "one-sided," but he nevertheless closed by saying that liberals should not "ignore the need for change." The speaker may have been attempting to put words in the mouth of "youth" and escape having them identified as his own, but the tenor of the criticism was too characteristic, and Kennedy's desire to identify with "youth" was too strong, for anyone to accept his charges as anything but his own.

The simple fact is that Kennedy had substantial help from organized labor in New York State in getting elected to the Senate in the first place (not to mention that labor's backing helped put his late brother in the White House, which didn't hurt Bobby either). Labor did not exactly elect Robert Kennedy singlehandedly, but it was most certainly instrumental.

The two most powerful leaders in New York's Liberal Party (without whose assured endorsement the Democrats would not have put up a candidate against popular GOP Senator Kenneth Keating in '64) were

Alex Rose, president of the Hatmakers' Union, and David Dubinsky, then head of the ladies' garment workers, both of whom were early Kennedy supporters and had solicited support for his nomination within labor and the Liberal Party.

Then there was the effort of the United Labor Committee, created by Kennedy's advisors to win the labor vote, and headed by two other labor bigwigs, John McNiff of the paper workers, and Robert Mazer, a legal advisor to several New York unions. Under their direction, the ULC set up a statewide organization to plump for Bobby, had local labor activists make daily reports of rank-and-file attitudes on the campaign to Kennedy headquarters, and coordinated New York state unions in a widespread, intensive campaign to steamroll the Kennedy candidacy among union members. Not only did the ULC effort boost Bobby's labor stock, it also blunted Keating's own popularity among workingmen.

For his part during the campaign, Kennedy faithfully endorsed labor's favorite legislative proposals—repeal of 14(b) and weakening of Landrum-Griffin—for which he received (at one labor gathering) "loud applause" and bundles of labor money to finance his Senate race. All told, during the campaign Kennedy received close to $25,000 from organized labor, including contributions of $10,000 from the New York State COPE and Dubinsky's garment union.

Kennedy may have talked of organized labor growing "sleek and bureaucratic with power," but the very platform he spoke from was built with labor money and support in his Senate campaign. Of course, he was discussing the ideological complexion of labor as a whole, not its practical political operations, but Kennedy still failed to mention labor's wholesale participation in a liberal-labor-Democrat coalition which has resulted not only in his own election, but also in victories for scores of other liberal lawmakers and, through this congressional bloc, in passage of a wealth of welfarist legislation.

By supporting candidates such as Kennedy, labor is able to influence the actual creation of liberal laws, and by giving its backing to other liberal-oriented interest groups it helps put pressure on lawmakers to pass this legislation. Labor regularly gives these groups the benefit of its financial aid, manpower resources and prestige, and through them plays a strong role on the liberal front. Yet, at the same time, the intellectual critics of labor report from their surface observation point that labor is inactive and uncommitted in the leftist fight. Typical of such analysis is this comment by Andrew Kopkind in the *New Republic:*

"For the security of an established place in American life, organized labor sacrificed its position for social change. The young Senate liberals today look more to the civil rights movement than to the labor hierarchy, as the instrument of progress."[7]

There can be no doubt that the young campus militants and leftist intellectuals who would have flocked to the labor picket lines in the 'thirties were found demonstrating for civil rights in the 'sixties, and this movement may indeed be viewed by today's "young Senate liberals" as a more appealing "instrument of progress" than organized labor. However, the relationship between the civil rights groups and labor must be considered before hasty judgments can be made. It turns out, upon analysis, that although all of labor may not have given endorsement to the '63 March on Washington and some locals may be guilty of racial discrimination, as a whole the AFL-CIO and its affiliated unions have contributed sizably to the civil rights movement in the 'sixties.

The ties between labor and other liberal bloc-organizations, including those in civil rights, are demonstrably strong. These are not the New Left or other radical outfits that have sprung up in the 'sixties, but those—like the ADA, Farmers' Union, Democratic Study Group, National Committee for an Effective Congress—that have been fighting the liberal-left's battles for some time; they represent those now labeled "Establishment" by the new militants. And these associations show that if labor—as writers Kopkind and Newfield charge—no longer provides the leftist ideological thrust it once offered, it now freely joins with those groups that still do. The result is that organized labor's political power is increased, not diminished.

(It is well known that some of labor's liberal allies disagree with the AFL-CIO on matters of foreign policy; these differences, however, have not dampened cooperation in domestic political activities. The subject of labor's relations with other members of the coalition will be covered more thoroughly in the section on "COPE's Allies.")

By broadening its own sphere of influence through its allies, labor creates wider acceptance for legislation which affects, first of all, the workingman. This was demonstrated in 1965 when the Washington lobbyist for the National Association for the Advancement of Colored People, Mr. Clarence Mitchell, testified on behalf of several civil rights groups in favor of repeal of Section 14(b) of Taft-Hartley; in his testimony, Mitchell acknowledged that his appearance was in return for the AFL-CIO's support of civil rights legislation. Other groups giving similar testimony included the Americans for Democratic Action and the National Farmers Union. If repeal of 14(b) failed, it was not because of any lack of interest or cooperation on the part of labor's allies.

In such a coalition, all sides benefit. While for practical reasons labor, civil rights and other special interest groups back each other on issues of parochial interest, they generally agree on the broader approaches to domestic legislation. All the members of this informal alliance are in favor of a greater federal role in domestic affairs concerning virtually everything from farming to air pollution, and none of these groups opposes increased federal spending—and taxing—to accomplish these programs.

It is obvious from the broad scope of the legislation supported by the AFL-CIO that the federation has chosen the legislative route, (as well as the political path) that the old CIO followed. Rather than concentrate its major efforts on legislation concerning the workingman's conditions—collective bargaining, wages, unemployment—the labor federation instead ranges its legislative cannons across the entire social front, advocating welfarist causes frequently having little to do with the union rank-and-file. If the AFL-CIO is not an activist force on the Left, its lobbying activism in the halls of Congress is nevertheless as intense as ever.

And joining with the labor lobbyists are the AFL-CIO's allies whose own legislative action is, more often than not, an echo of the AFL-CIO. Because this is an informal liberal alliance, with no rigid control or single governing doctrine, some of the groups will from time to time be on opposite sides of an issue. For example, the National Farmers Union, usually on labor's side of a legislative battle, favored a constitutional amendment altering the Supreme Court's one-man, one-vote legislative reapportionment decision, while the AFL-CIO opposed any such action. But, on the great majority of legislative and ideological issues the groups in the informal coalition are in agreement.

The special role of organized labor in this alliance, setting it apart—if not above—the other members, is professionally expert political enterprise. Through the talents of union political strategists legislators like the late Robert Kennedy are elected who will vote to pass the legislation the coalition members support. The civil rights movement may be a more attractive "instrument of progress" for the young liberals in Congress, but this should not obscure the fact that the majority of these liberals were elected to their seats with considerable assistance from organized labor and, specifically, from the AFL-CIO's Committee on Political Education. The political talents of the other groups, meanwhile, are negligible.

Beyond its vital role in the passage of specific legislation lies COPE's influence in the broad spectrum of American politics. This can be demonstrated by the part it played in the 1964 presidential contest. Lyndon Johnson's popularity may have been greatly responsible for the voters' pulling the lever for the entire Democratic ticket in most areas, but it was COPE and other labor political machines which made sure those voters were registered, that they received sufficient propaganda to convince them to back LBJ, and that they got to the polls on time. COPE, in other words, translated Johnson's popularity into hard, solid votes.

The liberal-labor-Democrat coalition, for all the flux it has recently undergone, remains secure. Although George Meany's personal endorsement of Lyndon Johnson's re-election twenty months before Election Day, 1968 and quick support of Vice President Humphrey hours after LBJ's decision not to run, may have been looked upon as a bit premature by some COPE allies, surely it will be a surprise if any of them end up backing a Republican. As with organized labor, it is not that these groups have nowhere else to go in a literal sense, but their situation is roughly similar to that of Eve in the Garden of Eden: even if Eve got irked and thought of splitting with Adam, what was she going to do —take up with the snake maybe? The liberal-labor allies are not about to embrace any reptilian Republicans.

Meanwhile, outside this tight little coalition, controversy continues to rage on the left as to the coalition's practical effectiveness and relevance to social change. Certainly the Black Power militants and the epileptic radicals of the New Left have dismissed coalition politics as a "sellout," but others among labor's critics-on-the-left—even while decrying labor's "complacency"—have not given up hope in the liberal-labor alliance.

Socialist thinker Michael Harrington, protégé of Norman Thomas and originator of the "war on poverty" concept, speaks of "a national [liberal-labor-religious-radical] coalition" which would form the front rank of a drive to restructure American economic and social life. And civil rights activist-intellectual Bayard Rustin says that without a "labor-Negro-liberal" coalition, "we have nothing."

There is evidence that AFL-CIO head Meany, in his attempted rejuvenation of the federation, has responded to some of the leftist critics by advocating increasingly liberal domestic legislation. In 1967, for example, he had the Executive Council pass a resolution calling for the establishment of a national health service program along the lines of the English system; the same year, Meany was one of the few liberals to speak out publicly and forcefully for open housing civil rights legislation, an issue even the Johnson Administration tried to soft-pedal.

If the AFL-CIO can break out of the slump which has led to accusations of complacency and impotence, and can placate some of its liberal-intellectual critics by becoming a more activist force on the domestic front, it could represent a more potent political force than ever before. An organized labor movement of 14 million-plus members working actively with other left-of-center organizations, coupled with an already-perfected COPE political machine, would constitute an economic power bloc heretofore unseen in American politics.

Such a creation must remain, however, a thing of the future. For the presidential-year election campaigns of 1968 labor will continue to stand in its accustomed position in the U.S. political system. Since the 1955 merger of the AFL-CIO, the Committee on Political Education, in informal alliance with other special interest groups, has aided considerably in building and expanding the congressional delegation which has been responsible for the passage of all liberal legislation during that time.

This is the vital part COPE plays—and will continue to play with earnest dedication—in fulfilling organized labor's role in contemporary American politics.

## CHAPTER THREE

# The COPE Heritage

THE presence of organized labor in partisan political activities has become so commonplace that professional politicians—whether national party chairmen or precinct captains—have come not only to accept but to expect this participation. COPE and the political personnel of the major unions are in politics up to their blue-collared necks and, while some in the non-union public might not be aware of labor's political power, they nevertheless seldom raise an eyebrow when unions endorse candidates, make large financial contributions, or send out workers to ring doorbells.

Not that this politicking is anything new, for the history of labor's political activities closely parallels the history of the trade union movement itself; one goal of the workingmen who formed the early guilds was the passage of local legislation which would better their lot. What has changed over the years, however, is the nature of political involvement —from local politics to national—and the degree of partisanship—from the old American Federation of Labor's official nonpartisan position to COPE's present-day overwhelming support of the Democratic Party.

As these degrees have shifted there has been occasional public criticism of labor entering politics as a large, well-organized, disciplined bloc. Back when the AFL, under its founder-president Samuel Gompers, first dabbled in politics in 1906, Sen. Henry Cabot Lodge of Massachusetts was moved to say, "The question of whether there should be a Republican or Democrat sinks into insignificance compared to the question whether Gompers shall dictate the choice of Congressmen. . . ."[1]

When the Congress of Industrial Organizations set up its Political Action Committee in 1944 there was such a public outcry that a PAC publicist could write, with only slight exaggeration, that "so great was the amount of space given to PAC by the nation's press that, had the entire PAC staff been assigned to nothing but the reading and analyzing of the clippings, they would have had no time left for anything else."[2]

The new, militant and pro-Democrat turn represented by PAC was a triumph for the left wing in American politics. Almost since the founding of the AFL these radicals had urged the federation to become the political, as well as the organizational, voice of the workingman and to campaign for a wide variety of socialistic goals. This Samuel Gompers steadfastly refused to do. Not only did he and his successor William Green have nothing but contempt for the militant leftists, but neither thought that organized labor should be used as an ideological-political vehicle.

Faced with this opposition from the AFL, the leftist segments interested in "capturing" the labor movement for their own purposes adopted two different courses of action. On the one side were those who favored the tactic of "dual unionism," that is, setting up their own labor federations to organize new workers and woo the others away from the AFL.

The other tactic used by the far left was the time-honored "boring-from-within" maneuver, that is, working quietly inside the AFL to pursue radical goals and change the federation's political policy. This was the tactic adopted by the Socialist Party of America, and also adopted by the Communists, who in 1921 established a front called the Trade Union Educational League to bore-from-within the AFL; eventually the Communist Party line was changed and the TUEL became the Trade Union Unity League and engaged in dual unionism.

But the far left's attempts to "capture" the AFL and to start a new labor movement met with only limited success until a group of dissident union leaders broke away from the AFL in 1936 to form the Congress of Industrial Organizations. Because they thought they could use the Communists as union organizers without getting hurt, the original CIO leaders allowed CP members and party-line followers to all but take over the new federation. Later the non-Communists found—belatedly but still in time—that they could not work with the Communists and were forced to undergo a housecleaning.

Before the purge, however, came the Political Action Committee and a new departure in labor politics. PAC, under the guidance of its chairman, Sidney Hillman, was vocal, demanding, well organized and disciplined. It set its sights on the Democratic Party and supported that party's ticket from top to bottom in most areas. During its first campaign in 1944, *Newsweek* columnist Raymond Moley summed up the major public apprehensions about PAC and accurately described the new turn which PAC had developed:

"The real issue" raised by PAC's activities, he wrote, "is the projection into American national politics of an organization, based upon a single economic group, whose purpose is the control of a major American political party and whose position in the national government, if this campaign succeeds, will be immensely powerful."[3]

The campaign was, of course, successful, with PAC emerging as the major organizational factor in re-electing Franklin D. Roosevelt.[4] The position of the CIO leaders was indeed powerful and the Democrats were grateful for the alliance.

When the Committee on Political Education (COPE) was formed in 1955, as a composite of PAC and the more education-oriented Labor's League for Political Education (LLPE) of the AFL, it carried on the tradition established by the CIO at the time when Communists were still in its hierarchy. PAC turned the last corner in labor's political activities and began a new degree of militancy and partisanship. Labor was committed to a firm political course and, when COPE was set up, it continued to follow this course.

Just as organized labor has progressed from the small craft guilds, the political action of labor has evolved into full-scale, full-time commitment; the degrees have changed, sometimes—as with PAC in 1944— radically, until labor has come to be accepted as the single most powerful economic-social bloc in politics. It was a long haul, filled with events and incidents that have affected not only American labor, but our politics and—through it—our destiny.

While the LLPE and PAC were COPE's immediate predecessors, the origins of the AFL-CIO's political arm go back much further than the twentieth century. One COPE publication, in fact, reaches back to the 1730s when, it says, "A political organization known as the 'Caucus,' composed mostly of shipyard workers but also including other artisans and shopkeepers, won for a time a firm grip on the town offices of Boston." Later the Caucus, together with "a party of debtor farmers secured control of the Massachusetts General Court . . ."[5]

The American Federation of Labor, with Samuel Gompers as president, was formed in 1867. From these first years until the turn of the century, the AFL worked together with other interest groups, such as the smaller and more radical Knights of Labor and William Jennings Bryan's Populists, to encourage lawmakers on both the state and national level to pass laws dealing with labor arbitration, factory safety, child and female labor. During this period the AFL was also working with both political parties, depending on which one agreed most with its goals; despite his personal lifelong allegiance to the Democratic Party, Samuel Gompers was at first willing to deal with the Republicans if they would deal with him.

This policy began to change in the early 1900s when the Republican Administrations of William McKinley and Theodore Roosevelt refused to give Gompers everything he wanted. Proposed legislation establishing the eight-hour day and a bill preventing courts from issuing strike-stopping injunction orders were defeated.

Following this setback, the AFL's Executive Council drew up a "Bill of Grievances" which protested the defeat of labor-supported legislation and called on President Roosevelt and Congress to remedy the situation by pushing the bills the AFL wanted. Gompers was not satisfied with the response this petition received and the AFL prepared to move into politics on a much broader scale.

There had been a variety of socialist-oriented splinter parties in the United States before the 1900s, but it was not until the formation of the Socialist Party of America in 1901 that these American leftists went into politics and propagandizing on a significant scale. As a primary source of strength, the Socialists, under the leadership of Eugene Debs, naturally appealed to Gompers and the AFL; it was to the workers all over the world that the Socialists, and, later, the Communists, were making their appeals, so why should America be different?

It *was* different, however, and largely so because of the strong character of the former cigar-maker, Samuel Gompers. A classic, libertarian liberal and a loyal Democrat, Gompers refused to have anything to do with socialism or increased government control. His libertarianism led him to recoil at the thought of the Socialist welfare state and when Debs and his followers came asking for AFL support, they got a firm rebuff.

A sizable drop in AFL membership between 1900-05, caused Gompers to re-evaluate the political stance of his organization. Until this time, the AFL had simply urged its members to get active in politics on the local level, leaving it up to the individual workingmen to support the issues and candidates whom they thought best represented their interests. With laborers successful through a third party in England and with Socialists at home urging a similar organization, Gompers and the AFL felt the need for a revision of policy.

The official policy then established and followed—somewhat loosely at times—by the AFL throughout its existence was one of nominal nonpartisanship. As articulated by Gompers this position was one in which unionmen worked for the "positive defeat of those who have been hostile or indifferent to the just demands of labor," and supported "the true friends to the rights of labor," or, as it has often been paraphrased, "support your friends, defeat your enemies."[6]

In 1908 Gompers induced the AFL to openly oppose the incumbent Republican Party. The bespectacled labor leader did not think that Teddy Roosevelt had improved and he saw no sign that the GOP presidential candidate in 1908, William Howard Taft, would be much better. During the course of the campaign, Roosevelt came out with a biting attack on the AFL's political activities, and Gompers replied with words which have since been quoted over and over by labor politicians:

"The American labor movement is not partisan to a political party; it is partisan to a principle, the principle of equal rights and human freedom."[7]

Just as COPE can today come up with gilt-edged phrases to justify its tooth-and-nail political fighting, Samuel Gompers had a few of his own. But, this statement was the summation of the nonpartisanship which Gompers sought to make the working policy with the AFL. The organization probably never did *officially* endorse a presidential candidate, and on the local level it often worked with conservative incumbents when the leaders realized they could get nothing better. However, Gompers' own Democratic loyalties—and, more important, his anti-Republicanism—did tend to moot the nonpartisan issue on a national level.

Shortly after the 1924 elections, Samuel Gompers, the founder and chief builder of the early American labor movement, died at seventy-four. He was replaced by the AFL's taciturn vice-president, William Green, a one-time Democratic state senator from Ohio, who made it clear that he meant to follow his predecessor's example in labor affairs.

Green had no great love for the Socialists and their utopian plans. At the AFL's 1928 convention in New Orleans, a group of visiting British labor leaders argued that the federation should seek the federal government's assistance in winning its demands from industry. Green's terse reply to this suggestion was:

"We want the government to keep its hands off our throat. We do not want more of government . . . we want less government." And he added that Soviet Russia was a perfect example of just what the AFL did not want in this country.[8]

That Green intended to follow the official policies of Gompers in action as well as words was made evident in the first presidential campaign during his tenure as president. For the 1928 elections, the AFL set up a Nonpartisan Political Campaign Committee to direct the election activities of its 3.5 million members and the motto adopted for this campaign was: "STAND FAITHFULLY BY OUR FRIENDS AND ELECT THEM, OPPOSE OUR ENEMIES AND DEFEAT THEM." In this year, however, nonpartisanship, or at least bipartisanship, was more of an accomplished fact than it had been in previous years. Despite later emotional propaganda to the contrary, Herbert C. Hoover was looked upon by many labor leaders as a true friend of the workingman.

Prosperity was still riding high in 1928 and the laborers' lot had improved with that of the rest of society. While it is a demonstrable fact that this complacency and tendency towards optimism was to lead to the weakening of the AFL in the 'thirties, this was beside the point in 1928. The nation was happy, "Black Thursday" was over the horizon, and a large percentage of workingmen and their union leaders looked upon the handsome, aggressive Republican Secretary of Commerce as their friend.

Less than a year after the Republican victory in 1928, the stock market disintegrated and Hoover, the man John L. Lewis had described as "the foremost industrial statesman of modern times," became the archetypical "reactionary" in the eyes of liberal and labor propagandists. In addition to marking the beginning of the near-end for the GOP for many years, 1928 started the decline in influence and prestige of the American Federation of Labor.

While the AFL had entered into national politics and gained sufficient power to force both major parties to pay attention to the political wishes of organized labor, its practical political success had been limited. The workingmen were anxious to "defeat their enemies and support their friends" in the Gompers tradition, but the AFL did not have the political expertise, the organization or the money to make this slogan an effective policy producing solid accomplishments.

In 1928, particularly, the fact that the AFL provided only limited information on "anti-labor" candidates and failed to distribute ample voting records on incumbents made political action difficult. Perhaps most indicative of the AFL's political amateurism was a letter sent out by President Green to state federations on September 17, 1928—a month and a half before Election Day—asking them whom they were supporting and opposing in congressional races.

The Hoover-Smith contest also pointed up some of the drawbacks— at least as far as labor's political militants were concerned—of the Green-Gompers "nonpartisan" policy. In 1928 the rank-and-file were confronted with two presidential candidates, neither of whom was readily identifiable as an "enemy" and both of whom, in fact, had been touted by labor leaders as the workingman's "friend." Moreover, neither party that year made a concerted bid for the support of the "labor bloc." In such a situation, it became extremely difficult for AFL leaders active in politics to make union members see the necessity of voting for (or against) either Smith or Hoover.

During the 'twenties membership in the AFL fell from a post-war high of 5,047,800 to a 1928 enrollment of 3,479,800. Part of this decline was due to the mood of complacency in the country as prosperity continued to rise: the workingmen figured that the unions had got all they could for them, and so they let their membership lapse. If, after the stock market crash and arrival of the Depression, the workingmen were to blame the AFL for not getting more for them and membership continued to dwindle away, such was the paradox of history.

If the AFL's membership was declining and indifference was rampant among the rank-and-file, the organization's prestige still held up; it was only after the start of the Depression that the old labor vs. employer hostilities erupted again and the AFL's stock fell even lower.

During this period the League for Industrial Democracy (LID) and its socialist allies intensified their efforts to gain support in the dissident unions of the AFL. One of the first targets was the huge, 500,000-member United Mine Workers. The president, John L. Lewis, may have been a Hoover partisan in 1928 and, as he claims, in 1932, but some of his underlings were on the opposite side of the political fence.

One of these was Christ J. Golden, president of the UMW's District 9 regional council, who in 1922 announced to an LID convention that anything other than "industrial democracy" in America would be tantamount to "semi-slavery." When Golden was criticized as a cohort of "Greenwich Village Reds" in the Mine Workers *Journal* he replied by saying that these people, his LID friends, were the most progressive friends the United Mine Workers had. And labor historian David Saposs has reported that at one time over half the AFL convention delegates from the United Mine Workers consisted of prominent Socialists.

The Socialists tried to move into AFL unions, as did the Communists. The CPUSA's chief tool for "capturing" American labor in the 'twenties was a front established by the party's leader, William Z. Foster, and called the Trade Union Educational League. When the TUEL began operations in 1921 it successfully disguised its direct affiliation with the Communists.

Building upon IWW dissidents, AFL Socialists and other "progressive" elements, Foster created an organization which had success boring-from-within the AFL and in promoting industrial unionism. In 1922, Foster openly aligned the TUEL with the Communist International. Few leftists of this day fully comprehended Communism and the general public even looked upon the CP as just another radical element. The open alliance of the TUEL with Moscow in 1922 drove off a few non-Communists, but many others welcomed the new move into politics and contributed to the success of the TUEL in gaining a foothold in many industrial unions. As Communist control of the TUEL became more dictatorial during the 'twenties more members began dropping out, and when a change in the Party line in 1929 transformed the TUEL into the Trade Union Unity League and the policy of dual unionism was followed, the Communists lost a great deal of their liberal support; to be sure, however, many of the unions they had infiltrated, notably the Auto

Workers and Mine, Mill and Smelter Workers, were later to loom large in the activities of the Congress of Industrial Organizations (CIO).

As the far-left was worming its way into American labor, it was also finding doors opening in Washington as the New Deal swept into power in 1932. The AFL had, for the most part, sat quietly on the sidelines during the Hoover-Roosevelt campaign and the workingmen, more intent on earning a meal each night, could not have cared less for political activism in the early days of the 1930s. To be sure, the sentiments of the great percentage of labor leaders were with the eloquent governor of New York, but even when FDR's cherished Social Security system bill came up for hot debate the AFL stood in opposition.

While the AFL was wallowing in the doldrums and its members were fighting to earn a living, the Socialists and radical unionists were learning important political lessons in the early 'thirties. The election triumph of Franklin D. Roosevelt and the subsequent welfarist legislation of the "First Hundred Days" showed the mixed elements of the American left that third parties were no longer necessary, for they could now work towards their goals through an established party. Long-time Socialist activist Upton Sinclair had run for the governorship of California in 1930 on the Socialist ticket and had attracted only 60,000 votes; four years later he ran for the same office on essentially the same platform, but this time as a Democrat, and polled close to a million votes to almost win the election. After this experience, Sinclair voiced the feelings of many of his fellow Socialists when he stated:

". . . it will be the Democratic Party and not the Socialist Party which will bring this great change to America. It will not be called socialism; its opponents will insist that it is communism, while its friends will know that it is industrial democracy."[9]

The political makeup of the New Deal in these days was such that a traveling British Laborite later wrote that "I had the impression that the New Deal was being run by men and women who had voted in the presidential election, not for Franklin Roosevelt, the Democrat, but for Norman Thomas, the Socialist, and Foster, the Communist."[10]

Sitting on top of this entourage was the liberal Roosevelt who had won the support of the Socialist intellectuals and the radical elements of labor simply through long and earnest cultivation. He had impressed the left with his speech nominating Al Smith in 1928 and with his later work as governor; in turn, FDR showed an early concern for lining up the allegiance of the left.

Roosevelt worked diligently to build friendships with organized labor, particularly the more militant and politically oriented segments. After his unsuccessful try for the Democratic vice-presidency on the ticket headed by Cox in 1920, FDR had taken a job with a Maryland insurance company where he was in charge of bonding labor leaders around the country. When he became governor of New York in 1930 he continued to cement his ties with labor, and two of his closest political advisors were New York's radical duo, David Dubinsky, long-time head of the ILGWU, and Sidney Hillman of the Amalgamated Clothing Workers. (Hillman's loyalty to FDR was later repaid with an appointment to the Office of Production Management.) When Roosevelt moved to the White House, these two men and members of their unions' leadership were to support the President to the degree that Norman Thomas bemoaned the fact that "old-time Socialists in the Amalgamated Clothing Workers and the International Ladies' Garment Workers were following Sidney Hillman and David Dubinsky into the New Deal camp."[11]

The enclave of members of the left in the Roosevelt Administration and the ties FDR himself had with radical labor were soon to affect the course of organized labor and, particularly, its political activities. When the AFL's Committee of Industrial Organizations broke away from the parent organization in 1936 to become the Congress of Industrial Organizations, the AFL accused the Administration of showing favoritism to the new union group. Considering the political complexion of Roosevelt's advisors and the fact that Dubinsky and Hillman were leaders of the embryonic CIO, this charge would not seem outrageous.

The decline in AFL membership which had begun in the 'twenties had not been arrested appreciably in the 'thirties. The ravages of the Depression had led many union men to become disillusioned with organized labor generally. To others, the conservative AFL did not seem to have the radical character necessary to match the New Deal, which they looked upon as the progressive savior of the workingman. A further and more specific reason for the AFL's decline in prestige and influence was its signal failure to organize workers in heavy industry.

The Depression had probably hit the industrial workers the hardest of all. Massive layoffs were common, wages were generally low, hours long and conditions sometimes deplorable—laborers in the big factories were often in bad shape. The AFL had generally resisted organizing, in a vertical pattern, industry-wide unions, preferring instead to rely on the craft guild concept, a more horizontal approach which included only skilled workers in a particular craft. While there were industrial unions, such as the Furriers, Mine Workers and Garment Workers, in the AFL, they were the exception to the Gompers-established rule.

The Communists, Socialists and other radical labor elements, on the other hand, had always looked upon the industrial unions as their base of power. Groups such as the IWW and TUEL saw the uneducated, unskilled, lower-class factory workers as just the right audience to respond to messianic leaders urging them to unite, since they had "nothing to lose but your chains."

In 1935 there was a dissident minority in the AFL, composed mainly of the heads of its few industrial unions, who advocated the federation's placing more emphasis on unionizing heavy industry. The Wagner National Labor Relations Act of that year had opened the door to greater opportunities for industrial organization and these AFL radicals meant to take advantage of it. In fact, these laborites, together with the lobbying efforts of their New Deal allies, had been the major force in persuading Congress to pass the historic Wagner Act. Section 7 of that Act gave labor the right "to form, join, or assist labor organizations, to bargain collectively through representatives of their own choosing, and to engage in concerted activities, for the purpose of collective bargaining or other mutual aid or protection." This provision, obviously opening the door for semi-skilled, unskilled and every other kind of worker, was the tool the dissidents needed to overcome the opposition of William Green and the other conservative AFL leaders to industrial unionism.

In November, 1935, a handful of AFL rebels, led by John L. Lewis, David Dubinsky and Sidney Hillman, met in Atlantic City to organize the Committee for Industrial Organization, a group which they intended would remain within the AFL to work solely on organizing factory workers. The chain of events which occurred in rapid succession after this meeting revolved around the implacable, orderly character of William Green and the impetuous, temperamental John L. Lewis: Green strongly disapproved of the new committee and told it to disband; Lewis resigned as AFL vice-president; the United Mine Workers' newspaper, egged on by John L., denounced Green's opposition; contrary to the wishes of Green, a steelworkers organization committee was set up, headed by Lewis lieutenant Philip Murray; Green ordered the AFL to suspend the Committee for Industrial Organization's member unions and its leadership; Lewis, Dubinsky, Hillman and the other ostracized radical leaders changed the Committee's name, kept the initials, and became the Congress of Industrial Organizations.

The CIO was formed around the nucleus of the ten unions Green expelled from the AFL.[12] Some of these unions were remnants of the old IWW (Wobbly) days (the Mine, Mill and Smelter Workers, one of the most Communist-dominated of the new CIO unions, was the offspring of the IWW's Western Federation of Miners), others had been organized and/or infiltrated by the Communists in the Trade Union Unity League (the United Auto Workers, formerly the Auto Workers Union of the TUUL, was deeply inroaded by Communists), and still others, such as Lewis' own Mine Workers, were heavily Socialist.

This wide array of radicals, differing in their degrees of leftism, did have two union goals in common. Their primary aim was to "organize the unorganized" in industry, and the second was to get the CIO in the thick of political battle, or, as the new federation's charter read, "to secure legislation safeguarding the economic security and social welfare of the workers of America . . ." To "secure" this legislation, one of the new federation's first acts was to set up an electioneering department, to be called Labor's Non-Partisan League (LNPL), with George L. Berry, president of the Pressman's Union, and Sidney Hillman, the Socialist head of the Clothing Workers, as its leaders.

The LNPL was a new departure for labor in politics and represented an alteration of the political course set long before by Samuel Gompers and continued by William Green. While not as successful or militant as its 1940s successor, PAC, the League was squarely in the Democrats' camp and did its best to make sure the Democrats were CIO patrons. The League's director, George Berry, had been named in 1935 as a "co-ordinator for industrial co-operation" for FDR's National Recovery Administration, and as for Sidney Hillman, New Deal speechwriter-turned-conservative Raymond Moley was able to write in 1944 that:

"The Hillman strategy since 1936 has been directed toward putting the leftist side of the labor movement into a dominant position in the Democratic Party."[13]

Hillman, Dubinsky, Lewis and the other leaders of the new CIO abandoned any remaining thoughts they had of starting a third, labor-socialist party, and aimed at working through the Non-Partisan League to influence the Democratic Party toward the leftist goals they favored. It was not difficult for the CIO to wield this influence as it had close connections with the Administration through, first, its own men in the New Deal, plus its League for Industrial Democracy (LID) sympa-thizers; the bond that finally soldered the CIO to the party in 1936 however, was a most ancient of all ties: money.

The year 1936, which saw FDR's first attempt at re-election, was still a Depression year and political contributions were hard to come by. Realizing this, John L. Lewis opened the coffers of the CIO wide to the Democrats and did the same with the treasury of his Mine Workers. It is not known exactly how much the CIO finally gave Roosevelt, but it has been estimated that the UMW alone gave well over half a million and that the other industrial unions, rich with dues from the newly acquired members, gave freely to buy their way to Washington. Whatever the exact total of the sizable contribution, FDR idolator Arthur Schlesinger, Jr., in his *Age of Roosevelt* series, writes that, "at a time when contributions from big business were falling sharply . . . labor enabled Roosevelt and [campaign director-Postmaster General James] Farley to campaign in the style to which they had become accustomed."[14]

Roosevelt, at the same time, was aware of the broad-based "grass-roots" support which was available for the asking through the huge industrial unions; and to ally with the CIO was a much more practical political move than to attempt to alter the firm non-partisan position of the AFL.

The CIO's Non-Partisan League, however, was not much more effective than the AFL had been, despite the Democrats' cooperation. Although it had money to dole out by the carload and the political intelligence of Sidney Hillman and George Berry to draw upon, the League could not fire up the workingmen to militant political action.

The most damaging blow to the LNPL's political influence came in 1940 when CIO president Lewis had his dramatic falling out with Roosevelt and all but ended his own career as a national labor leader. The most popular version of this story has it that the egomaniacal Lewis walked into the White House early in 1940 and modestly proposed to the President that he, Lewis, ought to have a place on the third-term Roosevelt ticket. "Which place will you take, John?," FDR supposedly replied. The elephantine CIO leader and Mine Workers boss stomped out of the room and later announced over coast-to-coast radio that he was supporting Republican Wendell Willkie and added that he intended to resign if Roosevelt was re-elected.

When FDR did win a third term, Lewis reneged on his vow and indicated he intended to stay on as CIO head; many of the delegates at the federation's '40 convention wanted to retain Lewis and prepared a campaign to draft him as president. The hard-line CIO leftists, led by Sidney Hillman and others who had gone down the line for Roosevelt, stopped this draft campaign, retired John L. Lewis, and promoted his former aide Philip Murray to the head of the CIO.

This family row within the CIO ended the LNPL, which Lewis had run with an iron hand, and created a temporary setback for the federation's political program. This was not by any means the end, for as a staff member of the Political Action Committee wrote four years later:

"Circumstance and the ego of a single individual caused the stultification of Labor's Non-Partisan League. But the organization which had given it birth, the CIO, remained and grew stronger with every passing day. And the leadership of labor had learned another valuable lesson in political action, which served them well in the next national crisis."[15]

By the time this statement was written in 1944, Lewis had quit the CIO, his former vice-president at the UMW, Philip Murray, having taken over the presidency. The next "national crisis" which the PAC pamphleteer speaks of came in 1942, when a conservative mood dominated the country and a Congress "openly at odds with the President" was elected. As an outgrowth of these election results, the CIO again organized an electioneering arm and created the Political Action Committee.

In the 1942 off-year congressional elections only 28 million people took the time to vote, although some 80 million were qualified. The Congress elected that year was markedly conservative and proceeded to act as a check against some of President Roosevelt's more radical programs. On July 7, 1943, the Executive Board of the CIO met in Washington "to evaluate the results of the 1942 elections, to evolve an effective plan to stem the reactionary tide, and to devise methods of putting that plan to work." The method devised was a Political Action Committee and at the CIO's biannual convention in November, 1943, president Philip Murray reported to the delegates on the formation of the new CIO adjunct:

"It is the function of the [Political Action] Committee to conduct a broad and intensive program of education for the purpose of mobilizing the five million members of the CIO . . . for effective labor action on the political front. . . .

"It is therefore the purpose of the CIO Political Action Committee to provide for the organization of labor's political arm. While the committee regards preparation for the crucial national elections of 1944 as a major task, it is also looking beyond 1944 and planning for a permanent political organization of labor. . . ."[16]

In a February, 1944, article in *American* magazine, Murray outlined further the purposes of the Political Action Committee which was to dominate the '44 elections:

"This is something new in American politics," he said of the Committee, "and it is a new departure for American labor to lead, and pour its funds into, a national movement devoted to the general welfare just as much as to the particular interests of labor groups. . . .

"We, of the CIO, and of labor generally, believe in the democratic system. We believe that the people, once they understand the issues, will decide them wisely. . . ."[17]

It was understood that PAC was to be the one organization which would help the people to "decide" the issues "wisely." After PAC's formation at the 1943 special session in Washington (the CIO leaders did not wait for the convention's formal approval of PAC before starting to work) the machinery for labor to "recapture" Congress was set in motion: the country was divided into 14 districts, leaders were chosen, a New York headquarters set up, meetings held, activities outlined, and old Socialist hand Sidney Hillman was named chairman of the new PAC.

The chairmanship of PAC was to be Sidney Hillman's "last hurrah" in the American labor movement. When he died in 1945 at the age of

58, Hillman had given most of his life to the development of his union, the Amalgamated Clothing Workers, and to the increased political radicalism of labor generally. Even his most bitter enemies credit Hillman with a blend of perceptive intelligence and hard-nosed practical militancy that led him to become one of the country's most effective and influential labor-political leaders.

His fatal flaw, however, was his open collaboration with Communists. While never a Communist himself and, in fact, sometimes a tough anti-Communist, Hillman nevertheless believed at times that alliance with the Communists could help his cause and that he could use them without being hurt himself. As a result of such naiveté, an otherwise capable and efficient labor administrator came to be looked upon by many as a foolish Communist "dupe."

Sidney Hillman's last—and most embarrassing—tie-in with the Communist left involved his position of leadership in the American Labor Party, a labor-liberal third party formed in New York State in 1936 to help FDR win a second term. The ALP from its beginning had been dominated by leftists of all sizes and types, not the least of whom were many prominent Communist labor leaders. This situation persisted until 1944 when the Communists made a bold move, with Hillman's tacit backing, to gain outright control of the ALP; this move outraged the more responsible liberal elements of the party and a full-fledged, blood-letting feud developed in the ALP ranks.

It was unfortunate for Hillman that the Communists chose 1944 to make their move and that the anti-Communists chose to vigorously oppose them. This was the year PAC was moving into national politics, under Hillman's leadership, and charges of Communist infiltration of PAC were being hurled daily. PAC's image was not helped any by Hillman's Red friends in the ALP.

The conflict between the Socialist-liberals and the Communists in the Labor Party became intense. At the 1944 ALP convention the leaders of the party's "right wing," led by Hillman's old crony David Dubinsky, a Russian-born Jew who had once been exiled to Siberia by the Czarist government, sought to have the Communists ousted from the party. When this position was defeated and Hillman's side had won, Dubinsky and his followers quit the ALP to form New York's Liberal Party, the left-wing gadfly in the state's politics.

As long as the AFL under the staunch anti-Communist leadership of William Green continued to dominate the American labor scene, the Communist conspirators in the U.S. had nowhere to go. But many of the unions belonging to the original CIO were already Communist-infiltrated by the time of the organization's birth in 1936, and it did not take them long to get a foothold in many more. As did Sidney Hillman, John L.

Lewis and his chief lieutenant—later his successor as CIO president—
Philip Murray, made the near-tragic mistake of thinking they could use
the Communists' organizing skills without paying the price of being
ruled from Moscow.

In the face of this attitude, Communists continued to march into the
CIO *en masse,* grabbing control of huge unions and securing positions of
leadership in the CIO itself. In 1944 the Special Committee on Un-
American Activities of the House of Representatives issued a report on
the Political Action Committee which showed conclusively that 21
union affiliates of the CIO—a majority of the member unions—were
dominated by Communist leadership, and that 18 of the 49 members
of the CIO's Executive Board were either outright Communists or duti-
ful followers of the party line.

The specter of Communism haunted the CIO and also PAC. Indeed,
the very idea for the Political Action Committee appeared to come, in
part at least, from the Communist leaders in the United States, and once
PAC was formed, the Communists threw their total support behind it.

Writing in the July, 1943, issue of *The Communist,* official monthly
publication of the CPUSA, national party chairman Earl Browder concluded that the party "must unite the CIO behind the leadership of Phil
Murray and his clear and correct program for the labor movement, and
we must work with every honest leading element who goes along with
Murray in the fullest collaboration, giving them our confidence and
support. . . . We must build the unity of all anti-Axis elements for the war
now, and for the 1944 elections, which are already a practical issue
today in the course of the conduct of the war." PAC was organized a
short time later.

In early 1944 the American Communist leaders received word from
Moscow that, in accordance with the new "united war effort" line, they
were to abandon the CPUSA as an open *political* party and refrain from
putting up candidates, or perform any distinctly political activities, in
the party's name. Instead, the U.S. Communists were ordered to promote their ideology by working as a well-disciplined faction within established, reputable political organizations. One of the groups they
intended to so subvert was PAC, and when the CPUSA obediently followed Stalin's dictate and "dissolved" itself as an open political instrument at its '44 convention, national chairman Earl Browder made the
significant statement:

"All of labor's present organized efforts looking toward effective political action must be deepened, strengthened and made broader and more
inclusive. All this must culminate in a great united effort in the 1944
elections. . . ."[18]

The Communists wasted no time in using their substantial power in the CIO to influence the direction of PAC: Sidney Hillman, who at the same time was openly collaborating with the Communists in New York's American Labor Party, was the top dog at PAC; R. J. Thomas, a man who held the presidency of the United Auto Workers only with the blessing of the Communists, was PAC's secretary; at PAC's national conference in 1944, nine known Communists were among the speakers; and so it went.

Some union men and a few liberals rose up to criticize PAC. William Mullins, a member of the Newspaper Guild, CIO, on the staff of the Boston *Herald,* wrote an article entitled "I Object to My Union in Politics" in the *Reader's Digest,* in which he stated: ". . . through my union's affiliation with the CIO, I find myself represented in politics, without my consent and against my will, by [PAC]."[19] And Socialist Louis Waldman wrote in the *Saturday Evening Post* that ". . . behind the cautious phrases of Mr. Hillman and his able lieutenants is the firm determination of PAC and the New Deal to capture the Democratic Party."[20]

By no means was the press entirely against PAC, much as the organization might have liked to make out. Most liberal papers of the day supported it, including the pro-Communist *PM,* which in one issue proclaimed "Hats Off: To Sidney Hillman and the Political Action Committee for carrying a great part of the burden of taking the issues of this Presidential campaign to the people."[21]

And when the press made charges against PAC, they were returned in kind by PAC staffers and its liberal friends, the favorite method of rebuttal being to make PAC's opponents look like some sort of secret agents for Adolf Hitler. When Republican vice-presidential nominee John W. Bricker, then governor of Ohio, criticized Sidney Hillman in one campaign speech, the *New Republic* pointed the accusing finger and said that Bricker has used the Goebbels technique, in a reference to the Nazi propaganda minister.

The CIO had set up its Political Action Committee for one purpose: to win a fourth term for Franklin D. Roosevelt and elect a Democrat-liberal Congress.[22] A conservative Congress had been elected in 1942 and in 1944 there was a conservative, nationalist attitude common throughout the land, and, while Roosevelt was still popular, many voters felt he was becoming too stale, physically weak and tired to warrant a fourth term in office.

The blossoming of PAC as a "front" for the Democrats obviously had the enthusiastic support of Roosevelt. Hillman had been one of FDR's closest advisors when the President was governor of New York and the Clothing Workers' leader had remained close to the Hudson River patroon after he came to the White House. As a reward for his loyalty

Sidney Hillman had been picked to head the Labor Division of the Administration's Office of Production Management. It was obvious to all who knew how badly Roosevelt wanted re-election (and feared defeat by Dewey) that the President was well aware of what his old friend Hillman and PAC were up to; whether or not Roosevelt was disturbed by the presence of Communists in PAC, he sorely needed its organizational support in 1944 and gave his blessing to Hillman's efforts on his behalf.

That such was the case was borne out at the 1944 Democratic convention in Chicago. The President did not wish Henry Wallace to be renominated as his vice-president. PAC wanted Wallace. PAC did not succeed in pressuring FDR into running with Wallace again, but they did successfully block the selection of FDR's first choice, James F. Byrnes, former Supreme Court Justice, then Economic Coordinator, later Secretary of State. When Roosevelt finally settled on Sen. Harry Truman of Missouri as his running-mate, he reportedly turned to an aide and said, referring to Truman's selection, "Clear it with Sidney." And a slogan was born.

The Republicans used and reused the slogan "Clear it with Sidney" throughout the campaign to indicate the power that PAC and its chairman held over the President. There was some argument at the time as to whether those exact words were ever uttered by the President but this was beside the point, for as one knowledgeable observer reported: "Whether Mr. Roosevelt actually said, 'Clear it with Sidney,' is not important. His directives to his leaders in the convention meant exactly that."[23]

Besides clearing vice-presidential nominations, PAC indulged in a wide range of activities, most still practiced by its successor, COPE. It hired a full-time staff of 135 to set up a political organization from Hillman's office down to the precincts; it published reams of literature (38 different pamphlets with a total printing of over 63 million); it registered voters; it "educated" the public; it distributed voting records (the Special Un-American Activities Committee found that PAC's 1944 voting record was a point-by-point duplicate of that circulated by the Communist Party the same year); and it supported candidates in the primaries and general elections.

In its endorsement of candidates, PAC performed almost exactly as does COPE today: it backed liberal Democrats to the hilt, opposed conservative Democrats in the primaries, and fought Republicans in general. However, to be on the safe side, PAC occasionally deviated from dogma and lent its backing to a handful of GOP incumbents. Two of the Republicans so blessed in '44 were Sen. Leverett Saltonstall of Massachusetts and Sen. George Aiken of Vermont.

To show their "open-mindedness," PAC leaders publicized their backing of Republicans. In *The First Round,* PAC promoter Joseph Gaer makes the statement that "in some states PAC supported conservatives, such as Republican [Sen.] Wayne Morse of Oregon.[24]

As for financing the multitude of operations it was indulging in, PAC was up against laws similar to those now governing COPE's spending. PAC could not use money from union treasuries in the general election campaigns (although they could, and did, in primaries), so it was necessary to go outside of this source and raise "voluntary" funds. The books of the organization show that it raised a little over a million dollars and spent around $600,000, but observers at the time thought both these figures to be ridiculously low.

It was only natural that such a group as PAC, bursting unprecedented on the election scene and organizing a well-disciplined and well-financed political machine in less than a year, should attract the attention of Congressional investigators. In addition to the 215-page report on PAC issued by Martin Dies' Un-American Activities Committee, two other congressional committees—the Senate and House Campaign Expenditures Committees—called Sidney Hillman to Capitol Hill to tell the lawmakers about PAC's activities. Pressure was also placed on the reluctant Administration to look into PAC's financial operations.

The outcome of PAC activity on the political makeup of the nation was profound. Franklin D. Roosevelt defeated Thomas E. Dewey convincingly. *Newsweek* magazine reported after the election, "For the first time in American history, labor had been the organizational vehicle of a Presidential candidate. . . . Without it [PAC] his [Roosevelt's] defeat would have been almost a certainty. . . . it provided what the Democratic Party had plainly lost—organization. . . . The results last Tuesday elevated Hillman—and Murray with him—to the highest political stature ever attained by labor leaders."[25]

On the congressional level PAC was able to wield tremendous influence and make the difference in countless contests by employing the same electioneering tactics that have made COPE such a success since the AFL-CIO merger. In the Democratic primaries it helped significantly to defeat such conservative House members as Joe Starnes of Alabama and John M. Costello of California, both members of the PAC-hated Un-American Activities Committee, and its power in Texas was so great that the chairman of that committee, Rep. Dies, decided not to stand for re-election. In the Senate, PAC aided the defeat, among others, of conservative Sen. Gerald Nye (R-N.D.) and, by pouring money and manpower into Arkansas, PAC influenced a primary which has had lasting effect on American politics: it defeated the Senate's "grande dame," Hattie Carraway, and elected the young and scholarly radical, J. William Fulbright.

PAC's hard-nosed politicking had alienated many persons and there was open warfare between Congress and the Hillman Committee. Over the next few years PAC maintained its extremely liberal goals and its alliance with the Democrats, but its methods became more subtle and low-keyed; it continued to drive a hard bargain with public officials, but carried on its activities behind closed doors, rather than in newspaper headlines.

The CIO had another problem which related directly to PAC, the presence of Communist unions as affiliates and Communist Party members in the federation's hierarchy. CIO president Philip Murray and the other non-Communist leaders of the organization realized that if the CIO was going to prosper and gain the respect of the American public they would have to rid themselves of the Communist albatross.

After the celebrations of VE Day and the Japanese surrender, it was not long before a new conflict, soon to be labeled the "Cold War," began and the American public became aware that its Russian ally of the war was not the friend it had been played up to be in the early 'forties. With opinion running strongly against the Communists and with former party members telling congressional committees about Communists in high places in Washington, the CIO itself underwent a long and painful Red purge.

Under the leadership of Phil Murray, the non-Communist CIO leaders chartered new unions to rival and to raid the membership of those that were Red-dominated. These leaders emphasized to the rank-and-file that the road to tomorrow was to the left, but not the tyrannical Communist left. Murray and friends—the Socialists, the LID grads and the other assorted leftists—booted the Communists out of the CIO so that they might gain respect and also be able to control their own federation. The Communists had become an intolerable presence in the CIO, the leftists who purged them were applauded by the public—socialism had managed to appear as an attractive, desirable compromise.

By 1950 the CIO ranks were, to the great degree, clean. The leadership of some Communist unions had been replaced, other unions—such as the Mine, Mill and Smelter Workers—had been kicked out wholesale and the Party members or line-followers who had sat on the CIO Executive Board had either changed their ways—as did Mike Quill and Joe Curran—or had been booted out by Murray. But many of the Communist-influenced CIO policies remained, and none were more lasting than those of the Political Action Committee. PAC had been something radically new: a national political organization directly aligned with, and sometimes controlling, a major party. And it was indisputable that this new direction had, to a large extent, been inspired and administered by Communists. With the AFL-CIO merger in 1955 the policies behind this direction were carried over, all but intact, into the Committee on Political Education.

Meanwhile, the American Federation of Labor would have nothing to do with PAC. The boisterous methods and coercive tactics of the Political Action Committee were incompatible with the AFL's Gompers-inspired tradition of supporting friends and defeating enemies on a local, nominally nonpartisan level. During the 'thirties and 'forties the AFL had continued to urge its members to become active in local politics, and gave some endorsements to congressional candidates, but the AFL stayed out of presidential elections and from 1944 on it maintained a good distance between itself and PAC.

An indication, in return, of what the CIO thought of the venerable American Federation of Labor can be glimpsed from a 1944 account in the strongly pro-CIO *New Republic* concerning a new world trade union organization proposed by Russia. The leftist publication, which referred to the AFL as "The Dowager Duchess of American Labor," criticized the AFL because it "passes the CIO with a haughty stare, and so far as the Soviet trade unions are concerned, they just don't exist at all." And in chiding the AFL for not joining with the Communists in a world-wide federation, the *New Republic* sneered that "The [AFL] is an august and numerous body, but its international labor activities have usually been confined to sending delegates to conventions and nothing more. The CIO is thought to mean business."[26]

One of the most enlightening comparisons of the political approaches of the CIO and the AFL has been provided by the late Phil Pearl, a life-long journalist-unionist who was director of public relations for the AFL in the 1940s and later an official with the AFL-CIO's Maritime Trades Department. While PAC never considered giving its support to a conservative candidate (other than Wayne Morse, that is) under any circumstances, Pearl disclosed the AFL did precisely this and caused a great deal of anger and bewilderment in the CIO when it did. Actually, the AFL was only being realistic instead of behaving like PAC's self-righteous ideologues, or, as Pearl described them, "shining knights in white armor."

Two examples of AFL-endorsed conservatives, Pearl related, were Sen. Pat McCarran (D-Nev.) and Rep. Hamilton Fish (R-N.Y.). Both these men were solid supporters of states' rights, free enterprise and other "reactionary" policies, and PAC, labeling them "anti-labor," worked for their defeat. According to Phil Pearl, the AFL supported McCarran because he was labor's "ace in the hole" on the Senate Judiciary Committee, of which he was chairman; when it came down to a one-vote difference on a bill the AFL wanted badly, McCarran would provide the vote—in committee, but not on the floor of the Senate where his vote would be recorded. According to Pearl, Fish allegedly played a similar role as a member of the important House Rules Committee. Fish received a letter of endorsement from AFL president Green whenever he ran for re-election. "We knew we couldn't get anyone better, from our point of view, in Fish's [congressional] district," explained Phil Pearl, "so we did our best to work with him."

Late in 1947 the AFL did create a nationwide political committee, called Labor's League for Political Education (LLPE), but it was far removed in operations and goals from the CIO's Political Action Committee. The AFL's main reason for establishing the LLPE was to fight passage of the Taft-Hartley Act; when this campaign was unsuccessful, the organization was kept in operation to distribute political "educational" literature to AFL members. It did not take a position on every issue that came along outside the field of labor legislation, as did PAC, nor did it dictate to its members whom to support and what "reactionaries" to oppose. Also, the LLPE had no organizational network, preferring to leave action decisions up to the members, stressing political education as the primary goal. It was, then, quite unlike both PAC and the modern-day COPE.

This situation remained for the next few years, with the LLPE educating its members on a decentralized basis and PAC beating its drums—albeit muffled—for its candidates and causes. When the Congress of Industrial Organizations and American Federation of Labor voted to merge in December, 1955, the new political arm of labor, the Committee on Political Education, took its name from the title of the AFL's Labor's League for Political Education. But its operating methods were taken strictly from the CIO's Political Action Committee.

The decision for COPE to follow in the footsteps of PAC, rather than the LLPE, did not come about easily and there continued to be disputes over candidates and tactics between the AFL and CIO right up to the first election day after the merger, in November, 1956. In the '56 Democratic gubernatorial primary in Kentucky, for example, the AFL backed the winner, A. B. "Happy" Chandler, whom the CIO had bitterly opposed. In Pittsburgh the CIO endorsed the Democratic ticket from top to bottom, while the AFL backed seven GOP candidates. And in Michigan the AFL opposed the CIO's darling, G. Mennen Williams, for the governorship, preferring his Republican opponent, Mayor Albert Cobo of Detroit.

Thus, while the individual state AFL and CIO organizations voted separately to merge, an eventuality that would force them to support the same candidates under the aegis of COPE, the battle over political position still raged between the two. AFL officials were quoted as saying, "The CIO-PAC used to shoot off its mouth too much . . . we [in the merger] are going to do things quietly, without a lot of boasts and threats and predictions of big victories."[27]

And another report commented that, "some members of the AFL-CIO council are determined that the new federation not be tied as closely to the Democratic Party as the old CIO was . . . other leaders want to stay clear of any AFL-CIO political action."[28]

But such was not to be the case. The CIO had laid the groundwork for continuing hostility towards the Republicans well and three months before the AFL-CIO merger, *Business Week* magazine reported:

"Although not yet unified, the labor bodies have already begun a coordinated attack on the Administration, its policies, and many of its appointees. The dominant theme of recent Labor Day addresses was political: criticism of the Republicans."[29]

(Also on Labor Day, 1955, President Eisenhower's Secretary of Labor, James P. Mitchell, was not invited to speak at a single labor gathering.)

Out in Toledo, Ohio, a CIO spokesman for that city's United Labor Committee stated that, "we will pick up anyone [to ride to the polls] on Election Day—Democrats, independents, non-partisans, everybody except Republicans."[30]

The CIO-PAC anti-Republican, liberal attitude was also evident in the composition of the leadership of the new Committee on Political Education. COPE was the only committee of the merged federation which had dual chairmanship, and one of these leaders was the head of the disbanded PAC, Jack Kroll. Kroll had succeeded to the top of PAC on the death in 1945 of his long-time friend Sidney Hillman. Kroll had been associated with Hillman in the Amalgamated Clothing Workers since its formation, and had been appointed by Hillman to be PAC's regional director for the states of Ohio, West Virginia and Kentucky when the organization was founded.

The other COPE co-chairman was James L. McDevitt, former head of the Pennsylvania Federation of Labor and leader of the AFL's Labor's League for Political Education at the time of the merger. McDevitt's opinion of the Republican Party can be seen in the following observation made in a laudatory biography published by the Pennsylvania AFL:

"The lengthening series of defeats suffered by the Republicans in Pennsylvania since 1946 is attributable in large measure to the zeal with which McDevitt translated this traditional labor policy [of Gompers] into methodical and aggressive practice."[31]

With such an openly pro-Democrat leadership, even on the part of the AFL's man, it is not at all surprising that the first COPE voting records, in 1956, found 43 Republicans and only 10 Democrats voting "wrong" a majority of the time in the Senate, and 175 Republicans and 59 Democrats on the "wrong" side in the House. Following on the heels of this revelation, in September, 1956, "COPE announced that the AFL-CIO 'might' endorse 25 Republicans in House races," and also reported that "they 'haven't yet found an acceptable Republican senatorial candidate' to support."[32]

It should have been obvious that the brand-new, merged federation and its electioneering arm were not going to "stay clear of any . . . political action," nor was it going to listen to the old-line AFL leaders who did not want to "be tied as closely to the Democratic Party as the old CIO was . . ." But these leaders who wanted the AFL-CIO to follow the old Gompers line of concentrating on labor legislation and participating only in local politics, still held out hope that the new organization would not get involved in presidential contests and risk alienating a President and his whole party. Even these dreams were soon shattered.

Dwight D. Eisenhower was one of the most "progressive" Republicans ever elected to the Presidency, a man always willing to listen to labor leaders and work with them when he thought they were right. And in James P. Mitchell, a former industrial personnel expert for the Army, he had a Secretary of Labor with a sympathetic approach to organized labor's problems. As a result of this cooperative attitude in the Administration some in the labor hierarchy, such as James C. Petrillo, head of the Musicians Union and member of the AFL-CIO's Executive Board, could state that, "if we ever had a friend in the White House, we have one now."[33]

But countering Petrillo was the old CIO crowd, men such as the Auto Workers' Walter Reuther and James B. Carey, head of the International Electrical Workers Union, activist ideologues who were irrevocably committed to supporting the policies and candidates of the liberal wing of the Democratic Party.

In the first week of September, 1956, the AFL-CIO's 23-member Executive Council met at the Pocono Mountain vacation resort of David Dubinsky's Ladies' Garment Workers' Union to decide whether or not to endorse a presidential candidate. Those favorable to Eisenhower, or opposed to the AFL-CIO's getting into politics altogether, voted against endorsement; the hard-line Democrats, led by Walter Reuther, vice-president of the merged federation, favored supporting the Democratic ticket of Adlai Stevenson and Estes Kefauver; AFL-CIO president George Meany, because he was dissatisfied with the platforms of both parties, opposed endorsement, saying, "Don't get me wrong. I'm not neutral— I'm against both parties."[34]

For two days the debate continued and finally a vote was called for.

The first vote taken was on the question of whether or not to endorse any presidential candidate, and the council voted 14 to 8 to do so. That decided, the AFL-CIO vice-presidents voted 17 to 5 to endorse Democrat Stevenson. The labor federation, in the face of a friendly Republican Administration, but aligned itself with the Democratic Party.

The larger implication of this alignment is not that it is with the Democrats, rather than the Republicans, or that it is ideologically liberal instead of conservative. It is that there is an alliance. The rank-and-file suffer from it, as does American labor, as a movement.

When union leaders place their federation (or union) at the disposal of one political party, two immediate results occur. First, the leaders become to a real degree servants of the party and thereby expend time and energy that could otherwise be used caring for the economic needs of their members and the organizational demands of their unions and the federation.

Second, and more important in broader political terms, the partisan labor federation becomes essentially dependent on the fate of the party; its fortunes rise and fall with those of the party, and if some factor completely unrelated to labor causes defeat of the party it makes no difference as far as the federation's political stock is concerned: the party lost, *ergo* the federation lost.

The chief victim, then, is labor's independence For the ability to get as much as it could for its members, from whichever party is in power, the AFL-CIO in 1956 substituted a dependence on—a servitude to—the Democratic Party. The CIO concept of political action had won out and the more moderate policy of the AFL was shoved aside. It made no difference whether the Democrats needed labor more than labor needed the Democrats: labor had cast its lot and the AFL-CIO's political policy was affirmed and set in motion.

The Committee on Political Education, a direct descendent of a group of Boston craftsmen calling themselves "The Caucus," had evolved in history to become a political force, representing one economic bloc, second to none in the land and second to none in American history. The COPE family tree took a long time in the growing, its roots are deep and the shade it casts covers all of American politics.

## CHAPTER FOUR

# The Men Behind COPE

THE history of American labor unionism is filled with conflicts between varying forms of political action, with socialist third-party proponents battling the pro-Democrats, and the CIO activists challenging the "non-partisan" AFL leaders. The conflicts were, however, more than matters of principle. The men behind the theories—the personal nature and character of each—gave the conflicts root and aided their development.

The principles were conflicting, to be sure, but the men who conceived and executed labor's political activities were their driving force; Hillman and Green may have had differing ideas on labor's political role, but a militant activist such as Hillman would probably rub against the grain of a complacent, tractable person such as Green in any circumstance. This is a primary reason why the labor movement has a history to be told in terms of the men who made organized labor a dominating force in American society and politics.

Since 1952 two men have overshadowed all others in the U.S. labor picture, George Meany, president of the old AFL and of the merged federation, and Walter Reuther, president of the UAW, the CIO and, after the merger and until 1967, a vice-president of the AFL-CIO. These two men are as totally opposite in almost every personality trait as were their predecessors, William Green and Phil Murray, and the conflicts Meany (the bluntly pragmatic administrator) and Reuther (the zealous ideologue activist) have engaged in are legion. In between their frequent disputes Meany and Reuther cooperated sufficiently to make the AFL-CIO—and its Committee on Political Education—a successfully going concern.

While these two personalities have long attracted the public's attention as the most powerful labor leaders, the immediate political course of the AFL-CIO had been placed in the hands of two other men, the late

James L. McDevitt, the first full director of COPE, and his successor, Al Barkan. There was never much conflict between these two men, since both were cast from the same mold; as was McDevitt, Barkan is a diligent organizer who quietly goes about his job of building an effective political machine and keeping it running smoothly. They are the unobtrusive, albeit staunchly liberal, type of men who do their jobs behind the scenes, more than willing to let their superiors—Meany and Reuther —hold down the spotlight in center stage.

These are the four men around whom have revolved the fortunes of organized labor and its political operations in the 'fifties and 'sixties. Due to the nature of the power and influence inherent in their positions, their contributions to the political makeup of the nation have been significant.

## GEORGE MEANY

The man who is generally credited with bringing about the bond between the American Federation of Labor and the Congress of Industrial Organizations is a big, bluff, cigar-smoking ex-plumber who decided when he took over as president of the AFL in 1952 that it was time for the two federations to stop fighting each other and to get about the business of organizing workers—as one federation. George Meany accomplished this imposing task in three short years.

William Green had been head of the AFL for 28 years before his death in November, 1952; Philip Murray, who had been in command of the CIO ever since his former boss, John L. Lewis, stepped down in 1940, died two weeks before Green. While these two men lived and continued to head their respective federations, there was no chance for cooperation, to say nothing of a merger.

For the rest of his life Green resented the unions and the leaders who had broken from his organization in 1936; even when Lewis came back to the AFL fold in 1946 the new-found palship was brief and the Mine Workers chief disaffiliated and set up shop as an independent a year later. But Green opposed Philip Murray just as much as Lewis: it was Murray who had been chairman of the Committee on Industrial Organizations' steelworkers organizational committee—the establishment of which led directly to the CIO's ouster from the AFL; and it was Murray, as head of the CIO, who had set up the Political Action Committee, the electioneering arm which cast almost as many slurs at the politically low-keyed AFL as it did at the Republicans.

Shortly after Murray died of a heart attack in his San Francisco hotel room on the eve of the CIO's 1952 convention, he was replaced at the top of the smaller federation by the Auto Workers' radical boss, Walter

Reuther. And when George Meany was elected to take William Green's place a fortnight later, the air was suddenly clear of the old personal antagonisms and the AFL president saw that it was then or never for the merger.

Meany's first official act on becoming president was to reactivate the Labor Unity Committee and following this he personally worked cease-lessly toward the goal of a merger. When the AFL and CIO leaders met to deliberate unity in February, 1955, after three years of negotiations and discussions, Meany thought that the talking had gone on long enough. Walter Reuther opened the meeting with a typically long-winded statement of principles; Meany in his turn rose and outlined the situation with characteristic bluntness:

"We can go after unity the long way or the short way. The short way is to merge into one trade union center which will protect the integrity of all affiliates. The long way is to solve all of our problems before merg-ing. Which will it be?"[1]

The conferees chose the short way, and Reuther agreed to step aside in favor of the larger federation's leader and take a vice-presidency. That December the merger was put on paper and after the official doc-uments were signed the jubilant Meany romped down to the grand piano in the lobby of the hotel meeting place and rippled off several choruses of the French ballad, "La Seine."

In the first ten years of the AFL-CIO's life George Meany managed, with the help of other leaders, to iron out most of the problems which had existed in 1955. He negotiated an agreement among affiliated unions preventing their raiding each other's memberships, a pre-merger activity which had dangerously sapped the unions' strength; he kicked five racket-infested unions out of the federation, including the AFL-CIO's single largest member union, Jimmy Hoffa's one million-plus Teamsters; he fought as well as he could against racial discrimination in union hiring and membership, and led the AFL-CIO into the position of a leader in civil rights.

Throughout the AFL-CIO lifespan, inevitably filled with the sharp clashes of personalities and ideas, George Meany has remained the un-disputed boss of Big Labor. Walter Reuther may have had an ambition to rule the labor world, and other leftist union leaders may not have always thought Meany to be "progressive" enough, but the dissident factions have had to either get out or put their differences aside and accept the bull-necked one-time plumber as the last word and supreme authority in AFL-CIO affairs.

Mike Meany, a husky, handsome plumber, was presented by his wife Annie with their second child, William George, on August 16, 1894. Born in a brownstone flat in Harlem and raised in a brick row house along the East River in the Bronx, George Meany grew up in the healthy, happy surroundings of an active, well-knit family of ten children. His father was prosperous and well liked, president of his plumber's union local and district captain for the Democratic Party; the Meany home was constantly filled with local politicians and unionists sitting and talking for hours about the trials and troubles of workers. As Meany later related about these gatherings:

"I can remember these men talking about something known as 'the organization,' and I may say to you that they did not pronounce it that way, they called it the 'organ-eye-zation.' But I can remember the reverence in which they used the term, and inculcated into my mind at that time was the thought that whatever the organization was, it was something with these men almost on a par with religion. I grew up with faith in the trade-union movement."[2]

Headily influenced by his father's faith in the Democratic Party and trade unionism, young Meany rejected schoolwork as boring and set out to sample the rewards that this faith could bring. He wangled a job from one of his father's union friends and at 16 became a plumber's assistant at $1.50 a day; by the time he was 21 he was pulling down $30 a week as a journeyman plumber and working on the construction of some of New York City's most notable landmarks, including Grand Central Station and the Commodore Hotel.

At this early age George Meany was not the active union member he was later to become. He seemed more interested in playing baseball as a semi-pro catcher and squiring young ladies to Tammany Hall dances than in attending union meetings. But in 1919 Meany became a family man, marrying a garment worker named Eugenia McMahon, and settled down to accept the responsibilities of life and union membership.

By 1920 he had become active enough in the plumbers Local 463 to be elected to the local board. Two years later he was named business agent for the local and in 1923 he was made secretary-treasurer of the New York Building Trades Council, a federation of several AFL construction unions. For the next few years Meany grew slowly in stature in the city's labor affairs and was recognized by his fellow workers as a capable leader and tough bargainer. When the Depression hit New York, Meany frequently worked with no pay at all and attempted to aid the financially destitute city unions.

In the Depression year of 1935 the leading candidate for the New York AFL presidency was a bartender from upstate who was thought to be unsympathetic to the economic plight of the Metropolitan building trades unions. To protect their interests, the New York labor leaders nominated Meany for the executive post, staged a whirlwind campaign, elected him, and the Bronx plumber was on his way to becoming a national union leader.

As labor's chief representative at the state capital in Albany, Meany worked diligently with facts and figures to sell the lawmakers on his bloc's legislative program. By the end of the first legislative session during his term as state president, Meany's success was measured by the unqualified admiration of liberal Democratic Governor Herbert Lehman and a record of getting the legislators to pass 72 of the 105 bills he had urged on behalf of the state AFL. Meanwhile, in New York City Meany fought and won a long fight with FDR's Works Progress Administration and its administrator, Harry Hopkins, over the issue of whether or not the WPA should pay union-scale wages to unemployed workers on its rolls. (Meany wanted it to and it did.)

It was also while he was state AFL president that Meany first became engaged in politics and began speaking out as a militant anti-Communist. The Democratic machine ensconced in its Tammany Hall headquarters had long held sway over the AFL locals, but Meany blunted this influence and delivered the bulk of the AFL labor vote to left-wing Republican-fusionist (later pro-Democrat), Fiorello La Guardia in the 1937 New York mayoralty race. This was at the same time that the "progressive" elements of the New York labor, led by the men's clothing workers' Sidney Hillman and the ladies' garment workers' David Dubinsky, were teaming up with various radical elements under the banner of the American Labor Party.

Refusing to go along with this leftist labor tide, in 1938 Meany attacked the ALP and its leaders as "political self-seekers, left-wingers, political renegades and non-laboring laborites."[3] At an American Legion Convention a year later, Meany attacked totalitarianism of the Left and Right, and clearly outlined his reasons for this life-long opposition:

"Labor has more reason to be vigilant in defense of democracy than has any other group or class. Organizations of working men and women formed for the sole purpose of raising the standards of life and work for wage earners cannot exist under any other form of government . . . Free trade unionism cannot exist where there is a dictator in control."[4]

In 1939 Meany gave up his New York State post to move to Washington as secretary-treasurer of the national AFL. The promotion proved to have its unpleasant aspects, however, as the rapidly aging William Green took special relish in keeping responsibility from his industrious young underling. After denying Meany any voice in the domestic affairs of the AFL, Green gave him the traditionally thankless task of watching over international union movements; in this position Meany's anti-Communism and good sense saved the AFL from acute embarrassment and added to his own prestige.

Moscow's labor leaders had devised a grand scheme for organizing an international union federation which would play upon the "united front" comradeship built up with the U.S. during the war, a feeling of jolly good will toward "Good Ol' Joe Stalin" which would bait the American unions and hook them into the proposed Communist organization. George Meany, however, wasn't biting. Despite the AFL's being chided by liberal U.S. publications as "the dowager duchess of American labor," Meany kept it out of the Communist-front World Federation of Trade Unions; a couple of years after the WFTU's founding in 1945 the much-chagrined CIO, which had joined, withdrew red-faced. When anti-Communist unions from around the world organized the International Confederation of Free Trade Unions in 1949, Meany was one of the founding fathers.

Meany displayed his antipathy to Communism in quite a different setting when the Taft-Hartley Act was passed in 1947 and the AFL was debating how to respond to the much-hated bill. The secretary-treasurer had sparked the AFL's fight against this act, an unsuccessful campaign which cost $1 million and led to the creation of the AFL's political arm, the League for Political Education; but just because he opposed the act itself, Meany was not about to follow the course others suggested and flout it entirely.

At their 1947 convention the AFL delegates discussed ways of coping with Taft-Hartley, particularly the provision of the law requiring union leaders to sign an affidavit that they were not Communists. John L. Lewis, who at this point in his wanderings was an AFL member, argued for open defiance of the law and accused the council members of being cowardly when they did not agree with him; turning to Green, Lewis said contemptuously, "I don't think the federation has a head, I think its neck has just grown up and haired over."

When George Meany stood to speak he showed the absurdity of trying to evade the non-Communist oath clause, saying, "Whether you like it or not, the fact remains that the Taft-Hartley Act is on the statute books. We know it is a bad law, [but] the only way it is going to be changed is by our representatives under that system."

Then, centering his fire on the irascible Lewis, Meany assaulted the former CIO boss's record: "With his right hand [Lewis] has upheld the position of the United Mine Workers in uncompromising resistance to Communism; but with his left hand he made fellowship with Harry Bridges, Julius Emspak, Michael Quill, Lew Merrill and all the other stinking America-haters who love Moscow." To make his own position on the issue perfectly clear, Meany concluded by saying, "I am prepared to sign a non-Communist affidavit. I am prepared to go further and sign an affidavit that I was never a comrade to the comrades."

(His feelings deeply hurt, Lewis sent William Green the following note shortly after Meany handed him his comeuppance: "Green, AFL. We disaffiliate. Lewis. 12-12-47.")[5]

Immediately upon taking over the leadership of the AFL in 1952, Meany let his Executive Council colleagues know that *he* was going to run the federation and was not going to succumb to the wishes of the bigger unions' leaders as Bill Green had done. One of his first administrative acts, taken before Green had even been buried, was to announce to surprised Executive Council members attending the funeral that he had chosen William Schnitzler, president of the Bakery Workers Union, to be the new secretary-treasurer; the unconsulted council members objected and muttered, but next day they voted 8-to-7 in favor of Schnitzler.

One of the favorite tactics of the larger unions' leaders under Green had been for them to threaten withdrawal from the AFL if they did not get their way, a strategy quickly rendered futile by Meany. When the new executive made a ruling on a jurisdictional dispute over the objections of Maurice Hutcheson, long-time president of the big Carpenters Union, Hutcheson said he would quit the federation unless the decision was reversed. Meany rose and said, "A motion has been made for withdrawal of the Carpenters Union. Do I hear a second? All in favor say aye."[6] The Carpenters and a thunderstruck Hutcheson were out in the cold. A week later Hutcheson humbly begged to be readmitted, and Meany smilingly agreed.

While the improvements George Meany made over the leadership of Green were significant, his greatest achievements came with the merging of the AFL and CIO and when, at the age of 59, he undertook to lead the largest federation of free trade unions in the world.

With the ten million member American Federation of Labor and the five million member Congress of Industrial Organizations officially joined in matrimony in December, 1955, the president of the new federation went about making it a going concern. AFL and CIO staffs, treasuries, committees and councils across the nation had to be meshed, the no-raiding agreement had to be enforced, and competing unions in each federation were urged to join together; factional disputes had to be dissolved, personality clashes muted and all were enjoined to work only for the progress of the now-allied American labor movement.

The problems of merging in the field of labor politics were indicated by the fact that in 1956 the local AFL councils and their CIO counterparts frequently endorsed opposing local candidates, although by 1958 this situation had been largely remedied. In 1957, under Meany's urging, the federation took another step forward when it expelled Dave Beck, the president of the Teamsters Union who had been convicted of misuse of union funds; later the same year, in an emotion-filled debate at the AFL-CIO convention, the delegates voted to expel the entire Teamsters Union and its president-elect Jimmy Hoffa. Meany had done all he could to convince respectable leaders in the Teamsters, one of the oldest and by far the largest union in American labor, to clean up their organization; when these efforts failed, he reluctantly led the fight to boot them out, realizing that to do otherwise would be to severely injure the public image of the AFL-CIO.

If Meany was able to skillfully handle the administrative problems of the federation and able to rid the organization of its more disreputable racketeering elements, he had much more difficulty solving the personal and factional disputes present in the AFL-CIO from its beginning. Many labor leaders at the time of the merger had been active when the CIO split from the AFL in 1936 and several on both sides had retained their hostile feelings. Nowhere were the differences between the two federations, even after merging, more explicit than in the personalities of George Meany and Walter Reuther.

Meany represents the traditionalist character of the American Federation of Labor, its relative conservatism in emphasizing the basic "meat and potatoes" labor issues of wages, hours and working conditions; he is not an ideologue, but an administrator who deals only with basic facts, blunt statements and plain realities. Reuther is the CIO: a militant, leftist organizer whose interest goes beyond collective bargaining to a wide spectrum of issues which he claims will aid the cause of society as a whole; while a capable administrator, Reuther would rather be on a picket line or a speaker's podium than behind a desk.

When the two federations were joined in 1955, Reuther stepped aside in favor of the president of the AFL (which was the larger of the two federations and had the votes to elect the AFL-CIO president, anyway) and took a vice presidency and the chairmanship of the Industrial Union Department of the new organization. Reuther did not enjoy being a second-rank official, but he never made any overt attempts to overthrow Meany and capture the leadership during these early days. Even so, he did frequently make life a little uneasy around the conference table of the Executive Council.

During the debate in the AFL-CIO's first year over whether the federation should endorse Stevenson, Eisenhower, or no one at all, Meany was one of those who preferred the latter course, saying he disapproved the platform of both parties. But Walter Reuther had led the successful floor fight at the Democratic convention for the nomination of Stevenson and Kefauver, and he was not about to see his prestige and influence with the Democrats sapped by an AFL-CIO refusal to endorse; he argued at length for a Stevenson endorsement, won the debate and subsequently had much more influence on the political direction of the AFL-CIO than did George Meany.

But the endorsement confrontation was only the beginning of

Meany's internal and public clashes with Reuther and, seven years after the merger, one publication was able to write that "repeatedly, Reuther has been reported about to bolt from the AFL-CIO and take his one million-member UAW with him."[7]

There came a change in this heated climate, however, and during the four-year period 1962-66 these frequent, vocal differences appeared to have been forgotten also. In 1962 Meany turned 68 and Reuther had every reason to believe his president would soon step down and that he, the ex-CIO boss, was still heir apparent. "Reuther has become a deliberate, well-seasoned politician," one reporter observed in '65, predicting that the redhead's "chances of taking over the mantle from George Meany as Number One man in American labor have improved substantially in the past two years."[8] Following Reuther's stormy 1967 resignation from the Executive Council it is difficult to recall these four years of relative harmony, but they were there nonetheless.

During the brief *entente cordiale* Meany and Reuther took to praising each other in an avalanche of adjectives and always wore sweeping smiles when together in public. To please Reuther's social conscience, Meany spoke out more often in support of liberal causes, and Reuther correspondingly muted his more radically activist traits.

An example of Meany's attempts to cooperate more fully with Reuther was his acceptance of Ralph Helstein, president of the Packinghouse Workers, as a CIO-wing candidate for the Executive Council in 1965. Helstein's union has always been one of the nation's most leftist and militant and, as late as 1959, one experienced labor chronicler noted that "this union has yet to take any action that is critical of the Soviet Union" and that "its official publications show that its executive board has adopted resolutions on Korea and other subjects following the Communist party line."[9]

President of the Packinghouse Workers since 1946, Helstein has himself been closely allied with a number of leftist groups, including the Ad Hoc Committee on the Triple Revolution. This utopian radical outfit burst on the scene in early 1964—a year and a half before Helstein's elevation to the AFL-CIO council—calling for a "redefinition of work" (aimed at downgrading the principle of a full day's work for a full day's wages), guaranteed annual pay and other, similar, leftist schemes. According to one reliable newspaper report, Helstein was not only a signer of the Triple Revolution manifesto but was one of the three men organizing the Committee.[10]

Because of such activities, George Meany had overruled the nomination of Helstein to the council in 1963. In the intervening years Helstein's case was strongly championed by his close ally Walter Reuther (Helstein was also vice-president of Reuther's Industrial Union Department) and in 1965 Meany relented and took no action against Helstein's nomination and election.

In politics Meany became more doctrinaire in his pro-Democratic loyalties and at one point all but read the GOP out of any labor consideration at all—something Reuther and the UAW had done years before. Speaking at the '65 AFL-CIO convention, Meany told the delegates that "we should take a good look at the Republican Party in this country and decide whether the labor movement should remain nonpartisan, as it has over the years." Even Meany's romantic "nonpartisan" delusion could not obscure the open rebuke to any and all Republicans embodied in these remarks.

On other fronts Meany sought to establish solidarity with the liberal Reuther by sending a delegation of union officials (including a personal representative from the AFL-CIO office) to participate in the Selma-to-Montgomery civil rights march, by lobbying hard for such Great Society measures as medicare, poverty warfare, aid to education, model cities and the food stamp plan. And in the labor legislative field Meany led the almost-successful congressional drive to repeal Section 14(b) of Taft-Hartley.

At the same time Walter Reuther appeared to be slipping into post-middle age with all the grace and mellowness of a born grandfather-figure. No longer did he rail against the "stodginess" of the old AFL leaders on the council, nor did he proclaim his positions in language implying their inspiration came from somewhere North of the Holy Gates; by no means did Reuther water down his liberalism, but between '62 and '66 he did first begin to exhibit a characteristic that had been lost on him in prior years: diplomacy.

This repeated series of curtsies and bows between Meany and Reuther climaxed at a 1965 federation convention unprecedented in its peacefulness. "Many were unwilling to give a plugged nickel for the chances of the AFL-CIO merger in 1955," *Washington Post* labor reporter Frank Porter wrote from the scene of the '65 conclave; "But there was little or no disagreement here yesterday when Meany said the marriage 'has been largely accomplished in substance and spirit as well.' "[11]

There were a few lingering traces of the old disputes, notably in debate over the federation's resolution on Vietnam. Meany and other hard-line anti-Communist leaders wanted the delegates to pass a measure supporting the Administration's policy down the line; Reuther argued for the inclusion of modifying language, placing the federation on record as urging peace negotiations with Hanoi. The Reuther-modified version finally passed.

(In one incident at the convention, anti-Vietnam demonstrators made their way into the galleries during a speech by Secretary of State Dean Rusk and president Meany ordered the sergeant-at-arms to "remove those kookies." Reuther's right-hand man in the UAW, Emil Mazey, later criticized Meany for what he termed "a vulgar display of intolerance" in ousting the protestors; Mazey, a bitter detractor of Meany, was not about to be a part of Reuther's conciliatory campaign.)

Because differences like this were resolved with seeming ease and amicability, the '65 convention took on the appearance of a genuine love-in. "It is more than Christmas that makes good will the dominant theme at this convention," wrote the *Post's* Frank Porter.[12]

But the bloom—if it was ever deeper than a surface gloss—was soon off the rosy romance. After a series of renewed squabbles over foreign policy matters, in December, 1966, a letter signed by the top officers of the UAW (Reuther, Mazey, vice-presidents Pat Greathouse and Leonard Woodcock) was sent to the leaders of the union's 1500 locals; the lengthy document questioned the federation's tough anti-Communist stance in foreign matters and, at a more "fundamental" level, charged that the AFL-CIO "suffers from a sense of complacency and adherence to the status quo and is not fulfilling the basic aims and purposes which promoted the merger of the AFL and the CIO."[13]

Two months later Reuther and the same three other UAW officers resigned from all posts they held in the federation hierarchy; this meant Reuther's stepping down from, among others, the Executive Council and the Operating and Organizing Committees, and Mazey's vacating the important AFL-CIO General Board. (The UAW officers did not resign their positions in the Industrial Union Department, however, and Reuther continued as its director; nor did this action affect UAW staff members also working for AFL-CIO departments, most notably the late Roy Reuther, COPE's voter registration expert at the time.) The collective resignation was viewed by several labor observers as a prelude to the entire union's pulling out of the AFL-CIO, and the UAW convention in April, 1967, gave its officers the power to take this action; however, expected Reuther-Meany showdowns were repeatedly avoided in the following months (Reuther did not show up at the 1967 AFL-CIO convention) and the UAW continued as an in-name-only AFL-CIO affiliate until May, 1968, when, after the UAW fell three months in arrears in its AFL-CIO dues payments, Meany had the union suspended.

If, as has been suggested, Walter Reuther expected to shock the federation hierarchy into action—*his* form of action—with the letter to local leaders and subsequent resignation, he must have been shocked by the response that he received. George Meany not only failed to register shock—he acted as if the switch had never been thrown. The essence of his reply to Reuther's actions and charges was to solidify his control over the federation, isolate Reuther's influence completely and, in a characteristically methodical manner, work to prove his voluble critic wrong.

Meany's first public action regarding Reuther's resignation was indicative of others to come, as it depicted cheery self-confidence, a touch of arrogant disdain, and a determination to prove the disgruntled ex-vice-president stood alone in his efforts to revolutionize the House of Labor. A bare 21 days after Reuther left the Executive Council Meany had him replaced. At a meeting of the council on February 24, 1967, William Pollack, head of the Textile Workers Union, was elected to fill Reuther's spot by what Meany said was a unanimous vote; some council members thought the federation might have waited awhile before filling the post, but Meany blithely opined that "when we get a resignation, we fill it." And that, Mr. Reuther, was that.

But simply replacing Reuther, no matter how audacious and final a move, could not dispel his substantive assaults on the AFL-CIO hierarchy; on this front, too, Meany went into prompt action. Reuther's charges revolved around the twin poles of AFL-CIO foreign policy and its growth and progress as the organizational embodiment of the labor movement. As far as Meany was concerned, the foreign policy dispute had already been resolved; at Reuther's insistence, an Executive Council meeting was held in November, 1966, expressly to review the federation's many resolutions on foreign matters, with the result that council members voted—again "unanimously"—not to change one comma in any of the foreign policy statements made by the AFL-CIO since the merger. (Reuther, who had called for this meeting and had had it postponed once, still failed to attend.)

But Reuther's charges of AFL-CIO "complacency" were another matter to president Meany, who, above all else, prides himself on his administrative and leadership capabilities. Meany is accustomed to having his deep-seated anti-Communism opposed (he being hardly a solitary target on this score), but when his performance as head of the House of Labor is questioned, he strikes back with a fury. Therefore, it was Reuther's assertion of "complacency" that was thrown back in the redhead's face, while his foreign policy criticisms—which, had they been left on their own, might have attracted him more support in and out of labor—were all but forgotten except among his most diehard left-wing idolators; here Meany scored a vital tactical victory.

In the months following Reuther's departure Meany worked assiduously to prove his nettlesome foe wrong in his scoring the AFL-CIO leadership for lack of action. Meany rallied and led the federation, concentrating on two separate fields where immediate results were most possible and would have the most impact: lobbying for Great Society legislation and organizing workers in important job areas and in big plants.

On Capitol Hill Meany often went beyond the Johnson Administration in calling for new liberal legislation; for example, when the White House was asking Congress for a 15 percent increase in Social Security benefits, Meany, terming it labor's most important legislative goal, was demanding a 20 percent hike. (Congress finally settled on 13 percent.) And while the Administration was downplaying its controversial open housing civil rights legislation in the 90th Congress, Meany was personally testifying before Congress in behalf of this bill, even though a majority of AFL-CIO members had expressed their opposition.

During 1967 the AFL-CIO continued its support of the organizing efforts among farm workers in the West and Southwest, even while Reuther's IUD was quietly cutting back its financial assistance to this drive. At the same time, federation organizers (with the customary helping hand from the National Labor Relations Board) were conducting an aggressive, sometimes cutthroat campaign to organize workers in the gigantic J.P. Stevens & Co. textile plants in the South, making it one of labor's most concentrated organizing efforts in years. And on the strike front, the UAW's shutdown at Ford Motors could never surpass the 22-union, five-company copper industry strike—begun in July, 1967, and extended into '68—for its militancy, insistence and coordinated bargaining assault.

Below the surface of such public activities was another Meany ploy: solidifying his own control of the federation and isolating Reuther by making him (and his charges) appear foolish and way off base. Meany's first move in this direction was having Pollack elected to succeed Reuther on the council, but he had to go beyond this and convince all the other council members—several of whom, although a minority, tended to agree with Reuther on many political and labor matters—that his course was the correct one and the one most beneficial to the labor movement.

Meany did this by making impassioned pleas for labor unity, by spotlighting the flaws in Reuther's charges and by personally exemplifying the attitude—perhaps in more extreme form—that he wanted reflected by the council members. Only a personality as forceful as Meany could have pulled this off, but indications of his success were visible in comments by federation officials at the council's meeting held three weeks after Reuther's resignation.

"Interviews with AFL-CIO officers" at the gathering, wrote the Los Angeles *Times'* knowledgeable Harry Bernstein, "made it plain that, as Meany hoped, they consider Reuther either naive or incomprehensible." Such former Reuther-backers on the council as A. Philip Randolph and Ralph Helstein were reported opposing the UAW leader's actions and charges, and another noted that "almost all of the UAW programs call for more labor cooperation than ever before, and you can't get cooperation while you are attacking the union for everything from apathy to ultraconservatism."

And an unidentified union vice-president gave this summary of Reuther's tactics:

"Walter is now isolated because he has tried two ploys and they both have failed. For awhile, he tried to be friendly with union men he basically regards as conservative, and he won some of them over. But others felt that he was just trying to improve his chances of succeeding Meany, and they resented what they felt was an insincere attempt at friendship. Now that he is using another tactic—that of the militant liberal—Reuther is losing even those he won over during his 'friendly' period."[14]

Meany's several strategies and activities following Reuther's departure were capped in a 1967 AFL-CIO convention which amounted to little more—or less—than a showcase for George Meany. His absolute control was abundantly in view and the 72-year-old labor chieftain was scarcely reluctant to bask in its glow; he paraded the federation's achievements with gusto and let forth blistering sarcasm at its detractors (without mentioning any names).

"The trade union movement is a more vital, a more vigorous and a more effective force for progress today than ever before in its history. I realize that in some quarters this view is considered highly unfashionable," was the way Meany began his speech opening the '67 convention.

"There are those," he continued, "who write us off as either obsolete or—in the terms of the current cliché—a part of the 'Establishment' and therefore unworthy of confidence as a progressive element in our society . . .

"The basic fact is that—year in and year out—while adverse forces have chopped away at the stems and branches of our structure, new growth has always emerged and the roots of the trade union movement have extended deeply and firmly into the ground of American life."[15]

Backing up Meany's metaphors, his thinly veiled personal attacks and his enthusiasm over the AFL-CIO's "vitality and vigor," were some hard statistics that gave him cause for some joy. The most important of these was the 1.5 million members the AFL-CIO had added to its ranks in the past decade, including some 800,000 in the last two years.

(Still, federation critics point out that the AFL-CIO represents a smaller percentage of the total national work force—a drop from 19.3 percent in '55 to 18.6 percent in '67—than it did ten years ago. But to some extent this is a numbers game. By including members of non-AFL-CIO unions and excluding members of the work force ineligible for union membership—professional men, farmers, self-employed workers, etc.—federation research director Nat Goldfinger could claim that "in the past year the number of trade union members in the United States has represented somewhere about 35 percent of those eligible for membership.")[16]

Adding to Meany's optimism over this membership growth was the fact that several job areas with vast organizing potential, notably the farm workers, public school teachers and white collar professional workers, had just begun to be opened up to unionization. And if a truce could ever be worked out between the AFL-CIO and the now Hoffa-less Teamsters Union, booted out of the federation for corruption in 1957, this would add another 1.7 million members to Mr. Meany's organization. (It would also counter the loss of the UAW's 1.5 million members.)

Another instance in which Meany's forcefulness was manifested at the '67 convention was the resolution on the Administration's Vietnam policy. Admittedly, with Reuther absent Vietnam critics had no strong individual to rally behind, but a proposal advanced by Charles Cogen, head of the American Federation of Teachers and an ADA National Board member, that the federation "take no position" on the war, attracted little more than a dozen supporters as the 1000-plus delegates affirmed their "unequivocal support" of President Johnson's Vietnam course.

There were, in fact, many who viewed the labor conclave as a barely disguised rally for LBJ. They had a point. After having been preceded to the speakers' rostrum by Vice President Humphrey, Secretary of State Rusk, Attorney General Ramsey Clark, Transportation Secretary Alan Boyd, HEW Secretary John Gardner, poverty boss Sargent Shriver, AID administrator William Gaud and consumer affairs director Betty Furness, Secretary of Labor Willard Wirtz half jokingly told the federation delegates, "I am delighted to be here at this first joint convention of the AFL-CIO and the President's Cabinet." And then, in the closing days of their convention, the delegates were addressed by the object of their praise, as LBJ came to Miami Beach to effuse over labor's support of the Great Society and call for more liberal legislation.

But those who saw the convention as an Administration victory in wooing labor leaders to the Great Society cause were looking at the spectacle through the wrong end of the telescope. It was so only because George Meany so willed it. Months before the convention Meany had personally endorsed LBJ's 1968 re-election, an action—considering significant rank-and-file antipathy to both the President and the Vietnam war—many considered somewhat presumptuous. Meany not only did not back off, but chose to turn his organization's convention into a rally for his candidate and challenged anyone to question him, much less stop him. No one of course did, as Meany's power was nakedly evident and absolute.

The relevance of all this to the fate of Walter Reuther was ably underscored by the *New York Times:*

"Mr. Reuther at one time could have carried with him ten former CIO unions if he walked out of the AFL-CIO. But no more. His erratic forays against shrewd George Meany have cost him support rather than gained it, and if he leaves the federation now he will be all alone."[17]

Meany had won all the preliminary rounds and it appeared he had the major battle in the bag as well. Even when the UAW did leave the AFL-CIO, this did not bring down the House of Labor around George Meany's ears; the master builder had taken care to shore up the house's underpinnings and seen to it that the sudden departure of 1.5 million members was not tantamount to complete collapse.

With the worrisome Reuther out of his hair, at least temporarily, and with his authority unquestioned, George Meany could leave the 1967 convention with his attention trained on the future and the problems organized labor expected soon to encounter. The uppermost item on this agenda was the election of Meany's candidate for President of the United States.

(When Meany's first presidential choice, Lyndon Johnson, abruptly declined renomination, the AFL-CIO chieftain did not skip a beat. Two days later Meany endorsed—again without consulting his Executive Council—Vice President Hubert Humphrey, long a personal friend of Meany and political friend of organized labor. Meany's avowed reason for backing HHH and urging him to enter the presidential race was because "in no other way can the American people be assured of an effective spokesman and advocate for the programs needed to continue the social and economic progress of the past eight years and to unite the American people behind the defense of freedom and democracy in the world.")

"We go into this campaign neither pessimistic or optimistic, but determined," Meany had told the '67 convention, labeling the 1968 elections "the number one problem labor faces." "There is no use trying to delude ourselves," he confided: "This is going to be a fight—1968 is going to be a real fight, and it's going to be a real test of the trade union movement."[18]

But George Meany has had a lot of tough fights in his lifetime, showdowns with enemies outside and inside organized labor. So far as is known, he has won them all.

Not the least of Meany's battles has been the grueling, tiring struggle to make the merger of the AFL and CIO work as an organization and as a force in American society; in short, he had to prove to the world that another Meany critic, John L. Lewis, was conclusively wrong when he said, in 1956, that the merged federation would amount to no more than "a rope of sand."

As 1968 dawned and the AFL-CIO girded for its campaign to elect a liberal Democrat, the merger had been a success and largely so because of Meany's perseverance and refusal to let it fall apart; by the sheer force of his uncompromising and dominating personality—however high-handed and arrogant it may have often been—he had held the AFL-CIO together and made it work for the benefit of its affiliates. On the occasion of the federation's twelfth anniversary, George Meany, the man who made the merger, was in firm control of the House of Labor.

# WALTER REUTHER

Whenever George Meany looked over his shoulder during the first years of the AFL-CIO, he saw dogging his footsteps an energetic red-head whose sharp, piercing blue eyes were set directly on the executive position which Meany held. Walter Reuther had worked and waited for a decade to take over the leadership of the CIO in 1952 and when, a bare three years later, he was induced to step aside and accept one of 27 vice-presidencies in the new merged federation, it was not an easy choice for such an ambitious man.

In addition to his vice-presidency and place on the Executive Council, Reuther was also made head of the AFL-CIO's Industrial Union Department, a strong, almost autonomous group consisting primarily of his old Congress of Industrial Organization member unions. But even this position could not salve Reuther's frustrated ambitions and in the first few years of the federation he argued frequently with Meany, on occasion threatening to withdraw his support and that of his United Auto Workers union. Then, after a brief period of harmony, the Reuther-Meany feud was renewed, the UAW president resigned from his federation offices and the union left the AFL-CIO.

Walter Reuther's union career has consisted of two separate, but interwoven and mutually dependent courses. As a labor organizer, he was the prime mover behind the illegal sit-down strikes and other ruthless tactics which "broke the back" of management at the Ford and General Motors auto companies in the 'thirties, two of labor's biggest organizing triumphs. In his role as a labor politician Reuther not only has been elected to positions of power within labor itself, but has made himself into one of the most potent "behind-the-scenes" forces in the national Democratic Party; he is a regular White House visitor, freely gives unsolicited—but nevertheless heeded—advice to Democratic leaders, and generally has as much, if not more, political power as had

Sidney Hillman when Senator Harry Truman's vice-presidential nomination was "cleared" with him in 1944.

Walter Reuther's political militancy and self-righteous moral dedication are a legacy from his German ancestors: his émigré grandfather, Jacob Reuther, quit his native Germany because he did not wish to see his sons conscripted into the army; Reuther's father, Valentine, was a Socialist activist who once ran for Congress on a ticket headed by Norman Thomas. As one friendly biographer says of this lineage, "In the Reuther family, it was almost as if one generation handed the brand to the next, and the new torchbearers raced off full tilt, carrying the light."[19] Walter just carried it further than any of the rest.

The immigrant Reuthers settled in the coal country of West Virginia and Valentine grew up to become, at age 23, the youngest president of the Ohio Valley Trades and Labor Assembly up to that time. His leftist activities included campaigning for Congress on the Socialist ticket and building up a friendship with "Big Bill" Haywood, leader of the militant Industrial Workers of the World. The household was the scene of continuous ideological debate in those earlier days of the labor movement, and when Walter Reuther was born on September 2, 1907, his father was making $1.50 a day at a brewery and fighting during every spare moment to organize workers.

While Walter was growing up, he and his three brothers, Ted, Roy and Victor, were made to share fully their father's intense interest in union and social problems. Every week Valentine Reuther would assign his offspring a topic for discussion; during the week the boys would do their "homework" at the local library and on Sunday they would retire to a back room at their home to debate the topic-of-the-week. Each was encouraged to find fault with the arguments of the others and to present his criticisms as forcefully as possible; it is said that while his three brothers were grandiose and colorful in the oratorical style of the day, Walter was sharp, calculating and to the point, with little side flourish.

Valentine Reuther impressed upon his sons his vision of the struggle the workers around the world were waging to win their rights, and his conviction that the only way to the future was with the Socialists. Walter was heavily imbued with this message and when he failed algebra in his first year in high school he decided to leave the stale world of the academy and strike out toward his goal of becoming a labor leader, an "organizer of the unorganized."

He found a job as a tool and die maker at the Wheeling Steel Co., but the pay was only $.40 an hour, and, true to his family tradition, Walter was outraged with the wage and other conditions. One condition he especially sought to change during his three years at Wheeling Steel was that of making the men work on Sundays. Finally, Walter organized a strike to protest this practice. When he reported to his job the next morning, Reuther was given his pink slip and found himself unable to get another job in Wheeling.

Having been shut out of a job in his home town, Reuther packed up and went to Detroit, the center of the new and booming automobile industry. He landed a job as a tool and die maker with the Briggs Manufacturing Co. He moved into a boarding house, exercised at the local YMCA, took long walks, and did not join his fellow-workers in their diversions of smoking, drinking and chasing women. This brand of asceticism, strongly influenced by his family's Lutheran faith, has remained with Reuther throughout his career, often earning him the dislike of other unionists who would have preferred Walter to be "one of the boys."

After working a short time at Briggs, and briefly at General Motors and the Coleman Tool and Die Co., Reuther made one of those bold moves which came to characterize his career. He answered a Ford newspaper ad for experienced tool and die workers capable of directing others; at this time Walter was 19, had limited experience, and had never been in charge of other men. When the personnel director at Ford expressed reservations about Reuther's qualifications, the young redhead summoned up all his glib persuasiveness and talked Ford into hiring him on probation; Walter got the job, starting at $1.10 an hour, and when he left six years later he was an acknowledged expert in his trade and boss of 40 employees.

During his days at Ford, Reuther picked up the strings of his education and completed a four-year high school course in two years. In 1930 he was joined in Detroit by his brother Victor and together they enrolled in Wayne State University, studying and going to classes in their off-work hours. While at Wayne the two brothers from Wheeling found time to organize and lead a Social Problems Club, a debating society which argued issues concerning the university directly and the world in general; when Walter was president, he took up his grandfather's old cause of anti-militarism and won reinstatement for a professor suspended because of his criticisms of the school's ROTC program.

Shortly after starting the Social Problems Club, the Reuther boys talked some of the group's more radical members into organizing a campus chapter of the League for Industrial Democracy, the leftist "think" group which was the offshoot of the disbanded Intercollegiate Society of Socialists. The Reuthers' next step to the Left came when they joined the Socialist Party in 1932. The Socialists were waging one of their most energetic and successful campaigns in this first Depression-era presidential election, and their idealistic zeal lured Walter and Victor into campaigning vigorously for candidate Norman Thomas.

The Ford Motor Company bosses were already irritated over Reuther's attempts to arouse the workers to organize, so that when he joined the Socialists to stump for Thomas, Walter again was the proud possessor of a pink slip. Unemployment did not disturb Reuther too much as he had accumulated a sizable bankroll through his spartan existence and he and his brother had their sights set on other lands to conquer.

Walter and Victor drew out their savings and headed for New York to meet with prominent leftists in the LID and Socialist Party. Having received the names of "contacts" and people who would befriend them in Europe, the brothers Reuther sailed third-class to Bremerhaven, Germany, in February, 1933. Upon landing, they purchased a pair of bicycles and proceeded to pedal their way through Germany, France, England and Italy, staying with fellow-Socialist radicals, relatives, or, if there was nothing else, sojourning in a neighborhood haystack. Along the way, the Reuthers transmitted messages and carried information for the anti-Nazi underground in Europe, a pastime which caught the eye of Hitler's Storm Troopers; once Walter and Victor were visiting their German grandmother and they were forced to escape the house by way of a rope ladder from a second story window while some SA guards searched for them in the cellar.

After nine months of travel around Europe, the Reuthers obtained visas to enter the Soviet Union, sold their bikes and in mid-December, 1933, took a train to Moscow. After a brief stopover in the Russian capital, they traveled on to Gorki intending to work in an automobile factory built with the assistance of the Ford Motor Company. This was shortly after the United States had recognized the Soviet government and the country was still attempting to establish a viable economy; it was not customary for the suspicious Stalin government to open the doors of the country to inquisitive foreign workers and it has never been fully explained just how the Reuthers found such relatively easy entry to Russia.

But find it they did and in short time the brothers had become completely absorbed in life at the Gorki auto plant. Walter was placed in charge of training burly peasants to do precision die and machine work and in time he was made boss of sixteen workers and regularly won bonuses for his imaginative ideas to improve production.

A little less than a month after their arrival in Gorki, Victor Reuther wrote—and Walter signed—a letter to some friends back in Detroit, a married couple named Gladys and Melvin Bishop, in which he glowingly described the conditions he and his brother had found in the "workers' fatherland." The letter has dogged the Reuthers throughout their careers and Walter has frequently been questioned about its flowery tribute to the Soviet Union:

". . . the daily inspiration," wrote Victor, "that is ours as we work side by side with our Russian comrades in our factory, the thought that we are actually helping to build a society that will forever end the exploitation of man by man, the thought that what we are building will be for the benefit and enjoyment of the working class, not only of Russia, but for the entire world, is the compensation we receive. . . ." Further on he stated that "in all the countries we have thus far been in, we have never found such genuine proletarian democracy," and he rhapsodized that "we are witnessing and experiencing great things in the U. S. S. R."[20]

The Reuther brothers have on occasion claimed that part of the letter was a forgery, but they have never singled out any section as an example except for the last sentence, which reads: "Carry on the fight for a Soviet America." Walter has tried to wave the letter away by saying it was written in "a burst of adolescent enthusiasm," but it should be noted that he was a 26-year-old adolescent at the time. The question of the complete authenticity of the letter notwithstanding, the Reuthers were very enthusiastic about their experiences in the Soviet Union.

Walter and Victor spent roughly a year in Gorki before setting out on a circuitous route back home. They went by train across the Siberian snows to Harbin, China, then on to India and Japan, all the while talking and working with leftist revolutionary leaders. In the fall of 1935 they obtained jobs on a tramp freighter and worked their way across the Pacific.

Back home, the two roving Reuthers were joined in Detroit by their youngest brother, Roy, the three working at a variety of jobs, but concentrating most of their time on assorted leftist activities: Victor and Walter both attended the Brookwood Labor College in upstate New York, a cited Communist operation; all three helped organize a meeting in Columbus, Ohio, at which the Communist National Student League and the Socialist Student League for Industrial Democracy were joined to form the American Student Union (at the conference Victor and Walter represented Brookwood, Roy represented Wayne State); Victor became a travelling lecturer for the pacifist Quaker Emergency Peace Program; Walter did some volunteer work for Anna Louise Strong, editor of the pro-Communist *Moscow Daily News,* helping her to raise money for the Spanish Loyalists; in 1936 Victor was teaching at the Southern Workers Anti-War Summer School at Commonwealth College, Mena, Arkansas, a pro-Red training camp which was indicted by the state for anarchy and flying the Hammer and Sickle in place of the American flag.

The jobs Walter Reuther held after he returned from abroad were once again in Detroit automobile plants. Union organizers in this industry had had a long history of failure, but in 1936 they were on the threshold of a major breakthrough.

The United Auto Workers, AFL, was small and ineffective, run by a president handpicked by William Green. When Walter Reuther joined UAW local 174 in 1936 it had fewer than 100 members, but he was eager to make it grow and found others who shared his feelings and would follow him. Reuther's first step as a labor activist was to be elected as a delegate to the '36 UAW convention in South Bend, Ind.

The Detroit firebrand made a spellbinding speech at the South Bend convention and impressed the delegates enough to get himself named to the UAW's executive council. Later at the meeting, the council voted overwhelmingly to leave the AFL and join forces with John L. Lewis' militant Congress of Industrial Organizations.

Newly infused with the cause of "organizing the unorganized," Reuther returned to Detroit to devote full time to unionism. He set up a headquarters, installed some rented furniture, and began to call organizational and strategy sessions. The tactic which he had decided on as the best to break management's opposition to unionism was the sit-down strike, a device relatively uncommon in the U.S. but which the Reuthers had seen employed with extreme effect in their travels abroad. At the battle meetings in the new Detroit UAW headquarters, Reuther began discussing likely sit-down targets.

The target finally selected was the Kelsey-Hayes Company, a plant employing 5,000 to produce brakes for Ford. In five days Kelsey-Hayes capitulated to the UAW. The sit-down concept of bargaining spread through Detroit like kerosene ablaze. In a few weeks, membership in Walter Reuther's Local 174 grew from less than 100 to over 30,000.

The next incident in Walter Reuther's career can only be described as an event on a cataclysmic scale, for not only did it represent a great leap forward for Reuther himself but it also started the snowballing trend toward compulsory unionism in all the big automobile companies. General Motors was then one of the biggest and its management leaders, Alfred P. Sloan and William Knudsen, were not prepared to welcome the UAW into their plants with open arms. The headquarters of their major obstacle to the UAW's organizing plans were located in the isolated "company town" of Flint, Michigan.

The "Battle of Flint" attracted world-wide press attention and was a hot topic for discussion in almost every American home. It began on February 5, 1937, and lasted 44 days, during which a few were killed in the rioting, hundreds were seriously injured, the Flint chief of police had to flee for his life, Michigan's Democratic Governor Frank Murphy sat on his hands and refused to send in National Guard troops to restore law and order, and President Franklin D. Roosevelt kept repeating, "But what can I do, what can I do?"

In the end, with many of their plants reduced to rubble by the sit-downers and with competitors snatching up lost profits, the General Motors management gave in to the demands of the UAW; at first they suggested that the workers vote on a secret ballot as to their choice of bargaining agents, but the UAW refused. The violent militancy of the CIO had won out where the orderly, rational AFL had failed. A major block in the auto industry's structure had been organized by the Auto Workers and the redheaded agitator from Wheeling had done it. As a reward for his good work, Reuther was made head of the UAW's new General Motors Department and he found the smell of success and power to be indeed sweet.

Reuther had had some powerful allies in the Battle of Flint, not the least of whom were battle-trained Communists looking for publicity for their cause as well as trying to create chaos. During the height of the battle, UAW organizer Wyndham Mortimer was forced to leave the scene because he was too openly and embarrassingly (for the UAW) pro-Communist; at another crucial point a group of industrious Communists, led by the CIO's Communist chief counsel Lee Pressman, dug up some smear material on a judge who had issued an injunction ordering the strikers back to work. And after the strike the CPUSA, quite expectedly, took full credit for the success and the party's Moscow headquarters sent a wire to its American representatives expressing pride in a job well done.

This was by no means to be Walter Reuther's last collaboration with the Communists, but it did lead a short time later to his expulsion from the UAW and a brief setback in his career. But, immediately after the victorious Battle of Flint, Reuther was riding high and he did not want to see the momentum lost. The next target was obvious and waiting. Henry Ford was one of the last living symbols of nineteenth-century laissez-faire business, a through-and-through opponent of unions—in other words, a natural target for Walter Reuther.

Reuther was to find Ford not as easy to crack as General Motors and, after an attempt at the River Rouge plant on May 26, 1937, it took four years to finally organize the corporation.

Through his string of dramatic battles, Reuther had become immensely popular with his fellow workers, and he understood the fickleness of popularity well enough to try to cash in on it. His first move was to run for Detroit city councilman on the Socialist ticket in 1937, and the result was disastrous, as he received 126,160 votes and ran fifteenth in the field.

This was to be Reuther's last public appearance as a Socialist. It was obvious to him, that if a man with his popularity could do no better than fifteenth in a city loaded with labor voters, it was time to give up on the Socialist Party. He wanted to quit the party right then in 1937, but

Norman Thomas prevailed on him to stay in the ranks at least through the 1938 elections, and Reuther honored the request. But then, we are told by pro-Reuther biographer Fred J. Cook, "Reuther's choice was one that many American liberals were making in those years. Since the Republican Party was primarily the party of opposition and the defender of the status quo, 'pragmatic idealists' like Reuther sought haven with the Democrats."[21]

This was a practical move on Reuther's part, with no ideological alteration or soul-searching involved. He realized that Americans had an inherent antipathy to third parties and saw the folly of attempting to gain political power with the Socialists. The Democrats were his ticket; they were riding high and he hopped aboard.

Before Reuther severed his formal connections with the far Left, they played a large part in his next political move, a wild, convulsive chain of events which resulted in new leadership for the UAW and a new position of power for Walter Reuther. The president of the United Auto Workers in 1937 was Homer Martin, an emotional, individualistic, strong-headed man who had graduated with a degree in theology from William Jewel College and was pastor of the Baptist Church in Leeds, Missouri, before being picked by William Green to head the UAW, when it was still in the AFL. Martin was an archetypical AFL leader and his relations with the young Reuther were no more amicable than an older Reuther was to have with AFL leaders of the 'sixties.

The only Communist faction (and in those days they were plentiful) Martin cooperated with to any degree were the followers of Jay Lovestone, the former CPUSA chairman who broke with Moscow in the late 'twenties to form his own group of dissident Marxists. When Martin was elected in 1936, Lovestoneites were picked for a number of top positions, including executive assistant and research director.

The pro-Stalinists, Trotskyites and other anti-Lovestone Communists who had come into the UAW from the disbanded Auto Workers Union wanted outright control of the union, however, and offered to promote Martin as a national labor figure if he would follow their counsel. Martin refused and these Communists launched a campaign to destroy the UAW president by branding him weak and irresponsible, by breaking up union meetings, and by calling "wildcat" strikes to tie up auto production.

In the summer of 1937, a few months before the UAW convention, Homer Martin denounced the controversial wildcat strikes and wrote General Motors, which had been the victim of 170 such strikes in five months during 1937, that it had the right to fire these strikers. Reuther, having thrown in with the Communists in his desire to see Martin deposed, promptly labeled his president a "sell-out" to management. Martin retaliated by expelling Reuther, his brother Victor and a handful of other young militants. In explaining the expulsion, Martin said the radicals were controlled by "an outside organization" which was trying to take over the union. Everyone knew he meant the Communist Party.

Walter Reuther was a confirmed Socialist, not a Communist. Years later ex-Communist Louis Budenz described how the CPUSA had tried to recruit Reuther in 1935-37, and how the radical activist had "balked when he was told that he would have to submit to the iron discipline of the party."[22] Reuther may never have joined the Party officially, but as with so many other CIO leaders, he believed he could associate with the Communists and use them and then throw them away and forget the whole thing. This is what he set about to do after Homer Martin had booted him out of the UAW; his first intent was to get rid of Martin and he didn't much care who helped him.

During the month of August, 1937, Reuther and his anti-Martin allies in a UAW Communist-organized faction called the Union Party, met twice with Communist leaders from across the country to plot Homer Martin's overthrow. The anti-Martin coalition, in which the Reuthers were central figures, received powerful and important help from Communists within the union. The strongest leader of the coalition was Wyndham Mortimer, and the well organized Communist core within the union supported and strengthened the coalition.[23]

When it came time to count delegates, however, Reuther found he did not have the votes needed for the coup. Despite Walter's efforts, Martin won all the battles for ballots and probably could have gained complete control of the union had not the national CIO leaders stepped in with a "compromise" solution.

At that time the Communists on the federation's national staff, led by general consul Lee Pressman, were influencing all decisions toward favoring their comrades in the affiliates, and the non-Communist CIO leaders feared the sight of blood spilled over internal factional fights. One result these forces at play had on the future of organized labor was president Lewis' insistence that Homer Martin compromise with his opponents by reinstating the UAW officers, including Reuther, he had expelled before the convention.

For the next year the two sides in the battle for UAW control attempted to outmanuever each other. In June, 1939, the Union Party held a rump meeting of the UAW executive board, on which their representation was minuscule, and charged Martin with weakness and ineptitude. Martin declared an emergency situation, convened the entire board, and by a majority vote expelled Reuther and all other office-holders who followed the Communists' lead in the Union Party.

Martin, with the support of the leaders of three-quarters of the local membership and with the backing of a solid majority on the executive board, asked the national CIO to keep hands off and to allow the UAW to purge its Communist elements. But Lewis came forth with another compromise "peace proposal." The UAW leader realized that anything short of complete expulsion would be meaningless and that Communist harassment would continue. With a burst of emotion, Martin resigned his post and took his most diehard followers out of the CIO to form a shortlived AFL auto union.

The bulk of the UAW membership, although opposing the Communist leaders, decided to stick it out with the union and the CIO. Lewis sent his top henchmen, Murray and Hillman, to Detroit to act as receivers for a bankrupt UAW, and the suspended officers were reinstated. At the 1939 convention the delegates elected the non-Communist, pro-Martin vice-president R. J. Thomas as president, Richard Frankensteen was re-elected vice-president, and George Addes became secretary. Walter Reuther was still only a member of the executive council, but his power was mightily increased.

With Homer Martin out of the way, Walter Reuther could concentrate elsewhere. One unfinished matter of business was the organization of the Ford Motor Company, and now he was going to accept nothing less than total victory over Henry Ford. The focus of Reuther's efforts was the Ford plant at River Rouge, near Dearborn, Mich., and after a bloody ten-day strike the mighty Henry Ford agreed to negotiate with a labor union.

All the while he was organizing Ford, Reuther kept one eye on the political front and maintained as many alliances as possible. During this time he was helping various groups raise money to support Communist-led troops fighting the Franco government in the Spanish Civil War, and as late as February, 1939, Reuther is known to have held a secret meeting in Detroit with Earl Browder, William Z. Foster and 18 other members of the Communist Party's national committee. The subject of this rendezvous was the future organization of automobile workers, and the final victory over Ford came just a short time later.

These ties with the Communists were matters of convenience for Reuther, something he hoped would serve him in his continuing struggle up the ladder of labor power. He still clung closely to the socialism he had learned at his father's knee, but for the public he was just a loyal Democrat, a dedicated liberal trying to lend the world a hand.

Reuther's union ambitions at this time were blocked by a man who was every bit as power-hungry as he, George Addes, the UAW's secretary-treasurer, who could match Reuther in militancy and liberalism. Both president Thomas and vice-president Frankensteen were little more than front men for the shrewd and conniving Addes. Walter Reuther searched desperately from 1939 to 1946 for the key issue with which he could ultimately topple Addes from power.

His first attempt came in 1941 and Reuther used anti-Communism to carry it out. Earlier that year, Communist-led unions had staged a wildcat strike in a California aircraft plant, even though the CIO had previously pledged not to strike the vital plant. At the August convention of the UAW, Reuther took a strong stand against the strikers, saying they should be fired. The Communists, quite naturally, supported the leadership and Walter Reuther learned that his former Red friends were not too big in the loyalty department.

Two years later it was the Communists again who provided an issue with which Reuther tried to defeat the leadership. At this time the official Soviet line was the "united front," everybody giving to the war effort and helping the U.S.A.'s grand ally, the Soviet Union. To speed up wartime production, American Communist chief Earl Browder proposed in 1943 that manufacturers adopt a program of "incentive pay": "It is patriotic to demand increased earnings based on increased production," said Browder in a strange demonstration of the Marxist dialectic. On the 1943 convention floor Reuther engaged Addes and Thomas in his best oratory, blasting them for following the dictates of the Soviet Union and "crucifying the workingmen." When a vote was taken, a Reuther resolution condemning incentive pay won easily. In the balloting for officers, Addes was re-elected by a slim 70 votes out of 7,422 cast; Reuther defeated Frankensteen for the first vice-presidency by close to 350 votes, and Frankensteen was installed as second vice-president. R. J. Thomas was retained as the presidential front man for Addes.

While Reuther was waiting for his next break to come, the Japanese surrendered in August, 1945. No sooner was the ink dry on the armistice treaty than President Harry Truman relaxed the wartime wage freeze, saying there could be wage increases as long as they did not cause prices to rise; no sooner were Truman's words out of his mouth than Reuther demanded that General Motors grant a 30 cent wage increase—but not raise the price of cars.

The workers bought the Reuther proposal, but GM argued that it was inconceivable that they could hike wages that high without a corresponding rise in auto prices. So the positions were taken, but Walter Reuther had an ace-in-the-hole and GM knew full well what it was. Reuther could close every single one of GM's reconverted plants, send the workers off on long vacations, and GM would sit and watch their competitors race ahead to grab up an eager market.

On November 20 that is precisely what Reuther did. He gave the signal, the UAW local leaders supported him, and upwards of 175,000 workers left their jobs. General Motors ground to a halt. Reuther was in his glory as he rode around Detroit in a sound truck to rally the workers, and stormed into bargaining sessions to lay down his 30 cent demand, take it or leave it. At one of these sessions, a General Motors negotiator, irked at Reuther's insistence, said to the redhead: "You are the fellow who wants to get the publicity out of this whole thing. You want to enhance your own personal political position. That is what the whole show is about."[24] The man obviously knew what he was talking about, but to gain political power, Reuther had to get his wage demand.

The strike dragged on for endless weeks, with both sides still unmoved in their positions. Then the workers were beginning to worry about getting back to their jobs and some of the other unions began to question Reuther's fuzzy economics. On January 10, 1946, a presidential fact-finding commission reported that General Motors could afford a 19-½ cent raise without a price increase, but Reuther denounced it as a meaningless compromise.

In January, 1946, the united labor front demanding the 30-cent increase began to crumble and several small unions signed contracts for 18-½ cent hourly increases. Reuther's biggest defeat came when the UAW workers at Chrysler signed for 18-½ cent raises and at Ford signed for even less, 18 cents. Meanwhile Walter's GM men were still pounding the pavement, carrying their drooping picket signs and muttering to themselves. Following 113 days of striking, the UAW signed with General Motors for an 18-½ cent hourly wage increase and the redheaded scion of the Socialist Reuther family went home crestfallen.

After he failed to get the wage increase he had "demanded," the prophets of doom wrote off any chances Reuther had of taking over the UAW in 1946. Walter did not listen and went immediately to the task of lining up convention support. He may have been detested by the UAW leaders, and maybe he didn't get all he had asked for from General Motors, but Reuther's obvious talent for leading men made him increasingly popular and respected among the rank-and-file. Even if he failed to get his demands, the workers still saw him as responsible for their 18-½ cent raises.

Another factor working in Reuther's favor at the time was the fact that it was the Communist UAW bloc which was keeping Thomas in power. With the war's end, the signing of the agreements at Yalta and Potsdam, and the takeover by the Soviets of Eastern Europe, America's wartime romance with "Uncle Joe" Stalin died and the "Cold War" was born. It was customary in the immediate post-war years for Communists to rise in union halls to embark on tedious political harangues and dialectical debates; however, the tirades only served to embitter the patriotic rank-and-file even more and eventually whenever a Communist rose to preach he was met by boos, catcalls and shouting from the non-Communist workers.

It was against this background of emotional and ideological conflict, that the United Auto Workers (which had been expanded during the war to include aircraft and agricultural implement workers) met in Atlantic City in April, 1946. Reuther reportedly did not sleep for four days as he went from caucus to caucus winning wavering delegates with the oratorical style he had learned long ago in those Sunday debates in Wheeling. Pro-Reuther conventioneers tangled with Thomas supporters in numerous fist-fights and shouting matches, and whenever a Thomas backer rose to speak in the convention he was greeted by the catcalls and jeers the rank-and-file reserved for Communists.

When the debate ended and the votes were counted, Walter Reuther had been elected president of the UAW by 124 votes, 4,444 to 4,320. But while the delegates liked the style of the fighting redhead, they still did not entrust him with total leadership: they elected R. J. Thomas as first vice-president, Richard Leonard, a pro-Thomas man, as second vice-president and kept George Addes as secretary-treasurer. Reuther was president, but the people he had to work with opposed him, and CIO president Philip Murray, who had backed Thomas and distrusted Reuther, commented that "Reuther's election is not a catastrophe. I would say Walter Reuther has been contained."[25]

The quality of the anti-Communism which Reuther had used to gain the presidency is indicated by his action immediately after the election; he took the podium and said, "I want now to extend my hand to George Addes, and tell him that together we can unite this organization."[26] The anti-Communist rank-and-filers who had put Reuther in office sat in stunned silence.

The Thomas forces refused Walter's outstretched hand. For the next year and a half, until the UAW convention in November, 1947, the internal battle continued, with Thomas and Addes accusing their new president of selling out to management and Reuther hurling charges that his enemies snapped to the beat from Moscow. In between the verbal assaults, CIO president Murray came to realize the extent of Reuther's personal popularity among the rank-and-file and concluded that it was senseless to continue sniping at a man with such obvious power. Murray came to the '47 convention to praise Reuther and bury Thomas, Addes and Leonard. Reuther's re-election was not even contested and enough Communists had been booted out of the UAW so that his antagonists were easily defeated. Walter Reuther was in firm control of the United Auto Workers.

With his position within his union secured, Reuther could safely turn his attention to other areas of activity, such as solving the world's ills and building his power in the Democratic Party. Ever since 1941 Walter Reuther had averaged roughly one glorious scheme per six months: there was a plan to limit personal incomes during the war to $25,000, a government Peace Production Board which would act as an "economic high command" after the war, and similar measures designed to further the government's control over the economy.

Writing about Reuther's ideological economics, James A. Wechsler said in 1948 that "Reuther belongs to the school of thought which visualizes an increasingly 'mixed' economy on the pattern of the American future—a society in which there is a far wider degree of public ownership but in which no wholesale liquidation of private industry is contemplated."[27]

If Reuther did not get all he wanted in the way of economic programs after his election, he did get his workers some healthy wage hikes. By the spring of 1948 UAW members had received increases of 16 cents an hour on top of the 18-½ cents of 1946; in 1949 he secured one of the first company pension plans when Ford agreed to a payment of $100 a month, including social security, to all employees 65 years old with 30 years of service, and lesser benefits for those with under 30 years.

Reuther's success at the bargaining table was equaled, if not outshone, by his political victories in the Democratic Party both nationally and in his home state of Michigan.

The Michigan party in 1947 was controlled by elements which the liberal labor leaders referred to as "reactionary," with the Republicans holding most of the state offices. Reuther, together with the state CIO Political Action Committee and other liberal groups, took over control of the state Democratic machinery and in 1948 elected their candidate for governor, G. Mennen Williams; Williams was subsequently re-elected for six more terms, as the labor-liberal coalition increased its power in the state.

(In later years, Reuther was to urge COPE to use tactics similar to those his troops employed in Michigan to take over other state Democratic parties; COPE followed this advice, albeit in a slightly altered version, under the plan called "Programs for Progress.")

At the same time he was being successful at the bargaining table and in the political arena in these first years of his UAW presidency, Reuther was diligently working to clean up his own union. One of the first tasks he embarked upon after securing complete control of the Auto Workers was to purge the Communists and racketeers from the ranks. He was successful to the degree that it almost cost him his life.

Reuther's effort to boot the Communists out of the UAW was not based so much on ideology or past opposition—although this surely played a part—but rather on their alliance with the Detroit underworld and the labor racketeers. Estimates indicate that in the years following World War II gamblers in the Motor City were doing a $75 million yearly business, $25 million of which was transacted in the auto plants through the numbers game, betting on the horses and baseball pools. While these rackets were inspired and administered by mobsters from the infamous Detroit Purple Gang, the Communists in the UAW openly collaborated in this operation and raked in profits of their own.

Walter Reuther, the strict Puritan and non-smoking, non-drinking ascetic, hated the rackets and found intolerable their working together with the UAW Communists. He went about the task of burning them out. He ousted most of the Reds by increasing membership totals in their locals and outvoting them, and in other cases he raided Red locals to start new ones free from the Communist taint. The Communists could not counter the Reuther offensive. By April, 1948, their power and membership in the UAW had been drastically decreased (although they continued to hold power in a few locals for a number of years).

On April 20, 1948, Reuther returned home late at night from a long, tiring executive board meeting. While he was in his brightly lit kitchen eating supper and chatting with his wife, a shotgun blast crashed through the window and into Reuther's right arm and side; his first reaction, as he lay bleeding on the floor, was that "those dirty rats"—the Communists and gangsters—had gunned him down. For five months Reuther lay in the hospital while his right arm slowly and successfully mended, and for ten years police officers and private detectives traced down every lead in trying to capture the would-be assassin, but came up empty-handed every time.

When he was lying in his hospital bed in 1948, waiting for his arm to heal, Reuther was visited by James Wechsler, the leftist editor of the *New York Post,* and the wounded labor leader told his socialistic ally about a new idea he had, a reunification of labor AFL and CIO. Speaking of the assassination attempt, he said, "I really think this thing shocked a lot of guys into realizing that unionism is more than a matter of nickels and dimes, and that personal interests and prejudices aren't as important as they seem."[28] After his recovery Reuther had to put this idea aside for a while and be content with what he had. He could go no further in labor politics as long as Phil Murray was still in office.

By 1952 the popular Murray was 86 years old and suffering from recurring heart trouble. His adherents in the CIO realized their leader would not be in office forever and had begun casting about for likely successors when the old Scotsman stepped down. Their thinking did not include Walter Reuther.

The CIO boss, like his predecessor and mentor John L. Lewis, had no great love for Reuther and what Murray termed his "phony economics." But the Murrayites knew full well that the Detroit firebrand would make a strong bid for the leadership whenever Murray vacated the spot and they were ready to go to great lengths to prevent this challenge from succeeding.

So the situation in the CIO stood when Phil Murray was found dead of a heart attack in his San Francisco hotel room just hours before the opening of the '52 convention. The stage was set for one of those free-swinging conventions which Walter Reuther loved so well.

The Murray followers, led by the Steelworkers, chose CIO executive vice-president Allan S. Haywood as their presidential candidate; the Reutherites, led by the Auto Workers, worked day and night rounding up delegates to back their leader. The debates were long and violent, tempers flared and fists flashed, and in the end Reuther beat out Haywood by 400,000 votes, 3,079,181 to 2,613,103. Reuther was on top of the CIO and in a masterful acceptance speech he managed to salve the wounds incurred in the bitter presidential fight; he had reunified the CIO and was now in a position to work toward the dream he talked of in 1948.

For the next three years Reuther and the newly elected AFL boss, George Meany, worked cautiously and deliberately toward the merger of their two federations. Although realizing the beneficial aspects the merger would have for all of labor, Reuther wanted to be sure that his federation, which was smaller by half than the AFL, would have an equal voice in the affairs of a combined organization.

When the papers were signed in December, 1955, making the AFL-CIO merger official, Walter Reuther's days as a one-union labor bargainer and organizer were over. Here was a brand new federation, composed of 15 million rank-and-filers, ready for political action, and Reuther realized what could be done with this potential. Although he was just a vice-president in the new organization—albeit, as former president of the CIO, unofficial *chief* vice-president—he knew that George Meany was not interested in guiding the political activities of the AFL-CIO and this was the void that Reuther planned to fill.

And Reuther wasted little time in putting his stamp on the new Committee on Political Education of the AFL-CIO. It was he who led the pro-Stevenson forces on the Executive Council in getting the federation's endorsement of their candidate over the objections of Meany and other old-line AFL leaders. In Michigan, in 1956, the CIO was supporting its old friend G. Mennen Williams for the governorship, while the AFL was backing the Republican mayor of Detroit, Albert Cobo; as an indication of the direction it was to take, COPE that year gave $11,000 to the Michigan CIO-PAC and $2,000 to the state AFL. (The Michigan CIO that year gave Williams $200,000, or 60 percent of his total expenditures.) Reuther and his UAW gave COPE financial contributions, staff members (his late brother Roy headed COPE's registration program), ideas such as the "Programs for Progress" (based upon the CIO-UAW takeover of the Democratic Party in Michigan), and ideological-partisan direction.

The traditionalist AFL leaders at the time of the merger, the followers of the Gompers principle of nominal nonpartisanship in politics who protested in 1955 that they "were determined that the new federation not be tied as closely to the Democratic Party as the old CIO was," had not figured on Walter Reuther. When he left the Socialist Party to join the Democrats in the late 'thirties, Reuther was determined that the Democratic Party was the vehicle through which he was going to see his leftist, collectivist plans realized; when the merger was affected, he saw to it that the political arm of the AFL-CIO was started off on the right track, the Democrat-liberal track.

Reuther's ties with the Democratic Party's liberal wing run so deep that there is substantial evidence he has consistently attempted to realign the party along even more leftist lines. It was Reuther who, at the 1960 Democratic Convention, led the fight for a strong platform statement urging federal intervention in the civil rights field, a move calculated to drive Southern conservatives from the party's ranks; the political committee of Reuther's UAW regularly contributes to liberal Democrats who are running in party primaries against conservative incumbents; in recent times, Reuther has quietly sought to give some aid and comfort to Vietnam "doves" and other foreign policy liberals in the party.

The corollary of Reuther's devotion to the Democratic left is his steadfast opposition to the Republican Party. In the accepted CIO tradition, he has continually refused to have anything to do with any GOP officials, preferring instead to label them "reactionaries" and bring about their defeat.

This is, then, how Reuther had his most profound effect on the Committee on Political Education. If he could not persuade the Executive Council to support his ideas on foreign policy or transform the AFL-CIO into the radical social "movement" organization he wished for, Reuther could provide COPE with money, manpower and a plan of practical political action; if the labor hierarchy was skeptical of Reuther, he could turn in the opposite direction and help establish a determined liberalism and practical activism within COPE's grass roots structure. This is the influence Reuther sought and that he had; additionally, this impact was made—and COPE's course set—early enough in the AFL-CIO's lifetime so that the subsequent fate of Reuther did not alter its effect.

Reuther thus became what might be termed the "political leader" of the young AFL-CIO. Leaders such as David Dubinsky of the ILGWU or the Hatters' Alex Rose may have had more political experience in number of years, and the COPE co-chairmen—Jack Kroll and James McDevitt—may have had more expertise in putting together a campaign, but Reuther was still the major federation leader most deeply and aggressively involved in political affairs and the one most thoroughly committed to a specific ideological-political program; when non-labor liberals sought a labor leader to serve on their committees or to sign their petitions, Walter Reuther was the first they turned to.

Other labor leaders may have had an abiding interest in national politics, but Reuther's role went beyond this as he frequently assumed the mantle of messianic crusader. As COPE represented, in name and function, the entire AFL-CIO, Reuther's successful battle to set it on a liberal pro-Democrat course at the very beginning marked him as the unofficial leader—if not the inspiration—of its subsequent activities.

Apparently, once this course was set with the 1956 Stevenson endorsement, neither Meany nor any of the other AFL stalwarts objected strenuously. Reuther certainly did continue to have political differences with the federation president, but these disputes were mainly over emphasis of issues and extent of political commitment, rather than over party loyalty. The nature of George Meany's political involvement up to the merger had principally consisted of his strong anti-Communism and adherence to the Democratic Party; he was not a social revolutionary like Reuther, nor was he seeking to use the Democrats as a vehicle for radical change: Meany's father had been a Democrat, he was a Democrat, he regularly pulled the party's lever, supported its candidates and let it go at that. Reuther of course believed the AFL-CIO should commit itself to pursuing progressive change on all fronts: that it not only should endorse and lobby for legislation, but should propose it and rally public (including the non-union public) support—in short, work for this change even to the neglect of basic labor legislation.

But these political differences, although not insignificant, were not those causing the continuing, growing rift between Reuther and Meany; the most substantial—and, in the end, disruptive—of these involved the federation's stand on U.S. foreign policy issues. However much they disagreed on political emphasis and commitment, Reuther could never question Meany's pro-Democrat loyalties. What he could not (and did not) quietly accept, even during the four-year period of harmony, was Meany's hardnosed anti-Communism.

It was no mere coincidence, then, that Reuther's resignation from the Executive Council in February, 1967, was preceded by an eight-month-long series of public disagreements with federation foreign policy. At first these disputes were thought to be no more than the old arguments warmed over, but they grew in frequency, intensity and scope until, as one report put it, Meany and Reuther did not "even have a way to pass the time of the day."

(Lurking in the background of the Reuther-Meany feud are two other men who have been immensely important in influencing the divergent principles and policies involved—Victor Reuther, international affairs director of the UAW, and Jay Lovestone, who holds the same post with the AFL-CIO; both men are judged to be more doctrinaire in their respective ideologies than are their bosses and may have added some fuel to the fire.

(Since coming to the AFL-CIO as Meany's chief foreign affairs expert, Jay Lovestone, the former American Communist leader, has set himself up as something of a minor potentate. Usually unavailable for interviews, seldom seen in public, Lovestone operates around the globe through a network of contacts and veil of secrecy that is the envy of every government's espionage agency; he is the man who initially composes all federation foreign policy statements and, abroad, works to strengthen anti-Communist unions while frustrating Communist organizing efforts. Because of the mystery shrouding Lovestone's operations, most accusations against him can be little more than speculation; the liberal-left has accused Lovestone of undermining "neutral" trade unions in Europe, of supporting "undemocratic" unions—although pro-U.S.—in Latin America, and generally hampering liberal desires to "build bridges" to the Soviet bloc.[29]

(Victor Reuther, Walter's fellow-traveller on their swing through Russia and Europe in the early 'thirties, is certainly Lovestone's most vocal and embittered detractor, calling him everything from Meany's "secretary of state" to a "handmaiden of the Central Intelligence Agency." If anything, Victor Reuther's pleas for policies affecting a *détente* with Soviet nations are more insistent than his brother's and he has, on some past occasions, made statements that have embarrassed Walter. While Meany reportedly keeps a close watch on Lovestone's activities, Victor Reuther has admitted to having a virtual free rein in overseeing the disbursal of the UAW's annual $1 million foreign expenditures.)

The first in this series of Meany-Reuther confrontations came in June, 1966, just seven months after the most harmonious AFL-CIO convention in history. Meeting in Geneva on June 1, the International Labor Organization, a UN-affiliated group composed of labor, business and government representatives from 115 nations, elected (by one vote) a Polish official as its first Communist president, defeating a Dutchman who had been the U.S.-favored candidate and was thought to be a shoo-in. In protest over the Communist victory, the U.S. labor delegation—

headed by Machinists' official Rudolph Faupl—walked out of the meeting, although the American business and government delegation remained.

Meany told Faupl that "if I were in your position, I would do the same thing." Reuther disagreed, vociferously. Reuther wrote the AFL-CIO president, objecting to the delegates' action having been taken without first consulting the Executive Council and saying the walkout was "a gross disservice to democracy."

What upset Meany most about the Reuther letter was its appearance in the *Washington Post* before it came to his desk. "Dear Sir and Brother," he replied stiffly, "the determination of whether or not I have violated the laws and policies of the AFL-CIO cannot be decided by any back-and-forth exchanges in the public press."[30] Where they should be decided, Meany believed, was in the Executive Council, and he called a meeting to debate and vote on the boycott; eighteen council members endorsed the boycott, six stood with Reuther in opposition.

Although one AFL-CIO official was quoted as saying that "this was a pretty bad day for Walter," few expected the ILO-walkout uproar to lead to a full-fledged feud.

Those who entertained such expectations were soon outpaced by rapidly moving events. On the day after Reuther's letter to Meany concerning the ILO boycott was made public, news broke which was to widen the rift. It was reported that the AFL-CIO had persuaded the State Department to refuse tourist visas to a group of Soviet labor officials seeking to visit the U.S. as part of an exchange program; the federation's reason for this action, according to the *Washington Post,* was "that admitting [the Soviets] would equate Soviet and American unions and lend unjustified status to the Russians."[31] Unimpressed by such Cold War logic, this incident only intensified Reuther's heated arguments over the boycott of the ILO.

The next development occurred two months later, when the Executive Council passed a strong resolution condemning anti-Vietnam demonstrators, saying, "Those who deny our military forces unstinting support are, in effect, aiding the Communist enemy of our country." After originally being reported as voting for the resolution, Reuther denied this and explained:

"I vigorously protested and objected to this statement as being intemperate, hysterical and jingoistic . . . Other commitments required me to leave the Executive Council meeting before this resolution was acted upon. Had I been present, I would have opposed this statement and would have voted against it."[32]

(Otherwise, the AFL-CIO said the council vote had been unanimous.)

Because of the increasing frequency and bitterness of these disputes, Reuther took the initiative in calling for a September, 1966, Executive Council meeting specifically to review the federation's past foreign policy statements. The meeting was postponed when Reuther suggested it be held following the November elections. When the council finally met on November 14, Reuther did not show up, saying his presence was required at a long-scheduled, week-long UAW executive board meeting.

This strange action may have privately irritated Meany and the other council members, but they were openly nonplussed. After examining nineteen federation policy statements made since the merger, the council declared that all of them "have been sound and have been justified by events." Moreover, the council statement went on, "we believe they have stood the test of time and therefore re-endorse them individually and collectively."[33] Among those backing the statement were such supposed Reuther allies as Jacob Potofsky, head of the Amalgamated Clothing Workers, and Reuther's Council protégé, the Packinghouse Workers' Ralph Helstein.

Forty-six days later the feud came to a head with a damning, lengthy letter from Reuther and three other UAW officials to their union's locals. Charging the AFL-CIO with a "sense of complacency and adherence to the status quo," the angry message criticized the federation's domestic policy, its administrative functions, and a major part was an itemized denunciation of its (meaning Meany's) foreign policy position. Following this blistering attack, the resignation of Reuther and the three UAW men from their federation offices two months later was anticlimactic.

The UAW administrative letter began by claiming that "there is no basic difference between the UAW and the AFL-CIO in the commitments to recent Communist aggression [i.e., Vietnam] and to struggle against all forms of tyranny that would destroy human freedom and enslave the human spirit . . ." It went on to state, however, that the officers believed "that the most effective way to fight Communism is to make democracy work. We believe that anti-Communism in and of itself is not enough . . .

"Together with many others in the labor movement, in church, civic and educational groups and with people knowledgeable in the field of international affairs, we have felt that the attitude of the AFL-CIO on most foreign policy questions has been narrow and negative and has not strengthened but rather weakened the free world's efforts to resist Communism and all forms of tyranny."[34]

Opposing principles on foreign policy was the wedge finally rupturing the tenuous working bond between Walter Reuther and George Meany.

The principles were deep-seated in both men and their opposition on foreign affairs had been growing even before the merger. The starting point of the feud—at least in public—could have been 1945, when AFL secretary-treasurer Meany personally kept his federation from joining the Communist-dominated World Federation of Trade Unions, which the CIO, with Reuther's robust support, briefly joined; since 1955 the two men have clashed on virtually every foreign policy question, from recognition of Red China and its admission to the U.N. to East-West trade and, most recently, conduct of the war in Vietnam. Differences of such importance and magnitude, in individuals forced to work so closely together, could not long be hidden or smoothed over by well-meaning mediators.

In the weeks and months following the UAW letter considerable information came to light which tended to discredit or, at least, dilute several of Reuther's charges. Some of this material obviously originated in the vicinity of George Meany, while other material appeared spontaneously, furnished by sources with no direct interest in the labor leaders' feud.

One of the first items concerned the favorite Reuther (Walter as well as Victor) allegation that Meany's foreign advisor Jay Lovestone had performed as little more than an agent for the Central Intelligence Agency (CIA) in many AFL-CIO overseas activities, allegedly transmitting funds and information for the CIA. Lovestone has said he has passed along pertinent information to interested government agencies, "as would any patriotic American," but both he and Meany have vehemently denied the AFL-CIO has used any CIA funds.

All the while the Reuthers were making these charges against Meany and Lovestone, few ever suspected that they themselves had dipped their hands into the CIA till on past occasions; one man who *knew* they had done this was Thomas Braden, a former aide to CIA director Allen Dulles, and he told about it in the *Saturday Evening Post*. Noting the anti-Lovestone charges, Braden wrote, "Victor Reuther ought to be ashamed of himself."

During the time he was in charge of CIA activities among anti-Communist unions in Europe, Braden related, at Victor Reuther's request "I went to Detroit one morning and gave Walter $50,000 in $50 bills. Victor spent the money, mostly in West Germany, to bolster labor unions there." In addition, Braden continued, "in my opinion and that of my peers in the CIA, he spent it with less than perfect wisdom, for the German unions he chose to help weren't seriously short of money and were already anti-Communist. The CIA money Victor spent would have done much more good where unions were tying up ports at the order of Communist leaders."[35]

With this startling disclosure, Walter Reuther admitted the transaction, pleading, "In this emergency situation 15 years ago, the UAW did agree reluctantly on one occasion to the request to transmit government funds to supplement the inadequate funds being made available by the American labor movement.[36] Many of Walter's liberal supporters could not help but wonder about his moral integrity after he had accused Meany of doing something he himself had done and had attempted to cover up.

Another point often made by Reuther, in the letter and elsewhere, concerned the federation's supposed lack of action in domestic affairs, particularly civil rights. There is, the UAW administrative letter asserted, "the need for deeper commitment and involvement of the whole labor movement in . . . the on-going struggle for equal rights and equal opportunity not only at the community level and through legislation but within the labor movement itself."

But even in civil rights, a cause long championed by Reuther and the UAW, the critic was revealed to have his own vulnerable spots, despite Reuther's personal role in leading countless demonstrations and organizing such private groups as the Citizens' Crusade Against Poverty (which has been less than successful).

A few weeks after the Reuther letter was mailed the *Detroit Free Press* published a U.S. Equal Employment Opportunities Commission report showing that the great majority of Negroes in the auto industry held the lowest-paying jobs available; the report revealed that 24 percent of the industry's male unskilled workers were Negroes, while only 2.4 percent of the skilled tradesmen were Negroes.[37] The United Auto Workers represents virtually all the workers in both classifications.

And, perhaps coincidentally, the following summer found the auto industry center of Detroit, Walter Reuther's backyard, torn by the worst riot in American history. Of course, the UAW could not be singly blamed for the riot anymore than could General Motors, but the outburst did indicate Negro frustration with unfulfilled promises of the sort Reuther is accustomed to make with some frequency.

Reuther's reaction to the riot was twofold: he immediately volunteered the aid of 600,000 UAW members in helping to clean up the debris and he joined with Detroit business, civil rights and church leaders to form the New Detroit Committee (NDC), a civic group dedicated to bettering race relations and alleviating poverty conditions in the city's ghettos. The UAW clean-up crew never appeared and Reuther's "seeming disinterest" in the committee, reported *Newsweek,* was one of its "serious problems"; after his initial pledge to work with the NDC, the publication continued, "he has barely been heard from since on civil rights."[38]

(For what it's worth, when a Black Power militant, the Rev. Albert B. Cleage, resigned from the New Detroit Committee, charging it with failure to "deal with indigenous residents as equals," he singled out Reuther as an example of "paternalism." "Walter Reuther has attempted to dictate to the black community ever since the UAW came to power," the Rev. Cleage challenged; "He has been a Jekyll and Hyde—a liberal around the country, and in Detroit, where he tried to control political power, he is a ruthless despot.")[39]

The third area in which Reuther has repeatedly criticized the AFL-CIO is that of organizing non-union workers and on the general subject of how the federation is administered. In the UAW officials' letter they saw "the need to demonstrate the will and the commitment of adequate resources essential to the full mobilization of the American labor movement in an all-out organizational crusade to extend the benefits and protection of organization to millions of unorganized among industrial, construction, office, technical and professional workers. Today, the AFL-CIO represents a smaller proportion of the American labor force than at the time of the merger in December, 1955."

While acknowledging that the AFL-CIO's share of the work force had declined in percentage figures since 1955, Reuther's foes still found room to rebut their critic:

* During the same period Reuther charged that the AFL-CIO's percentage of the labor force had declined, his own United Auto Workers had added only 1,000 new members, thus failing to improve its own percentage of members among the auto industry's work force;[40]

* A major UAW organizing failure was among the industry's white collar office workers, with precious few signed up in the field Reuther accused the AFL-CIO of failing in;

* On a larger scale, the Reuther-headed AFL-CIO Industrial Union Department (IUD) launched a widely publicized organizing campaign in 1967, but it was sharply cut back when Reuther could not get the IUD unions to cooperate and contribute funds;

* Perhaps the most convincing rebuttal offered by Reuther critics concerned his position as head of the AFL-CIO's Organizing Committee, largest (in terms of budget and staff) headquarters department in the federation: in the three years preceding his resignation as its chairman in February, 1967, Reuther did not call a single meeting of the committee.

(One job area Reuther specifically blamed the AFL-CIO for not organizing was that of farm workers. Although the IUD had initially been interested in unionizing these laborers, in December, 1967, the *New York Times* reported that "the [Industrial Union] Department also has quietly cut off financing for farm workers organizing in Texas.")[41]

The presence of such evidence, tending to dilute Reuther's charges in the three main areas of his criticism—foreign, domestic and worker organizing policy—was obviously beneficial to Meany in his campaign to win the support of the Executive Council and, at the same time, isolate his foe. Judging by the comments of other council members, this information (plus whatever else Meany saw fit to use) worked in achieving the president's goal. For, with such former council allies as Randolph and Helstein openly questioning his actions and with sympathetic newspapers observing that if he pulled the UAW out of the AFL-CIO "he will be all alone," it was evident that Walter Reuther was, in the words of one union chieftain, "a stranger in the House of Labor."[42]

Reuther has apparently accepted the oblivion he helped create and has little hope of seeing the AFL-CIO accept his way of thinking. Even as head of the nation's second largest union Reuther remains a powerful and prestigious figure in organized labor, but he has made enemies of some important men and the loss of his presence in the AFL-CIO was not universally grieved.

(Ironically, the man most observers are betting on to succeed Meany is one whom Reuther helped somewhat in his elevation to the federation council, Steelworkers' president I.W. Abel; Reuther is well-liked by the Steelworkers' rank-and-file and during Abel's 1965 campaign against incumbent president David McDonald, an old Reuther nemesis, the UAW boss made it clear whom he would like to see as winner. Since his victory, the toughly liberal Abel has demonstrated ability to get along with all elements of organized labor and has reportedly greatly impressed Meany.)

In politics, Reuther's main concern now, as always, is maintaining the power of the liberal wing of the Democratic Party; this is his one goal for 1968. As it is also COPE's goal, the '68 campaign will find the committee and the UAW, long its strongest supporter, still fighting for the same goal, although perhaps separately. It is a true sign of Walter Reuther's initial influence on the AFL-CIO's political operations that, no matter how intense his feud with its leaders, the federation's political committee is found in his corner on Election Day.

# JAMES L. McDEVITT

When leaders of the two union federations first discussed merging in the early 'fifties, the subject of what political course the AFL-CIO would take was uppermost in their minds.[43] The CIO men wanted to follow in the activist role of PAC, while the AFL stalwarts held out for the noncommittal, low-keyed Gompers method of political action. In the course of time it was the CIO tradition which the Committee on Political

Education followed, but at the birth of the AFL-CIO an attempt was made to please both sides in the political dispute and COPE was the only committee of the new federation with a dual chairmanship. Jack Kroll, head of the Political Action Committee, and James McDevitt, chairman of Labor's League for Political Education, were to jointly direct the political fortunes of Big Labor.

Jack Kroll was a unionist in the radical and militant CIO mold, an activist who had had a quarter of a century's experience in labor politics before he took over PAC on Sidney Hillman's death in 1945. He had been with Hillman since the early days of the Amalgamated Clothing Workers, and when the Political Action Committee was formed in 1943, Hillman quickly appointed his long-time ally to the post of director of Region V in the PAC organizational scheme. In this position Kroll was responsible for the CIO's political activities in the states of Ohio, West Virginia and Kentucky. The liberal, pro-Democratic attitude of the CIO which Kroll brought with him to COPE was to help set the same pattern for the AFL-CIO in its early years. When he resigned from his position with COPE in 1957, the committee was already well on the way to following in the footsteps of PAC, an occurrence which did not meet with any strong objections from the AFL's man at COPE, James L. McDevitt.

The Pennsylvania Federation of Labor had a long history of being one of the more militant and liberal state organizations in the American Federation of Labor. Even before the AFL's birth, Pennsylvania workers had been active in politics, organizing the Workingman's Party for Andrew Jackson in 1828 and later forming the Knights of Labor group; in 1881 the first convention of the AFL was held in Pittsburgh.

The original constitution of the Pennsylvania Federation[44] (it was subsequently reworded) read like something straight from Karl Marx: ". . . a struggle is going on in all nations of the civilized world between the oppressors and the oppressed of all countries; a struggle between the capitalist and the laborer, which grows in intensity from year to year . . ."[45] And the leader of the PFL during the first thirty years of the twentieth century was James Hudson Maurer, a militant Socialist "whose memory is still revered by Pennsylvania labor men." Maurer, the modern-day Pennsylvania labor publicists claim, "knew how to blend the idealism of the Socialists of his day with the pragmatic approach of trade unionism."[46]

It was in this context of leftist political activism that James L. McDevitt was born and raised. In 1938 he was elected to the presidency of the Pennsylvania Federation of Labor, a job he continued in for two years after he was named chairman of the national AFL's Labor's League for Political Education in 1951. McDevitt, the grandson of an

Irish immigrant, was the product of two generations of Pennsylvania workers, a "labor politician" who did his best to see that the Democrats were served during his tenure as Pennsylvania union leader and as a national labor political organizer.

The youngest of five children, James L. McDevitt was born on November 3, 1898; his mother died when he was three and he was raised in the household of an older married sister. He was educated in Philadelphia parochial schools and by the time he was ten years old he was holding down a variety of after-school odd jobs. When he turned 15, James was ready for the outside world and quit school to take a full-time job as a clerk and delivery boy for a hardware store.

In 1916, at the age of 18, McDevitt joined the "family trade" and became a plasterer's apprentice, a field he served in various capacities for the next twenty years, with a time out in 1918-19 to serve with the Army in France. Upon his discharge he resumed his work as a plasterer, joining Local 8 of the Operative Plasterers' and Cement Finishers' International Association, the renamed offspring of the union his grandfather had helped organize over forty years before.

McDevitt's career as a laborer was shortlived, however, as his fellow unionists recognized his talent for organizing and in 1923 elected him recording secretary of Local 8. A year later he was voted president of the Local and in 1925 named business agent. From 1925 until 1938 he represented the Plasterers' Union and the Pennsylvania Federation of Labor in assorted positions. He was appointed by the Roosevelt Administration as a Labor Member of the Philadelphia Regional Labor Board and as Labor Relations Director of the Works Progress Administration in the Philadelphia area.

The split between the AFL and the CIO in 1936 hit Pennsylvania labor perhaps the hardest of any state. John L. Lewis' United Mine Workers and the recently organized Steelworkers, under Philip Murray, were the two huge unions forming the bulwark of the Pennsylvania Federation of Labor; when both these unions pulled out of the AFL to join the new organization, the Pennsylvania federation was severely weakened and feelings between the two factions were bitter. Therefore, "in 1938, when AFL leaders in Pennsylvania needed someone to hold together a state federation badly split and demoralized by the departure of the CIO unions, they turned to McDevitt."[47] And James L. McDevitt at age 40 became the sixth president of the Pennsylvania Federation of Labor.

During his 15 years as head of the PFL, McDevitt helped to increase the number of its affiliated unions from 28 to 1,438. In 1947, in reaction to the Taft-Hartley Act, McDevitt persuaded the state organization to set up a Permanent Committee on Political Action, a well-disciplined outfit which worked hand-in-hand with the CIO's Political Action Committee in 1948 to put the state in President Harry Truman's column and defeat eleven Pennsylvania congressmen who had voted for Taft-Hartley.

In 1951 the AFL was looking for someone to replace the resigning director of its League for Political Education, Joseph Keenan, someone who could organize the AFL's political activities as a counterbalance to PAC's operations. They chose James McDevitt, purportedly because of "his vast knowledge of the intricacies and mechanics of politics,";[48] another factor must have been his ability to fire up union men to political action and organize them to work as a force in electing liberals (usually Democrats).

McDevitt became co-director with PAC's Jack Kroll of the Committee on Political Education in 1955; when Kroll retired in 1957 McDevitt was made national director, a position he held until his death in 1963.

The political outlook which James McDevitt brought to bear on COPE was formed in his early years for, as he later remarked, when he was growing up he became a Democrat "because in Republican Philadelphia it was the only thing a sincere trade unionist could be."[49] (There were a lot of trade unionists in Philadelphia at this time and a lot of them must have been very insincere, as they voted to keep the city Republican.) This attitude was no doubt influenced by the political complexion of the state AFL led by the Socialist Maurer, in the 'twenties and 'thirties.

The young McDevitt's anti-Republicanism led him into conflict with the national AFL president, William Green, almost from the moment he took over the Pennsylvania Federation in 1938. In that year's elections Green was supporting the incumbent U. S. Senator from Pennsylvania, James J. Davis, a Republican; McDevitt persuaded the PFL to back Davis' opponent, George H. Earle. Green questioned the wisdom of the newly elected state president, but the two endorsements stood and Earle, then Governor of the state, was soundly defeated. A Philadelphia newspaper columnist wrote following the GOP sweep of the 1938 elections that McDevitt was "crying all over the back lot"[50] because of the victories.

This antipathy to the GOP even extended to liberals in the party. In the midst of the 1940 presidential campaign between Franklin Roosevelt and Wendell Willkie, a liberal Republican, for example, McDevitt said in one speech that the contest offered a basic choice between "the New Deal philosophy as personified by Roosevelt and arrogance, selfishness and greed as personified by Willkie. . . ."[51] Following FDR's victory in this campaign McDevitt wired the President that "at a time when labor movements are being crushed in many other nations under ruthless dictatorships, your successful struggle against reactionary forces in America gives us a new confidence to carry on, not only the beloved principles of our government but also the great philosophy of the New Deal program made possible by your courage and broad vision."[52] (The President later thanked McDevitt with positions on the War Labor Board and War Manpower Commission.)

McDevitt's determination to elect liberal Democrats to national office was, if anything, surpassed by his efforts in Pennsylvania state politics. During his fifteen years as president of the AFL, we are told in a ridiculously flattering biography[53] published by the Pennsylvania AFL, "he was constantly embroiled in one battle or another with the state's Republican administration." In attempting to justify this opposition, McDevitt said in one speech that "we know from recent bitter experiences that labor and social legislation becomes the first target for Republican machines. Both in Harrisburg and Philadelphia the attack against labor legislation was almost immediate under these political puppets who place personal obligations above the desires of the citizens of our community."[54]

The Permanent Committee on Political Action, which he set up in the mid-forties, provided McDevitt with a strong force with which to implement his desire to put more Democrats into office, so much so that his idolators claim that "the lengthening series of defeats suffered by Republicans in Pennsylvania since 1946 is attributable in large measure to the zeal with which McDevitt translated this traditional [Gompers] labor policy into methodical and aggressive practice."[55] This statement is supported by the fact that in 1948 eleven "blacklisted" Pennsylvania congressmen were defeated and the "reform" Democrats, led by Joseph P. Clark, in succession mayor of Philadelphia and U. S. Senator, took over the state and ran it according to the wishes of labor for the next twenty years.

This series of Republican losses in the state was not accomplished by the AFL working alone, however. At a time when the rest of the American Federaton of Labor was keeping a good distance between itself and the leftist CIO and its Political Action Committee, James McDevitt and the Pennsylvania Federation were working with the state PAC in perfect harmony. The political goals of the two state federations were so similar that years before the AFL merged with the CIO in 1955 (after waiting until the Communists had been purged from the CIO), "the [Pennsylvania] Federation, in fact, had frequently gone on record in favor of unity [with the CIO]."[56]

Although cooperation with PAC was minimal during McDevitt's years as head of the League for Political Education, when he became co-director of COPE he was back in harness with his old political bedfellows. And just so that there would be no doubt as to the control and direction of the new political arm, McDevitt announced to the membership in the summer of 1956, "Do not differ with the movement [the AFL-CIO] with respect to issues or candidates. We will not stand for it."[57]

Asked after he took over his position with COPE in 1955 to describe his new job, McDevitt replied that he was just doing on a national scale "the same sort of thing we did in Pennsylvania. It's a bigger job, and a bigger challenge."[58]

That McDevitt was supremely able to meet this challenge is attested to by the fact that in the first election after his becoming co-director of COPE, labor added four Senate and fourteen House votes it considered "friendly"; in the first election after he took over as National Director in 1957, eleven pro-labor Senators were added while the House bloc was increased by thirty. McDevitt was indeed doing the "same sort of thing we did in Pennsylvania" where he had been responsible for "the lengthening series of defeats suffered by Republicans."

James L. McDevitt was not a political philosopher or theorist. He was a superb organizer. In his fifteen years as Pennsylvania state AFL president he took a federation consisting of a handful of union affiliates and built it into a force of over 1,000; he set up a labor political arm in the state which had continued success in electing liberal Democrats to office. Because his fellow COPE director Jack Kroll left the committee after only two years, it must be considered that it was McDevitt who, by using the skills he learned in the back rooms and at the grass roots of Pennsylvania, built COPE from a paper outline into the "smoothest political machine in the land."

It was James L. McDevitt, the anti-Republican labor politician from South Philly, who started the motor on that machine.

# AL BARKAN

The man who took over the reins of COPE on James McDevitt's death in 1963 is an archetype of the professional labor political strategist. The basic facts of Alexander Barkan's life are summarized by his official COPE biography in seven bland sentences and the rest of his public record is equally sparse. Barkan has spent his adult life as a fulltime Union Man, first organizing the unorganized and later organizing the organized into a fighting political machine.

Lacking the flamboyance of a Reuther, the authoritativeness of a Meany or the colorful personality of a Jim McDevitt, Barkan has not attracted the public spotlight that beamed on many of his predecessors and contemporaries in labor politics. Instead, Al Barkan has preferred to remain in the background, making few remarks for publication and shunning personal publicity, and performing like any Good Union Man should by running his shop the best he knows how. Al Barkan's job is, after all, to win elections and this requires work, determination and subservience.

As the national director of the Committee on Political Education Barkan is strictly an administrator, the man who makes the day-to-day decisions on COPE affairs and delegates authority to other staff members. With the fundamental ideological and partisan bias of the committee well established by the time he took over, there was no need for Barkan to perform as his militantly liberal pro-Democrat CIO and COPE predecessors had in the 1940s and 1950s. And with the AFL-CIO Executive Council and convention delegates dictating the major decisions on legislation to support and programs to follow, Barkan does not act as a policy-maker on the grand scale.

It is up to Al Barkan, then, to see that the AFL-CIO members are registered to vote, that they are "educated" on the issues, and that they know which candidates support the federation's position; on another level, Barkan sees to it that the rank-and-file *has* candidates to support in primary and general elections. This is not to imply that Barkan is absent of political ideology and that he is nothing more than a labor bureaucrat; he is most definitely a confirmed and committed liberal Democrat who has no intention of deviating—or encouraging deviation—from COPE's partisan position.

Al Barkan is employed, however, to win elections for organized labor, and this he has proved himself extremely capable of doing. Just one year after he was thrust into the COPE leadership after the sudden death of McDevitt, the committee's forces scored the biggest triumph in their history. Before the 1964 elections Barkan had written that 20-25 more liberals were needed in the House "to break out of the horse latitudes and achieve a legislative record of greatness"; in the '64 voting COPE helped elect over twice that many new liberal congressmen. Add to this a Senate pro-labor bloc increased to 63 and a landslide victory for President Johnson, and Al Barkan's record in the first election during his tenure as national director looks very good.

Barkan received his training as a man who gets things done while organizer for the Textile Workers Union of America (TWUA) in New Jersey. Born in Bayonne, N.J., in 1909 and graduated from the University of Chicago, Barkan joined the Textile Workers Organizing Committee (one of the first creations of the newfound industry-oriented CIO) as an organizer in 1937, and a short time later was made a subregional director for the committee in the Northeast.

A few years after enlisting in the fight to organize the unorganized textile workers as a CIO-affiliated union, Barkan signed up with the Navy. After his 1945 discharge he was appointed veterans' director of the CIO Community Services Committee; one year later he left the national CIO office to take the post of executive secretary of the New Jersey state CIO council.

Some indication of Barkan's political leanings and commitment can be found in the historical background of his union and state labor. Before and since their creation as a union, the textile workers have been one of the most militant and politically active segments of American labor. The early agitation for the organization of these workers came from such leftist labor groups as the "Wobblies" and the Ladies' Garment Workers; the bitter and bloody strikes in Patterson, N.J., in the early 'twenties were instigated by the Communists, were financed by the League for Industrial Democracy, and had as one of their foremost goals the organizing of textile workers in that area. In later years TWUA members were extremely active in local political affairs in those states, especially New Jersey, where they had a strong membership.

The New Jersey state CIO was and remains one of the most determinedly radical of any state federation. Several years passed after the national merger before it finally got together with the state AFL, only to break away from that federation again in 1963; as of 1967 the two New Jersey federations were still very cool to each other. One immediate outcome of the moderate-radical AFL vs. CIO state feud has been the absence of united labor backing for New Jersey political candidates, with 1966 being a typical year as labor split several different ways in endorsing senatorial candidates.

This was the milieu from which Al Barkan came to COPE. After two years of working for his home state CIO, Barkan had left in 1948 to rejoin the TWUA, serving for seven years as its national political action director. Barkan's experience and skill in directing the TWUA's political fortunes impressed national labor leaders enough to select him as COPE assistant director, under co-directors Kroll and McDevitt, when the committee was established in 1955. (This appointment, it should be noted, also served to strengthen the CIO's hold over the infant COPE; with CIO man Kroll as one director and with an AFL director who was more in tune with CIO tactics than with his own federation's, the addition of Barkan to the uppermost COPE hierarchy can only be viewed as a strategic victory for the CIO political activists on the AFL-CIO Executive Council.)

From that point Barkan's rise to top-level COPE power was mere formality. When Kroll retired in 1957, Barkan became COPE deputy director and when McDevitt died in August, 1963, he was appointed to run "the smoothest political machine in the land."

Upon taking command of the committee, Barkan moved quickly to prepare for the next year's elections by continuing to push the regular COPE activities while innovating new programs and bringing in new personnel. Barkan and his deputy director, Joe Rourke, for example, devised and put into effect the marginal district project, placing special effort into congressional districts where a conservative had won in 1962 by a margin of less than 5 percent of the total vote. Barkan also worked with Roy Reuther, on loan to COPE from the UAW, in improving and perfecting the vast voter registration effort.

Barkan's drive and imagination did not let up following the triumph of 1964. Just two months after these elections he sent to local COPE leaders a 92-page list of the municipal elections to take place in over 100 cities across the country in 1965; in an accompanying memo Barkan urged local COPEs to become active in these usually ignored odd-year campaigns because "of their potential effect on state and national elections in 1966."

To further aid in preparation for elections to come, Barkan and his aides came up with what might be considered the most revolutionary idea in political action in many years: the use of computers to keep close tabs on the political status (i.e., registration, party, precinct, address, etc.) of every one of the AFL-CIO's members. This system will not only allow COPE to keep in closer touch with its members, help it to register more voters and win more elections, but has the practical effect of sizably reducing mailing and list maintenance costs.

As the crucial 1968 presidential campaign approached, Barkan, acting on a poll showing over 50 percent of AFL-CIO members now live in the suburbs, worked out a plan for organizing a COPE operation in the previously untouched areas beyond the city limits. Calling suburbia "the new frontier of politics," a COPE brochure outlined the Barkan strategy and described the precise function of the new-style organization:

"A suburban COPE can be to the community what the grievance committee is to the workplace. It can take up arms for union members and the citizenry at large on important local, or neighborhood, issues."

With the greater part of his time occupied with working on the many COPE activities and projects, old and new, it is understandable that the reticent Barkan is not given to granting interviews or holding press conferences. Even in his infrequent public utterances, Barkan remains the very model of the labor political leader.

He will protest, for instance, that COPE is really non-partisan and interested only in protecting the interests of the workingman. But despite this caution and unwillingness to talk about his job or the position of his committee, Barkan has displayed in several statements the distinct mark of a liberal pro-Democrat expected in a leader of COPE.

Barkan is capable of making the statement, when asked why COPE does not back more Republicans, that "we just don't find enough Republicans, on the basis of their record, who warrant our support."[59] Yet, this assertion—which is dealt with at length in this book's section on choosing candidates—fails to explain why COPE finds it impossible to support such liberal Republicans as New York's Nelson Rockefeller, Michigan's George Romney, Oregon's Mark Hatfield or Illinois' Chuck Percy.

Another indication that Barkan has no intention of seeing COPE deviate from its hostility to GOP candidates was a statement made shortly before the AFL-CIO officially endorsed Lyndon Johnson for the presidency in 1964. Asked if it was not more or less a "foregone conclusion" that COPE would be working for LBJ, in view of the fact that the AFL-CIO (jointly or separately) had never before backed a Republican, Barkan admitted it was true the federation had not backed the GOP, "but it is not mandatory. It is voluntary, like all of our endorsements."[60] Yet, a short time before making this statement, Barkan had written with obvious approval that "all the professional polls show President Johnson running well ahead of any so-far mentioned Republican candidates."[61] (Note that this was written even before the GOP nominated arch labor foe Goldwater.) COPE's political actions may be voluntary, but they are also predictable.

No, Barkan's anti-Republicanism goes much deeper than "the basis of their record." One indication is his attitude toward growing GOP strength in the nation's large cities, areas where the most liberal of Republicans are to be found. It would seem that COPE—if it were truly dedicated to "liberal progress"—would welcome this development and back left-of-center GOP candidates against hack politicians run by an entrenched Democratic machine. But Barkan doesn't give it a thought.

In the summer of 1964 he warned union members that the Republican Party is "throwing $9.5 million" into city campaigns and that the GOP "is invading traditionally Democratic areas [i.e., cities] in hopes of siphoning off enough votes to supplement usually strong outstate Republican voting, and thereby achieve victory."[62] A year later COPE opposed liberal Republican John Lindsay in his successful New York mayoralty race and in 1967 Barkan directed COPE's massive assistance campaign for Philadelphia's Mayor James Tate, running against a Republican—Arlen Specter—who was probably more liberal than the Democrat.

Al Barkan is safely in the COPE mold. A product of the militant-activist political tradition of the CIO, he is a committed liberal Democrat and an expert, imaginative organizer who skillfully uses basic political tactics, blended with modern technology and ideas, to win elections for the AFL-CIO's candidates.

It has been Barkan's fate to preside over COPE during the biggest (1964) and worst (1966) years in its history. Just as he did not rest on his laurels after the '64 COPE sweep, but went right back to work, Barkan did not let the '66 defeats overly faze him; after briefly wondering what went wrong after such a mighty COPE effort, Barkan went about trying to find the answer. Part of the solution was provided in the results of the AFL-CIO-commissioned Kraft Poll—bad communications with members, no suburban organization, wrong approach on issues— and Barkan saw to it that these findings were acted upon.

With characteristic methodical dedication, Barkan and his staff swallowed their pride, admitted COPE had been doing some things wrong, and began making corrections. None of this activity was designed to boost the name of Al Barkan, but was aimed at helping to improve the political fortunes of the labor movement which he had been serving all of his adult life. Barkan was showing that he is still the Good Union Man.

## CHAPTER FIVE

# The Mechanics of COPE

THE national nucleus of the organization which Al Barkan heads occupies about one-half of the sixth floor in the eight-story AFL-CIO Building in Washington, D.C. The federation's headquarters is on 16th Street, one door away from famed Lafayette Park (where financier Bernard Baruch had a bench "reserved" for his outdoor meditations and conferences). And just across Pennsylvania Avenue from the park, resides the President of the United States.

The Washington headquarters of the free world's largest federation of trade unions houses all the numerous and complex staffs, departments, committees and computers which make the organization tick. From George Meany's resplendent office on the eighth floor, down to the receptionist who greets visitors in the vast muraled lobby, everyone is involved in the operation and success of one of the most powerful and wealthy member-organizations in America.

In 1967 the American Federation of Labor-Congress of Industrial Organizations reported an average per capita union-by-union paid membership of 14,300,000 spread out over 126 affiliated national and international unions ranging from the Associated Actors and Artists to the International Woodworkers of America. The 14.3 million per capita figure given in the *Report of the AFL-CIO Executive Council* for 1967 represented an increase of nearly one million over the previous two years (in 1965 the paid membership was 13,500,000); this was the largest increase in dues-paying members since the AFL-CIO merger. Using this 1965-67 membership increase as ammunition, at the '67 AFL-CIO convention president Meany challenged the federation's detractors by proclaiming:

"The essential truth is that—year in and year out—the trade unions of this country, as represented in this federation of ours, have constituted and will continue to constitute the vital main force of the progressive movement in America . . . The evidence is there—in abundance—for those who care to look without the blinders on. . . . Since our last convention, the membership of AFL-CIO affiliates, as reflected in per capita payments to the federation, has passed well beyond the 14 million mark—to a level of 14.3 million, according to our most recent figures. This represents a gain of almost one million since 1965."

The five largest unions in the federation in 1967 were the United Auto Workers, with 1,325,000 members; the Steelworkers, with 952,000 members; the Machinists, with 740,000 members; the Carpenters, with 700,000 members; and the Brotherhood of Electrical Workers, with 658,000. Two of the fastest-growing unions are the Federation of Government Employees (from 132,000 to 196,000 in '65-'67) and the American Federation of Teachers (from 97,000 to 125,000), two relatively new unions organizing in virtually "unorganized" professions which stand to gain many more members in the next few years. Another field in which AFL-CIO organizers are working diligently is that of farm workers and migrant laborers; as of 1967 the Farm Workers Organizing Committee (FWOC) reported only 1,000 per capita paid members, but in the one-year period July 1, 1966—June 30, 1967, the national AFL-CIO gave over $140,000 to the organizing committee to help in its efforts of building a union of farm workers.

As the membership of the AFL-CIO increases, so does its revenue. In its 1967 "Report," the Executive Council stated that the federation received $11, 382, 172.17 in per capita taxes from the member unions for the fiscal year, July 1, 1966 to June 30, 1967. This figure represented an increase in tax revenue of $194,952.32 over the previous fiscal year. (The tax levied on the five largest unions in '66-'67 were: Auto Workers, $947,899.75; Steelworkers, $813,823.64; Machinists, $640,739.75; Carpenters, $588,000.00; and Electrical Workers, $561,-528.31). The net worth of the federation in 1967 was reported to be $5,698,000.37, a two-year increase of $800,000. In view of this, it is not preposterous to state that Big Labor is also very Big Business.

The system of control over this expansive and expensive federation is complex and somewhat deceptive. From the outside, the procedures by which the AFL-CIO's officers and policies are selected would seem reasonably democratic, but these same processes have been called into question by federation critics and one detractor has labeled the system "cronyism, not representative leadership."[1] The degree of actual freedom of choice and democracy within the 14.3 million-member organization is, of course, something best known in the upper echelon of the federation, and detailed accounting must await public exposure of the books and records.

On paper, the AFL-CIO's decision-making apparatus is roughly similar to that of major political parties: delegates to a local convention elect delegates to another convention, who in turn elect delegates to still another convention. Within the AFL-CIO's affiliates, local unions will pick representatives to the union's national convention, where officers of that union and delegates to the federation's national convention are selected; and it is at the bi-annual AFL-CIO Convention where the broad policies of the organization are decided.

At the federation's conventions each national and international union has votes equal to its paid membership and delegates proportionate to its membership to cast these votes (e.g., the Auto Workers had 1,324,-793 votes and 24 delegates at the '67 convention; the Air Line Dispatchers Association had 852 votes and one delegate). In addition, each department of the AFL-CIO has one vote, as does every state federation and as do, also, the "central bodies" of such heavily unionized areas as Akron, Ohio, and Flint, Michigan. By this system of delegate apportionment, at the 1967 convention there were 939 delegates representing 126 national and international unions, 5 federation departments, 46 state bodies, 176 central bodies, 16 local unions directly affiliated with the federation, and 3 fraternal delegates from other nations.

It is, by far, the delegates from national and international unions who have the decisive power at an AFL-CIO convention, and it is their selection which has been most criticized. In the majority of affiliated unions, top officers and delegates to the federation convention are not elected by a direct vote of the rank-and-file, but by a "representative system" comparable to the system whereby state legislatures once picked members of the U.S. Senate. Each local within a union will select representatives to the union's convention, and these men—theoretically reflecting the membership's view of matters—decide the policies and officers of their union and, in part at least, the future of the AFL-CIO through the naming of delegates to the federation's convention.

At AFL-CIO conventions, the process of democracy would seem to break down a bit more. The federation's top officers and its program are chosen in a manner roughly akin to party presidential nominees and party platforms, but, then, the AFL-CIO is supposedly not a political organization; historically, labor federations purport to represent the views of the common workingman and are presumably organized to protect the interests of the rank-and-file. This would not seem to be the case with the AFL-CIO.

One well-placed individual who has questioned the federation's process of electing officers (and, through them, its policies), is Edward Swayduck, president of the Amalgamated Lithographers of America. Writing in the union's publication, *Lithopinion 4,* Swayduck took the federation to task on the subject:

"As for the AFL-CIO itself, its affairs are run by officials many of whom have not been directly voted upon by any labor rank-and-file group for a generation. The 29-member executive council includes many incumbents close to their seventies, who have not faced direct elections since they were young men. The often-heard motto is that 'Nobody dies and nobody resigns.' They win their offices first, by personal selection by the top AFL-CIO hierarchy, and are then voted on at national AFL-CIO conventions by delegates who have been elected by other delegates at national or international union conventions. Once on the executive council, the custom is to leave them on it. This makes for a top governing council subservient to the top officership and out of touch with the membership . . .

"Is labor so big and delicate and precious and refined and vulnerable and prissy that its officials can't be elected the way we elect the President and the Congress of the United States? Does it take more courage for labor's national officials to face the rank-and-file in direct elections than it does for our highest government officials to face the public?"[2]

Swayduck's attack was by no means a voice in the wilderness. Prior to the federation's 1965 convention, criticism (including, in the upper ranks of the AFL-CIO, that of Walter Reuther) was centered on the nine men on the Executive Council who were no longer even elected officials of their unions and instead held titles equivalent to "president emeritus." To calm the restive critics, President George Meany induced eight of the nine old men to step down in favor of "young blood," with one of them—Harry C. Bates, president emeritus of the Bricklayers—refusing to budge. Meany didn't want to push old AFL crony Bates on the matter and let him stay, a move promptly denounced by Mr. Reuther.[3]

Others besides Reuther were dissatisfied. Meany had expected the eight retirements to be the kind of housecleaning which would silence the critics who had pointed out that the average age of council members pre-convention was older than that of the current Supreme Court (which was 63). When it was computed that the average age of the replacements was 59, the critics saw no need to maintain silence on the subject.

In gaining the eight letters of resignation, Meany was responding to only a portion of the complaints put forth by critics such as Edward Swayduck. Swayduck's basic charge, that the federation's hierarchy, not the rank-and-file, ruled organized labor with an iron hand, had evidently made little effect: the replacements for the eight resignees were picked by the council itself.

Beside naming the members of the Executive Council, the delegates to the bi-annual federation soirées also determine AFL-CIO policy to a limited degree. By voting on a long list of policy resolutions (written at federation headquarters and usually passed intact), the convention voters provide the AFL-CIO executives and staff with a broad policy outline for the next two years. In 1967 well over 200 resolutions were voted on, ranging from encouraging women to vote to Vietnam. An example of the generalities contained in these statements is the '65 resolution on political education, which stated:

"To stimulate political interest, political education and political action among trade unionists as an essential ingredient in a democratic society, we call upon each affiliated national and international union and each state and local central body to render all assistance and support to the policies and programs of the AFL-CIO Committee on Political Education."

It is left up to the directors and staff of COPE to interpret and carry out their resolution, and elect candidates who support the legislative program which is also resolved by the AFL-CIO convention delegates. In this manner the actual functions of the labor federation are removed another step from the rank-and-file. The delegates the membership elects at local conventions elect other delegates at national union conventions who go to the AFL-CIO convention and elect leaders—chosen by the existing leadership—who govern the federation within broad outlines provided them in the resolutions; it is these leaders and the appointed directors of the numerous departments and committees in the federation who make the important daily decisions and have the biggest voice in the direction of the AFL-CIO.

At the top of the chain of command are the 27 AFL-CIO vice-presidents comprising the Executive Council (with the federation's president as their chairman). They meet regularly to discuss immediate policy and make all major decisions. Originally there was provision in the federation's constitution for an executive committee to the council, composed of the president, secretary-treasurer and six council members. The design of the committee, constituted to meet every two months, was for its members to discuss and formulate policy recommendations to the full Executive Council.

Following the '65 AFL-CIO convention, however, the executive committee became virtually extinct; no new members were named to replace those who had retired, no meetings were called and the committee was no longer mentioned on the AFL-CIO letterhead. These developments did not escape the eagle eye of Walter Reuther, who years before had argued for establishment of the committee in the pre-merger discussions with George Meany.

In the December, 1966, letter from the four Auto Workers officials to local UAW leaders, the failure to convene the executive committee was labeled a violation of the AFL-CIO constitution and used as an example of Meany's "heavy-handed" control of the federation. Subsequently, in a list of suggested changes for the AFL-CIO, the UAW hierarchy called for re-establishment of the committee to "make it a meaningful, functioning committee."

George Meany responded to this suggestion at the 1967 AFL-CIO convention by proposing and having passed an amendment to the federation's constitution which did away with the executive committee completely. The official reason given for the change was "to simplify the government of the federation with the end in view of increasing its flexibility and efficiency."

Next to the Executive Council in the AFL-CIO hierarchical ladder is a body called the General Board, consisting of all council members plus the president (or principal officer) of each affiliated national and international union and the heads of the federation's trade and industrial departments. As conceived at the time of the merger, the board was to meet at least once a year to debate perplexing policy questions referred to it by the Executive Council. But here again, under the autocratic control of Meany the board fell into disuse and this, too, attracted the attention of critic Reuther; the UAW letter urged that the General Board "share fully in leadership responsibility in shaping major program and policy decisions and in insuring their effective implementation."

And again Meany replied to Reuther with a constitutional amendment; at the '67 convention the AFL-CIO delegates voted to delete from the constitution the provision that the General Board meet "at least once a year." As is now provided, the board meets only when Meany or the Executive Council decides it will meet.

The council and, to a far lesser degree, the board have some control over the headquarters departments and committees of the AFL-CIO, and all these adjuncts have a council member or international president as titular head; George Meany, however, is the one leader in the headquarters building every working day and he more than anyone else knows what is going on in every room. The function of the assorted departments and committees is to oversee the activities of the AFL-CIO membership within their particular spheres of influence: the Metal Trades Department works only with unions in the metal mining or construction fields, and the Committee on Political Education (COPE) deals with all unions in promoting political activism.

At the top of the COPE chain of command is the AFL-CIO Executive Council and General Board, with President George Meany acting as chairman of COPE and William Schnitzler as secretary-treasurer. Beneath these comes the COPE administrative committee, composed of the 27 council members plus the presidents of 15 unions, and the COPE operating committee, consisting of representatives of 64 international unions (secretaries, presidents, or delegates). The operating committee establishes the broad guidelines for COPE activities and draws up the plans for all major projects. This committee reports quarterly to the administrative committee which must approve all of these projects before COPE can go to work on them. (The Council and Board must also give the nod to important COPE projects.)

Once these red tape roadblocks are cleared, the national headquarters staff at COPE puts the plans into action. This staff, headed by National Director Al Barkan, has 30 members, including field representatives and the secretarial pool, and has a higher salary budget than any of the other departments or committees. (In fiscal year 1966 COPE paid $430,-333.24 in salaries.) The positions on this staff, the duties of each, and the persons who held the top posts in early 1968 follow:

* National Director, Al Barkan, makes all day-to-day decisions for COPE and delegates authority to his staff. The director takes his orders on major policy from the hierarchy above and passes them down to his staff.

* Deputy Director, Joseph Rourke, implements the orders of the director and sees that Barkan's commands are obeyed.

(There formerly was a COPE assistant director, second in line below the national director; when this official resigned in late 1967 there was no immediate plan to fill the post and its functions were distributed among other COPE staff members.)

* National Field Coordinator, Earl Davis, works with the area directors in coordinating activities of national and local COPEs; also administers the political projects involving minority group members, such as voter registration drives among Negro citizens.

* Publications Director, Ben Albert, writes and oversees the production of all COPE pamphlets and brochures, including the bi-weekly "Political Memo," and acts as COPE's public relations and press information man.

* Comptroller, Walter Bartkin, with a staff of four, is in charge of getting money from the AFL-CIO affiliated unions for COPE's "educational" activities, and handles all other funds for COPE operations.

* Research Director, Mary Zon, with an assistant and staff of three, compiles the election and legislative information needed for political activities.

* Women's Activities Directors, Mrs. Esther Murray for east of the Mississippi and Mrs. Margaret Thornburgh for west, coordinate COPE's projects involving female union members and wives of the rank-and-file; the WADs publish their own political memo, put out their own brochures and have a program of political action which draws on the special talents of women.

* Area Directors are assigned to nine divisions of the country where

they administer and watch over the COPE activities in their area; these nine men work with the local COPE leaders to see that the national policies are carried out.

&ast; Secretarial pool of six to write letters, answer phones and get coffee for the regular staff.

Below the national level, each of the 50 state AFL-CIO organizations has its own committee on political education, working directly with the state labor hierarchy to coordinate statewide political activities. The state COPEs have a staff—although sometimes smaller in number—similar in positions and duties to the national headquarters, raise their own money (most states have a member head-tax used for political action), and have their own action program. The state political directors take their cue on major policy from the national headquarters and work with COPE field directors in implementing these plans; the state COPE leaders generally make policy on local programs, with some suggestions from national headquarters, and put these into effect on their own.

Each state is broken down into smaller COPE organizations, operating the political activities in a particular geographic area—either a city, county or congressional district—depending on organizational convenience. In a metropolitan area, for example, there will usually be a city labor council, composed of representatives of the city's AFL-CIO unions, having a political committee; in a suburban area the organization will probably be on a county level, and in a rural or sparsely populated section the labor forces will normally organize within a congressional district. (Combinations are also possible: Several city or county COPEs could work together in a congressional district COPE.)

These COPE organizations work through their area's unions to coordinate the political activities of the rank-and-file. As nationally AFL-CIO head George Meany is titular chairman of COPE, on the state, city, county and congressional district level, the leader of the COPE organization will be the man in charge of the corresponding area's labor council, an arrangement showing the importance all of organized labor places on political activities; moreover, to facilitate the collection of moneys for political activities (whether by per capita head-tax or "voluntary" contributions), it is not unusual for the financial officer of either the state or local labor council to act in the same capacity for the area COPE. Usually, local COPEs will get most of their finances from the state political group, but some raise supplemental funds from area rank-and-file.

The lowest rung on the COPE ladder is the committee on political education within a local union. Not every local in the nation has a political committee, and national COPE officials are reluctant to guess how many do; it is safe to assume, however, that the great majority of the AFL-CIO's 60,000 affiliated local unions do have such a committee, or else work closely with the labor council's COPE in their area, through a union officer in change of political activity.

Organization of a committee on political education in grass roots unions receives priority attention in COPE's *How To Win* handbook. "In the beginning," it tells the membership, "you do what humans have been doing ever since they realized that two heads are often better than one: You form a committee." In further outlining the establishment of this committee, the handbook avers that "normally," a local union COPE includes:

1. The officers and executive board members. (*The participation of the leadership is vital to success.*) [All italics are theirs.]
2. Stewards and/or grievance committeemen. (*They are constantly in touch with the members; they know the people; and the people know them—an important fact when it comes to recruiting volunteers and collecting COPE dollars.*)
3. Members from the community services, education, welfare and legislative committees. (*Their areas of interest are ones which bear directly on the political process.*)
4. Any other members who are interested in politics and good government, and are willing to work. (*These are as important as the others, for they will be people with the inclination to perform the difficult, time-consuming jobs that need to be done.*)

The representatives of the union's community services, education, welfare and legislative adjuncts, will advise the political committee in these fields. The leadership will appoint other members to head up committees within the local COPE dealing with registration, precinct organization, women's activities, candidate screening and public relations.

The most influential participants in the union's COPE are the "other members," those "with the inclination to perform the difficult, time-consuming jobs that need to be done." These are the unpaid, hardworking individuals who do the hundreds of "nuts-and-bolts" jobs which arise in political action, or else recruit volunteers to do them. From doorbell-ringing to envelope-stuffing, these rank-and-filers represent the backbone of the COPE structure. Without these millions of volunteers, all of national COPE's directives, guidelines, propaganda, money and activity would be utterly useless.

As to the question of control over these members' political activities —whether national COPE's control over state operations, or a state's over a local affiliate—it is difficult to pinpoint the nature and extent of such control. The national COPE staff, quite naturally, denies any control exists, with one spokesman telling the writer, "When you're asking people to do something on a volunteer basis, you can't get after them with a whip."

In the realm of volunteer political action, tight control is undoubtedly not imposed and would be wasted if it were. National, state and local COPE directors are aware that no matter how great their enthusiasm *they* cannot ring all the doorbells, register all the voters, get all the people to the polls and distribute all the propaganda necessary to win elections. They must depend on the rank-and-file to perform these vital functions, and to start pushing the membership around or ordering them to run up and down mounds of dirt (as in the military) would only serve to upset the delicate balance between the leaders and the troops. The most that local or state COPE leaders can do is train and encourage campaign workers, and hope their blandishments take hold in the workers' imagination and produce victory.

The control which does exist within the COPE structure is of a much more sophisticated variety and concerns not political activity but political ideology and direction; not the fact that rank-and-filers work, but whom they work *for* is decisive. But, here again, control is used discriminatingly, as there is a question as to how much is actually needed.

Organized labor has progressed to the point in its political "education" where most of the leaders, if not the members, think along the same ideological and party lines. The men who run the state or local COPEs are most likely every bit as liberal and pro-Democrat as Al Barkan, the organization's national head. These men are veterans of the labor movement and are fully aware of labor's commitment to the Democrats and its role in the liberal-labor alliance. Even though their thinking may be basically "sound," to reinforce it, national COPE conducts "leadership clinics" to train local leaders in methods of financing, organizing and propagandizing; buttressing these efforts are the committee's field directors, men who work closely with grass roots COPE leaders.

A demonstration of a local leader's political bias being equal to—if not a step ahead of—the national leadership, occurred in South Dakota in 1960. At the state federation of labor's annual convention, AFL-CIO President Meany made a speech in which he called for the "retirement from political life" of the state's conservative Republican Senator, Karl Mundt. But, prior to the Meany directive, state labor's political leader had denounced Mundt in more damning terms, calling him a "spokesman for the National Association of Manufacturers,"[4] and demanding his defeat. Meany's declaration was, at most, redundant.

What sophisticated control there is in COPE affairs occurs in the selection of candidates and policies by the AFL-CIO and international unions. This control is most evidenced in the system of delegate selection and voting on officers and policy found in both the federation and its affiliates, outlined previously. As was seen—particularly in AFL-CIO affairs—the rank-and-file is far removed from the actual physical process of making these decisions.

An illustration of this control is found in the Street Case, the past decade's most celebrated legal battle between union membership and leadership, with a group of workingmen challenging their unions' right to spend dues money for political purposes to which the members were opposed. In the "Stipulation of Facts" in this case (points on which both the union appellants and member plaintiffs agreed) it was flatly stated:

"The determination of the legislative, political, and ideological programs and activities of the labor union defendants, Railway Labor Executives Association, Railway Labor's Political League, the Machinists Non-Partisan Political League, the AFL-CIO or the latter's Committee on Political Education . . . does not involve participation by the plaintiffs, intervening plaintiffs and the class they represent; the views of the plaintiffs, intervening plaintiffs and the class they represent have not been sought; and they have not ratified such activities or programs, nor have they acquiesced therein."

Stripped of legal verbiage, what the unions were admitting in this particular stipulation is that in the process of choosing the political programs and candidates supported by labor and union dues money, the rank-and-filers do not participate, their views are not sought, nor do they ratify or agree in these activities. Of course, the unions claim, the "representatives of the membership" will fulfill these functions as convention delegates. But this argument is of dubious merit—to say nothing of dubious democratic practice.

If most of the AFL-CIO membership gets short shrift in determining federation policy, its leaders do not. These men lead delegations to the convention and have a controlling influence in the casting of ballots on policy matters. The continued liberal pro-Democrat coloring of the federation's political complexion attests to the amicability of affiliated union leaders in going along with the AFL-CIO hierarchy on these decisions.

To help convince any slackers among the leadership that its ways on policy matters are sound, COPE has its various means of influencing endorsement of political candidates. In its election year voting records, for instance, COPE can pretty much make an incumbent it opposes appear "anti-labor" while those it likes come out smelling of roses in springtime; for opposition candidates without such a record, there is always the propaganda aimed at the "right-wing," big business or the Republican Party in general.

COPE denies it uses something called a "blacklist" (its leaders abhor the word), but other politically conscious elements—by no means anti-labor—see things differently. When a 1960 COPE "Political Memo" denounced seven U.S. senators for what it termed "wrong" votes in the session of Congress just ended, the *Washington Post* recognized this for what it was and headlined a news story on the "Memo": "COPE Puts 7 Senators on Blacklist."

And if local COPE leaders ever persist in defying national authority, dire consequences await. If a state or local COPE organization endorsed a presidential candidate other than the one backed by the national AFL-CIO, President Meany could yank the rebellious group's charter. (The same fate would also await any city or county COPE which bucked the state COPE on a gubernatorial or senatorial candidate.) Such action would only be taken in the most extreme cases, COPE leaders contend, and they cannot remember it ever having happened.

What AFL-CIO powerhouse Meany did do on two occasions in the 1966 campaign was completely to bypass the state labor leadership and give financial assistance from COPE's treasury to candidates the state AFL-CIOs had not endorsed. In New Jersey's badly split AFL-CIO no agreement could be reached on an endorsement in the state's senatorial race between incumbent GOP liberal Clifford Case and Democrat Warren Wilentz; finally some old AFL unions backed the sure-loser Democrat, and the CIO unions scattered to the winds. Fed up with such goings-on, Meany ordered COPE to send the pro-labor Case $2500. In the Maine senatorial race, the state AFL-CIO had endorsed the Democrat opposing the lady Republican incumbent, Sen. Margaret Chase Smith; but George Meany saw matters differently and had the boys at COPE send Mrs. Smith another $2500.

Instances of the local leadership challenging the decisions of national COPE (or, as in the above cases, vice versa), however, are rare. Everyone in the organization's chain of command realizes the necessity of cooperation if success is to be achieved, and few boats get rocked. The problem facing national COPE is not, therefore, one of making sure the local leaders endorse the right candidates or follow the proper course of action. The principal challenge to COPE is seeing that the millions of AFL-CIO workingmen follow these endorsements and participate in the programs established by their leaders.

## CHAPTER SIX

# COPE and the Workingman

## The Problems Faced by COPE

T HE relationship between the Committee on Political Education and the 14.3 million rank-and-filers in the AFL-CIO falls into two broad categories. The first consideration is that of worker participation in COPE's political activities. This encompasses COPE's ability to get workers active in a campaign and COPE's ability to contend with those members who oppose labor's political involvement in the first place. Secondly, and most important insofar as tangible benefits are concerned, is COPE's effectiveness in having union members (and their families and friends) vote for the candidates endorsed by the AFL-CIO.

These categories, though distinct in nature and importance, are themselves influenced by a number of problems confronting COPE on all sides and casting a gray shadow over all its relations with the workingmen on whom it relies for support. One of the reprimands offered by labor's contemporary critics is that the AFL-CIO has "lost touch" with the membership, a factor, these detractors claim, which is evidenced by rank-and-file apathy to labor's political activities. In the congressional elections of 1966, says the *Wall Street Journal,* "the message came through clearly that unions had failed to make contact with their members."

The *Journal* went on to quote an unnamed "labor politico" as commenting, "We aren't reaching our young people. We don't seem to be speaking their language.[1]

This apparent breakdown in rapport between the AFL-CIO hierarchy and the grass roots laborers is based upon a series of problems, all related to the success of COPE. These may be separated into the leaders' difficulty in communicating to the membership the goals and aspirations of COPE, the question of whether or not COPE's direction is endorsed by the rank-and-file, and the degree to which the union membership wishes to assert its independence, supporting or rejecting positions taken by the labor leadership.

In an age which has made "alienation" a byword and provided hundreds of scholars a full-time living studying this phenomenon, it should not be surprising that a form of alienation—or as it is often characterized, "lack of communication"—should plague the halls of the House of Labor. COPE's communication with the membership concerns both member participation in campaigns and getting members to vote for favored candidates.

The communication difficulty reared its hydra-head in 1966 as never before and COPE leaders viewed it as one of the primary causes for the congressional defeats; the members, one labor political operative said after the elections, "don't seem to understand what we're trying to do." In COPE's confidential report on the elections to the AFL-CIO Executive Council, it commented that the membership had a "short memory" when it came time to vote for supporters of the Great Society; many labor voters were caught up in the general wave of antipathy to LBJ and opted to reject Administration candidates, forgetting, said COPE, the "many services" these same representatives had rendered them.

As one step toward rectification of the situation outlined in this confidential report, the Council ordered COPE to examine the political attitudes and social-economic status of the rank-and-file; the result was the Kraft Poll of AFL-CIO union members, released in 1967. Meanwhile, COPE proceeded to use its customary "selling" method, blanket propaganda, telling the membership just who and what the AFL-CIO was supporting, and why. Throughout 1967 its propaganda lauded President Johnson and the Great Society programs, carefully explaining to the workers (who complain of high taxes just like anyone else) that the projects of the Administration cost money.

This line of propagandizing was followed up in COPE's reporting on specific legislative proposals for the 90th Congress. "Whether you're a young pup or an old gaffer," it wrote of LBJ's proposed 20 percent social security benefit increase—to which many young workers had objected—"the President's social security proposals are better than money in the bank. But, they'll also cost you a few bucks."[2]

The effort to sell its candidates and issues brings up the problem which COPE must sooner or later consider: whether the labor rank-and-file is growing more conservative than its leadership and is now rejecting the AFL-CIO's liberal legislative program because of its high cost and the infliction of government control (rather than because they do not "understand" it). In the opinion of the *Wall Street Journal,* "the union membership and the general public have moved to the right of the labor movement's historic political position, so that the union leadership no longer is attuned to the sentiments of the labor force . . ."[3]

While the situation may not be as dramatic as the *Journal* would have its readers believe, there was evidence, in the 1966 elections at least, of the rank-and-file exhibiting tendencies to vote for conservative candidates who in previous years would have been anathema. Thousands of workers obviously voted for California's Ronald Reagan, a former union leader (of the Screen Actors Guild) who campaigned on a platform calling for a reduction of federal control of the State and the individual; another example would be the election of Michigan Sen. Robert Griffin, the man who co-authored the Landrum-Griffin union policing bill, and in 1966 ran on a platform promising protection to the workers from union bosses. "I found in this campaign," said Griffin in a post-election interview, "that there was a growing tolerance among the rank-and-file toward Republican candidates; I received a far better reception at the plant gates in 1966 than I did, say, ten years ago. I believe this is found because there is now a younger generation of union members who don't buy the anti-management, anti-Republican propaganda of the labor leaders."

COPE itself, however, prefers to believe the success of candidates like Griffin among the rank-and-file in 1966 was more a case of a reaction called the "white backlash." "Your enemies are trying to throw dust in your eyes," wrote COPE before the elections, in an attempt to stave off a feared worker backlash vote, "extremists, hate-peddlers and the fear-ridden are trying to blind you to the real issues of the 1966 political campaign. They're counting on something called 'backlash.' "[4] After the results were in, the indescribable "something" became very precise for COPE, as it reported, " 'Backlash' is for real," and blamed the defeat of Sen. Douglas in Illinois and Pat Brown in California partially on this factor and its effect on the working voter.[5]

To define such a voter reaction as "backlash" (a term created by liberals to discredit Sen. Goldwater in 1964) and to say this behavior is solely predicated on racism and prejudice is a gross underestimation of the workingman's intelligence and constitutes blatantly demagogic propaganda. Union members are, after all, also home owners and are as opposed as any citizen to having the federal government place regulations on them—in the form of so-called "open housing" legislation, the supposed "backlash" issue of '66—concerning the rental or sale of their private dwellings. This sentiment was documented in the Kraft Poll, which showed 46 percent of the AFL-CIO members questioned in opposition to open housing legislation, 43 percent favorable; this was, COPE alleged, the only AFL-CIO legislative position a majority of the polling sample opposed.

It is difficult to know completely what else the poll told COPE about the rank-and-file. The *Wall Street Journal,* in breaking the story of the previously secret poll, said it portrayed the membership as taking on a "conservative cast" and that "labor's traditional goals are far out of line with union members' main interests."[6] Not so, said Al Barkan, writing that the poll demonstrated to COPE that union members "support the President's legislative achievements and endorse the legislative goals of the AFL-CIO and the President."[7]

Most of the discrepancy over interpretation was caused by COPE's failure to release the poll's complete results. Those figures it did reveal listed the rank-and-file as supporting the AFL-CIO on such items (described as "some of the major issues of today") as medicare expansion, air and water pollution control, truth-in-lending, increased minimum wage and improved workmen's compensation. But, while proudly displaying the statistics on these issues, Barkan did admit that elsewhere the poll disclosed "some uncertainty and unease among unionists, notably concerning jobs and economic security, some areas of civil rights and Vietnam . . ." Because the COPE-released results did not fully elaborate on this remark, it must be assumed that non-reported figures indicated some new conservatism among the rank-and-file; it would seem unlikely that COPE would suppress figures showing workers in agreement with the AFL-CIO.

Additionally, those figures revealed by COPE tended to indicate that the more controversial an issue was, the less worker support it received. Open housing is one example, repeal of Section 14(b) and aid to education are others. Next to housing, education aid received the lowest support (67 percent) of the public (i.e., not labor-oriented) issues listed in COPE's report. The matter of 14(b) repeal is truly surprising—and amusing: the poll turned up only 54 percent backing repeal, 23 percent in opposition, and, after all these years of labor propaganda on the subject, another 23 percent who were "not sure."

It is apparent from the poll that there is no wholesale "Goldwaterism" rampant within the AFL-CIO rank-and-file. It is equally apparent that the labor leadership can no longer take it for granted that the preponderance of the membership is as automatically liberal as they are.

For those critics of labor who say the AFL-CIO is not moving far enough left, the possibility of workers today becoming more conservative must come as something of a shock—if they bother to acknowledge it at all. "But the AFL-CIO under Meany," counters left-Socialist labor critic Sidney Lens, "*has* created a great vacuum between itself and the forces left of center, especially the New Left."[8] Such an analysis may fit neatly with Mr. Lens' desire to see a leftist labor movement reincarnate, but it does not quite fit in with the current situation which shows little—

if any—sentiment among the rank-and-filers for the militancy of the New Left, bearded as it is in Communist-oriented dogma similar to that which they fought so long to overthrow in their own ranks in the 'forties.

The AFL-CIO leadership shows no signs of placating its leftist critics by going whole-hog with the New Left ultra-liberalism (and thereby losing substantial support among its increasingly conservative membership). It probably will continue to promote liberal legislation in a subdued manner, without taking to the streets in riotous demonstrations, and work quietly within the liberal-labor alliance to support this legislation.

This procedure would probably not satisfy hostile and impatient critics such as Lens, who don't mind seeing "commitment" exhibited even if the cost be self-destruction. Federation spokesmen are aware of these charges and rebut them by defending their "creeping" approach to radical legislation: "We may be making slow progress," said one AFL-CIO henchman in an interview, "we may be too committed to gradualism—but dammit, it's progress."[9]

What Sidney Lens and his fellow labor critics of the Left want, of course, is more spectacular progress, of the type Walter Reuther is capable of producing in banner headlines. "Reuther intends to re-establish these ties with the far Left," writes Lens, "firm them up . . . Reuther may very well be the bridge, the man who forges a labor-liberal-radical coalition more independent of the establishment . . ."[10]

There is some cause to question just how much support Reuther himself has for his leftist ideals within his own United Auto Workers. Discussing Reuther's plans to move the UAW into the field of organizing the poor, the *New York Times*' knowledgeable labor columnist A. H. Raskin mused:

"The real question is whether his own rank and file will back any large-scale diversion of the UAW's funds and energies into such a drive. The gulf between the social aspirations of the union leadership and the middle-class property consciousness of much of its membership has been reflected in the spotty election support for union-endorsed political candidates in Michigan."[11]

These growing behavior trends among union members indicate not only a growing political conservatism but also a new-found desire to assert their independence of labor leaders. This display is found in labor politics as well as in other relationships between the AFL-CIO hierarchy and the grass roots. In 1966 politics, the workingman's feeling of independence from his rulers was exhibited in abundance in Michigan, where voters split their tickets by electing Gov. George Romney (first on the ballot, labor-opposed), then switched to elect two labor-endorsed Democrats for Secretary of State and Attorney General, the second and third spots on the ballot, and finally went back to the Republican side in the fourth spot to vote for Sen. Griffin.

Commented a Griffin aide after the '66 voting: "From now on there will be an enormous drifting vote within the rank-and-file not committed to any party or any faction."[12]

A non-political but equally dramatic situation in which this independent mood has surfaced is in contract negotiations. The Landrum-Griffin Act gave union members the final say on approval of contracts, allowing them a secret ballot to disapprove or ratify new labor-management pacts. The outcome, according to *Times*man Raskin, is that "the Government's labor troubleshooters estimate that about one-tenth of all their active cases now involve situations in which the union rank-and-file spurns agreements its leaders consider good enough to accept. That means about 800 cases a year . . ."[13]

The suggestion proposed by Raskin and others opposed to such union democracy is a weakening of Landrum-Griffin and a return to the policy of allowing union leaders to sign contracts without consulting their membership. Such is the position of contemporary liberals on the subject of union democracy.

With this challenge and a series of conditioning factors confronting it, COPE seeks to establish a working and voting relationship with the 14.3 million members of the AFL-CIO, their families, their friends. COPE must recruit workers to take part in campaigns, signing up volunteers at the same time it answers critics of its political commitment, and then convince those not campaigning to vote for labor-endorsed candidates. Because the campaign and voting manpower it can marshal for approved candidates is COPE's most influential weapon, it is understandable that relations with the workingman demand great attention from COPE leaders.

## The Workingman as Campaigner

As concerns COPE's all-round efforts, the most vital link in its rapport with the workingman is inducing participation in political activities, from getting voters registered to babysitting on election day. It should be stated at the outset that it is totally impossible to know even approximately what percentage of the AFL-CIO membership is available to COPE for campaign purposes; no figures exist and no one will hazard a guess. An added factor in the problem is the relative enthusiasm of workingmen for attractive candidates and their apathy toward unappealing—however liberal—candidates.

All of which means that the number of union member participants in any campaign is numerically indeterminate and varies from campaign to campaign, candidate to candidate.

COPE confronts the problem of enlisting campaign workers in the very beginning of its *How To Win* handbook. "No committee," it writes, "can roll very far without one more essential ingredient: Live, warm human bodies and alert human minds to perform with you the many tasks demanded by political activity." And in the second chapter COPE offers suggestions on getting warm union member bodies to attend organizational meetings and take an active part in the campaign.

Use announcements and posters on bulletin boards, advertisements in your union newspaper, and announcements mailed to the members about a week in advance of a meeting.

Then follow up with as many *personal* invitations (by phone or in the plant) as the COPE committee members can extend.

In most meetings you'll want to tell your audience about a particular problem so that they'll *do* something—help in registration drives, make COPE contributions, get out the vote. . . .

If you're looking for political action as the result of your meeting, have a workable plan ready. . . .

All of us are human; we like praise for a job well done. Keep this in mind, and pass out the laurels—in your oral report at the next meeting, and in your local union newspaper.

Recognition of the jobs that people do will keep these people coming back for more assignments.

The extent to which the membership responds to such blandishments and marches out of the meeting full of enthusiasm and ready to carry out action directives, is the unanswerable question. While COPE reported in 1966 on receiving only $750,000 in voluntary contributions, this is not a good indicator of participation in that year's campaign: if COPE had to depend on that much money and manpower for its operation, it would be no better off than any other independent political action group. A better gauge would be the approximately 65-80 percent of the AFL-CIO membership who regularly back labor-endorsed candidates. It would not be unreasonable to guess that within this average figure is a "hard core" of about 30 percent of the 14.3 million AFL-CIO members who donate a portion of their time to COPE activities.

(There is no question, however, of the active support COPE receives from union officials. A staff member at the National Chamber of Commerce recounted to the writer a story told by an industrial executive: it was always hopeless, the executive had said, to negotiate a contract during an election campaign because all the union leaders were unavailable and out campaigning.)

Substantiating this calculated figure—representing about four million workingmen—are the polls that have been taken concerning the attitude of workingmen toward labor union political activities. Invariably, these polls have shown, the rank-and-file overwhelmingly supports labor's participation in practical politics, even if they do not always back the favored candidates or take an active part in all campaigns.

The most thorough poll of this type was taken by Wayne State University which studied the attitudes of United Auto Workers members toward many facets of political action and the 1952 presidential-year election. Among the topics covered in this poll, the results of which were printed in a book entitled *When Labor Votes,* were several questions regarding the worker's opinions of labor's political activities and organized labor's influence on government.[14]

For obvious reasons, this poll cannot be taken as the final word on union members' political attitudes in 1968; it was published in 1956, concerned the 1952 elections and is limited to a sampling of members of one union, the United Auto Workers. For other reasons, however, the poll's findings are still given considerable weight by students of labor and by national COPE officials.

One such reason is simply that it is the most exhaustive poll of its type known to have been conducted in recent times. Subsequent polls, including the 1967 Kraft study, have not probed as deeply or extensively as the Wayne State Poll and what findings they have uncovered have generally confirmed the Wayne pollsters' analyses.

The fact that the study group was UAW members is also important here. As the pollsters themselves comment, "As a result of the years of [UAW] union educational effort and constant emphasis by the organization's leaders, they are probably a jump ahead in political understanding and readiness for political action. Consequently, what is found to be true of them, we believe, may be indicative of potential political behavior and attitudes in much wider labor circles."

The creation of COPE and the intensification of political activism "in wider labor circles," would seem to bear this observation out; COPE and most politically attuned unions are, in 1968, generally as well-organized, dogmatic and disciplined as the UAW was back in 1952, and this would have had an obvious impact on the attitudes of AFL-CIO members. A factor not to be forgotten in this "political maturity" is the influence the UAW's Walter Reuther had on COPE and the lessons the committee borrowed from his union.

The Wayne State Poll found that not only was there widespread support for the UAW's political activities, but that opposition to this activity had sharply declined. The pollsters recounted stories told by UAW "veterans" describing this drop-off: "Ten or fifteen years ago," the old-timers told the pollsters, "in union meetings or workers' education classes, there could always be found sizable numbers of workers expressing in no uncertain terms their opposition to *any* participation in political action by the union . . . and what is equally important, such remarks would be enthusiastically applauded by other workers present. Such remarks are rarely witnessed today, according to these 'veterans'."

The observations of the veterans are supported by the results of the poll. Fifty-five percent of all UAW members interviewed expressed the opinion that unions should have "more to say" in the operation of the government, through political activity and lobbying, and only 14 percent said labor should have "less to say." More important was the fact that the same sample produced 19 percent who believed business should have "more to say," and 41 percent who thought it should have "less to say." In other words, combining the figures, there were 42 percent of the UAW members who thought unions should play a larger role in politics, without also thinking business should, and only 6 percent who wanted business to have more say, unions less.

As to degrees of pro-labor faithfulness, the poll uncovered that 55 percent of the auto workers questioned were "strongly pro-labor," meaning they believed it all right for both labor and business to work for candidates, but wanted to see labor have more of a say in government and business less.

Commenting on these findings, the authors of *When Labor Votes* point out:

> It should be remembered that this is a picture of the political orienta-
> tion and allegiance not of union leaders and intellectuals but of rank
> and file UAW members, by the tens of thousands. What it signifies is
> that somewhat more than half of these union members definitely view
> the labor union as representing their broad political interests . . . and
> they want the unions to have greater influence on government. Most of
> the members of this majority group see business (and newspapers) as
> offering political leadership that is not to be followed, and they want to
> see the political influence of business curtailed. The evidence suggests
> that most of these people see the political world in terms of opposed
> goals and group interests as between labor and business. The findings
> indicate that the unionism of these UAW members extends a long
> distance beyond simple job-centered concerns. . . .

Although there is no more recent reliable poll examining these attitudes (the Kraft Poll did not take this matter up), this assessment by
the Wayne State authors has been well in evidence in succeeding years.
COPE has regularly used propaganda aimed at Big Business to arouse
the rank-and-file, and in its attack on the "right wing" COPE goes to
great lengths to show how businessmen are purportedly giving financial
support to this enemy. This is in line with the poll's finding that work-

ingmen tend to "see the political world in terms of opposed goals and group interests."

And despite any new independence found among union voters, there has been surprisingly little increase in the number of workers wanting labor to alter its traditional political role. Not only has there been a notable lack of demand for such action at conventions (union or AFL-CIO), but there has been, in recent years, comparatively little public complaint by rank-and-filers concerning the political activities of their unions and the federation—although numerous opportunities to do so have been presented.

However, just as labor participation in politics goes back in American history to the start of this century, so do workers' objections to this participation. When the AFL first became involved in its tacit non-partisan campaign approach, there was then a rank-and-file outcry demanding cessation of this activity and/or support of more Republicans. When the CIO established its Political Action Committee, the cry increased at times to a loud roar (this was obviously the time the UAW "veterans" referred to, when members would rise in meetings to denounce political activity).

One of the most damning indictments of the CIO's radical approach to politics was provided by William Mullins, political editor of the Boston *Herald* and long-time member of the CIO-affiliated Newspaper Guild. Writing in the *Reader's Digest* in 1944, Mullins declared:

"Through my union's affiliation with the CIO, I find myself represented in politics, without my consent and against my will. . . . Unions do not need partisan politics. . . . A union is not a political proposition. It is an economic and human proposition. . . . My main point is the effort of the Political Action Committee to transfer my *union affiliations* into *political opinions*."[15]

Twelve years later, with the merger of the AFL and CIO pending and creation of a political organization a lively topic of discussion, a number of top-ranking labor leaders—primarily from the old-line AFL unions—raised objections. Some AFL leaders thought it acceptable for the new federation to indulge in political action, but not on the loudly partisan level the CIO had followed. Others believed politics—like religion—should be a matter left strictly to the discretion of the workingman. Both factions were silenced by the concentrated barrage of the CIO's Big Guns—led by Walter Reuther—as the AFL-CIO Executive Council voted to continue the pattern set by PAC.

One powerful grass roots labor leader, George Hinkle, a UAW member who was Indiana Commissioner of Labor in 1956, objected to political partisanship for financial reasons:

"There are millions of Republicans in organized labor who are being forced to pay the campaign expenses for Democratic office seekers as a condition of employment. If they do not pay their union dues, they do not have a job; and if they object to this sort of use of their dues money they are insulted, baited and labeled anti-labor by the very same labor leaders who claim to be defending their individual rights and freedoms. I am not opposed to unions participating in politics, as long as they finance their candidates with money which is solicited on a non-compulsory, voluntary basis from the membership."[16]

This contention that organized labor uses compulsory union dues money for partisan political activities to which many dues-paying workers may be opposed, formed the basis of the most concentrated, well-organized attack by rank-and-filers on the political operations of their unions in the past decade. This was a court case originated in Atlanta, Georgia, by six rail employes against a slew of railroad unions, the AFL-CIO, COPE, and their officers, which eventually wound up in the Supreme Court.

The focus of the suit, commonly called the Street Case, was put in these terms in the appellees brief filed with the Supreme Court in 1959:

"The major question presented to the Court for decision is: May unions under cover of a union shop contract authorized by the Railway Labor Act, force minority employees to *accept* and *pay for* political and ideological representation by unions whose views are repugnant to and opposed by such minority employees?"[17]

In other words, can Congress force workers to support a political party, issue or candidate they oppose? In states not having right-to-work laws, every employee in a union shop must join a union to hold his job, he must pay his dues, and his dues money is used for political purposes to which he may be in opposition; railway employees, such as those involved in the Street Case, are not covered by Section 14(b) of Taft-Hartley, but by a Railway Labor Act provision ordering all rail workers to join unions, pay dues, and perhaps be forced to financially back politics they don't like. In an echo of William Mullins' objections to the CIO's Political Action Committee, the attorneys for the Street appellees asserted:

"Congress has no constitutional power to require an employee to *accept* and *pay* his 'collective bargaining representative' as also his political and ideological spokesman. . . . A labor party (in deed if not in name) cannot be created through funds exacted under a union shop agreement."

Organized labor's usual rebuttal to such charges is that, while some small part of a worker's required dues charge may pay for repugnant (to the worker) politics, he is still free to electioneer on his own, as he chooses. To this, the Street Case attorneys argue that the workers' "participation through their union representatives negates and destroys the effectiveness of their individual participation. It is worse than being merely 'paired' off against themselves. Their self-appointed 'spokesmen' —the union—speaks so loudly that their individual voices cannot be heard. In this clearest possible violation of their freedom of association, the individuals are so thoroughly submerged by the mass which they are compelled to finance that their individual identities and views cannot be recognized."

This case presented a perfect opportunity for Earl Warren's Supreme Court to demonstrate its true liberalism and concern with the civil rights of unionized workers. Both the Georgia superior court in Macon, and the state supreme court in Atlanta had ruled in favor of the worker appellees, but the U.S. Supreme Court took the easy road out. Reversing the state court's decisions in 1961, it ruled to send the case back to the state for the purpose of receiving evidence as to what portions of the dues were being spent for political activities. Seizing an escape route, the unions offered to settle out of court by paying the appellees back *all* money they had given in dues since joining their unions.

Another well-publicized attempt by individual workers to rally the rank-and-file in rebuking their unions' free-wheeling expenditure of dues money for partisan politics came in 1955, during the course of the Street litigation. Three local union leaders, two from the Auto Workers and one from the Steelworkers came to Washington to testify before a Senate Committee on Constitutional Rights concerning what they considered to be an unconstitutional use of their union dues money.

The chairman of the Senate Committee, Sen. Thomas C. Hennings (D-Mo.), who was counting on labor support in his re-election bid the following year, refused to hear this testimony, and the three workers from the upper Midwest appealed to GOP Sen. Carl Curtis for a hearing. Curtis and Sen. Barry Goldwater called a press conference in December, 1955, and the complainants told their stories to a large assemblage of newspaper, television and radio correspondents. One of the workers, Walter Brauninger, a UAW member from Chelsea, Michigan, saw the situation in this light:

"A great problem exists and it must be recognized. A solution must be found. The unions grew big by doing a good job, economically speaking, that needs to be done. They have gained the faith and confidence of a vast majority of the members because of the job that is being accomplished from the standpoint of economics.

"The union bosses are now taking advantage of this faith and confidence, built up in a few short years, and are turning the power given to them, and confidence bestowed upon them, into a political purpose. I consider this to be a betrayal of the rank-and-file membership.

"I believe they are doing things in politics which the members have never asked or wanted them to do. I believe there are many Democrats as well as Republicans among the union members who feel that this political coercion and this cynical use of hard-earned union dues for purposes never contemplated by the union members as a whole, is undermining the basic structure of the labor movement."[18]

Clarence Bridgeman, one of Brauninger's fellow protestors and a member of the United Steelworkers from Marquette, Michigan, told the press conference of a unique experience a couple of years before when his own money was used to defeat his candidacy for public office. Bridgeman was running as a Republican for the county clerk's post in Marquette County and he sought out the leader of his local to discuss his candidacy.

"I was told," reported Bridgeman in Washington, "in clear language that I was running on the wrong ticket. . . . My union leadership came out openly and strongly for the entire Democrat slate. To me, this meant my own union was opposing my candidacy on the Republican ticket, and more important, that a part of the union dues which I had to pay in order to keep my job covered were being used in the Democrat campaign against me."

Despite the newspaper coverage and other publicity these rank-and-file protests received, the ultimate effect was minimal. A special Select Committee on Improper Activities in the Labor or Management Field was established in the Senate to hear testimony on the notorious Kohler and Perfect Circle strikes. Sen. John McClellan's Rackets Subcommittee held further hearings on labor bosses' conduct. As a result, some suggestions from both committees were incorporated in the Landrum-Griffin Labor-Management Bill of 1959. As for labor's political activities, there was little or no alteration in operation.

Most frustrating to those workers who had dared speak out must have been the absence of spontaneous support from their fellow rank-and-filers. The three men who came from Michigan and Wisconsin to air their objections, and the appellees in the Street Case arguing against financial coercion, all found precious little moral backing at the grass roots of organized labor.

Since that time, there has been virtual silence on the subject from the rank-and-file. When Sen. Everett Dirksen began his Senate campaign to defeat repeal of Section 14(b) in 1966 he received tons of mail from union members all across the nation supporting his drive; while these letters were concerned mostly with the issue of open vs. union shop laws, the tone of many showed a widespread objection to any form of dictation, on any topic, from labor leaders.

"I am a union man and a Democrat," wrote a man from Minnesota, "but I want to keep my right to choose between a union or no union. It's my only chance to protect myself against crooked union officials and those who feel I work for them instead of the company . . ." Another AFL-CIO member wrote to complain that it was "the labor bosses, not the members" who so fervently wanted right-to-work repealed.[19]

And Sen. Robert Griffin (R-Mich.) is convinced that his campaign victory over "Soapy" Williams in 1966, and his large vote in working-class precincts, was due in part to union voters' resentment over having the state AFL-CIO foist Williams on them and order them to vote for the ex-Governor. In one position advanced by Griffin in his speeches to rank-and-filers, he insisted "I believe that spending dues money collected in a union shop for political purposes is an invasion of a worker's civil rights, as much an invasion as any concerned with Negroes." Some 42 percent of Michigan's laboring voters obviously did not disagree with this position strongly enough to forsake support of Griffin.

Significant though these expressions may be, there still has been little tangible, concerted effort on the part of rank-and-file union members to change the partisan political position of their unions or the AFL-CIO. Among the more practical reasons for this absence may be the time involved in mounting such an attack, especially in the courts (the Street Case was in state and federal courts for twelve years), the cost involved in court fights or union convention challenges, and, perhaps more important to the workingman, the threat he would face in terms of losing his job or position if he dared face down his union. (The president of the local to which Walter Brauninger, one of the protesters who went to Sen. Curtis, belonged told him: "Why don't you find a job in a plant where they're all Republicans and where they don't have a union?")

Underlying the more practical reasons, however, is the inescapable truth that a solid majority of union members actually see nothing (or very little) wrong with the heavily pro-Democrat activities of their unions and the AFL-CIO, an observation confirmed by the Wayne State study and the Kraft Poll 15 years later. Though they may not all be wildly enthusiastic about ringing doorbells every spare minute and they may not all vote for every labor-backed candidate, this majority does maintain the "right" of labor to participate in politics—in many cases enthusiastically endorses it; most important, the allegiance of this great number far outweighs the objections of the few. For every courageous protestor like Brauninger, Bridgeman, or A. B. Street, there are dozens more who feel like a Michigan UAW member, Lewis Daniels, who told reporters for his union's newspaper:

"The future of the common man depends on the election of Democratic candidates . . . A couple of workers—workers, mind you—were critical of Democrats in 1966! They should be ashamed of themselves;

they were rejecting the only party that really did anything for workers. They forget too easily."[20]

The sentiments of Brother Daniels were found to be in evidence among the great majority of UAW members by the Wayne State University group when they examined laborers' political attitudes in the mid-fifties.

The loyalty and devotion of a majority of rank-and-file members to their union was also mentioned by the legal authors of the appellees brief in the Street Case. Speaking on the subject, they said, "While some tough-minded individuals, such as the named appellees, may resist regimentation, it is probable, as Congress, the unions and the railroads all have realized, that the great preponderance of employees, upon being told they must join the union, will join—not just in a *pro forma* sense, but in a genuine sense."

The 1967 Kraft Poll tended to confirm that the majority of workers still join their union in "a genuine sense." Statistics pointing in this direction showed that: 64 percent of the AFL-CIO members polled "quickly referred to their [union] membership when asked to list affiliations with various public, private, church or job-related organizations"; 20 percent—"a surprisingly high figure," said COPE—attend "almost every" union meeting, and another 14 percent attend "quite frequently"; 63 percent read their union publications "a lot"; and George Meany came out fourth when workers were asked to name their "most reliable source of information," trailing only President Johnson, TV newscaster Walter Cronkite and *Time* magazine—all with considerably more exposure than Meany.

Such demonstrable loyalty, or "genuine" adherence, by a majority of the workers to their union (and federation) does not necessarily mean the rank-and-file agrees with their union's every individual political action. A bloc of workers—perhaps even a majority—may disagree with labor's choice of a candidate in a specific election, but rather than object to the union endorsement itself the dissidents have shown they will simply vote for his opponent. This is what happened with Ike in '52 and '56, Reagan in '66 and Bob Griffin the same year.

Likewise, the mere fact of the total absence of unionists' objection to labor's political participation by itself strongly indicates there is not sufficient disagreement over individual candidates to merit active, blanket opposition. Most of the same workers who voted for Eisenhower (or Reagan, or Griffin) obviously did not view this "nonconformity" as cause to condemn labor for endorsing the opposing candidate, or any candidates.

The situation in the AFL-CIO today, as concerns members' backing of their organization's political activities, is undoubtedly similar to that in the UAW in the 'fifties. For example, the Kraft Poll found that 58 percent of its sample identified themselves as strong Democrats, 16 percent as Republicans, 17 percent as independents and 9 percent said they were "not sure." While it is certainly possible that a worker who is rabidly pro-Democrat may not want his union to behave the same way, there is little evidence that such a sentiment exists to any significant degree.

Barring any such untapped reservoir of opposition, it may be estimated that there is within the AFL-CIO today a bloc of between 50-60 percent of the membership who approve (at the very least, tolerantly so) labor's political participation; there is another 15-20 percent who can be "swayed" by the attitudes of the majority to support—perhaps less enthusiastically—the labor political position. It is reasonably safe to conclude that in a preponderance of its activities COPE has the support of between 65-80 percent of the AFL-CIO's members. This support is not uniformly active, nor is its lasting cohesion guaranteed, but, more often than not, it is there.

If there is then any growing rebellion against union leadership dictation, as Sen. Dirksen's right-to-work mail and Sen. Griffin's 1966 experiences might suggest, it is something to be quickly captured and exploited by those in politics who wish to see a rank-and-file truly independent from the political dictates of the pro-Democratic labor leaders.

There is a great deal of room to question, however, just how much so-called independence there is and just how far it extends in politics. In 1968 and the election years to come, will union voters demonstrate more and more independence from the leadership's announced positions, or is this independence a sometime thing? In other words, will the workingman throw off for good the political chains his leaders have, at least since the formation of the CIO, bound him with, or will his freedom be only an infrequent exhibition to be found in rare and unique circumstances?

## The Workingman as Voter

These questions of workingman voter independence lead directly to the second general category within COPE's overall relationship with AFL-CIO members: its ability to induce union members, their families and friends, to follow their leaders and cast votes for the candidates and policies supported by the AFL-CIO.

Shortly after formation of the AFL-CIO, George L. O'Brien, Assistant General President of the Brotherhood of Railway Carmen, referred to this relationship in terms of the then-popular television quiz show which awarded contestants a top prize of $64,000:

"This year, 1956, will be the first year in which all labor organizations in the United States will be united in their political efforts. The leaders of our political parties are very much alive to this fact and consequently are now centering their attention on watching every activity of the leaders of the trade unions. The reason for this close study is quite obvious—the combined membership of labor today is estimated to be *seventeen million*. Without doubt organized labor constitutes a tremendous block of votes, which in the opinion of this writer could very easily decide a national election—IF—they would but vote unitedly.

"The $64,000 question is, will they? Will the rank and file of labor listen to the advice of their leaders on political candidates? Will these same rank and filers follow the advice given and cast their votes accordingly?"[21]

This high-priced question has still to be answered. Until someone devises a method of determining the vote of every workingman voter, it will remain insoluble. On the subject of rank-and-filers voting or not voting for labor-endorsed candidates and the degree of independence shown by union voters, the answer for now must—like Mr. O'Brien's question—be a numerical composition.

For the most exhaustive study yet done of labor union members' voting behavior one must again turn to the Wayne State University examination published in *When Labor Votes*. Overall, this study found, members of the United Auto Workers supported the labor-backed presidential candidate in 1952, Adlai Stevenson, over GOP rival Dwight Eisenhower, by a margin of 3 to 1. Within the polling sample (828 workers in pre-election, 351 in post-election sample, many of them the same) 75 percent of the UAW members voted for Stevenson.

The poll had found that 80 percent of its pre-election sample had declared as Democrats or Democrat-leaning, 11 percent had said the same of the Republican Party, and 9 percent had claimed "independence." In view of these statistics, it can not come as any surprise that 39 percent of those questioned before the '52 elections who said they intended to vote for Stevenson, explained they were going to do so principally because he was "running on the Democratic ticket." (The second most cited reason for Stevenson support was that he would be "better for workers" and favored Taft-Hartley repeal.) And after the election, 52 percent of those who actually voted for Stevenson gave his Democratic label as their "main reason" for doing so.

This diehard allegiance to the Democratic Party is most instructive, not in its reflection on the presidential race, but its influence on secondary contests. Eisenhower was extremely popular in all segments of the public, including the working classes, and while the dedicated Democrats in the UAW—a more activist, pro-Democrat union than any other—may have given Ike only 25 percent support (at least in this poll), nationally, according to the AFL-CIO, he received 48 percent of the union vote.

But on the lower rungs of the ballot the story is different. Some 98 percent of the workers in the Wayne State polling who voted for Stevenson voted a straight Democrat ticket, and among those backing Eisenhower the percentage casting straight GOP ballots dropped to 55 percent. If this polling was a true sample, therefore, 13 percent of all UAW voters stuck with the Republican ticket all the way. "These findings clearly indicate," it is concluded in *When Labor Votes*, "that auto workers in the Detroit area were decidedly more Democratic than their votes for Stevenson and Eisenhower would suggest." This display of some independence in voting for top political offices, and concurrent adherence to the labor-backed candidates on the lower office levels, is a phenomenon which has persisted among union voters, most recently in Michigan's 1966 voting.

Another factor having to do with union voter "independence" uncovered in the poll is that it is not those workers most interested and concerned with politics who exhibit this freedom. In fact, the report stated that "it is also true that members with high political interest tend to agree most with the union politically," and the poll found 38 percent of its sampling in the "high political interest" category. At the same time, the poll found 21 percent who were judged "not pro-labor," in that they did not share their leaders' distrust of business and wholehearted allegiance to the union, and among this group 61 percent backed Eisenhower, 29 percent Stevenson.

It would seem safe to assume on the basis of these findings that what political independence is to be found among labor voters lies within that segment which belongs to a union only because it must in order to retain a job. These members probably do not regularly attend union meetings, are reluctant to walk picket lines, ignore labor propaganda, and vote in opposition to labor candidates—perhaps sometimes only out of spite. This segment is comparatively minor (21 percent, as compared to 55 percent "strong pro-labor" in the Wayne State sample), but it is something for labor-opposed candidates to build upon.

One fairly common trait of union voters in evidence in the two Stevenson-Eisenhower contests, was that a portion of labor voters will sometimes fail to cast a ballot at all, rather than back an unappealing Democrat. The liberal, popular Eisenhower provided millions of union members a "respectable" Republican for whom they could vote in good conscience, but many others, deeply inculcated by their leaders with the glory of the Democratic Party, could only "support" Eisenhower by not voting for Stevenson.

A COPE analysis of the 1956 Eisenhower-Stevenson race commented on this behavior in these terms:

"It is not true that there were substantial shifts from Stevenson to Eisenhower in the so-called labor wards of the big cities. Preliminary checks of the voting pattern in these wards indicates a small decline in the vote for Stevenson over 1952, but no corresponding increase in the vote for Eisenhower. In other words, there was some withholding of ballots."

This pattern has continued to haunt organized labor to this day. COPE believed this to have been a main factor in the defeat of pro-labor candidates Sen. Paul Douglas of Illinois and "Soapy" Williams of Michigan in 1966, and an influential factor in several other races.

"In state after state," said COPE's own report of the '66 voting, "the Democratic vote failed to come out in numbers comparable to 1962, the last off-year election. The most extreme example occurred in Detroit, where Governor Romney actually polled 11,000 *fewer* votes than in 1962, but the Democratic gubernatorial vote plummeted by 152,000.

"In blue collar and middle income wards, the pattern was the same in many cities as in Detroit, notably in Chicago, Philadelphia, Denver, Milwaukee, Phoenix, Minneapolis, Cincinnati, Louisville, Memphis. More than through actual voter defection, then, liberal candidates in these areas were hurt by the stay-at-homes."[22]

The means to counter such behavior is, of course, COPE's "get-out-the-vote" drive on Election Day. But a large "stay-at-home vote" is, like a sizable "independent" union vote, a sometime thing and will occur only when the "opposition" can offer candidates and issues that will either win over union voters or cast enough doubt on the quality of the labor candidate to persuade the workers to "sit out" the balloting. With active interest on the part of labor voters, the COPE campaign to get them to the polls can swing the election.

Speaking of the decisive question of how loyal union voters are to union-backed candidates, in 1957 COPE's then deputy director, Al Barkan, was able to look at the Stevenson-Eisenhower contest of the year before and, despite the unusually large labor vote for Ike, find cause for optimism. Using a study by the Survey Research Center at the University of Michigan as his source, Barkan observed:

"Union members voted 52 percent for the Democratic candidate for President (Stevenson) who was recommended by the AFL-CIO General Board and 48 percent for the Republican candidate. The contrast with the voting behavior of the general public, of which union members are a part, is marked [Ike got 57.8 percent of the total vote]. The contrast with the voting behavior of the non-union 'workers' was even greater.

"While 52 percent of the union 'workers' voted for the candidate recommended by the AFL-CIO, only 35 percent of the non-union 'workers' voted for the same candidate. Sixty-five percent of the non-union workers voted for the opposing candidate, while 48 percent of the union 'workers' voted for the same candidate.

"More detailed study confirmed the findings. In those unions which expressed a clear political preference in their publications, whose leaders took strong stands and gave direction to their members, the vote for backed candidates was higher than in unions in which this was not the case."[23]

Barkan's point is an obvious and important one—the Democratic Party has long held faith in it—but it bears constant repeating, if only for the benefit of those who see a growing "freedom" or "selectivity" among union voters. If there were no union endorsements of candidates, if there were no coordinated union political activity on behalf of one candidate or one party and if leaders and members were left to function politically as individuals, there would be a greater diversity of voting patterns among rank-and-file balloting. There is no known study, comparing voting between union and non-union workers, since this 1957 report, but subsequent national elections confirm Barkan's observation that where and when unions do endorse there is a greater degree of conformity among labor voting than when there is not.

(Again it should be noted that the 1956 presidential election of which Barkan spoke presented an incumbent GOP candidate who was widely popular more as an individual than as an ideologist or Republican. The degree of union voter conformity could be expected to be much higher in contests where the focus was on distinctly Republican-Democrat candidates and issues.)

Statistics from the last three presidential contests show first of all that labor voters are as susceptible as the rest of the public to a particular candidate's relative attractiveness, as interpreted by the general populace. Eisenhower went over big with a large segment of the labor bloc, Goldwater scared them off in droves. This should not dim the pro-Democrat bias of the large majority of union voters, however—even Ike, the great war hero, had to struggle to make a dent in the labor vote.

Eisenhower did not do well at all in what might be called the "hard core" labor precincts, areas with an unusually high concentration of dedicated union members. He received only 32.6 percent of the vote, for example, in the four solidly labor precincts of Chicago in 1956; 42 percent in the auto workers' stronghold of Wayne County, Michigan (Detroit); 44.4 percent in the four towns of Allegheny County, Pa., with their large number of steel and mine workers (this same area gave Ike but 36.5 percent in '52); and in the labor wards of Milwaukee,

Eisenhower received 42.5 percent in 1956 (up from 32.6 in 1952).[24]

In other cities with a large percentage of labor voters, Eisenhower did score better. In the labor wards of Hartford, Conn., Ike received 51.4 percent of the vote in 1956, while Hartford city itself was giving Stevenson 54.9 percent of its votes; in New York's Erie County, containing the Democratic stronghold of Buffalo, Ike racked up a resounding 63 percent; and in heavily industrial Montgomery County, Ohio (Dayton), the GOP standard-bearer received 58.4 percent of the vote.

Sen. Barry Goldwater, on the other hand, did poorly in labor areas all across the board. The smears about the 1964 Republican presidential nominee, created by COPE and others, worked their wonders in a very tangible way. In the labor precincts of Hartford, Goldwater salvaged 21.6 percent of the votes (Hartford city, surprisingly, was ahead of the labor voters in Democratic-bias, awarding Goldwater a bare 16.6 percent), in Erie County the Arizonan got 33.3 percent, and in Dayton 34.3 percent.

Actually, as low as these Goldwater figures may appear, his labor vote average was only a few points below his national vote percentage total. Goldwater's vote fluctuated wildly in labor strongholds, with the GOP candidate doing comparatively well in some (30.7 percent in Baltimore's labor wards) and getting drubbed in others (14.2 percent in Chicago's labor wards). Overall, however, it would appear that union voters were only slightly less taken aback by the avowed conservative candidate than was the rest of the country.

Because of the overriding personal issues involved in both the 1956 and 1964 presidential races, neither could be said to represent a wholly accurate view of labor voting and each must be judged in its own particular context. Perhaps the most recent election presenting a reasonably objective view of union members' party and organizational loyalty in voting for national officeholders is the 1960 contest between John F. Kennedy and Richard Nixon. A race between a moderate-conservative and moderate-liberal on traditional Republican vs. Democrat grounds, and without substantial personality clashes (it is difficult now to remember there was not always a "Kennedy Myth"), the '60 presidential sweepstakes was hard fought until the final moment and was decided nationally by a scant 113,000 votes out of close to 60 million cast.

With such a close contest it can be assumed that union members followed the '60 campaign as closely as the rest of the electorate— viewing the televised debates, reading the newspapers and listening to the arguments put forth by their leaders and COPE's propaganda. Organized labor went down the line behind Democrat Kennedy and in some vital areas labor political activists may well have been the deciding factor in swinging electoral votes to JFK; Illinois' bloc of 26 electoral votes, for example, went to Kennedy because of the large pluralities he racked up in the labor precincts of Chicago, and Michigan's votes were decided in the auto worker neighborhoods of Wayne County.

The overall picture of 1960 voting shows Nixon getting a vote averaging in the 30-40 percent range in heavily union sections. In comparison with Eisenhower's 1956 totals, Nixon's vote drops sharply in these areas which Ike had either carried or done respectably in. Sen. Goldwater, on the other hand, is down from Nixon (although the drop here is not as sharp as that between the Nixon-Eisenhower votes), generally about 10 percentage points. A few comparative figures follow:

|  | EISENHOWER ('56) | NIXON | GOLDWATER |
|---|---|---|---|
| Pueblo Co., Col. |  |  |  |
| (Pueblo) | 53.4 | 42.4 | 39.8 |
| Bridgeport, Conn. |  |  |  |
| Labor Wards | 52.9 | 33 | 21.3 |
| Wayne Co., Mich. |  |  |  |
| (Detroit) | 42 | 33.8 | 25.9 |
| Franklin Co., Ohio |  |  |  |
| (Columbus) | 65.8 | 59.4 | 46.1 |
| Cleveland City | 45.4 | 29 | 17.2 |
| Mahoning Co., Ohio |  |  |  |
| (Youngstown) | 52 | 38.2 | 27 |
| Pittsburgh, Pa. |  |  |  |
| Labor Wards | 45.7 | 29.9 | 22 |
| Milwaukee, Wisc. |  |  |  |
| Labor Wards | 42.5 | 25.2 | 19.9 |

There can be no denying the wide gulf between the Eisenhower and Goldwater totals in these areas, and most other labor centers, but the personality issues involved in these races must militate against any attempts to show a pro-Republicanism among union members in 1956 or an anti-conservatism in 1964. As the Wayne State Poll observed, although more auto workers than usual did vote Republican for the top spot on the ticket in 1952, they were far more Democratic than those solitary figures revealed.

The 1960 contest saw a middle-of-the-road "solid Republican" incumbent Vice President vying with an untried Liberal Democratic Senator, and union members were presented an opportunity to display their true party loyalty and obedience to their leaders. The result was a labor vote varying between 65 and 80 percent for Democratic candidate Kennedy and low response to Republican Nixon, despite the heavy inroads made by Eisenhower just four years earlier.

There has been no accounting of labor votes since 1964 which reveals anything new about union members' voting behavior. What figures are available tend to confirm the view that in unique contests the labor vote will scatter with the winds. In Michigan's 1966 Senate race, GOP candidate Robert Griffin was able to carry the heavily unionized community of Battle Creek with 56.1 percent of the total vote, but in the Detroit township of Hamtramck he made off with a minuscule 19.2 percent; he could carry the union cities of Saginaw and Flint, and still get only 24.8 percent in River Rouge, a Detroit suburb housing a huge Ford Motor plant and thousands of auto workers.

The Kraft Poll dealt only passingly with the question of workers' candidate-party preference, but even so it offered some valuable insights. The poll was taken in January, 1967, a time when President Johnson's popularity was at one of its lowest points and the Louis Harris Poll showed only 43 percent of the public giving the President a "good job" rating; with such widespread disenchantment, it might have been expected that LBJ would not have fared too well when the Kraft pollsters matched him against each of four potential GOP challengers and asked union members to pick their favorite, or else declare "not sure" or "neither."

On the contrary, Johnson did extremely well against his Republican adversaries, receiving less than majority support in only one case. Matched against George Romney, LBJ was the favorite of 46 percent while the Michigan Governor, who was then at the peak of his popularity, was liked by 30 percent (meanwhile, 19 percent were "not sure," 5 percent said, "neither"). Paired with Richard Nixon, it was LBJ, 55 percent, and Nixon, 22 (with 15 percent not sure, 8 percent neither); California's Ronald Reagan received 16 percent support, as against Johnson's 60 percent (17 percent, not sure, 7 percent, neither); and Nelson Rockefeller attracted 20 percent, LBJ 55 percent (18 percent, not sure, 7 percent, neither).

The Kraft Poll clearly shows that, with one slight exception, a majority of AFL-CIO members still hold a fundamental political-party loyalty, demonstrating it by supporting a then-unpopular Democratic President. Also eminently noteworthy is the continuing wariness the rank-and-file exhibits toward all Republicans, with liberal Romney—the "most attractive" to the membership, according to Kraft—receiving only 30 percent support at a time when his popularity was riding high and LBJ's was on the decline.

From such an avalanche of figures, statistics and addenda here presented, certain basic conclusions may yet be drawn as to COPE's and organized labor's ability to "line up" the labor vote. Most important is that there is some significant degree of "discriminatory voting" among union members when it comes to selection of top government officials. It is here, on the upper rungs of state and national office, that any "independence" is found in this voting bloc, and the heavy labor vote for GOP candidates such as Eisenhower, George Romney, Sen. Robert Griffin and a handful of others equally successful testifies to this.

But, the "independent" phenomenon is found strictly at the highest levels. At the same time that Ike was making deep inroads in labor wards in 1956, union members were deserting the Republican ticket after this ballot and returning a Democratic Congress to Washington. When Romney and Griffin led the Republican ticket in Michigan to a small landslide in 1966, taking a large number of GOP state legislators with them, union voters were able to buck the tide and make their votes count in returning a Democratic Secretary of State, Attorney General (both of whom were at the top of the ballot wedged in between governor and senator) and a solid phalanx of city, county and judicial officials.

The figures available on union members' voting for elective offices do not necessarily correspond to the faith laborers place in the endorsements made by organized labor. The exact motivations for voting overwhelmingly for Democratic candidates may rest more upon party loyalty than the lone factor of union endorsement, although it is probably impossible to separate the two, the labor leaders having had a great deal to do with creating and reinforcing a pro-Democratic bias among the rank-and-file in the first place.

Even careful, scientific studies of public attitudes toward political endorsements by pressure groups are not very helpful. A 1963 poll taken by the Purdue University Communications Research Center, asking a cross section of voters in five states (California, Connecticut, Illinois, Kentucky and Pennsylvania) whom they relied on most for political information, produced some interesting answers: 32 percent said business leaders were those they "most likely would believe" and 4 percent said labor leaders belonged in the same category.[25]

Obviously, labor leaders do not make endorsements and spread propaganda for the general public, and there is no reason to expect people outside organized labor to place full confidence in this propaganda, least of all to find it "most likely" to be believed. More revelatory on this subject, perhaps, is the finding made in the Wayne State Poll, that, of the total sample of auto workers, 49 percent said they trusted voting recommendations of labor groups the most, and a corresponding percentage stated they distrusted business endorsement more than any other.

The conclusion reached from these statistics in *When Labor Votes* confirms the observation by COPE's Al Barkan, when he said that "the vote for backed candidates was higher than in unions in which this was not the case." "The 49 percent naming labor groups" as the most reliable endorsee, said the Wayne State group, "can be considered clear positive support of union endorsements, especially by contrast with the decidedly smaller percentages naming other groups as trusted."

And the Kraft Poll's discovery that union members consider their federation's president, George Meany, to be a leading "most reliable source for information" could be interpreted to mean that they also consider his (and, through his, COPE's) word on candidates to be authoritative. Meany came in fourth in this ranking, behind LBJ, TV's Cronkite and *Time;* two of these others made no political endorsements (at least overtly), and LBJ and Meany pretty much agree on who should get elected. Thus, as for their "most reliable" information outlets, union members put most of their faith in sources solidly on the Democratic side of the fence.

But, perhaps the actions of most Democrats in seeking a labor endorsement makes the whole question moot. One does not crawl on his hands and knees toward an oasis that is dried up unless it is a mirage; politicians know full well that organized labor's political effectiveness is no mirage.

Whether it is due to union endorsement, personal sentiment or the side of the bed they got out of on Election Day morning, the majority of union members do give their votes to labor-backed candidates. Despite some fluctuations—or "independence"—in balloting for top offices, there is a "sure" labor bloc of between 65 and 80 percent which can be counted on by pro-labor Democratic candidates. The direction of this vote is found most convincingly in the tallies Richard Nixon received in labor wards and in the repeated success of lesser Democratic office-holders.

COPE national director Al Barkan is optimistic on the percentage of labor votes a candidate may receive, all things being equal. In a 1964 interview he said, "If 70 to 80 percent of our membership will follow the endorsement made by COPE, we think that is good." He elaborated further on his convoluted wording when asked if this was what COPE "generally" received: "Yes, when we have a good candidate, a popular candidate."[26]

Barkan might have explained this by saying that when there is no great popular hero (such as Eisenhower) running as a Republican, or when the Democrat-labor forces do not botch up a campaign (as they did in Michigan's '66 Senate race), COPE can count on up to 80 percent of the union members' vote.

It is most likely this figure will remain fairly constant in the election years immediately ahead. The AFL-CIO and its adjunct COPE are both aware of the special problems now facing them in the political arena, those of communications, policy and "independence" tendencies of labor voters. Whatever difficulties these new factors may present, they can be overcome with concentrated effort—and COPE is noted for this type of activity.

Within the 65-80 percent of AFL-CIO members following the labor leaders' policy there is the activist bloc which will gladly participate in the campaign itself. Whether they are ringing doorbells, sealing envelopes, telephoning voters or advising a candidate, they are the workers who form the backbone of the COPE campaign.

## CHAPTER SEVEN

# The COPE Campaign

## PART ONE: *The Big Picture*

A COPE campaign is a many splendored thing. It unobtrusively rolls along during the winters of odd-years, perks up in the spring and summer of election years, and explodes full-blast as the fall Election Day approaches. Union members may face the drudgery of stuffing envelopes, may be the candidate's closest political advisors, or, as in many cases, union leaders have themselves been candidates for office.

The campaign itself can function on any of a number of levels. It can be above or under ground, out in the open with the labor banner boldly waving, or silent and discreet, with everyone denying any "labor blitz." The COPE campaign may supplement the activities of a political party, or, as has happened in some instances, supplant a party with a labor precinct organization.

In her excellent work on the *modus operandi* of the old Political Action Committee, *The CIO and the Democratic Party,* Fay Calkins describes five distinct types of labor campaigns.[1] Most of these, perhaps in modified form, can still be found to persist; they are:

*Supplementing a campaign. In the 1950 Ohio Senate race between incumbent Senator Robert Taft (R) and Joseph Ferguson, PAC wanted very much to defeat the "anti-labor" Taft and was willing to go all out for his Democratic adversary. However, labor in Ohio, though well-organized and active politically, was not a deciding influence in state-wide politics, nor was the state's Democratic hierarchy overly friendly and cooperative with the PAC forces. Therefore, in the '50 race labor ran its own campaign for the Democrat, independent of, or supplementing, the party's effort.

*Exerting pressure through balance of power. In Ohio's 18th Congressional District, meanwhile, a majority of the voters and labor union members were located in the largest of the district's three counties. Here the county Democratic chairman was cooperative towards labor because PAC's political activities could swing the large county's vote, and thus the election, as it did in 1950. In this instance, organized labor was able to gain concessions from the party because of the balance of power it held at election time.

*Fighting a machine. Chicago's Democratic organization was the most powerful political force in the city in 1950 and no decisions were made without its approval; it saw no reason to seek labor's counsel, even though some union leaders were part of the machine. PAC's only recourse here was to run a candidate to its liking in the primaries, an unsuccessful effort this year, but one which, if victorious, would have forced the machine to start paying attention to labor.

*Taking over a local party. The Democratic Party in Illinois' 16th Congressional District in 1950 was weak and split into factions. By building alliances with other interest groups to form a solid coalition, the strong local PAC group was able to take control of the local party, rather than supplement it or provide the balance of power. But, although it gained a position in which it could strongly influence internal party matters, PAC was still unable to elect a Democrat to Congress.

*Taking over a state party. Through assiduous precinct work, organized labor in Michigan, with the cooperation of other "reform" elements, was able to gain control of the Wayne County (Detroit) Democratic Party machinery and, from this base, control the state. PAC was responsible for revitalizing the Michigan Democrats, taking the state out of the "sure-Republican" category and ruling the party for over twenty years.

With some variance in form, these same basic campaign approaches can be found in contemporary labor politics. Generally speaking, it may be said that where the Democratic Party structure itself is strong and liberal, and there are not a great number of union members, labor will usually be found supplementing the party's activity; in a similar party situation, but with a strong union organization, labor will probably hold a balance of power in an election and will be able to gain concessions from the Democratic hierarchy. But, where the Democratic leadership, as in Chicago, is either conservative or principally concerned with perpetuating the machine through patronage, labor will be found fighting the ruling order; in some rare cases, it will cooperate with the machine in hopes of being thrown a few crumbs.

Instances of organized labor completely taking over a local or state Democratic party—as in Illinois' 16th District, or Michigan—are infrequent and, where they do exist, are usually kept well-disguised. This will typically occur in areas where the Democratic Party has long been weak and inactive, a factor contributing to Republican success; labor, with a few allies, will organize a campaign to take over the party through election of party officials (precinct committeemen, convention delegates, etc.) and move it into action.

The most common forms of COPE campaigns found today are supplementing party activity and gaining concessions from the party through labor's standing as a balance of power. In traditionally Democratic areas, with a small percentage of union members, labor's political activists will frequently supplement the party's campaign by working quietly on their own in liberal wards. This is what happened in a primary contest in Florida's newly-created 10th Congressional District in 1962, when a "pro-labor" state senator, Sam Gibbons, fought it out with a segregationist retired military officer; labor was solidly behind the liberal Democrat and he won easily.

In the steel center of Erie County, Pennsylvania, the situation is somewhat different. Labor is well-organized in the area and very active in county Democratic politics, as was the case in the 1966 congressional race in which freshman liberal Rep. Joseph Vigorito was running for re-election. "In 1966 labor supplemented my campaign," said Vigorito following the race, "they had their own organization, and I had mine. We worked closely together and kept each other advised as to what we were doing so there would be no duplication of effort."

In its analyses of the 1966 elections, COPE listed Vigorito's victory as one of those in which it helped raise the incumbent liberal's margin of victory over the 1964 figure. Vigorito does not dispute this claim and frankly acknowledges that "labor's contribution to my campaign in 1966 was very great. They gave me financial help—direct contributions and their own spending—they donated workers in the campaign and they put out a lot of literature promoting my campaign."

Ohio's Democrats and organized labor leaders, in the meantime, have reconciled the differences evident when both groups futilely attempted to unseat Senator Taft in 1950. As labor has steadily strengthened its organization, membership rolls, and *espirit de corps,* the Democratic leadership has become increasingly aware of its political potential, and COPE now holds a balance of power in state politics.

The most immediate evidence of COPE's lofty position is the standing of the Ohio AFL-CIO president (and, hence, COPE chairman) as Democratic floor leader in the state senate. State Senator Frank W. King, a former Toledo bricklayer, was elected to head the senate's Democrats in early 1965 and a short while later was named AFL-CIO head; when Republicans objected to this conflict of interest, King announced he would remain in the senate and was re-elected to his party post without opposition. Speaking of the unified Democratic phalanx King had built up in the Ohio state senate, one report noted:

"King could not have achieved this cohesion merely as the Party floor manager. But in his other capacity as the labor leader, he is in a position to deny important union endorsements to Democratic senators when they come up for re-election. And they know it."[2]

With its state chairman holding a ranking post in the Democratic hierarchy, Ohio COPE finds itself in the comfortable position of being able to wait until aspiring officeholders come humbly to ask for its campaign support. Its organization has yet to replace that of the regular Democratic Party, but there is little need for such action: in its present status, COPE can work concessions from the party, gaining support for its legislative proposals and other goals, and then go out to electioneer in the labor wards while the party takes care of the rest.

COPE did just this in the May, 1968, Ohio primary, in pulling off one of the first major upsets of the political season. By effecting a strong alliance with the state's Democratic leadership, and by making extraordinarily effective use of computerized voter registration checks, Ohio labor was able to defeat the longtime incumbent Senator, conservative Democrat Frank Lausche, and nominate a young liberal, former Rep. John Gilligan. This was a dramatic display of the political club organized labor could wield.

A traditional free-swinging battle between the political forces of organized labor and an entrenched Democratic machine took place in Philadelphia during the bitter mayoralty primary fight in the spring of 1967. The long-dominant party machine, led by City Chairman Francis R. Smith, had scuttled incumbent mayor James Tate and nominated city comptroller Alexander Hemphill as the organization-approved candidate. The frequently feuding AFL and CIO unions in the city promptly united to back the primary fight by Tate, one of the few Philadelphia Democratic politicians who had listened to labor while the rest of the party hierarchy was largely ignoring it.

As the heated campaign built up steam, union halls were converted into Tate-for-Mayor headquarters, union men were selected to act as Tate's campaign committeemen, a Washington campaign consultant firm was hired to assist labor's activities, national COPE sent down a deputy director to help out, and a union local president who was labor's only elected ward chairman taught other union members the finer skills of practical politics and helped set up a campaign organization in each of Philadelphia's 66 wards.

The results of labor's effort staggered even the most seasoned political observers, as Tate racked up a victory margin of more than 70,000 votes over Organization Man Hemphill. And when it came time to receive the laurels, COPE was among the first in line: "The virtually solid support from the city's labor leaders and thousands of union members," wrote the *Philadelphia Inquirer,* was a main factor in the Mayor's triumph; "they not only helped to man the polls for Tate but were believed to have raised $100,000 toward the Mayor's campaign war chest."[3] (Tate went on to win another "underdog" victory in November, again with considerable help from COPE.)

Another form of COPE's fighting an established Democratic party with which it disagreed occurred in Texas' 7th Congressional District in 1962. The incumbent representative, conservative Democrat John Dowdy, had proof that organized labor forces were the main supporters of his primary challenger, young liberal lawyer Benton Musslewhite: campaign workers were coming in from Austin, 100 miles from the 7th District; funds for Musslewhite were coming from out-of-state; labor politicos were attempting to change the minds of Dowdy backers; and Musslewhite's literature was almost an exact duplicate of that distributed by labor's gubernatorial primary candidate.

Yet, whenever during the campaign Dowdy claimed his adversary had strong labor backing, Musslewhite would complain that the congressman was trying to smear him as a "labor candidate." At one point, Musslewhite's father, a popular and powerful figure in the District, asked a large audience, "Why is John Dowdy saying these things about my boy, why is he accusing him of courting labor; John Dowdy has stayed in our home, he knows my son personally and he knows he wouldn't hang out with people like that." And Dowdy aides acknowledge that this passionate plea, together with Musslewhite's own denials of COPE support, won some sympathy votes for their opponent—although not quite enough.

When the results were in and Dowdy had won an eyelash victory, a COPE election report candidly acknowledged, "In the [Texas] 7th Congressional District, only 41 votes separated us from an important victory. COPE-backed Benton Musslewhite, a young liberal, former football star at Southern Methodist, ran strong against five-termer John Dowdy, an anti-everything Dixiecrat." Two years later when Musslewhite ran for the same seat the Dowdy forces circulated this COPE quote and won a handy 12,000-vote victory.

There have been instances where this form of COPE "underground" campaign has been successful. In a situation with conditions similar to those in Texas' 7th District, COPE in 1962 contributed mightily to ousting a conservative Democrat in an Atlanta, Georgia, congressional district and winning behind young liberal Charles Weltner. The 1966 victory of Miami Mayor Robert King High in Florida's Democratic gubernatorial primary was, despite his loss in the November elections, a stunning liberal-labor upset over the long-entrenched state Democratic organization.

As will be noted, many campaigns of this type are waged by COPE in

Southern states, where its primary objective is wresting Democratic Party control from conservative old guardists; this strategy has met with mixed success, but it is an important part of labor's effort to make the national Democratic Party uniformly liberal. (For another aspect of this strategy, see this chapter's section on selection of candidates.)

All of the COPE campaign examples described thus far have begun with a well-organized, active labor political force taking the initiative. An instructive demonstration of what happens when the situation is reversed, when a candidate goes to labor to ask its assistance in a campaign and helps prod a local COPE into action, is found in New York's 34th Congressional District in 1966.

In the Democratic landslide that swept New York State in 1964, former undertaker James Hanley slipped into the 34th District seat with 51.2 percent of the vote. This district consists of the city of Syracuse (fourth largest in the state) and its suburbs, a heavily industrialized area with an estimated 40,000 union members in 127 locals, all governed by the Greater Syracuse Labor Council. Despite the working-class complexion of the area, Hanley's district showed—in '64 and '66—an approximately 70 percent Republican voter registration and the GOP has regularly held the majority of elective offices. Walter Riehlman, the Republican whom Hanley defeated for Congress, had served since 1946. The force behind the consistent GOP success was a well-run, tightly controlled party organization with uncommon power in the city. Labor had consistently gone along with the Republican leadership—"played ball with them," as one liberal Democrat termed it. The Labor Council would endorse national Democratic candidates, but this was little more than "lip service," with no concurrent political activity.

The two exceptions to this attitude were the auto and electrical workers' local unions who—taking their cue from an activist national leadership—tried to buck the complacent tide of the other Council members and energetically campaigned for liberal candidates.

In 1964 Hanley had received the Council's endorsement, but, except for the UAW and IBEW, this support was described as "wishy-washy" and uncoordinated by one Hanley aide. But, with Lyndon Johnson leading the Democratic ticket across New York State, defeating dozens of incumbent Republicans in his wake, Hanley did not actually need much organizational strength to win. Hanley does believe, however, that what he prefers to call his "independent" approach helped him to win the votes of the rank-and-file; he was not a candidate tied to any "machine" or interests, Hanley would tell union audiences, and he would go to Washington, he said, to represent them as individuals and taxpayers, not as members of one economic bloc.

When liberal Democrat Hanley got to Washington he proceeded to chalk up a 100 percent perfect COPE voting record at the 89th Congress, a record the Representative's advisors hoped would prod Syracuse labor into more political interest and activity. Because of his district's traditional Republicanism and the absence of Barry Goldwater on the ticket, Hanley's re-election in 1966 was by no means assured, and no matter how "independent" Hanley tried to appear, this approach would be meaningless in labor wards if there was no organization to back it up.

Hanley's aides soon realized that, despite their boss's pro-labor voting, the Labor Council had not changed its ways and was not eager to shake its political inertia. In 1965 the AFL representatives on the Council wanted to back the Republican organization's candidate for mayor; the CIO men, led by the auto and electrical chieftains, walked out in disgust to return only when it was agreed to give at least tacit, unenthusiastic Council backing to the Democrat.

With the 1966 elections looming in the not-too-distant future, Hanley's political strategists realized the need for a change in the Council's attitude. They reasoned that Syracuse labor must become fully committed in terms of endorsement and grass roots politicking, if Hanley was to have a chance at returning to Capitol Hill. In the winter of 1965-66, the Hanley advisors devised a plan of action to build a fire under the Labor Council and its affiliates, and help them construct a well-organized campaign operation.

The first step in this plan was to establish personal contact with the Council members and officers, explaining the situation to them in these terms: if Hanley were defeated, labor would stand to lose a great deal; his record and ideology were in complete accord with labor's thinking and he had given his vote on issues important to labor; additionally, a Hanley re-election victory would be a great psychological blow to the Syracuse Republican organization and might possibly pave the way for more liberal Democratic victories. At the same time, Hanley's aides (and, later in the campaign, Hanley himself) attacked his GOP opponent as being a member of the local Establishment "elite," one whose family had a "proprietary interest" in the congressional seat (his uncle held it for 20 years).

"We took labor into our confidence," one Hanley advisor later described. "We explained to the leaders what was at stake in the election and what they stood to lose if they did not work and re-elect Hanley. We made them a part of our campaign. Before, labor had always been asked by the Democrats a month before elections for some cash or its support; it was taken for granted and never made to feel an important part of the campaign. We did not do this; we showed labor why it should support Democrats—something the leaders had always known before, but which no candidate had ever taken time or bothered to explain. We described this obligation, made them feel an important part of the campaign, and got them active."

After going to the Council leaders, the Hanley strategists used the leverage provided by the activist UAW and IBEW—the latter having the largest membership in the district—in attempting to plunge the rest of the AFL-CIO affiliates into the political swim. It took some doing, but after the election one aide commented that "the other unions in the Council were stimulated by these two; without them, the others would never have gotten off their feet."

As a further inducement to prod the Council into an active campaign, the Hanley advisors contacted the presidents of the international unions which had locals in Syracuse; these leaders were given a similar explanation of labor's stake in Hanley's future and were urged to get their Syracuse locals moving. Contact was also established with the national AFL-CIO and COPE, and a federation regional director was put to work helping the Labor Council to set up an electioneering organization; the leaders had to be shown how to run a full-fledged campaign, as they had not done this for over twenty years.

The Council's first substantial move in getting into the thick of battle was a successful testimonial dinner it held for Hanley in June, 1966. The fete not only provided the candidate with sorely needed cash, but represented a psychological victory for his hard-working advisors as they saw their assiduous wooing of Council leaders finally begin to show results.

The new-found political enthusiasm in the Labor Council was contagious, quickly spreading to the rank-and-file. A registration drive was launched (financed by national COPE), with labor responsible for signing up approximately 10,000 new voters. A telephone bank was installed, manned by workers and their wives, and used both to contact voters and recruit volunteers. Literature was printed by the Council and individual unions, promoting Hanley's candidacy.

Concurrent with the labor activities were Hanley's own campaign and the operations of the Hanley for Congress Committee. All the candidate's actions in this race were carried out independently of the Democratic Party structure, a strategic move that later benefited the party when Hanley led the ticket and carried several Democrats into lower office.

There were labor representatives on the Hanley Committee officially acting as liaisons with the Syracuse Labor Council (although, of course, Hanley's aides maintained their own contacts with the Council). Some special projects in which labor played a major role—notably the registration drive—were carried out under the aegis of the campaign committee, rather than COPE, with the two groups working closely together and sharing facilities.

Hanley's managers also insisted on control over the spending of as much labor campaign money as possible. The normal procedure, nationally, is for COPE and individual unions to spend their political funds themselves in areas where the union leaders feel they can produce the best results; Hanley's aides, however, insisted that *they* knew what was best in spending and they told local labor, in effect, "If we can't spend it, we don't want it." For starters, national COPE contributed—by way of a donation to New York State COPE—$3,000 to the Hanley treasury, with most union locals and some internationals following suit.

Hanley's reason for insisting on control over his campaign and wanting his own committee to predominate, was not only to prevent his being labeled a "labor captive," but also to allow him to win the votes of the union rank-and-file. There are two basic appeals a candidate can make to organized labor, Hanley's advisors theorized, and the best way is a blend of the two. You can gain the support of labor leadership by endorsing their "structured" goals, vowing support of legislation, promising patronage, and offering help toward realization of their other dreams; or you can appeal to the "unstructured" goals of the union membership, approaching them as citizens and taxpayers, and vowing to represent their interests by passing legislation to provide a better economic and social life for their families.

A Hanley aide candidly admits that "if we had made a straight leadership pitch we would have been murdered." But, Hanley *did* approach the labor leaders first, in requesting their support, and obviously he *did* satisfy their "structured" wants or else he would not have received a 100 percent COPE rating and the enthusiastic support of the Labor Council. But he publicly submerged the union leadership, making them appear subservient to his own campaign committee, thus succeeding in convincing the rank-and-file that he was not a hip-pocket candidate of their leaders, but was more interested in representing them, first and foremost, as private citizens.

Representative Hanley's efforts to get labor active in his campaign in 1966—taking leaders into his confidence, cajoling them, prodding the Council to work—showed results on Election Day. Hanley received 85,238 votes, raising his total vote percentage to 54.9. His Republican opponent was far behind with 59,728, and the remaining votes were split between candidates of the Conservative and Liberal parties.

In the victor's opinion, labor deserved credit for both working among the membership and for spreading its influence throughout the whole community. "In our campaign in 1966," Hanley summarized, "labor influenced a great many people and deserves credit for a part of the victory. In registering voters and getting out the vote, they were very influential. They focused on their own people, but I believe there was a rub-off on the general public." And as for labor's impact on the results as compared to the party's, one Hanley advisor declared: "By rallying around Hanley, labor can claim as much a part of this victory as can the Democratic Party. Labor's expanded role in 1966 certainly qualifies them for great credit in this victory."

The Hanley incident is instructive in demonstrating the great effect organized labor can have in a campaign once it decides to take an active part. The Greater Syracuse Labor Council had been politically lethargic until the Hanley people explained the situation to them, took them into their confidence, and—with an assist from national labor leaders—got the locals "on the stick." Liberal Democrat Hanley could have just as easily lost this historically Republican congressional seat in 1966, but labor's increased activities and new enthusiasm for practical politics was instrumental in his re-election.

An interesting comparison to this campaign is COPE's role in a Maryland congressional race in 1958. Here labor politicos literally took over an apathetic local Democratic party and won a smashing upset victory.

Maryland's First Congressional District is composed of nine counties along the East bank of the Chesapeake Bay—the "Eastern Shore"—and is as solidly conservative as was its incumbent congressman in 1958. Republican Representative Edward T. "Ted" Miller had first been elected to Congress in 1946, had built up valuable House seniority and rapport with his constituents, and had every reason to feel assured of re-election in the '58 off-year voting.

COPE had a different idea: it saw an opportunity to silently invade a congressional district, whose Democratic organization was largely indifferent, and ruled by an over-confident GOP, and sneak off with the loot before anyone knew quite what was happening. The Eastern Shore does not contain a great many union residents, but there were enough dedicated unionists willing to work to build a tightly knit political operation. Under the guidance of COPE operatives imported from the heavily unionized areas around Baltimore and Washington, D.C., Eastern Shore labor was molded into a sophisticated political machine.

The organization's first step was to card-catalogue every eligible voter in the First District, separating those it knew would go Republican from those it thought (and/or knew) would back Miller's liberal Democrat opponent, Tom Johnson. The rest of the campaign was spent lining up potential Johnson voters, registering them, propagandizing them and, finally, getting them to the voting booths on Election Day.

Meanwhile, the Republican Party and Miller forces drifted complacently along, with many GOP supporters not even bothering to vote in November, so sure were they of success. The labor organizers had succeeded in keeping their intensive activities from being detected by the Republicans; what goings-on the Miller backers did notice were dismissed as either non-partisan registration efforts or the lost-cause industry of the union member minority.

Imagine, then, the surprise when Democrat Johnson won over Miller, (the incumbent for twelve years) by a scant, but conclusive, 780 votes. Recounts were demanded, "vote theft" charges hurled, and the labor blitz denounced—but the results stood. The COPE operatives, by keeping their activities out of public view and concentrating on "friendly" voters, had pulled off a liberal victory in definitely conservative country.

Several variations of COPE's "Operation Eastern Shore" were carried out elsewhere in 1958 campaigns (and later formed the basis for such efforts as the anti-Dowdy Texas primary in 1962.) In the Wyoming Senate race between Republican incumbent Frank Barrett and youthful university professor Gale McGee, for example, COPE poured in money, manpower and organizational assistance to win an upset liberal victory, defeating a supposedly "sure" Republican. McGee may have later denied he owed his victory in any large share to COPE's activities, but his subsequent words and liberal actions belied his denials; at one point he went so far as to write in a union publication that "in short, labor speaks for all"[4]—seemingly unusual sentiments for a senator from the non-union state of Wyoming.

By making concentrated efforts in nominally Republican, low-population states, COPE can build a close-knit, smoothly functioning organization around a small number of industrious union members, and achieve a position of political power that is far more difficult to come by in more populous states. A significant part of this power derives from the great impact COPE's financial lode can have in these areas: it can strongly influence elections here for a fraction of what it would cost in larger states—winning elections at a "bargain rate."

And, due to the traditional Republicanism of most sparsely populated states, organized labor can, because of its active political operation with sizable fiscal resources, gain concessions from the Democrats that would be denied in many heavily unionized, populous states with a strong, independent Democratic structure. Moreover, in such union strongholds as New York State, Pennsylvania, Illinois, and New Jersey, there are actually *too many* rank-and-filers and individually strong labor leaders for COPE always to work effectively.

Political factions will develop among big-state unions; personally powerful labor leaders will want more of a voice; disputes arise over endorsements, and political contributions are hoarded by unions and their locals in hopes of buying concessions from politicians. The result often is that COPE expends as much energy attempting to unite state unions and their leaders behind its candidates, as it does in fighting the opposition.

The one top-heavy union state not in this category is Michigan and here exists the most blatant example of organized labor taking over a state Democratic Party and running the party and the state government like a labor fief. Even though in recent years small factions have developed inside the state's labor hierarchy and some independent voting has been exhibited by the rank-and-file, the state Democratic Party is still essentially a labor party, with Gus Scholle, state AFL-CIO head, and Walter Reuther the two most powerful Democratic leaders in Michigan.

The dramatic tale of organized labor's capture of Michigan's Democratic structure has its beginnings in the spring of 1948, at a time when the party was controlled by the relatively conservative Old Guard and the state regularly went Republican in national and most state elections. After careful analysis of the state's Democratic Party structure, Michigan CIO Political Action Committee chairman Gus Scholle saw a way to seize control through election of party officials.

PAC's first two steps were to form a coalition with other liberal interest groups similarly disenchanted with the complexion of the party, and to convince CIO members that this form of political action was the most effective. Joining PAC in the takeover coalition were liberal, reform-minded Democrats already in the party, segments of non-CIO unions (part of the AFL and Brotherhood of Railway Trainmen), Polish and Negro political groups, the League of Women Voters, and Americans for Democratic Action. Although all these groups played an instrumental role in the coalition, because of its greater numbers and political organizing skills, the CIO Political Action Committee was, and continued to be, the dominant member.

Assuring Michigan union members that this was the best approach was not an easy task for PAC. Many of the rank-and-file were so thoroughly disgusted with the state's Democratic hierarchy that they saw a leftist third party as the only alternative. To those dissidents, the PAC leadership explained:

"We are not accepting the Democratic Party in Michigan as it now is. Our purpose in going into it is to line up with its liberal elements and remodel the Party in a progressive force. . . . It is our objective in adopting this policy to remold the Democratic Party into a real liberal and progressive political party which can be subscribed to by members of the CIO and other liberals. We therefore advise CIO members to become active precinct, ward, county, and congressional district workers and attempt to become delegates to Democratic conventions."[5]

PAC's plan was to grab the party's reins through control over the state party convention and the Democratic State Committee which was selected at the convention; these two groups made all major policy decisions in the state party and absolute control was essential for the PAC plan to work. What the coalition had to do was elect its men as precinct chairmen, officials who would then go to congressional district conventions where delegates to the state convention were named. Fortunately for the coalition, and more so for organized labor, a majority of state convention delegates would be elected at district conclaves in the Wayne County (Detroit) area.

PAC's first political target was the precinct elections in Detroit, and it "advised" all its shop stewards and local presidents to run for party posts. In 1948, 1,240 candidates filed in the 1,748 Wayne County precincts, 1,000 of whom represented coalition members; 720 were elected. Because, as with the Republicans in Maryland's Eastern Shore in '58, the Old Guard Democrats had no idea what PAC was up to (PAC workers in the precincts identified themselves, even to CIO members, simply as Democrats), they had not bothered to field candidates in many of the state's precincts. Therefore, when the state convention was ready to convene, the liberal coalition claimed a majority of the delegates and the Old Guard was caught completely off guard.

When the existing Democratic leadership refused to acknowledge the liberal delegates and sought to postpone the convention, the coalition went ahead and held its own state conclave with 1,243 delegates in attendance, far more than the Old Guard could round up. Sixty-eight liberals (twenty of them CIO members) were promptly named to the state committee. Young liberal G. Mennen "Soapy" Williams (the winner, with CIO support, in the Democratic gubernatorial primary) was named gubernatorial candidate, and the Old Guardists were finally forced to capitulate; following Williams' election in November, the *New York Times* editorialized that "Scholle, rather than the governor, was real head of the convention."[6]

Following the coalition's 1948 coup, the Old Guard Democrats began an intensive campaign to end the Scholle rule at the 1950 convention. They fielded and elected more precinct chairmen than in '48 and confronted the liberal coalition head-on at the district conventions in September, 1950; at one district meeting a liberal presided using a baseball bat as a gavel and at others there were burly rank-and-filers (some armed) acting as bouncers to toss out Old Guardists who had won their precinct posts with questionable petitions.

Members of the ousted hierarchy complained bitterly about the coalition's tactics, with one telling a Detroit newspaper that at a district convention he had "just watched socialism take over the Democratic party by Communist processes." And later a former Democratic National Convention delegate, Mrs. Nellie Riley, said flatly that "Socialists are in complete charge of the Democratic party machinery."[7]

It was no contest at the 1950 state convention, since the liberals had a solid bloc of 750 delegates out of the 1,243 in attendance, with the CIO claiming 486 of them. All members named to the state committee were again from the liberal coalition, "Soapy" Williams was again named gubernatorial candidate, and the Democratic Old Guard was decisively a party minority, minus any party voice as the coalition settled down to a long reign over Michigan's Democratic Party.

The benefits organized labor received through its dominant position in the coalition are indicated by the line in the 1950 state Democratic platform reading, "The Democratic Party believes that the prosperity of the whole state depends on the health, security, and dignity of the working man."

The leftist politics of the state's labor leadership were also reflected in the new Democratic direction. As reported by author Fay Calkins, a CIO researcher at the time, in 1950 the Michigan party's "campaign publicity might have sounded like class warfare to Marx." The irony is that liberal Governor Williams was the wealthy heir to a shaving cream fortune and state Democratic committee chairman Neil Staebler was president of an oil company. Class warfare, like any other, has its privileged sanctuaries.

The decisive CIO influence was due not only to labor's advantage in numbers and political skills, but its financial largess; in 1950 the Democratic Party reported contributions to state-wide party candidates amounted to $328,519.68, of which $211,550—or 64 percent—was donated by the CIO's Political Action Committee.

As can be seen, labor was the most powerful member of the coalition, but as happens in practical politics there were powers within powers and true control over the state's Democrats (and, therefore, over the state government during the 'fifties) was vested in a small number of labor leaders. All influential decisions were made by the state PAC executive board. The board was composed of 15 members, nine of whom were from the United Auto Workers (and headed by Walter Reuther); the remainder of the positions were distributed among the steel, chemical, amalgamated clothing and utility workers' unions, plus union regional directors or presidents residing in Michigan. Labor political power in the state was broken down even further, however, as the board's "main work was performed by about five of its most active members, located in Detroit. This was the core of PAC leadership."[8] Walter Reuther and

August Scholle, as two of Detroit's leading citizens, were assuredly the most vocal and forceful members of the five-man group.

Scholle, whom onetime CIO employee Miss Calkins describes as "militant, aggressive and ruthless," was, in no particular order, Michigan PAC chairman, president of the state CIO council, its chief operating executive, and regional director of the national CIO; to this day he maintains he is not a "labor boss." As for Walter Reuther, he was just making good on his pledge to the 1947 UAW convention that "political action shall have first call upon my time and energy as president of this international union."

For all the labor influence and activity, the general public was largely ignorant of the nature of the CIO's operations. PAC's campaign workers continued to identify themselves only as Democrats, and persons making inquiries at PAC concerning political developments were referred to party headquarters (where, most likely, another PAC member would pick up the phone).

Throughout the 'fifties the labor-led coalition solidified its hold over the Democratic Party, re-electing Governor Williams by ever-increasing margins, and replacing two Republican senators with liberal Democrats in the meantime. In 1954, the late Patrick McNamara, president of a pipefitters' union local in Detroit, rode into the Senate on Williams' coattails, beating out longtime GOP incumbent Homer Ferguson. And in 1958, labor, by then represented in politics by COPE, elected state attorney general Philip Hart over Republican Senator Charles Potter, who had been carried into office in the Eisenhower landslide of 1952 (not even the Scholle-Reuther combine could prevent Ike from sweeping Michigan in both '52 and '56).

COPE's power showed signs of sluggishness in 1961, when young upstart Jerry Cavanagh was elected mayor of Detroit over the labor-supported incumbent Louis Mariani. This was not a staggering blow, as Cavanagh proved as liberal a mayor as labor could want. But, because he owed COPE nothing for his success, his independence from the AFL-CIO rankled its leaders. The victory of the aggressive Cavanagh, and his popularity among Detroit's young voters and Negro residents, did hold dark portents for COPE. In the '61 campaign labor had stuck with the old pro, Mariani (a man it had put into office and who did its bidding), rather than retire the incumbent when polls showed his challenger to have wider appeal. This tendency to rely on shopworn labor "friends" was to have more severe repercussions in the 1966 Senate race.

Before that campaign, however, Michigan's labor politicos were dealt a solid blow with the 1962 election of Republican Governor George Romney, a victor over incumbent Democrat John Swainson, a labor favorite. Despite his small share of union members' votes in 1962—he received only 51 percent of the total popular vote—Romney owed much of his first election's success to the careful steps he had taken before opening his campaign to neutralize the expected opposition of Michigan labor leaders. Fervently denying any political ambitions, in 1960 Romney had been the leading force in organizing a state constitutional convention which revamped Michigan's archaic state government. Giving him full support in this drive were Walter Reuther and a host of other powerful AFL-CIO leaders; when these same men came back to attack him during the '62 campaign, Romney had a number of glowing praises from the constitutional convention days to show that they had not always opposed him.

Romney's 1962 victory, and re-election (with a higher percentage of rank-and-file votes) in 1964 and 1966, were no distress to labor compared to the election of Robert Griffin to the Senate over labor godhead "Soapy" Williams. Organized labor's infatuation with Williams notwithstanding, after 18 years many people were tired of his smiling, bow-tie image and his brand of liberalism which sounded as if it had been lifted out of mothballs in Hyde Park. Because Williams (and evidently his COPE advisors) were out of touch with political attitudes, interim Senator Griffin, the son of an auto worker, was able to attract more than enough rank-and-file votes to defeat the shaving-cream millionaire.

Much as Griffin's victory can be attributed in part to tactical errors and out-of-date politics by the COPE-Williams forces, there is evidence that Michigan voters, now that they finally know the facts, are concerned about labor political power in their state and are therefore highly selective among Democratic candidates. Awareness of this new sentiment was evidenced by a Democratic candidate in a special 1967 state senate primary in Detroit who said he did not want formal union support because "too many people feel the party is labor dominated."[9] Interestingly enough, the candidate was a member of the largest Auto Workers local in the union and his father was a UAW regional director. (Still more interesting, the UAW-member candidate who disavowed labor support lost the primary to the son of imprisoned Teamsters' boss Jimmy Hoffa, who had all-out Teamsters' backing in the primary. You figure it out.)

The victories of George Romney and Robert Griffin signal no monumental loss of AFL-CIO power within Michigan's Democratic Party. In terms of numbers, organizing skill and finances, labor remains the most influential element in the party. "Reuther and Scholle's power in state politics was weakened as a result of the '66 elections," said Senator Griffin in a post-election interview, "but much less than might be assumed."

In Michigan, as in other areas of the country where labor has led an assault wave into the political arena, COPE has dug a secure enough position to outlast any momentary storms of reversal. Abundant possession of the three basic commodities of money, manpower and political skill has allowed Michigan COPE and its cross-country kin to make their imprint on local, state and national politics. It will take a great effort in most areas to erase this mark and balance labor power.

The broad outlines of how this position has been achieved in certain parts of the U.S. have been described. Within each individual COPE campaign—whether in Eastern Maryland or West Texas—are the separate parts of the whole, the multiple activities composing the COPE campaign.

## PART TWO: *The Voter Registration Drive*

It would hardly seem necessary for anyone to have to tell political activists that all their efforts are wasted unless eligible persons are registered to vote. Surprisingly or not, this basic step in practical politics is ignored by most political action organizations, including—in most areas of the country—the two major parties.

For politicians or campaigners to assume everyone interested in the outcome of an election will get himself registered is dangerous; perhaps foolhardy. People forget, are "too busy," don't know where to register, don't know when to register, or are confused by the whole process and end up sitting home on Election Day.

COPE does not make this mistake. It tells its membership that "all your talk adds up to nothing . . . if you can't vote. *And you can't vote if you're not registered!* So that's the important first step in politics: Registration." And the reason behind this emphasis is stated in another COPE pamphlet:

"The overwhelming majority of the 37 million adults who did not vote in the 1960 Presidential election, including the 22½ million who failed even to register, are the natural allies and friends of the Labor Movement. A good percentage are our members and their families."

To prevent recurrences of such a situation, COPE now has a year-round registration drive aimed at having as many union members, their friends and families, eligible and registered to vote as is possible. This is *the* COPE activity which consumes more time and receives more attention than any other. It also uses up a sizable portion of the COPE budget, as local labor registration drives have been traditionally financed almost totally by National COPE through money received from the AFL-CIO's "Special Purposes" fund (and the money comes from members' dues payments, as this is considered an "educational" expense).

And federation leaders consider the drive important enough to enlist the aide of an "outside pro" to head the COPE project; for the past three major election campaigns, this individual was Roy Reuther, Walter's late brother, who spent the rest of his time serving as a UAW department official.

In the mid-sixties COPE's registration program began undergoing a revolutionary change which promises to make it even more effective. Data processing computers are being used in selected "pilot" areas to catalogue voter information and sort it into pertinent categories. The use of computers will undoubtedly be expanded, and while this may save COPE vitally needed time and money, it will never fully replace the work of campaign volunteers—the heart (and feet) of the registration drive.

COPE workers urge voters to register and then see to it that they get registered. There are constant reminders to the rank-and-file in union newspapers, on shop bulletin boards, and in mailboxes; volunteers will make repeated phone calls to members and their wives at home; shop stewards will ask their men about their registration status—and then more reminders, calls and questions will follow. The COPE registration drive is nagging, prodding and, probably to some unionists, a distinct nuisance—but it gets the job done.

The philosophy and approach behind the drive has been put in these words by AFL-CIO President Meany:

"When you pay a candidate's bills, you are not so sure where the money is going . . . But when you spend your money to get people registered, and then spend a lesser proportion to get them out to vote, you know you got a vote in the ballot box.

"Of course, we are a little bit choosy when we choose districts in which we want to better these votes in the ballot box, so that when they go in we have a pretty good idea how they are going to vote."[10]

What Meany means by "choosy" is that when COPE goes about its voter registration tasks there is a certain priority in whom it approaches. There is a definite descending order of population groups on which COPE will concentrate its efforts; this does not mean, however, that in an especially active local drive all groups could not be contacted at the same time, or that in a less enthusiastic campaign just the first two groups would be reached. The four groups in order of COPE priority are:

* Union members. COPE's first concern is that the members of AFL-CIO unions have their names on the current registration rolls. Members are the target of the largest share of propaganda, they receive the most personal reminders by labor leaders and are the surprised hosts for the greatest number of doorbell-ringing COPE volunteers. Before it will do

anything else in the drive, COPE must see to it that its own members have been signed up.

* Union members' families. With the members themselves enrolled COPE volunteers will move on to the wives, children, relatives, or anyone else living in a member's home who is eligible to vote. Names of those persons are normally placed in the COPE card file along with information on the member, so many will be contacted at the same time as the unionist; if not, they may expect a phone call or letter soon afterwards.

* Other residents of labor wards. After contacting union members and their families, COPE workers will branch out into the residential neighborhoods in which these people live. Next door may be a retired union member, a member's relative, a non-union worker, or similar individuals who most likely would support labor-backed candidates. Door-to-door visits and phone calls into these areas are COPE's most effective means of reaching potential friendly voters who might otherwise be bypassed.

* Other labor-oriented voters. If COPE workers have time, money and stamina remaining after contacting the preceding three groups, they will register other voters who have shown inclination to endorse liberal pro-labor officials at the ballot box. By checking recent election returns, COPE can fairly accurately define where these voters reside and can direct its registration project toward their districts. Usually the neighborhoods will house members of minority groups, or perhaps it will be an area bordering a university and housing liberal-oriented students and professors. Although a last-priority item, a COPE voter registration drive in such districts has often proved profitable.

Even though COPE goes after "its own" first and foremost in the registration project, national headquarters urges workers to make the drive community-wide by joining with other organizations, including even the Chamber of Commerce and Republican Party. Certainly no politically concerned group should overlook the value of a concentrated registration effort, but "cooperation" with COPE has its limits; in registration drives enlisting the aid of diverse organizations, COPE will most often continue to function independently, concentrating on union members and never going near any area or voters who may be potentially Republican.

In researching her book, *The CIO and the Democratic Party,* author Fay Calkins was told by a Chicago Political Action Committee precinct worker of a tactic which is undoubtedly still practiced by COPE volunteers: "Of course, I don't want to register Republicans. I get a line on a person's sentiments by asking around and by talking with him. If he is a Republican, I tell him he can register at the polls on election day."[11] In fact, it was impossible for Chicago voters to register on Election Day.

While avoiding potential Republican voters like a contagious affliction, local COPEs may join with other liberal interest groups in a further attempt to register the pro-labor voters living outside labor wards. Particularly helpful in such an effort are "minority organizations," including Italian-American and Negro groups, the Americans for Democratic Action, and League of Women Voters. These organizations will have contacts in liberal districts that COPE probably would not have, and their efforts in these neighborhoods greatly benefit the cause of labor candidates.

A second, but equally important, prong in COPE's registration drive is to seek legislation changing state and local registration laws to make it easier for workingmen to sign up. In a COPE manual on how to conduct a drive, the rank-and-file is advised that "one of the first steps your Registration Committee should take is an evaluation of registration procedures in your area." The reason for this study, COPE continues, is that "failure to register is generally not an indication of a lack of interest in voting. It is in many cities a result of inconvenience of hours and location of the place of registration."

The changes COPE seeks include: extension of the number of days, and hours in the day, during which voters may register; where registration is confined to one day of the week, having this fall on a Saturday, a non-working day when more union members could register; enlargement of the number of registration places in the neighborhood; approval of "roving registrars" who may register voters door-to-door; approval of "mobile registrars" who may travel around neighborhoods, registering voters in trailers; allowing registrars to come into a place of work, registering working voters on the spot.

The potent effect of COPE's two-pronged registration drive is attested to by the number of voters COPE has had a hand in enrolling, the thoroughness of labor's volunteers and the success and comments of political candidates whom the drive has benefited.

Shortly before the 1964 presidential election, a COPE leader estimated in an interview that 65 percent of the 13.5 million members then in the AFL-CIO were registered to vote before that year's drive began and that this figure would probably be raised another 5 to 10 percent as a result of the '64 drive. Figuring that COPE got a bare 5 percent increase—to 70 percent of the members—this would represent 9,450,-000 registered AFL-CIO members. If only half these persons were married and their spouses were also contacted by COPE, this would be another 4,725,000 labor votes signed up. And if COPE registered only one relative, friend, or other resident of a labor neighborhood, for each registered union member, an additional 9.4 million voters would be placed on the rolls.

The total of these three figures is 23,625,000, a low estimate of the number of voters COPE has had some hand in getting registered. In 1964 this figure represented one-third of the total voting electorate—such is the success and importance of COPE's registration drive. (Of course, many of these voters would have signed the rolls without COPE's urging, but COPE still figures prominently in getting many others on the books.)

Although COPE undoubtedly has occasional difficulty in getting ample volunteers to do the tedious routine work in a registration drive, tales recounting the thoroughness of labor precinct workers are many, and the zeal of these few is duplicated by unsung rank-and-filers across the country. In her *The CIO and the Democratic Party*, Fay Calkins quotes an industrious big city labor registrar as saying, "My precinct is mobile because there are so many students and roomers in it. But I know whenever a new person moves into the neighborhood. I got sixty new registrations before this [1950 Chicago] primary and eighty before the general election."[12]

Al Barkan once told an interviewer the story of a COPE worker in charge of voter registration in 10 Oklahoma counties in 1964. A few days before an important election, Barkan recounted, the man reported to COPE that in his bailiwick "all but 26 of the members of AFL-CIO and the adults in their families were registered. He had that thing broken down so that he knew that, of the 26, six of them were illiterate and were too embarrassed to put their 'X' down, 11 wouldn't vote for religious reasons. Two people were in Alaska and—I don't know what was the matter with the other seven but he had the thing broken down to the point where he knew."[13]

While political candidates and their assistants are generally close-mouthed on the role labor plays in their campaigns, COPE's registration drive—when it is in their behalf—is one point on which most are effusive. Following the re-election of Sen. Gale McGee (D-Wyo.) in 1964, one of the senator's aides exclaimed "We had one of the highest voter turnouts in recent election history in Wyoming last fall, and a great deal of this turnout was due to the registration efforts of labor. Organized labor, through COPE, registered and turned out voters that otherwise would have stayed at home."

One COPE election-time registration campaign was so well-organized, successful and influential that the national AFL-CIO had a film made to record it. This drive took place in Wisconsin in 1958 and was prompted by two important liberal vs. conservative election contests, one for governor and another for the Senate. In 27 of the Badger State's industrial cities COPE set up a mammoth card file indexing every labor ward resident, including all union members and their families; phone banks were set up, manned by women volunteers and professional operators (from the Communications Workers' Union), and thousands of phone calls were made into union homes urging the residents to register. The result was a pro-labor Governor (now, Sen. Gaylord Nelson), Senator William Proxmire, two new liberal congressmen and a friendly state assembly.

A similarly extensive COPE registration drive was conducted prior to the 1960 Tennessee Democratic primary where incumbent pro-labor Sen. Estes Kefauver was being challenged by a conservative Democrat. COPE went to work for "Keef" by setting up a central card file of union members in the state's four largest cities. Over 200 COPE volunteers were kept busy cataloguing some 65,000 rank-and-filers and making a like number of telephone calls. Union membership lists were checked against registration rolls and delinquent members told to get their names down. The result was the greatest concentration of registered union voters in the South, as 80 percent of Tennessee's AFL-CIO members were enrolled, and in one city the number of rank-and-file wives registered rose from 50 to 70 percent.

Said Kefauver after he gathered 65 percent of the primary votes that August: "I want to express my appreciation for the effective efforts of labor, working through their fine organization, COPE. . . ."[14]

Elsewhere in 1960—although COPE later lamented that many "natural allies and friends of the Labor Movement" did not register that year—COPE's drive for new voters was enthusiastic and produced some startling results. During one day's registration activity in Missouri's St. Louis County, said one report, 85,077 voters were enrolled by COPE; in Allegheny County (Pittsburgh), Pa., 43,490 new Democratic voters were registered by labor workers; in California, COPE made special appeals to unregistered but eligible Mexican-American voters, and managed to sign up over 100,000 from this minority group.[15]

COPE's voter registration drive in the 1960 presidential year also saw the inauguration of a new method of financing this project. By a vote of the AFL-CIO Executive Council it was decided to ask each affiliate union to "voluntarily" contribute five cents per member to support the campaign to enroll potential labor voters. In all, a report stated, COPE spent upwards of $600,000 in the '60 drive, with any deficit made up out of the Committee's "educational" funds.

Two years later COPE made another alteration in its registration drive operations. For the 1962 off-year congressional elections Roy Reuther was brought in to direct the effort; at the time Walter's late brother was director of the UAW Legislative Department, but he subsequently moved on to head the union's Citizenship Department, a quasi-political arm directed at getting auto workers active in politics. Reuther's job—he performed the same task in the '64 and '66 campaigns—was to oversee fund-raising, analyze registration and voting patterns, and direct COPE's drive into the areas where it would have the most benefit.

Except to provide financial and advisory assistance, national COPE relies on the work of local volunteers in getting the registration job done. Perhaps the greatest help national gives to local COPEs comes in the form of suggested organizational strategy and directions on how to set up and conduct the registration project. Having been thoroughly tested through trial and error over the years, the COPE outline for the drive is both detailed and to the point. The following are quotations from COPE's two principal manuals on the subject, its all-around handbook *How To Win,* and a specialty pamphlet entitled "A Step By Step Plan For Organizing and Conducting an Effective Register and Vote Campaign at the Community Level."[16]

*Organization*

The [City or County] Central Labor Body should establish a city or county-wide AFL-CIO COPE Register and Vote Committee. . . .

Appropriate sub-committees headed by experienced people should be appointed to plan and handle such essential over-all features of the Register and Vote Campaign as: publicity and literature; recruitment of volunteer workers; a speakers' bureau; organization on the community and precinct level; finances and fund raising; transportation; telephone crew. A full-time person should be appointed to direct and coordinate [the campaign]. . . .

In each district, ward, or township a chairman or co-chairman should be appointed and a steering committee selected . . . the district steering committee should divide the congressional district into smaller organizational units such as wards or in the case of suburban areas into townships. . . .

The precinct leader is the key to the success of the entire register and vote campaign. . . . He should attempt to enlist additional volunteers to assist him and should be responsible for the conduct of register and vote activities within his precinct. . . .

*Getting Volunteers*

[Note: while these instructions are used by COPE to recruit volunteers for the registration drive, they are equally applicable to any portion of the COPE campaign.]

Thousands of citizens who would be glad to volunteer time in a political campaign never get to do so . . . *because no one ever contacts them.* And contacting them is the simplest job in the world. They're no farther away than your telephone . . . Here are the highlights of the telephone recruiting plan:

Install controlled telephone banks . . .

Project a postal zone map on your city precinct map. Block out high priority zones where union members are concentrated and those wards where the highest percentage of unregistered are located. This is where your register-and-vote campaign should concentrate.

Mark these zones or areas on your city's Telephone Address Directory [a cross-index telephone directory listing by street address and number].

Supply each operator with a prepared telephone dialogue urging persons to volunteer, and with marked pages of the cross-index phone directory for her or him to call. Also, give operator telephone report forms.

Instruct operator to phone only marked zones and to *skip 10 names* between each recruited volunteer worker. Operator is to strive for one volunteer in each block.

*Information*

If you're going to conduct a registration drive, find out immediately what the registration laws are for your state or community. . . . While you're at it, get all the information you can about voting—how to transfer registration from one precinct to another, absentee balloting, etc . . .

*Central Card File*

There is no use kidding yourself. You can do everything else this handbook recommends, but if you do not have a ship-shape card file, and if you do not use it properly, you're not going to have a meaningful, successful political program. The central card file is the heart of your operation. . . .

Here are steps you should follow in setting up a city or county COPE central card file:

The city or county COPE chairman requests from each affiliated local union a list of names and addresses of its members . . .

To process the cards from the membership list, copy the last name first [on 3 x 5 card] . . .

Next, copy address on to card, including the city, county and ZIP code . . .

Add telephone number . . .

Using a city directory,[17] look up the name of the member's wife or husband, or any other family member eligible to vote, and write it in the space provided . . .

Find with your precinct [map] the number of the ward and precinct for each member . . .

Check each card against the roster of registered voters you get from the Board of Election, marking each with an "R" if they are registered, or an "N" if non-registered, for the union member and all eligible family members.

Copy all this information identically on a second and third [3 x 5] card, each of a different color.

Separate the cards of the registered from the non-registered in the ward and precinct file. . . . Place in the non-registered file all cards from each of the three different files on which either the member or one of this family is shown as not registered.

*Follow Through*

Once you know who the unregistered union members, or their relatives, are you can do something about it.

The local union should, of course, contact them in the shop. But you should also have a precinct organization to do the door-bell pushing. This organization should be able to provide baby sitters, transportation or any other kind of assistance to help get them out to register . . .

*The All-Out Drive*

Send COPE representatives from each precinct to the Registrar of Voters office to copy onto a file card the names and addresses of each registered voter in the precinct. Once you have a card for each registered voter . . . you arrange your cards by blocks, streets and house numbers.

The blockworker then goes from house to house, pushing each doorbell for which he *doesn't* have a card. . . .

If the person is eligible, the blockworker provides all the necessary registration information, and gives all the help he can to get the potential voter to the registration office . . . the blockworker should make out a card for the person noting on it all pertinent information.

*Publicity*

Every technique of advertising and promotion should be used to alert union members and other citizens to the importance of registering. Here are the major methods you should employ:

Radio and television. These should give free time for: five or ten-minute talks . . . about the importance of registration; spot announcements giving dates, places and times for registration (and the phone numbers to call for transportation or baby-sitters, if needed).

Newspapers. These should give free space for: a box, preferably on the front page, each day throughout the drive, showing the number of days left in which to register; "Register-to-Vote" cut-off slugs at the end of stories, columns, editorials, etc., instead of regular rules; editorials and cartoons on the "register-so-you-can-vote" theme; news stories about the registration drive; ads giving registration information.

Business firms and advertising agencies. These should be asked to cooperate with the following: inclusion of registration slogans in newspaper ads, or the sponsorship of ads exclusively devoted to registration; registration announcements as part of their regular radio and TV advertising; donation of space in car cards and on billboards for registration messages; window displays in stores, banks, utilities, etc.

Clergy. Ask the clergy to mention the citizenship responsibility of registration in their announcements and church bulletins. . . .

Handbills. Print a simple, attractive flyer or handbill with registration information for distribution: door-to-door, as inserts with organizational mailings, on store counters, as bill inserts by department stores, on street corners. . . .

Stamps. Print "register-so-you-can-vote" stamps and urge organizations and businesses to stick them on all their mailing envelopes.

You need free publicity for an effective registration drive, so you'll be asking a lot of people to cooperate with you . . . to get this needed help, you must be prepared to give.

Newspaper writers, and radio and TV commentators . . . have a lot on their minds . . . the easier you make it for them to write or broadcast your story, the better your chances to get it in print or on the air. Here are some of the basic materials you should prepare: a mimeographed or printed sheet listing all pertinent information on registration . . . ; a sheet of short "register-so-you-can-vote" slogans and plugs suitable for use in advertising, fillers in newspapers, etc.; sample spot announcements for radio and TV; short announcements for organization bulletins; sample registration boxes for newspapers and advertising agencies.

In the *How To Win* handbook's section on voter registration, COPE closes by suggesting that "where there is other information you need to know . . . contact the city-wide Register and Vote Committee." After the thorough, detailed outline COPE has just presented, such advice would hardly seem necessary!

National COPE headquarters in Washington has available additional instructions, advice, propaganda and other items to assist local rank-and-filers in their registration drive, but much of this goes unused. City and county COPEs have demonstrated in past campaigns that they are able to take the outline national provides them and conduct a well-organized and successful drive on their own. Examples abound to illustrate this resourcefulness, and following are just two of these concerning two different parts of the drive.

In the spring of 1966 the COPE organization in Montgomery County, Md., a suburb of Washington, D.C., sent two flyers to every unregistered voter in the county. In urging eligible persons to register, one flyer alluded to a recent congressional and legislative redistricting in Maryland, saying, "Your vote is worth more this year. It's worth more because for the first time in Maryland's history Montgomery County—where *you* live—will be fairly represented in the state legislature and the U.S. Congress." This plea ended by saying simply, "Remember, if you don't register you forfeit your right to vote and to have a say in what happens in *your* county and *your* state."

This particular flyer was trying to cash in on a political situation organized labor had been instrumental in helping to create. In state after state, the AFL-CIO has been a leader in taking to court congressional and state legislative districting arrangements it believes to be unconstitutional, in light of the Supreme Court's revolutionary 1962 *Baker vs. Carr* decision; the national AFL-CIO has buttressed this drive by opposing any congressional legislation or constitutional amendments which would alter this high court decision. The result of the nationwide redistricting demanded by the courts has been to give more representation to heavily-unionized areas. Labor—through COPE—has tried to capitalize on this development, as in Montgomery County, Md., by making concentrated efforts in the areas with increased political power.

The second flyer sent to all unregistered voters in Montgomery County was a professional-appearing leaflet setting down requirements for registration, places and times to register, and the local COPE phone number to call with any problems. Evidently this drive met with success, as the overwhelming majority of COPE-backed candidates in the county won in November, 1966.

The other example of local COPE resourcefulness concerns enlisting the aid of volunteers. In the registration drive outlined in *How To Win,* COPE suggests telephoning as the best means to acquire volunteers; the Harris County (Houston), Texas, COPE may have made some phone calls in 1962, but its directoi came up with a few new twists to get union members enthused about volunteering for political action.

In a letter to Harris County rank-and-file members, the director began by attacking one of the county's two congressmen, a conservative Democrat then in a primary battle against a labor-backed liberal: "Labor has a good opportunity to remove Bob Casey as Congressman this year, if we will work. As you know Bob Casey has voted right only three times in the three and one-half years he has been in the Congress, so let's retire him." After telling the workers when and where to meet to organize the drive, the writer suggested that workers needn't worry about not living in Casey's district; referring to Houston's other congressman, the letter stated, "Everyone can work on the project, because Congressman Albert Thomas has no opposition in the Democratic primary."

Whether in contacting all unregistered voters in a county, or going outside a congressional district for volunteer workers, COPE organizations on the local levels have proved themselves eminently capable of producing results. And now, to this already efficient registration operation is coming further sophistication in the form of data processing computers, an improvement capable of having great effect on COPE's future fortunes—and on the future of American politics.

For some time international unions and large locals have made use of computers for addressing mailings and otherwise reaching the membership. In 1964, for the first time, some labor groups used computers to prepare information for a voter registration drive; the Texas AFL-CIO, for example, rented computers to provide "walk lists" of unregistered voters in El Paso and San Antonio.

Realizing the potential in widespread use of a computerized voter registration drive, national COPE held a series of 12 regional conferences in 1965 which were devoted for the most part to explaining the value of data processing computers to local COPE leaders. COPE's leaders were well aware of the cost involved when a local body set up a computerized program, but their argument was:

"We believe it is possible for us to use present day data processing technology in our political efforts, that we can utilize machinery that is presently available to perform the time-consuming tasks that are so vital to our success and upon which our whole political program is based."

Following these briefings, the computer approach to practical politics was tested in 1966 in the state of Pennsylvania, the San Francisco Bay area and the Washington, D.C., area where 65,000 union members in the capital and suburban Maryland and Virginia were indexed on IBM cards. In the Pennsylvania pilot project, 41 international unions with locals in the state sent the names of 750,000 Keystone State rank-and-filers to the Washington headquarters of the International Association of Machinists, the AFL-CIO affiliate with the most elaborate computer set-up. At the IAM offices, a UNIVAC machine processed this data and returned lists with the members' names, precincts, streets, telephone numbers, and status of registration.

These lists were then passed back to local COPE leaders in Pennsylvania who divided them up among volunteers, and house-to-house canvassing of unregistered AFL-CIO members began. The result of the revolutionary effort was a whopping 80 percent rate of registration among the state's union voters.

Despite the proven success of the computer project, there is still the problem faced by many state and local labor political organizations which cannot afford the $6,000 estimated price tag national COPE places on the necessary equipment, or even the rental charge of $50 per hour. To dispel gloom over such figures, COPE advises that "organizations contemplating a data processing system start on a minimum basis with rented or leased equipment" and urges locals to "plan your system as simply as possible to fill your present needs, but with capability to do more elaborate jobs in the future."

As a guide for grass roots political directors, national COPE has published a pamphlet—entitled, with tongue firmly in cheek, "Machine Politics"[18]—in which it outlines a sample computer operation. "Our objective," the pamphlet begins, "is to utilize available machinery to perform the clerical work. This will make possible better and more efficient personal contact work." The primary functions of the system COPE envisions would be the ability to handle a large number of names and associated data; the capability to "manipulate this information automatically to produce the desired information, for instance, the names and addresses of unregistered union members in Ward 6, Precinct 21"; and "to perform more efficiently than manual labor."

The data-processing hardware in which COPE advises its local committees to invest, includes a key punch machine for imprinting information on cards, a storage file for these cards, and a machine to sort the cards into the various categories desired. Based on a 65,000 union member card file, COPE arrives at the cost of $6,000; this figure includes the above basic equipment, plus the fee paid to a professional computer service to process the cards and record the desired information on other cards or magnetic tape.

COPE envisions the suggested hardware as a computerized version of the central card file system outlined in *How To Win*. This encompasses an ambitious program to achieve a maximum union member vote through machine-coordinated propaganda, increased registration and Election Day voter turnout.

When the computerized registration project was instituted statewide in Pennsylvania in 1966, COPE leaders realized some side benefits they had not anticipated. One was the cooperation among individual unions in submitting membership lists to one central authority. As a holdover phenomenon from the "old days" when interunion raiding between AFL and CIO unions was a common fact of life, internationals and locals both have guarded their membership rolls as if they were state secrets. In freely surrendering their lists to COPE, Pennsylvania unions not only broke this clandestine tradition, but made COPE, rather than the unions, the focus of political activity.

Commented Walt Davis, national COPE assistant director, on this development: "This is the kind of unity, the kind of identity the labor movement needs."[19]

The computerized approach to registration will also improve organized labor's bargaining power within the upper echelons of the Democratic Party. If any Democrat would ever dare question COPE's political clout, the labor politicos could quickly whip out their files of computer cards and show the skeptic just how many of the rank-and-filers were registered and were strong Democrats. A Democratic Party leader in Pennsylvania, following COPE's 1966 registration drive in his state, stated:

"Labor has been labeled a paper tiger and hasn't been able to fight back. If now it can show that 80 percent of its people are registered, and how they're registered, it will get broader respect from the men in the legislative halls.[20]

The greatest benefit of all, however, and the development having the greatest importance for the nation's political structure, is the increased effectiveness and efficiency data-processing computers will add to a registration drive already leading the country in these two qualities. Of course, Republican and Democratic organizations, and other political action groups, can also invest in computers to improve their operations, but the fact that COPE is the first to use the system on a widespread basis and the first to realize the full implications of this new technology, is indicative of the labor committee's imagination and ambition.

And even if other political organizations purchase computers and put them to work, they may never be able to match the results COPE can get from data processing. No other group has yet the immediate rapport and working relationship that organized labor has with members it wishes to contact—for any purpose; this is an elementary reason for COPE's repeated political success, and a more efficient means of making this contact will only enhance its advantage.

The area where this enhancement will be most productive is voter registration. National COPE is quite aware of its position as the leader in political sophistication and progress, and minces no words in making the rank-and-file similarly aware:

"The now commonly accepted notion that a widespread registration campaign is the vital prelude to a political battle was fostered and developed by organized labor . . . Now, as we move toward the 21st century, labor has another vital contribution to make to the practice of politics. It is the adaptation of modern technology and techniques to political procedure."

The employment of computer technology is, first of all, characteristic of COPE's adaptation to, and willingness for, improvement and change. It also indicates the continuing stress it places on voter registration. Rather than be content with letting union members, their families, and neighbors get to the polls on their own, or with making a cursory stab at a registration drive, COPE mobilizes all its many resources for a concentrated, year-round campaign to get every single eligible voter it believes will support labor-backed candidates registered to vote.

This concern is Number One at COPE headquarters; it is the strong foundation of the COPE campaign.

# PART THREE:
## Choosing a Candidate (*Usually Democrat*)

Next to having eligible persons registered to vote, the most basic need in a political campaign is a candidate. It is the COPE candidate—rather than the issues—around whom the campaign is centered. It is he who will stir up the voters, and who will—when successful—carry the labor banner into the legislative halls.

COPE, of course, will not always have final choice of political candidates, and in many instances it has been forced to work with less than "perfect" candidates simply because it could get nothing better. But

COPE has its ways of actually choosing the candidate, and has even more ways of influencing the choice a party may make. Therefore, if COPE cannot get a "100 percent pure" candidate, he will most likely be at least 99 and 44/100 percent pure, and a Democrat (a factor making for 99 percent of his purity, in the eyes of most labor leaders).

Some of the methods COPE uses to select a party nominee have already been touched upon in its approach to campaigns; these plus unmentioned others comprise an essential activity of national COPE and one it wishes the rank-and-file to undertake.

COPE's first concern is that union members become active in practical politics, including establishing a local union COPE, conducting registration drives, convincing their union brothers whom to vote for. A second concern is for the AFL-CIO membership to become active in the political process itself. Join a political party, COPE urges, become a precinct official and have a voice in internal party affairs; "The power to nominate," it says emphatically in *How To Win,* "is as important as the power to elect."

This approach can be seen most clearly in areas such as Michigan, where labor has elected its own people to vital party posts and taken over the party structure for itself; when COPE participation in a party reaches this scale, choosing an acceptable candidate is a mere formality. But, even in states and districts where labor's inter-party strength is not dominant, there will be "labor men" in party positions who will be listened to, consulted; through them labor will exercise a strong influence over the party's functions. It will not be caught standing outside waiting for the party hierarchy to make up its mind.

The end result of this participation in the upper ranks of the political party most labor activists choose to join is that at the 1964 Democratic National Convention fully 10 percent of the delegates were leaders of international unions or union locals, while many other delegates were rank-and-file union members.

In heavily unionized locales, a powerful supplement to the voice of union members within a party will be COPE's political position independent of the party. A strong labor organization, able to operate effectively at campaign time, will undoubtedly be sought out for advice by the party when it comes time to select candidates. Such an independent position and the capability to act as a balance of power requires, however, that a local COPE remain formally non-committed to one particular party; without such formal non-partisanship, its support could be taken for granted, a situation avoided by maintaining the possibility of backing a candidate of the other party.

Such genuine non-partisanship is hardly ever the case. From the Democratic National Committee on down to the neighborhood precinct committeeman, labor's political power is openly acknowledged and its voice respected. The party politicians, when they are not labor men themselves, realize the danger of nominating a man thoroughly unacceptable to labor and know they would do so at the party's own risk. Labor's balance of power and internal influence are usually capable of obtaining an acceptable compromise candidate from the party.

When compromises cannot be made, COPE's recourse is to the third basic method it uses in choosing candidates: running its own men in primaries. This was the course taken when Texas COPE attempted to unseat Rep. John Dowdy in 1962, and when Philadelphia labor united behind incumbent mayor James Tate in 1967, achieving his nomination over the opposition of the regular party organization.

The primary route to candidate selection does not always bring labor success, and in this practice local union politicos realize they proceed at the risk of seeing their COPE lose any position of power it might hold. Fully aware of the chance involved, the Committee's *How To Win* advises its local troops on "How To Win a Primary." The indispensable essential in this operation, the handbook stresses, is organization:

> Your COPE—or any other organized group—can hold the key to who will be the candidate of a given party [in a primary].
> That's because *a handful of organized voters* can make the decision for *a mass of unorganized voters.*

COPE continues by giving an intriguing example of how a well-organized group, although a numerical minority within the total electorate, can sway a primary election. "Take 100 voters in a normal American precinct," *How To Win* begins. "Only about 50 percent of these turn out in a typical election."

> These 50 voters will fall into a pattern whereby some 25 are regular backers of the majority party; some 15 will back the minority party; and the other 10 will scatter their votes as unenrolled voters of either party.
> In the typical district, then, the victory for the predominant party is generally predictable: It starts with a majority, and usually ends up with from 55 to 60 percent of the vote.
> The 25 regular voters of the majority party, then, are the decisive voting bloc in this electorate of 100.
> When it comes to the primary, however, not all 25 regular supporters of the majority party will turn out to vote.
> As a matter of fact, if 20 to 30 percent of these come out for the primary, it's a high percentage.
> That means that of the 25 voters we're talking about, only five or six—or, at the most, 10—will vote in the primary.

To win the primary, then (which is almost identical with winning the election in some 300 out of 435 Congressional Districts across the country) you must get a majority of the five or six—or, at the most, 10—out of 100 eligible to vote in the election.

That means you must get the votes of three or four—or, at the most, six—in this electorate of 100.

Needless to say, this optimistic breakdown is a bit oversimplified and presupposes a totally disorganized opposition. In very few areas of the country can labor alone muster up enough voter strength to override a party choice, and primary challenges of the party structure are not a common COPE practice. It will undertake this course of action only when the party candidate is completely unacceptable (as with John Dowdy) or when the party machine completely ignores labor's counsel in political matters (as in Philadelphia).

However, there is another, a more sophisticated, brand of primary campaign, and this is the type COPE most likely speaks of in the example quoted. This variety occurs in areas where top party control has been diluted by law (with leadership positions limited to executive caretaker functions) and primaries are the customary route to nomination. In such instances COPE's demonstration example may be operable and its basic point well taken:

"If you have 20 active people in a precinct of 1,000, you're well on the way to controlling the primary machinery that nominates candidates . . . An organized group *within a political party* has many advantages over an unorganized group, all of whose members are outside a political party."

What happens when the opposition within the same party is equally well-organized, *How To Win* does not say. After all, the grass roots politicos should have *some* surprises.

With three courses available to it for the actual act of naming a candidate, COPE has a system of procedures available for judging the qualifications of would-be officeholders. The standards a candidate must meet before gaining the support of COPE, local or national, are found in fundamental form in the legislative program of the AFL-CIO; a contestant for the presidency or for Congress must measure up ideologically to the program of national AFL-CIO, a state legislative candidate must meet the requirements of his state's labor council.

This process, explains one COPE official, begins with "the convention of the AFL-CIO itself, which establishes the broad, general policy areas in which the AFL-CIO finds itself in support or opposition on various issues. Out of that derives the AFL-CIO's position on legislative issues, and out of the record of officeholders on these legislative issues derives the position on candidates for public office."

Judging from appearances, therefore, it seems COPE will endorse that candidate who is most in agreement with the AFL-CIO legislative program. Despite the overall accuracy of this judgment, it omits the essential ingredient of just *how much* COPE expects a candidate to agree with labor policy. Although COPE endorsement practices vary from area to area, one comment heard most often on this facet of COPE operations is that the organization all too often expects an all-or-nothing commitment from the candidates seeking its support; either you back us all the way, or we don't back you at all, COPE seems to be saying in many cases. This sentiment was well expressed by an aide to a Southern Democratic congressman:

"The worst thing of all about labor in politics is that you can't be 90 or 95 percent for them—you have to be 100 percent or they'll be out to get you next time. They won't accept anybody at all unless they've 100 percent on their side."

Supporting such expressions of personal opinion are documented instances of this practice being used. In 1966 two candidates who were otherwise—in varying degrees—pro-labor, including an incumbent with a high COPE voting rating, did not receive labor support in their campaigns apparently only because they had failed to support repeal of section 14(b) of the Taft-Hartley Act.

One such case involved Ted Kupferman, the liberal Republican seeking the seat formerly held by John Lindsay, elected mayor of New York in 1965. Kupferman's candidacy offered labor a golden opportunity to display its self-proclaimed "bi-partisanship," in view of his GOP liberalism in a district which had demonstrated itself receptive to this type of candidate. When Kupferman first ran for the seat in 1965, to fill out Lindsay's unexpired term, he was denied COPE support, with the *New York Times* explaining that "one of the factors mitigating against Mr. Kupferman was his disclosure that he no longer advocated repeal of Section 14(b) of the Taft-Hartley Act."[21]

Kupferman was elected in '65 by a comfortable margin, and went on in the remaining days of the 89th Congress to chalk up a 100 percent "perfect" COPE rating in his votes. When it came time for endorsements in 1966, however, COPE ignored its own rating system and gave its support to Kupferman's opponent.

In Texas in 1966, labor had a good shot at retiring the GOP Senator, John Tower (whom COPE had rated at 0 percent for the 89th Congress), but it was faced with a Democratic candidate, state attorney general Waggoner Carr, who in the past had proved conservative on many issues. President Johnson had placed defeat of Tower (who had won the LBJ Senate seat in a special 1961 election) high on his priority list for 1966, so he brought Carr to Washington to have a chat with

COPE's Al Barkan in an attempt to straighten matters out and get him labor backing. According to columnists Evans and Novak, the following exchange occurred during the meeting:

"Al Barkan . . . quizzed Carr in a long, private session about his well-known conservative views. Carr replied that he would support President Johnson on Great Society issues in the Senate.

"Well then, asked Barkan, how about the repeal of section 14(b) of the Taft-Hartley Act? Carr said he was sorry, but he just could not support repeal of 14(b).

"Barkan's reply to that ended any chance that labor will go all-out for Carr in the election."[22]

(The irony of these two examples is that by the time they occurred, repeal of 14(b) was virtually a dead issue. It had been defeated in a Senate filibuster in 1966, in the face of the most liberal, pro-labor Congress in two decades. Yet labor still continues to make this issue an ultimate criterion for endorsement.)

These and following examples show that the "all-or-nothing" concept of candidate approval is frequently a working policy with national and local COPEs. However, as will also be seen, this is not an exclusive rule. More than half the incumbents backed by COPE in 1966 had less than a 100 percent voting record and in one case the labor candidate's rating was only 32 percent; in most of these instances local COPEs decided they would rather try to win with a less-than-perfect candidate than sit out the campaign.

It is just this either/or dilemma that leads COPE to urge workers to participate in the political process. If labor can control or strongly influence party candidate selection processes, the question of accepting a less-than-perfect candidate is largely dispensed with; then local COPEs can "shop around" to find a candidate who will do his "all" for labor.

Following the wishes of the labor leadership "100 percent" can pertain to candidates as well as issues, as one Philadelphia congressman discovered during that city's bitter 1967 Democratic mayoralty primary. Rep. Joshua Eilberg, who had squeaked into his first congressional term in 1966 with only 51.1 percent of the votes, decided during the primary to remain loyal to the Democratic organization's candidate, rather than back the incumbent mayor who was enjoying the support of organized labor.

According to a report in the *Philadelphia Inquirer,* Eilberg was closeted with a handful of city labor leaders who "reminded that labor represented the handful of votes that separated Eilberg from his Republican opponent last fall.

"When Eilberg remained unmoved, they promised him that his current term in Congress would be his first and last."[23]

Another variation of the "all-or-nothing" theme involved Sen. Wayne

Morse, the ultra-liberal Oregon Democrat with a 96 percent COPE rating for 1966. In the early months of 1966, the iconoclastic Morse had decided to oppose the AFL-CIO on two important issues. When the International Association of Machinists struck the nation's airlines, Morse proposed legislation permitting the seizure of the airlines by the government, a move promptly criticized by the AFL-CIO leadership and by labor newspapers in Oregon.

Morse brought up this attack a few months later when federation lobbyists attempted to persuade him to alter his opposition to a minimum wage bill. Before the two AFL-CIO men could get around to expressing their views on the bill, Morse exclaimed:

"By the way, I read that editorial in the Portland labor paper calling me a strikebreaker [for the airlines proposal]. Tell George Meany I know where it came from.

"Because you supported me don't get the idea that you own me. Tell Meany that I'll fight for labor when it's right and I'll fight against labor when it's wrong . . . Name any other Senator who has been as staunch a champion of labor when you were right and needed help. Name any other Senator who stood up and made the kind of speech I did against 14(b).

"Don't call me off the floor [for discussions] again, and tell Meany to go to hell."[24]

(Morse was up for re-election in 1968 and Oregon labor began the campaign supporting his primary opponent, Bob Duncan. However, when Sen. Lister Hill (D-Ala.) announced his retirement, and Morse became next in line as chairman of the Senate Labor and Public Welfare Committee, the AFL-CIO called off its anti-Morse effort so as not to further alienate the potential head of the committee dealing closely with its legislative fate. Morse won the primary by an eyelash.)

To protect themselves against the type of independence from labor displayed by Wayne Morse, some zealous labor political leaders will exact promises from candidates, having them state that, if and when elected, they will back labor's program down-the-line. And in some instances, these promises have taken the form of a written pledge.

The first time such a document came to public light was in Minneapolis, Minnesota, in 1955. An enterprising city alderman put one of the city's newspapers onto the story of a "labor loyalty oath" being extracted from COPE candidates, and the *Minneapolis Star* reported the story Dec. 30 and 31, 1955; on August 30, 1956, the *Star* again reported the oath's use, and the next year the *Minneapolis Tribune* documented COPE's demands of sworn loyalty. The oath given to candidates receiving support from the Minneapolis-St. Paul COPE reportedly read:

"I hereby agree that if I receive the endorsement of this committee I pledge to actively support the program and platform formulated by the Labor Movement on city, state and national issues. That I will join a caucus of all other Labor-endorsed candidates which is pledged to abide by unit rule on all matters of organization or on basic labor issues. That I will clear all campaign literature through this committee and will cause to have distributed only that which is approved. If it is found at any time that I have failed to meet the obligation outlined above, I agree that I forfeit this labor endorsement."

The most celebrated case of a "loyalty oath" being used to enforce COPE's "all-or-nothing" demands involved labor's Number One goal of 14(b) repeal and a 1964 primary in Baltimore, Md. The candidate in question was Rep. Clarence Long, a liberal Democrat (1966 COPE "right" rating of 88 percent) with insignificant primary opposition. Long had stated on many occasions that he opposed right-to-work laws, but this was not enough for Baltimore COPE leaders. Before getting their endorsement Long was requested to sign an oath, stating:

"I pledge my support to the Trade Union Movement in their fight to eliminate Section 14B from the Taft-Hartley Law, and my vote will be on this issue in accordance with labor's position."

Long refused to sign the document and COPE refused to endorse him or list his name on the "Workingman's Ballot" it circulated on primary election day. Not being one to accept such abuse silently, Long took the issue to the floor of the House:

"This attempt to make a Congressman trade his vote for a political endorsement demonstrates a lack of respect for Congress. . . . Now I do not favor right-to-work laws; it is quite possible that when this [repeal] bill comes to the floor I will vote to outlaw them. But I can never sign away my future vote. . . .

"The day I must pledge my vote to get elected to Congress is the day I shall leave Congress to take up some other line of work."[25]

Naturally, after such public exposure of one of its seamier activities, national COPE officials were embarrassedly apologetic and the chairman of Baltimore COPE was reprimanded. But in their comments on the matter, COPE staffers seem to imply as much criticism of Long as of their Baltimore man: "Inevitably," said one COPE spokesman, "in any organization, ours or anybody else's, somebody is going to pop off, and when he does somebody is going to make a big fat issue out of it just as Mr. Long did."

(Long won his primary race—scoring up to 12 to 1 in some labor wards. In the general election, an embarrassed and chastened Baltimore COPE backed Long . . . no loyalty oath asked.)

Another practice labor has used to insure that successful candidates it had endorsed follow the "labor line" when in office is placing union personnel on the official's staff. This tactic was widespread when the CIO's Political Action Committee was a political force in the 'forties, and it continued under COPE in the late 'fifties. But, because of press exposure and hostile public reaction to such "labor domination," it has abated in recent years.

The 1966 *Congressional Staff Directory*,[26] a quasi-official listing of staff personnel on Capitol Hill, lists only 36 individuals (out of about 1800 major staffers) with labor union connections, and many of these ties are of little consequence; a congressman's press aide, for example, could be expected to be a member of the American Newspaper Guild. (At the same time, the "Staff Directory" is by no means a complete listing of every staff member's every affiliation; Hill personnel submit their biographies to the publication, including and omitting whatever they wish.)

The simplest way for COPE to have candidates who will meet AFL-CIO standards is for it to find men willing to run, build them into leading contenders, win the nomination for them and go into the campaign with a ready-made product. An outline of how this may be accomplished is found in *How To Win,* as it asks its field workers to remember that "your project is to get good men into office, and that's a long-term proposition"; the handbook then presents a rudimentary step-by-step advancement chart:

"So get your man to run for the school board—or the public service commission. These elections serve both to give him campaign experience and to get him known."

"Then you can run him later for county commissioner or the city council, for the State Legislature or for Congress."

The practical result of this strategy is the number of candidates elected to recent Congresses who had past records of union affiliation. This labor bloc in the 90th Congress included:

Sens. William Proxmire (D-Wisc.) and Warren Magnuson (D-Wash.), both members of the American Newspaper Guild;

Rep. Jeffrey Cohelan (D-Calif.), former secretary-treasurer of Milk and Dairy Employees local in Berkeley;

Rep. George Rhodes (D-Pa.), member of Typographers' Union and former president of Reading, Pa., Federated Trades Council;

Rep. John Dent (D-Pa.), past president of United Rubber Workers local and member of the union's international council;

Rep. Joseph Karth (D-Minn.), international representative for Oil, Chemical and Atomic Workers Union;

Rep. Joseph Minish (D-N.J.), member of International Union of Electrical Workers, CIO organizer, and executive secretary of Essex-West Hudson (N.J.) AFL-CIO Labor Council;

Rep. Edward Garmatz (D-Md.), member of International Brotherhood of Electrical Workers.

Among the former union personnel defeated in 1966 were Rep. John Race (D-Wisc.), a one-time Machinists local president, and Rep. Paul Krebs (D-N.J.), who had served as shop steward, secretary, and director of political action and education for the United Auto Workers in the region covering New Jersey.

Barring such easy acceptance of candidates, however, COPE must pass judgment on the men who are vying for a particular nomination or office. The means for judging a man's suitability for COPE endorsement depend upon his electoral status: if he is already an officeholder, COPE will weigh his existing record, plus his position on upcoming issues in which the AFL-CIO has taken an interest; without this record, COPE must screen the candidates by means of questionnaires and/or "hearings" before the leadership board determining the COPE endorsement.

The most common method of judging the record of an incumbent candidate for national office is the COPE Voting Record, a document compiled at the end of each session of Congress. These records purport to establish a congressman's position in relation to organized labor by giving him a "right" or "wrong" listing, depending on how he voted on issues on which the AFL-CIO took a position. Although COPE is not the only special interest organization to make use of the "rating game," its practice is by far the most dubious.

Following the adjournment of each Congress, COPE officials consult with representatives of the AFL-CIO's Legislative Department to decide which votes in the session to use in the ratings. The votes are selected and each representative's and senator's individual vote on the issues is recorded, a "W" (wrong) being noted if the official opposed the AFL-CIO stand, an "R" (right) if he agreed with the federation.

The votes are chosen ostensibly to gauge a congressman's affinity for organized labor's interests; they are not, however, all votes on labor-oriented legislation. In COPE's ratings for House members in the 89th Congress there were only four votes out of the 13 used which directly related to workingmen (three votes on 14(b) repeal, one on minimum wage); of the 12 votes used to judge senators the same year, only two pertained to the rank-and-file (14(b) repeal and wages for construction workers on federal projects). The remainder of the issues COPE used in '66 covered a broad range of social legislation, from federal rent subsidies to a procedural vote on the rules of the House of Representatives.

The two other large organizations employing a similar vote rating are Americans for Democratic Action (ADA) and Americans for Constitutional Action (ACA), two unabashedly ideological groups who judge members of Congress on their liberalism and conservatism and use a wide variety of legislative votes in doing so. COPE, meanwhile, contends that its ratings represent how congressmen stand on the interests of one economic bloc—unionized workingmen—and it is the only bloc-oriented organization to do so (the National Chamber of Commerce and NAM put out no voting ratings). If it used only votes involving specifically labor issues, COPE might have some validity to its claim, but the inclusion of matters far distant from the rank-and-file destroys the reality of the vote ratings reflecting a congressman's labor position.

COPE's defense is that union members are citizens and therefore have an interest—determined in AFL-CIO legislative endorsements—in all social and economic legislation. This assumption is undoubtedly true of any person in the United States, which is why we have political parties, nominations of candidates and free elections—for the citizens to express their feelings on social and economic issues. In this particular instance COPE is doing nothing less than presenting itself as an alternative to the political parties and arbitrarily deciding what is good and what is bad for the captive rank-and-file.

Also, in the selection and presentation of the votes chosen, COPE employs a little trickery. Take, as an example, the 13 votes used to judge House members for the 89th Congress (1965-66). The first three listed in the official COPE Voting Ratings were votes on the repeal of section 14(b) of Taft-Hartley.

The first of these is said by COPE to be a vote "on a motion to take the repeal bill away from the Rules Committee and to bring it up for House action." There was, however, a great deal more involved in the motion than this, and it concerned House parliamentary procedure more than it did 14(b) repeal: under the motion in question, repeal would have been brought out of committee under a rule allowing only five hours of House debate and permitting only amendments to the bill approved by the House Speaker. The motion passed, the bill was brought to the floor and the Speaker proceeded to rule every proposed amendment as "not germane" except for one inconsequential move to change the date of enforcement. (Incidentally, the rule delegating this autocratic power to the Speaker was abandoned in the 90th Congress.)

The next two repeal votes used by COPE were virtually identical measures and were taken within moments of each other in the House; the first a move by repeal opponents to send the bill back to committee, the second on final passage. And as most members voted the same on both (the labor forces got 223 on the first, and 221 on the second), COPE was able to give those "anti-labor villains" *two* wrong votes instead of just one.

On its Medicare vote COPE again distorts the issue through over-simplified, inflammatory language, saying the vote was "on a motion to recommit, in effect to kill, the [Medicare] proposal." The recommittal motion contained explicit instructions for the committee to substitute another Medicare program which was equally comprehensive, but would have required voluntary participation and would have been financed out of general government funds (not Social Security). But COPE explains none of this.

Another interesting item in COPE's ratings is its traditional "public power" issue, an egalitarian holdover from the activist 'thirties when labor saw itself as the representative of the "little men" in the fight against the Big Corporations. In 1966 COPE listed a bill appropriating construction funds to Maine's Dickey-Lincoln power project as its "public power" vote; commenting on this bill, the objective *Congressional Quarterly* noted that "supporters of the bill, including the Interior Department in its report, made clear that one of their major objectives in seeking the project was to bring federal power to New England for the first time."

Probably there are a few AFL-CIO leaders who would go simply wild with joy at seeing federal power come to New England for the first time and watch those nasty ol' Private Utilities bite the dust, but it is hard to imagine the rank-and-file dancing in the streets. What conceivable relevance this issue might have had to union members would seem to involve the increased unemployment this project would cause among coal workers, due to the reduction in coal consumption with the advent of water power. This is why the United Mine Workers opposed the bill. The AFL-CIO, however, is apparently more concerned with outdated public vs. private power social issues than it is with unemployment.

The last item worth mentioning in COPE's 1966 Voting Records is the verbiage in the Senate and House votes listed as "War on Poverty." After a glowing review of the poverty war, COPE claims "an effort, opposed by the AFL-CIO, was made to hamstring . . . the war on poverty," and lists the vote supposedly representing this grim "effort." But, all that the vote—in both Senate and House—concerned was the right for state governors to veto federal poverty projects in their states; not funds, not programs, merely the right of state chief executives to determine what is best for their constituencies.

For all the broad range of legislation covered in the COPE ratings, the organization still mentions only a fraction of the votes cast in one session of Congress; the 1966 ratings for the House included 13 record votes out of the 394 cast during the two sessions of the 89th Congress and in the Senate COPE used but 12 out of 493 record votes. And it is on these few votes that an incumbent's labor record stands or falls, as far as COPE is concerned. The only alternative to presenting just a fraction of the votes, of course, would be an impractical and cumbersome complete rundown. For this reason, COPE—as with the ADA, the ACA and other organizations using ratings—chooses only the issues its leaders deem the most appropriate.

What COPE does with the results of its bi-annual compilations is to employ a unique numbers game which is *not* practiced by any other rating organization. Rather than add up the "right" and "wrong" totals for one session of Congress, COPE takes these totals and adds them on to the corresponding figures a congressman has accumulated since he came to Congress, or since 1947. Therefore, on COPE's '66 ratings Sen. Clinton Anderson (New Mexico Democrat elected in 1948) has a score of 57 "right" and 8 "wrong," instead of the 10 "right" and 1 "wrong" he received for just the 89th Congress; on the same scoreboard, Sen. Robert Kennedy (D-N.Y.) was judged to have 11 "right" and no "wrong" votes as he had served in only one session of Congress since his 1964 election.

When the newly formed AFL-CIO Committee on Political Education prepared for its first national election campaign in 1956, it published voting records for incumbent congressmen which included votes cast in the preceding five Congresses, or back to 1947. This period contained some 913 votes in the House of Representatives, out of which COPE selected 19, or 2 percent, to judge the 10-year record of veteran representatives.

There was much criticism at the time of COPE's use of so small a percentage, plus its inclusion of votes taken 5 to 10 years before and its open distortion of the issues involved. Ignoring this criticism, COPE has continued to add to the original 19 votes at the end of every session of Congress, until in 1966 there was a total of 79 issues scored upon for senators and 77 for representatives. (Of course, congressmen not having served since 1947 are scored from the time they do enter.) The total for senators can climb even higher, as COPE will include House votes if a senator was formerly a representative.

The plain effect of this stockpiling of votes over the years is that incumbents COPE does not like will come out looking much worse than if the votes from just one session had been used; it is far more effective for a labor political leader to be able to say: "Senator X has voted against us 75 times!" than if he had to say the Senator has voted "wrong" 12 times. Big numbers are always more impressive, especially to hard-working laborers.

(The Americans for Constitutional Action uses in its ratings a similar cumulative figure, but keeps this separate and distinct from another figure representing a score for the session of Congress just ended.)

And this is precisely how national COPE intends its voting statistics to be used. On the last page of the 1966 Voting Record COPE declares: "If the voters have full information about the record of candidates running for office, they will vote for the best one . . . AFL-CIO members have a right to know how their Representatives and Senators actually voted on the important national issues. That is why we have distributed a record of key congressional roll call votes prior to each national election."

There are several dubious implications in this message. First, COPE implies that its records provide rank-and-filers with "full information" on congressmen's records, a questionable claim in view of the small percentage of votes selected for the record. Secondly, when COPE says AFL-CIO members have the "right to know" how congressmen "actually" voted, it appears to be telling the membership that, unless COPE gave them this information, some mysterious force would keep it from them and they would never know.

After compiling the purported "full information" on congressional voting in its bi-annual records, COPE relies on a newly instituted and highly sophisticated method of distribution to get the "word" to the grass roots. Prior to 1966, national COPE prepared a master voting record for all members of Congress and shipped millions of copies across the country to local COPEs everywhere.

In 1966, however, the distribution procedure was changed. National COPE still prepared the master record for all congressmen, printing a few thousand copies, but then sent prepared offset printing plates to each state COPE organization, thus allowing state committees to run off as many of their own copies as needed. This new process saved national COPE time, money and confusion; state COPEs no longer needed to send to national for additional copies, and then wait for them to be published and shipped, but could simply print more on their own printing presses.

What was done with the approximately 15 million copies of COPE's 1966 Voting Record when they reached the grass roots can only be generally described. As noted previously, they come in very handy when a local labor politico makes a speech and they can damn a congressman for voting "against labor" X times, or, on the opposite scale, can praise someone for voting "with labor." They can also be put to good use when an incumbent candidate opposed by labor makes a campaign speech; local COPE representatives can attend the speech and, referring to the voting records, ask the candidate why he voted "against labor" on a certain issue, or why he voted "against" the War on Poverty (when all he did, for example, was vote in favor of keeping the governor's veto).

And the records are used in determining endorsements. National COPE may have little to do with the routine of picking candidates on the local or state level, but its bi-annual review of incumbents' votes are certainly a strong determinate in this process. The COPE Voting Records are by no means the final word in defining suitability of candidates for labor backing, but their contribution to the process is significant.

Even when an incumbent candidate's "pro-" or "anti-labor" record has been judged by COPE, as time approaches for a local committee to bequeath its endorsement there may be other measures taken to determine whom to endorse. The two methods used most frequently are questionnaires sent to the candidates, and "hearings" before the endorsing board or the area's union membership.

The former procedure consists simply of sending a candidate—incumbent or first-timer—a list of questions inquiring into his position on issues which the AFL-CIO has taken a stand on. The wording of the queries will undoubtedly be slanted—commonly called "when-have-you-stopped-beating-your-wife" type questions—to make someone not agreeing with labor appear an extreme reactionary. A number of special interest groups (including the American Farm Bureau and League of Women Voters) use the questionnaire method of eliciting candidates' views and most employ the biased question, but in the majority of cases the replies to COPE's questionnaires are given a broader circulation (through union periodicals and mass distribution) and have a greater impact (due to size of union membership) than do any other group's.

The COPE "hearings" take a number of forms. They can be held at a state or district COPE convention, where delegates will hear candidate speeches, or the hearings may take place before a gathering of the local COPE leadership. Whatever the nature of the meeting, the candidate invited to appear is expected to present his views on labor-sponsored legislation and this position theoretically determines COPE's endorsement.

Although convention delegates may hear candidates' speeches it is repeatedly made clear to the rank-and-file that it is their leaders who make the final endorsement decisions. Enforcing leadership control over this matter, *How To Win* warns local union COPE workers that, in talking with and questioning candidates, "make it clear you are promising nothing as far as your support is concerned."

"Endorsements," the manual emphasizes, "are made by State and City or County Central Council COPEs."

Because of the overall unanimity on political policy and the many candidates found among labor leaders and representatives of the rank-and-file, there normally is little question or dispute over candidates receiving support. The rare cases of internal COPE dispute on this matter that have arisen offer an intriguing glimpse of how confused and disoriented the endorsement procedure can become.

In August, 1966, a spokesman for New Jersey's industrial unions told a reporter there was "terrific support" among these unions for incumbent Republican Sen. Clifford Case; meanwhile, some other state labor leaders were worried lest a strong Case election showing, with COPE backing, would pull in Republican congressmen whom labor opposed: "It's not that we love Case less," they said, "it's that we love Democratic congressmen more."[27] The 1966 AFL-CIO convention called to decide the New Jersey Senate endorsement was unusually stormy, with the building trades unions unable to get along with the industrial groups and no decisions being reached. In the end, most CIO unions backed Case, as did the railroad unions, with some AFL groups backing the Democratic candidate and others remaining neutral.

Labor's role in the 1966 gubernatorial race in New York State was even more confusing. Traditionally, the Empire State's labor unions have supported the candidates endorsed by the Democratic Party and the state's left-wing third force, the Liberal Party; under normal conditions, office-seekers on the Democrat ticket had Liberal backing and there was no problem over whom labor would work for. In 1966 things were far from normal: the Liberals would not support the Democrats' gubernatorial seeker, Frank O'Connor, and put their backing behind Franklin D. Roosevelt, Jr. As a result, the biggest New York City unions, notably the ladies' garment workers, clothing workers and hat makers—which had helped create the Liberal Party in the early 'forties —were split down the middle. What happened in most cases was for the Liberal Party-inclined unions to remain neutral and let the membership go where they wanted.

Democrat O'Connor, who might otherwise have expected strong COPE support, had his labor strength further dissipated by the popularity of incumbent Gov. Rockefeller among the rank-and-file, especially among workers in the building and construction trades. As the campaign evolved, O'Connor was found with the endorsement of such unions as the machinists, auto workers, teamsters, longshoremen, textile workers, meat cutters, communication workers, and public employees; the final winner, Rockefeller, had backing from the barbers, building service and trades employees, steel workers, electrical workers, firemen and utility workers.

Examples of such dissension in the labor ranks are the rare exception, with COPE's list of 1966 political endorsements showing only the above two instances of CIO and AFL unions having differences over candidate preference. (The unaffiliated United Mine Workers, Teamsters and Railway Labor's Political League have strong political power independent of COPE and make individual endorsements; frequently these three groups will be found supporting Republicans or conservative-moderate Democrats whom COPE will be avoiding.)

Another stratagem COPE sometimes employs in putting its influence to maximum effective use is the withholding of endorsements. This ploy is common in the South, or other nominally conservative states, where COPE backing could mean the kiss of death for a candidate. Alabama's Sen. John Sparkman is a liberal by Southern standards and when he was challenged by a strong conservative in the Democratic primary in 1966, COPE gave him full support; in his general election race against a popular Republican, however, COPE made a big thing out of *not* endorsing Sparkman.

Wrote Sparkman's unsuccessful GOP opponent, John Grenier, following the election: "Whether the refusal to endorse [Sparkman] in the general election was a stratagem adopted specifically to assist in his re-election, I do not know. I am confident that the withholding of endorsement was beneficial to my opponent since the [Alabama Labor] Council has a liberal reputation and I have the impression that Alabamians like to think of themselves as conservatives."[28]

Whether strategically withholding an endorsement or giving enthusiastic support, COPE's procedure in selecting a candidate is sophisticated, diffuse and—on the surface—somewhat complex. But, in analyzing the maze of systems of choice and methods of candidate approval, one unassailable fact comes clear: the result is, 99 percent of the time, exactly the same—liberal Democrats are supported, Republicans (including liberals) are opposed.

"The entire pattern of labor's participation in politics since the formation of the CIO in the 1930's," wrote Raymond Moley in 1962, "is a partnership arrangement with the Democratic Party."[29]

This is not quite true, argues COPE director Al Barkan, who claims that "we just don't find enough Republicans, on the basis of their position and the basis of their record, who warrant our support." However, he continues, "In the Senate state COPEs have supported Case in New Jersey, Javits and Keating in New York, Margaret Chase Smith in Maine and Kuchel in California."[30]

Barkan, in his rush to proclaim COPE's bi-partisanship, forgot a few things: New Jersey COPE, as has been seen, did not give Sen. Case its formal support in 1966, nor did it do so in his previous race in 1960 (when it remained neutral); Maine COPE endorsed Sen. Smith's Democratic opponent in 1966, even though she had a record of agreeing with the AFL-CIO 59 percent of the time; New York State COPE did not back former Sen. Keating in 1964, and many unions were instrumental in his defeat by Robert Kennedy.

In 1966 COPE did not endorse the Republican running in any one of the 33 Senate races.[31] Sen. Caleb Boggs of Delaware, with a 45 percent COPE rating, was supported by the railroad unions, but opposed by COPE; Sen. James Pearson (Kan.) was backed by the United Mine Workers, but opposed by COPE; and Sen. John Sherman Cooper, one of the Senate's most liberal Republicans and recipient of a 58 percent "right" voting record from COPE in '66, was supported by the railroad unions, but Kentucky COPE made no endorsement.

Barkan's protest that COPE simply cannot find more Republicans to endorse "on the basis of their position and the basis of their record," is also proven empty when 1966 House endorsements are scrutinized. True, in '66 COPE did endorse 15 GOP House candidates (out of 435 House seats), and these ranged from Rep. Frank Horton (R-N.Y.), with a 75 percent COPE rating, to Rep. Tom Pelly (R-Wash.), with a seemingly low 32 percent score for '66.

If COPE expects these endorsements to prove its alleged bi-partisanship, it might also expect to have its party loyalties examined by noting the liberal Republican incumbent representatives it opposed; these include (COPE rating noted for 1966):

Rep. Theodore Kupferman (N.Y.), 100 percent

Rep. Robert Stafford (Vt.), 37 percent

Rep. Silvio Conte (Mass.), 40 percent

Rep. William Widnall (N.J.), 36 percent

Rep. William Ayres (Ohio), 36 percent

Rep. Arch Moore (W. Va.), 42 percent

Admittedly, none of these representatives—except for Kupferman—could be called, on the basis of their COPE scores, rabidly pro-labor. But each of them does have a higher rating than COPE-endorsed Rep. Pelly of Washington State, and each of them comes from a traditionally Republican district. Endorsement of these six House members would have brought the number of COPE's GOP candidates to a minuscule 21, but their ommission from this list hints that the tacit bi-partisanship which COPE pretends to is lacking in field support.

Labor's anti-Republican posture is certainly nothing new and probably elicits little public surprise. This is evident throughout the long history of AFL and CIO operations in practical politics, and got off to a running start when the two federations merged: COPE in 1956 supported Stevenson against Eisenhower, meanwhile giving endorsements to 18 Democrats running for the Senate (no Republicans), 7 Democrats for governorships (no Republicans), and 125 Democrats for the House (2 Republicans).

The COPE-Democrat liaison moved smoothly along in like manner until early 1966, when political observers were shaken from their easy chairs with George Meany's pronouncement: "If we are looking around for a party to adopt or control, we don't want the Democratic Party, because they can't deliver."[32] The White House had announced unions should seek no more than a 3.2 percent increase in wages (with a like limit placed on business price increases) and the AFL-CIO Executive Council ignored the guideline, saying "neither wage nor price restraints are tolerable in a free society except in the gravest national emergency." Then the congressional Democratic leadership failed in its goal of repealing section 14(b), and labor suspected the reason lay at the White House, with one union boss commenting, "If President Johnson had put as much emphasis on the repeal of 14(b) as he did on his wife's beautification bill, we would have gotten repeal."[33]

In short, organized labor was a little bit piqued over Democratic performance. Some press observers saw it as more than a momentary hostility, however, with *Time* magazine going so far as to opine that Meany's denouncement "brought the smoldering feud between labor and the Democratic Party close to open warfare."[34] And the *Washington Evening Star*'s respected columnist, Gould Lincoln, interpreted the AFL-CIO president's remarks in political terms:

"Meany has not so far announced that labor would form an independent political party. It is going back to the unaligned position it held under the late Sam Gompers, supporting Republican and Democratic candidates it liked, and avoiding endorsing presidential candidates of any political party."[35]

With press comments such as these bursting forth all around him, President Johnson became a little fearful that columnist Lincoln's prophecy could possibly come true. Vice President Hubert Humphrey was quickly dispatched to a labor conclave in Washington, where he told the assembled union delegates:

"We Democrats need the labor movement. I don't mind telling you that the Vice President has been your friend and I don't mind telling you that the President of the United States is your friend too. We are not going to let you down."[36]

Other events later showed that Humphrey's bouquet was little more than an embarrassment and the press "analyses" were little more than exercises in fantasy. Scant days before Meany's "can't deliver" pronouncement, the AFL-CIO Executive Council (ruled by the same Mr. Meany) had released a statement saying that the Senate Republicans' fight to retain section 14(b) of Taft-Hartley "raised once again the question of whether [GOP minority leader] Dirksen's party is the anti-labor party, the party that stands unalterably opposed to any social progress legislation."[37]

Of Meany's alternating hostility to the Republicans and the Democrats in early 1966, it is the latter which was proved momentary while the former remains the semi-official AFL-CIO and COPE policy: that November only 15 Republicans were COPE-supported in campaigns for national office, and in March, 1967, Meany announced he was ready then to endorse President Johnson (whose party a year before had been accused of not being able to "deliver") because "I feel that we have made greater progress under this Administration than any Administration in my experience . . ."[38] George Meany's political machinations often rival those of Harold Stassen in their astuteness.

The general public, indeed, should be aware that organized labor is happiest with the Democratic Party and its candidates. What is not always understood, however, is the full nature of labor's ingrained aversion to Republicans. This sentiment is found, not in the mere fact of endorsements of Democrats, but more so in the refusal to back seemingly acceptable GOP candidates and the reasons given for doing so; COPE, more often than not, judges candidates purely on party labels, rather than personal credentials. Consider the following examples:

* In 1966 Oregon's liberal Republican Governor Mark Hatfield, whose administration had promoted a number of laws benefiting union members, gave up his state post to run for the Senate; COPE chose to oppose him, with United Auto Workers' president Walter Reuther going so far as to give a blank check to Hatfield's Democrat opponent, Robert Duncan.

This action should hardly have surprised Hatfield. When Hatfield was running for his second term as governor in 1962 COPE had opposed him, even though the state AFL-CIO's executive board had voted for his endorsement. The reason given for the COPE convention's reversal of this decision was that Hatfield would "be campaigning with and for" the GOP candidate against incumbent Sen. Wayne Morse, a liberal Democrat sometimes idolized by Oregon's labor leaders.[39]

* At the 1964 Republican National Convention, Pennsylvania Gov. William Scranton had gone down to the wire in opposing Sen. Goldwater for the GOP presidential nomination, loudly denouncing conservatism along the way; back home in the Keystone State, under Scranton's leadership the legislature had passed pension and wage legislation. None of these performances, however, could dissuade COPE from battling Scranton on the political front.

At the 1964 state AFL-CIO convention, a resolution was passed denouncing a "concerted Gov. William W. Scranton-Chamber of Commerce onslaught," accusing Scranton of being behind an effort to pass a state right-to-work law (which, in fact, he opposed and would veto, he said, if it ever passed the legislature). While acknowledging Scranton's battle with Goldwater, COPE claimed he had "refused to disassociate himself from Goldwater ideologies." The irony of this hostility was that

Scranton was not even up for election in '64 and, under Pennsylvania law, could not run to succeed himself in 1966; but he *was* the most prominent Republican in the state and, in COPE's eyes, this was a perfectly justifiable reason for the attack.[40]

* George Romney is a third example of a liberal Republican governor who has been responsible for legislation favored by organized labor (notably a minimum-wage bill and a construction-safety measure), but has been regularly assaulted by Michigan's AFL-CIO in return. At the 1966 COPE convention Romney heard himself denounced as an "anti-hero . . . long on vetoes, short on performance," and saw the convention delegates endorse his unknown Democratic opponent Zolton Ferency by a vote of 561-7. This in spite of Romney's having received an estimated 48 percent of the rank-and-file vote in his 1964 election.

Michigan COPE and its leaders, Walter Reuther and Gus Scholle, felt it necessary to damn Romney and railroad the convention for Ferency because the governor's senatorial ticket-mate was Robert Griffin and because of the latter's possible victory over labor idol "Soapy" Williams. For Williams to have a chance in November, Romney, the demonstrated "friend" of the workingman, had to be fought as hard as Griffin. Here the Michigan AFL-CIO proved that power politics come first.

* In New Mexico's gubernatorial race in 1966, organized labor attempted a "divide-and-conquer" strategy against the Republicans. In a fairly even GOP primary, COPE had given its backing to a moderate Republican, David Cargo, and this endorsement plus union men's "crossing over" to vote GOP helped in Cargo's victory over his conservative opponent. In the November campaign, however, COPE shifted its course and endorsed the liberal Democrat candidate, a move calculated to leave Cargo without much popular support. The strategy backfired for labor, as Cargo won with backing from both conservative Republicans and the rank-and-file.

* Perhaps the perfect specimen of convoluted, manufactured, obscure reasoning employed by a labor organization in explaining opposition to a Republican was offered in 1956 by *Labor,* the mouthpiece for Railway Labor's Political League. The item concerned the New York State campaign to fill the seat of retiring Sen. Herbert Lehman (D). New York City Mayor Wagner was pitted against State Attorney General Jacob Javits, a Manhattan liberal who had the support of many individual unions. The logic provided in a special edition of *Labor* for refusing to consider a Javits endorsement deserves to stand as a model of organized labor's anti-Republicanism:

"The big issue in the current Senate campaign is just this: Should Empire State voters send to Washington an outstanding liberal—Robert

Wagner—who'll play on the same aggressive Senate team that Herbert Lehman has helped to lead so long?

"Or should New York voters send to the Senate a Republican who'll be forced willy-nilly into a minor role under the reactionary Old Guard team that utterly dominates the GOP? . . .

"The undoubted 'party line' assistance that a new Republican senator from New York would give to organizing the Senate under the GOP Old Guard is the second big reason why the rail unions appeal to all New Yorkers to elect Bob Wagner instead."[41]

Since his coming to the Senate, Javits may not have achieved the power he would have liked, but he has undoubtedly been effective. Perchance Bob Wagner would have been more effective, but it is difficult to see how he could have been more liberal. The point is, however, that in choosing a candidate in the '56 race, labor did not look at the Republican contender's credentials or judge on his individual record, but instead opposed him solely because of the nature of the Senate Republican leadership.

(Another aspect of this Senate race which casts doubt on Al Barkan's contention that COPE has supported Javits, is that in 1956 national COPE contributed $5,000 to Wagner, nothing to Jake.)

Each of the Republicans in these instances—Hatfield, Scranton, Romney, Cargo and Javits—are generally considered to be liberal by all relevant standards, and each has demonstrated his desire to work for legislation sponsored by the AFL-CIO; in addition, in each case (with the possible exception of 1966 newcomer Cargo) the liberal GOP candidate was strongly favored to win. Therefore, a COPE endorsement of their candidacies, which obviously would not have required compromising the AFL-CIO legislative requirements, would have yielded double benefits for the committee: 1) a winner, and 2) a demonstration of its purported bi-partisanship. Non-endorsement only served to leave COPE on the losing end and further demonstrated its Democratic loyalties.

In numerous other cases Republican candidates have even been denied the courtesy of a "hearing" before labor groups. "In three campaigns in Utah," says that state's Republican Sen. Wallace Bennett, "I have only been able to get inside a union hall once; I cannot even get inside to present my views." Sen. Bennett's assessment of this development is that "the unions only let their members hear the people they want them to hear."

Bennett's observation would also pertain in important measure to Michigan in 1966. When the state COPE met in September, the three-day convention was dominated by attacks on the Republican Party, particularly on interim Sen. Robert Griffin and the Landrum-Griffin bill.

Griffin had not been invited to the convention (while Gov. Romney and all Democratic candidates had), but he appeared at the convention hall on the meeting's last day anyway, explaining, "I've been attacked from this podium, and I think it only fair that I have a chance to reply to those attacks." A sergeant-at-arms was dispatched to bring COPE chairman Gus Scholle to meet with Griffin.

While waiting for word from Scholle—whom he had called "Soapy" Williams' "political boss"—Griffin was physically shoved from the hall by one delegate, who shouted, "What the hell are you doing here?" He was told by another COPE representative, "I don't think the delegates want to hear both sides," and a third delegate berated the Senator, saying, "I've heard all your views and I'm not interested in hearing them again." Gus Scholle did not want to hear Griffin's views, either, as he refused to leave the podium. "That's too bad," commented Griffin when told of Scholle's misanthropic tendencies toward Republicans. "I think it's very unfortunate that the [COPE] leadership is giving further evidence of one-man, one-boss rule."[42]

A few weeks earlier the Michigan AFL-CIO had refused to invite Romney and Griffin to the traditional Detroit Labor Day rally, at which President Johnson was to be the featured speaker. By this time undaunted by and inured to labor hostility, the GOP duo not only showed up at the rally (where Scholle grudgingly gave them back row corner seats on the presidential platform), but rode in LBJ's motorcade (with Romney in the Johnson car) and showed up at the head of the receiving line for the President at the Detroit airport, forcing the official AFL-CIO greeters back to the third and fourth positions in line.

Boss Scholle's only official comment on these Romney-Griffin activities was to say, "If we had gate crashers at our homes, we'd call the police and have them thrown out. These guys stab us in the back 364 days a year and then want to celebrate Labor Day with us." Romney continued his efforts to get a hearing at any labor gathering he could gain admittance to, whether by "gate crashing" or invitation. And his reception was usually good. Indeed, Scholle was forced in desperation to use the ultimate weapon of a COPE boss, when he said to Romney in reference to the rank-and-file: "I can't let you talk to them, George. You'll snow them."[43]

Republican Rep. George Hansen had a little different experience when he sought to express his position before union members in his Idaho district in 1964. "During the campaign," he recalls, "I was invited by the local AFL-CIO to a meeting where I could present my ideas and platform. This was supposed to be a 'bi-partisan' hearing—where both candidates would be heard and then the unions would decide whom to support. Well, when I got there the hall was decorated with banners, bunting and Democratic propaganda; there were huge pictures of President Johnson and signs saying, 'Vote Democrat.' But most interesting of all is that they had up posters for my opponent and also had his literature spread all over when they hadn't even asked me for any of my literature. I didn't get the impression that this meeting was very bipartisan."

A form of labor anti-Republicanism common in Southern states finds COPE, in races between relatively liberal GOP candidates and Democrats with racist tendencies, making no endorsement at all, rather than go with the Republican. This is what happened in the 1966 Arkansas gubernatorial race where Winthrop Rockefeller, liberal brother of New York's liberal governor, ran against Democrat Jim Johnson, an avowed segregationist running with support from the White Citizens Council. At the AFL-CIO nominating convention in the summer of 1966, there was some sympathy for Rockefeller (and also a good deal for racist Johnson), and "Win" did end up, says one advisor, "getting a great many union votes in November," but still COPE could not bring itself to endorse this liberal GOP candidate despite the nature of his opposition.

The Virginia Democratic primaries of 1966 brought about what the *AFL-CIO News* referred to as "the emergence of a New South," with the defeat of incumbents Rep. Howard Smith and Sen. A. Willis Robertson, two foremost members of what is commonly referred to as the Old Dominion's "Byrd Machine." The lone survivor of the liberal Democrats' purge was the son of the man who helped start the "machine," Sen. Harry Flood Byrd, Jr. COPE had gone all out to defeat all three conservative Democrats, especially Byrd as the symbol of the "machine," and after "young Harry's" primary victory one COPE spokesman complained that "the labor movement, with a little more help, could have made a clean sweep."

Opposition to Byrd apparently had its limits. In the fall campaign, Virginia COPE backed the liberal winners of the Democratic primary purge, but took no position in the race between Byrd and Republican Lawrence Traylor, a "moderate" who had gone on record as opposing right-to-work laws and favoring other measures calculated to win labor support; a nice try, but Virginia COPE, like its kin across the nation, is just not interested in GOP candidates.

However, labor's strategy in these Southern cases is something more than the usual desire to keep down the Republican population in Washington. Here labor is doing nothing less than attempting to remold the national Democratic Party into an even more liberal cast. A first step in an undertaking of this nature, obviously, would be to cleanse the party of its more conservative members, and this COPE has been trying to do since at least 1960—with mixed results.

As has been seen, Walter Reuther had a little to do with getting this operation rolling. This was indicated in 1960 when an unnamed union president was quoted in the *Wall Street Journal* as saying "political realignment" was Reuther's "big pitch" and that the others were going along with him.[44]

One major Reuther contribution to the purge (or "realignment") attempt has been his quadrennial fight for a more liberal civil rights plank in the Democratic presidential platforms. No matter how noble Reuther's ideals may be on the subject, or however justified the positions, the practical political effect of the liberalized planks has been to drive Southerners from the Democrats' ranks.

Another stratagem in the purge has been the "Programs of Progress." These projects, instituted on a state-by-state level by local COPEs, comprise an effort to liberalize Southern Democratic parties at the grass roots level of state government; this then is meant to provide a compatible base from which liberal Democrats can be elected to national office. This is a continuing COPE effort, not widespread or all-encompassing, but selective; COPE can pick and choose the Democratic targets for extinction and slowly build a more liberal, pro-labor national party.

There are some defenders of COPE bi-partisanship who are fond of arguing that labor is generally Democratic because—however much realignment Reuther may think necessary—this is where most of the liberal candidates are to be found. Organized labor, they argue, still has shown a willingness to listen to GOP candidates and give consideration to their endorsement. These defendants usually will point to a spate of press stories (sometimes their own) to buttress their argument and will remind doubters that some labor leaders are "good Republicans."

One of these so-called good Republican unionists is James A. Suffridge, president of the Retail Clerks International Union and a member of the AFL-CIO Executive Board; when Suffridge announced in 1964 that he just couldn't bring himself to support Sen. Goldwater, the press treated it as a major GOP defection. "Retail Clerks' Chief To Vote for Johnson," headlined the *Washington Post* in an article which began:

"James A. Suffridge is that rarity, a labor leader who is a Republican. He was still Republican after a visit to the White House yesterday, but he announced that he would vote for President Johnson in November."

Upon further questioning of the union chief, reporters discovered just how good a Republican Suffridge was: yes, he admitted, he had voted for Jack Kennedy in 1960, and, no, he had never voted for the Republican who had represented his Virginia district in Congress for ten years. He also conceded that a round-the-world trip with the then Vice President Lyndon Johnson, and the friendship that ensued, had not a little bit to do with his 1964 support of LBJ.[45]

Another lightning bolt supposedly revealing new-found GOP support within organized labor, struck the public press in 1966. An issue of the *Machinist,* publication of the IAM, had high praise for 18 Republican officeholders, remarking that "they are Republicans of a new breed, capable of attracting city voters. Their records are worthy of serious consideration."

Forgetting for a moment that the Machinists only mentioned 18 out of the 173 Republicans in the House and Senate at the time, when election time rolled around in 1966 not all of the "new breed" GOPers were as "worthy of serious consideration" as they had been a few months before. Of the six incumbent GOP senators mentioned in the IAM publication, only three were up for election in '66, and none was endorsed by COPE (which represents all unions, including the IAM, in politics), and two of the eleven House members running for re-election were denied COPE backing.

Organized labor's aversion to Republican candidates may grow into outright hostility in the majority of cases, but in some areas of the nation conservative Republican office-seekers have reported a polite reception by local labor. A number of congressional candidates say they have been invited to COPE candidate hearings where they found an attentive, if not sympathetic, audience, and others recall friendly receptions on plant gate handshaking tours. In a 1965 interview, one of the Senate's most conservative members at the time, former Sen. Milward Simpson (R-Wyo.), recalled:

"I have always had a good rapport with labor in my state. When I was a young boy working in the coal mines in Montana, I belonged to a union and I have always felt close to the workingman and always tried to protect his interests.

"When I was governor of Wyoming we passed some of the best labor laws in the country; they are still on the books and have satisfied labor and management. During my campaigns I never had local support, but the local unions have always invited me to their meetings to speak and debate."

The president of the Wisconsin AFL-CIO rejected the "all-or-nothing" principle and told the state's Republican convention in 1966 that labor and the GOP should develop closer ties. "Labor is not looking for 100 percent endorsement of its program," the spokesman explained. "We feel any member of any party who is 100 percent is not giving full consideration to legislation pending before him. He is using it for aggrandizement and further campaigning."[46]

But the Simpson, Wisconsin and other similar incidents are the exceptions to a well-established rule. It is a rule evidenced in labor's treatment of liberal Republicans such as Mark Hatfield, George Romney and Margaret Chase Smith; it is a rule established over thirty years of a solid alliance between organized labor and the Democratic Party. "I think labor will continue to align themselves with the Democratic Party," says Rep. James Hanley (D-N.Y.), "because, over history, the party has been the father of the progressive legislation labor stands for."

And also, Hanley omitted to say, because the party's candidates are willing to go to quite some lengths to placate organized labor in order to secure this support. When asked in 1965 for his comments on COPE's role in practical politics, Vice President Hubert Humphrey offered only the most lofty phrases:

"America faces the finest opportunities and some of the most serious challenges in its history. To do justice in both requires spirited efforts by as many of our citizens as possible.

"Broad participation in the electoral process is essential on the part of America's workingmen and women as well as by all other groups in our society. The AFL-CIO Committee on Political Education has played an outstanding role in assuring such participation. Labor has a vital stake in America; it has the right and the duty to exercise its fullest franchise."

A few short months after this ringing endorsement of the "American Way," the Democratic Vice President of the United States stood before an audience of labor union members and stated: "We Democrats need the labor movement . . . We are not going to let you down."

The difference between the two Humphrey statements, and the two Humphreys who spoke them, is the difference between theory and practice.

In theory the participation of organized labor in politics may appear a desirable expression of concern for government exhibited by an important bloc of American citizens. Of course, the AFL-CIO is politically independent: it does not share offices with any other political organization, it does not entirely support nor is it supported by any such organization, and there are few national leadership or personnel links between it and a political party.

Vice President Humphrey says the Democrats, in practice, "need" labor's political support, and AFL-CIO president Meany responds by giving his personal endorsement (can his Executive Council be far behind?) to Hubert Humphrey a full five months before HHH may or may not receive the same blessing from his own political party; Meany did not even grant the Republicans the courtesy of waiting to see whom they might nominate.

In return for the loyalty of men like Humphrey and the liberal legislation such as that passed in the 89th Congress, organized labor will give full support to Democratic candidates. More important still, it will remain openly hostile to Republicans, no matter the degree of their liberalism.

When the time comes in the COPE campaign to endorse a candidate, and the elaborate machinery for approval and selection is put into motion, all of the effort often seems unnecessary: the result is virtually uniform. The next step is to "sell" the candidate and his platform, and, in the meantime, downgrade the opposition; this procedure requires the mobilization of COPE's most visible enterprise: propaganda.

# PART FOUR: *COPE's Propaganda Arsenal*

When George Meany conceded that the "one handicap" labor faced in the 1966 congressional election campaign was that "we didn't have Goldwater against us," he was offering more than a post-election observation. His words—and the reasoning behind them—reveal just how much organized labor depends on propaganda for its political successes.

Starting at national COPE, labor's political propaganda transmission belt runs all the way to the smallest local in the AFL-CIO. There are brochures, pamphlets and flyers; newspapers published by national, state and local unions; radio broadcasts, television programs, public speakers, private man-to-man conversations—millions upon millions of words, words, words.

The two targets for the propaganda words are the union members and the general public. But, as with its voter registration drives, COPE's first concern is to use its propaganda to convince the workingmen belonging to AFL-CIO affiliates.

Convince them of what? Basically, that the labor leardership and the decisions it makes are right and in the best interests of the rank-and-file. As pertains to COPE and labor's political activities, the effort must be made to indoctrinate the workers in the idea that COPE's approach to politics, its political position and its choice of political candidates, are all correct and to their benefit.

"COPE represents you," Meany tells the rank-and-file in the foreword to *How To Win*. "Its responsibility is to engage union members in the political process that makes democracy work—registration, voting and education on issues."

The gap existing between the moment of registration of a voter and the moment he actually casts his ballot, is more than one of time. During this period the undecided voter must make his decision on candidates and issues, changing from an uncommitted "?" to a definite "X" whose final choice can tip the balance of power in American government.

To help fill this gap COPE carries out the "education" part of its title.

Lest there be any trace of lingering confusion, this is not education of the idealized type parents believe their children receive in the class-rooms. COPE's interpretation of the word could, in fact, be called "anti-education," as it leaves no room for alternatives or questions in present-ing its political positions.

In the midst of the hot 1966 Senate race, one Michigan voter became so irate over COPE's version of education that he wrote the *Detroit News* suggesting the organization change its name to "the Committee on Polluted Elections."

To accomplish the goal of an indoctrinated rank-and-file, COPE must use its propaganda both to build up the labor position and to discredit the opposition. It is a fact of political life, however, that the most expedient means to getting voters on your side is to give them something to vote *against,* rather than attempt to build a positive case.

And this basic tenet has been converted to a working policy at COPE. In presenting the case for workingman support of Democratic candi-dates, labor's propagandists may make passing reference to the positive accomplishments of incumbent liberals (e.g., the "flow of progressive legislation enacted in 1965") and during the 1966 campaign a few editions of the "Memo from COPE" were devoted entirely to specific issues, such as "Education—A Bonanza." But these are, judging by COPE's own words, secondary issues.

When the AFL-CIO held its biannual convention in San Francisco in early December 1965, a resolution was passed calling on union mem-bers to "render all assistance and support to the policies and programs of COPE." But this resolution was not justified at the convention by *first* mentioning the records of the men it wanted elected. As COPE itself reported the resolution's passage:

"Warning against the resurgent political strength of right-wing and conservative forces, the AFL-CIO convention urged all unions and union members to total effort in behalf of liberals in the 1966 congres-sional elections."[47]

By not first mentioning  the liberals' qualifications, issues or accom-plishments, COPE demonstrated in black-and-white the negative nature of labor's approach to politics. Rather than an honest debate on the merits of two opposing candidates, COPE prefers to label its adversary a captive of "right wing" elements, and in place of an honest debate on issues, COPE will opt for a free-swinging attack on "extremist tactics."

It is, after all, much easier and far more expedient for the propa-gandist to build an image of his opponent as evil, and continually rein-force this image through distortion and half-truth, than it is to test his ideas against his opponent's in the light of public debate.

In the early days of the labor movement, its propagandists seized on the issue of "class struggle" and proceeded to dump their invective on the "ruling class," the "elite," and most often, on Big Business and the "robber barons" who controlled the country's wealth. The intensity of this single-minded assault persisted and had such an impact on the minds of the workers that in 1950 a study group from Wayne State University found:

". . . that somewhat more than half of these [United Auto Workers] union members definitely view the labor union as representing their broad political interests . . . and they want the unions to have greater influence on government. Most of the members of this majority group see business (and newspapers) as offering political leadership that is not to be followed, and they want to see the political influence of business curtailed. The evidence suggests that most of these people see the political world in terms of opposed goals and group interests as between organized labor and business."[48]

And appeals to the mentality here described are still to be found in labor propaganda. "One of the major objectives of the Big Business drive for control of State and Federal governments," says one COPE publication, "is to pass legislation to cripple and shackle Unions so that they can no longer effectively bargain for wages, hours, working conditions and fringe benefits. The Enemies of Labor reason that when Unions are so chained down by anti-labor laws that it becomes impossible to successfully bargain for the workers, then the Unions will cease to exist."[49]

However, in these days of corporate direction, profit-sharing and Henry Ford endorsements of Lyndon B. Johnson, the old business vs. labor battlelines have become somewhat blurred and labor's propagandists have had to create a new bugaboo, "right wing extremists." And once more the labor powers forego appeals to the judgment or common sense of the workingman in favor of mouthing emotion-laden slogans.

The attack on Big Business has by no means been halted, but it has been given a new twist: "Economically," says a COPE anti-rightist pamphlet, "the right wing has a powerful base in big industry and big finance. Its leadership interlocks substantially with leadership of the National Association of Manufacturers and U.S. Chamber of Commerce."[50] The assault on business has become but a part of the general war on the right wing, the vogue among labor propagandists.

In December, 1961, two of America's most powerful labor union leaders strode into the office of the Attorney General of the United States and laid on his desk a detailed, 15-page memorandum outlining how the U.S. government could and should use all its power and influence to fight the growth of the "radical right." "What are needed," said the memorandum, "are deliberate Administration policies and programs to contain the radical right from further expansion . . ."

The document then went on to list five possible offensives the Administration could take against the "radical right": 1) have the Defense Department (or Senate Armed Services Subcommittee) conduct investigations of "radical right Generals and Admirals"; 2) have the Attorney General list radical right groups on his list of subversive organizations; 3) stop the "flow of big money to the radical right" through investigations of certain groups' tax-exempt status by the Internal Revenue Service, and radio programs' free air time by the Federal Communications Commission; 4) have the federal government call a conference of states in which the paramilitary group, the Minutemen, are active "to see what action could be taken under state laws"; and 5) have the domestic Communist problem "put in proper perspective for the American people, thus exposing the basic fallacy of the radical right."

But this should not be solely a government operation, the memorandum argued. Organized labor, together with other private agencies, "must carry the prime burden in this struggle." "Indeed," it added, "in the long run the extent of participation by private agencies in this struggle is more likely to determine its outcome than anything the Government can do."

Since the day this paper was dropped on the desk of Attorney General Robert Kennedy by Walter Reuther and his brother Victor, international vice-president of the UAW, organized labor has led a virtual crusade against any political force which could remotely be classified as "right wing." Labor has done more than share the "prime burden" in the Reuthers' "struggle." Its efforts have far overshadowed anything done by other organizations, private or federal.

(The Reuther Memorandum most assuredly was well received in the upper echelons of the Kennedy Administration, and the IRS and FCC especially were put on the warpath against "right wing" groups, but their legal grounds were so shaky and results so minimal that the attack quickly abated. Perhaps the most significant victory of the anti-right campaign was the discontinuation of anti-Communist training in the armed services.)

COPE's first task in the struggle was to pinpoint the right-wing "evil" and get the word to the rank-and-file. It did this through articles in its regular publication, "Memo from COPE," and through special pamphlets, such as "The Target is You."

"A new and ominous challenge confronts American trade unions and threatens their security," this hatchet-work began. "Everywhere the forces of the right wing are churning distrust of free democratic institutions, unions among them." There followed an attack on the familiar "right wing" organizations (Birch Society, Manion Forum), individuals (the Rev. Billy James Hargis, Dr. Fred Schwarz), and business groups such as "the grand-daddy of conservatism, the National Association of Manufacturers," and "its Siamese twin of reaction, the U.S. Chamber of Commerce."

After describing the evil from which "no community escapes," COPE admonished the rank-and-file to "begin now in your community to establish a coordinating committee to combat the right wing . . . The challenge has been hurled at us by men and organizations determined to wreck the trade union movement. It can be ignored only at our own risk."

The most popular tactic employed by COPE in its early anti-right propaganda was the same strategy liberals a decade before had accused Sen. Joseph McCarthy of practicing: guilt by association. In a 1964 filmstrip called "The Extremists"[51] (available to any union member for $3.00), COPE executes this tactic more effectively than "Tailgunner Joe" ever managed. In its film, COPE describes what it calls "the building that houses extremism": in the cellar are shown the Nazi Party and segregationist National States Rights Party; on the main floors are the Birch Society, Manion Forum, Life Line, Dan Smoot Report, the Rev. Billy James Hargis, and the Rev. Carl McIntyre; and in the penthouse are the widely respected publications, *National Review* and *Human Events*. Q.E.D.

The ultimate absurdity of this guilt by association tactic was shown in a chart appearing in the September 9, 1963, COPE "Memo," a diagram so ludicrous that it is difficult to describe. The chart depicts the links between the John Birch Society and "other rightist groups" in the following manner: listed in the middle column are individuals who have been, however remotely, connected with the JBS or any of its by-activities; on the left is a list of "rightist organizations," including respected organizations as, for example, the Committee of One Million Against Admission of Red China to the U.N. (which has several liberal Democrats among its sponsors) together with such disreputables as Conde McGinley's anti-Semitic rag, *Common Sense;* and the column on the right lists several businesses, colleges, professional groups and government agencies all tied to the "right wing" conspiracy, including such extremist strongholds as Harvard University and the State Department.

COPE then proceeds to link everyone and everything together in a maze of black lines. After completing this enterprise, COPE's line-drawers stood back to contemplate their creation and sadly concluded that "it is impossible to trace all the lines on the chart." One conservative editorialist took a look at COPE's guilt-by-association effort and concluded that the chart "reveals less about the far right than it does about the people at COPE."

With its subject defined and the black lines drawn, COPE had to concentrate its attack in a single political direction. And the biggest target it could find was GOP presidential nominee, Sen. Barry Goldwater, the first public figure to feel the full wrath of COPE's anti-rightist crusade. The AFL-CIO General Board launched the Goldwater assault when it endorsed President Johnson in September, 1964, saying the election of the Republican standard-bearer would "heighten the risk of an atomic holocaust" and that his domestic program would be "an invitation to depression and economic disaster." And individual union bosses soon took up the cry, with the then president of the United Steelworkers, David McDonald, telling his union's convention:

"I think [ Goldwater] actually despises the poor people of our country. So I tell you quite frankly, if you want to destroy our great union all you need to do is support Goldwater for President. And if you want to be unemployed and live in filth and degradation go out and support Goldwater."[52]

For its part COPE was, if anything, even more harsh on the Arizona Republican than the union heads. One COPE project was a series of small pamphlets each dedicated to one "issue" in the presidential campaign; the piece in this series on the issue of "Peace" featured a Goldwater caricature on the cover, dressed in armor and brandishing swords, and inside the reader was asked: "How about you? War . . . or peace? Goldwater . . . or Johnson?"

A brochure aimed specifically at the workingman, this one depicting a cowboy-type Goldwater sticking up a cowering figure labeled "Labor," asserted, "Trade unions are at the crossroads. One turn leads to destruction. It is marked Barry Goldwater."

The net effect of the anti-Goldwater smear campaign among the rank-and-file was profound. Researching for an article in *Harper's* magazine, noted labor writer Herbert Harris found at the grass roots that "COPE has been mounting an ideological campaign unprecedented in sweep and verve," and that the workingmen were responding. "You know," said one Connecticut labor leader in an open distortion of one of the senator's statements, "that Goldwater wants to give the decision to use nuclear weapons to commanders in the field."[53]

And a short time later, a rubber worker told Harris: "At the lunch break, when we get talking about the election, the thing that keeps coming up most often is that Goldwater is the most likely to get us into war." A machinist nearby concurred, saying, "When Goldwater said he wants the generals in the field to signal when to drop the bomb, he lost it right there."

COPE also made strong use of its Voting Records, which in 1964 showed Goldwater had supposedly voted against the interests of labor ("wrong") on 53 issues since coming to the Senate in 1952. Basing himself on his grass roots research, writer Harris described how COPE leaders "break these [votes] down into simple colloquial specifics." "Would you," a local COPE leader asked a gathering of rank-and-filers, "vote for a man who says $1.25 an hour is too much for you to earn," and "who wouldn't let the poor blind and crippled have another four bucks a month," and, getting down to the real "gut" issues, "would you vote for a guy who would take your union away from you and let management push you around in the old 'take it or leave it' way?"

To what extent the anti-Goldwater assault was responsible for Lyndon Johnson's racking up an estimated 70 percent of the union vote is unknown, but, as this was the main thrust of COPE's '64 campaign, undoubtedly was a major factor in the LBJ sweep; after all, Johnson himself acknowledged the influence of the COPE effort when he stated after the election that "no group worked harder for a Democratic victory" than did labor.

The AFL-CIO certainly did deserve a great deal of credit for the defeat of Goldwater and the "right wingers" it claimed constituted his base of support. Soon after the election, however, the COPE propagandists began to worry that the Johnson victory might have been too overwhelming and that the rank-and-file might be led to believe the "extremist enemy" slain. The "right wing" had proved to be too productive a target for COPE to forsake it after the '64 elections, and immediate steps were taken to warn the membership that the "menace" was still lurking in every dark corner. COPE had to demonstrate that the so-called extremists were 1) still active, and 2) still active in the Republican Party.

"In 1964, the right-wingers took a shellacking at the polls," admitted a COPE pamphlet published in early 1965. "Their presidential candidate, Senator Goldwater, was routed." And then came COPE's clincher: "But out of their crushing 1964 defeat, the extremists—John Birchers and others—learned a valuable lesson. They learned that sound and fury from a national platform are no substitute for planning and organization at the ward and precinct level. They've been planning and organizing ever since. . . . If the right wing is to be stopped at the polls—if we are to keep Congress in liberal hands—YOU will have to help."[54]

The war was on again.

The belaboring of the right wing continued and the range of targets was broadened. Not only were the old, familiar standby rightist bugaboos—the Birchers, H.L. Hunt, *et al.*—objects of the labor broadside, but new groups, publications and individuals were mixed into the "rightist" stew.

Sen. Goldwater's Free Society Association, for example, was labeled in one COPE "Memo" as a group organized "to unify the rightist elements that formed the core of Goldwater support in 1964," and COPE warned in ominous tones that a potential "long-range purpose" of the FSA was to "pick the GOP presidential nominee in 1968." (A difficult objective, in that FSA is an issue study group with no organization other than its tiny Washington staff.)

Another labor publication alerted its readers that the right-wing "message is still ignorance and a rejection of our basic democratic values, but the package has been done up in a new label, many times with good taste and appeal." And it found this subversive appeal all around:

"Television programs present well-scrubbed young people singing; slick magazines offer good writing and shun Eisenhower-was-a-Communist idiocies, while book clubs aim at the conservative businessman and suburbanite with brochures that would not shame the Book-of-the-Month Club."[55]

One unlikely group to feel the wrath of labor's propaganda artists in 1966 was Moral Re-Armament, a worldwide youth organization which promotes morality, nationalism and respect for law through films, plays and touring companies of musicians and singers.

Two consecutive '66 issues of *Steel Labor,* organ of the United Steelworkers, devoted considerable space and effort to attacking MRA. The August, 1966, issue used one-third page in "exposing" the MRA-televised musical program, "Up With People," as an effort of the "anti-union right wing [to] branch out into TV." And an editorial in the following issue referred to MRA as "death warmed over" and spoke of the organization's "utter dishonesty, not to speak of its dubious claim to 'moral revolution.' " ("Up With People" does not even mention unions; what seems to have upset *Steel Labor* is the MRA insistence that people stand on their own two feet and that there be a fair day's work for a fair day's wage.)

But the purpose of COPE's propaganda is political. It can reveal, expose and denounce as many extremists as it wants to, and it all will be quite futile if some political dividend is not achieved. In 1964 COPE's dividend came in the form of a crushing Goldwater defeat, and in the escalated war on the right wing prior to the 1966 congressional elections the dividend-goal was defeat for *all* Republican Party candidates.

COPE and its labor political allies go after conservative Democrats too, since their basic target is conservatism wherever it may exist; but in bringing this attack into the realm of practical politics where it could pay off in a labor-oriented Congress, the propagandists must attach the "extremists" to one particular party.

Conservative Democrats—especially Southerners—get their share of abuse from organized labor, but in nowhere near the same intensity as that given the Republican Party, which is portrayed by COPE as the home-sweet-home for the various "extremist" elements. The intention of labor's propagandists following the Goldwater defeat was to convince the rank-and-file once and for all that the Arizona senator was but one "GOP rightist" and that, in fact, the entire Republican Party, from coast to coast, was rife with right-wingers.

The key to the '66 version of this strategy was the headline on the "Memo From COPE" for July 25, 1966, proclaiming, "Primary Wins Show Rightists Still Hold GOP." The first paragraph of the accompanying article trumpeted this theme:

"It's a comeback year for Goldwater Republicans in GOP primaries —so much so that it suggests the all-out shellacking right-wingers took in 1964 failed to shake their grip on party organizations in most areas."

All the evidence COPE offered of this "grip" was the successful effort of nine conservative Republican congressmen, defeated in 1964, in gaining the nomination for a 1966 race. Viewed objectively, these nine primary victories would not seem to offer proof of a nationwide "rightist hold" on the Republican Party, but this was the tune COPE had chosen to play for '66 and it was playing it full blast.

Other labor publications followed COPE's lead and launched their own attacks on alleged dominance of the GOP by "extremists." "GOP Primary Results Show Resurgence of Goldwater Wing," echoed the *AFL-CIO News,* warning its millions of readers that "the ultra-right-wing Goldwaterites are far from losing their grip on the Republican Party on the basis of primary elections to date. . . . The Goldwater conservatives have no intention of relinquishing control of the Republican Party without a fight."

And *Steel Labor* thus quoted Steelworkers president I.W. Abel, one of labor's truly wild men on the subject of conservatism, trumpeting to the union's '66 convention:

"The enemies of democracy who would stifle your freedom, shackle you with dictatorship and launch an orgy of national hate are still very much alive and kicking.

"The disciples of John Birch and American fascism are moving ahead with a carefully calculated program to delude the American public and to seize control of our nation. In several senatorial and congressional races that take place next November this reactionary element may very well hold the balance of power."[56]

If COPE's anti-right campaign was not as fanatical as Abel's utterances, it was more diverse. It openly distorted important issues, ignored Democrats, and freely waved aside the facts, in its drive to make the "extremists" and the Republican Party one and the same in the minds of the rank-and-file.

"Extremists Cement Grip on Dixie GOP," screamed one headline on a "Memo From COPE." "Right-wing Republicans, many of them John Birch Society members, have tightened their grip on the GOP in the South," the story read, and it went on to paraphrase a *Los Angeles Times* survey purporting to show that "along with Birch Society support and participation is support and participation by out-and-out racist groups—notably in Mississippi, where the Ku Klux Klan and White Citizens Councils have been attracted by the surging Southern GOP."[57] (Unreported by COPE: Mississippi's only Republican candidate worth mentioning, former Rep. Prentiss Walker, a self-acknowledged racist, received virtually no support from national GOP organizations; the one candidate in the South in 1966 who *did* have open White Citizens Councils support was Arkansas gubernatorial hopeful Jim Johnson, a Democrat. COPE responded to this extremist challenge by refusing to endorse his liberal Republican opponent, Winthrop Rockefeller.)

Another COPE "news" item sought to prove that "an overwhelming majority of Republicans in the U.S. House are still clinging to the Goldwater line despite the American voters' crushing rejection of it in 1964." The article listed the GOP congressional votes opposing such measures as creation of the power-grabbing Department of Urban Affairs and the repeal of 14(b) (opposed by over 50 percent of the American public) as evidence of a "rigidly reactionary" Republican congressional delegation.[58]

What is interesting about this particular COPE anti-Republican item is that, while the votes in 1964 may have rejected the "Goldwater line," the same voters obviously did *not* reject the "reactionary" congressmen cited in this article. As these representatives presumably ran in '64 on the same conservative principles later evidenced in these votes, COPE apparently expects a congressman to run on one set of principles and vote on another.

To implant the idea in the minds of the rank-and-file that the GOP is a bastion of anti-labor power, COPE propagandists placed the blame for defeat of 14(b) repeal and the drive for constitutional amendments on reapportionment and school prayer almost exclusively on the shoulders of the familiar "rightist-Republican coalition."

"Rightists Urge Last Push to Save 14b," was a headline in one COPE "Memo," listing Senators Strom Thurmond (R-S.C.) and Carl Curtis (R-Neb.) as two "reactionary" senators who were campaigning to defeat the labor-supported repeal bill. Unmentioned in COPE's stories were such supposedly outstanding liberal congressmen as Sen. George

McGovern (D-S.D.) and Rep. Charles Weltner (D-Ga.), who also voted against labor's wishes on repeal.[59]

Still another "Memo From COPE" reported the organization of a Committee for Government of the People, describing it as a "front group for the nationwide drive behind the Dirksen amendment to kill the Supreme Court one-man, one-vote rule." This item, headlined "Rightists Aid Dirksen Drive to Kill 1-and-1," sifted out four members of this committee whom COPE claimed had ties to "rightist organizations," including the Birch Society, Manion Forum and Young Americans for Freedom.[60]

Again COPE's attack was typical for what it failed to tell the rank-and-filers. Unmentioned were liberals such as Senators Frank Church (D-Idaho), Hugh Scott (R-Pa.) and Rep. B.F. Sisk (D-Calif.), all of whom had well over a 50 percent COPE rating, and all of whom were national co-chairmen of this so-called "rightist" committee.

In 1966, organized labor devised an entirely new wrinkle in the propaganda attack on right-wingers, and reached new depths of personal abuse. Sensing a negative reaction—the so-called "white backlash" —among the American electorate, including the union rank-and-file to the violent and disruptive civil rights demonstrations, the labor propagandists leaped at every opportunity to label a candidate who spoke out against these demonstrations as a "racist."

The most extreme use of this tactic was found in a letter sent to all members of the United Steelworkers of America on Oct. 21, 1966, signed by the hot-headed president of that union, I.W. Abel, and two other top officers.

"Reports reaching us," read the inflammatory epistle, "show that many of our good union members have deserted labor's proven friends and embraced the candidacies of sworn enemies of the union. It happened in Maryland, Louisiana and Georgia. It could happen in California and Illinois and elsewhere.

"What has prompted good, reliable union men and women to do this? Apparently they have permitted their justifiable concern over recent racial rioting to affect their better judgment in choosing candidates. . . .

"We should be short-sighted indeed if we did not recognize that many of the traditional enemies of labor—from the far left and the far right— are today actively agitating and exploiting the unrest that exists among Negroes and other minority groups.

"These forces are not trying to solve our racial problems; they are trying to magnify them. They oppose men like Governor Brown in California and Senator Douglas of Illinois because they don't want solutions. They want turmoil and hope to create it by arousing Negro against white, and white against Negro.

"If our members fall for this engineered confusion and allow the extremists to trick them into voting like the Birchers or Communists would like them to vote, they will only help defeat your friends and allies in Congress on November 8."

Put more simply, the Steelworkers' leadership was saying that either you vote for the union-backed candidate or else you are a racist, or, perhaps, a "Bircher" or a Communist. Senator Goldwater, in a post-election comment, referred to this letter as being itself racist.

Also note that the letter mentions no "racist" candidate by name, alluding only to an evil "they" who were opposing Democrats Brown and Douglas. Obviously, this tactic is much more effective than directly challenging the platforms of Ronald Reagan and Charles Percy. (In the Steelworkers' lexicon, Dr. Martin Luther King should also have qualified as a "racist," since in 1967 he said that Sen. Percy—Douglas' opponent —was the only Republican he could then support for the presidency.)

The Steelworkers' attack was quickly seconded by the eager propagandists at COPE. "Your enemies are trying to throw dust in your eyes," they wrote in the bi-weekly "Memo" two weeks before the election. "Extremists, hate-peddlers and the fear-ridden are trying to blind you to the real issues of the 1966 political campaign. They're counting on something called 'backlash.'

"They're trying to tell you the issue is hate, or fear, or prejudice, or property, or who shares your neighborhood. . . .

"Don't be blinded by the dust-throwers of prejudice. Don't risk your progress and your welfare. Vote for candidates who know the real issues and who have proved, when the chips are down, they're your friends."[61]

In another part of the same "Memo" the reader is asked, "Who really is behind the race hate injected into the 1966 campaign?" Quickly the answer is supplied and the final twist given: "It's all the groups ranged against you and your welfare and your union—the John Birch Society and other extremists, the racists, the 'right-to-workers' and their allies. . . .

"It's happened before. Real issues have been hidden in smokescreens of lies and propaganda. . . . It happened only 30 years ago in Germany."

Such is the demagogic reasoning of COPE's propagandists: a supporter of right-to-work laws is a racist or maybe a neo-Nazi; and they're all behind the Republican Party.

As if its anti-right, anti-Republican campaign were not effective enough, 1966 brought new evidence of labor's increasing propaganda ties with the Democratic Party. Four days before Election Day 1966, the United Auto Workers took out an almost full-page advertisement in several metropolitan newspapers[62] endorsing the Democratic Party *in toto:*

"America has moved forward to unparalleled prosperity. Month after month after month since Jan. 20, 1961—the day John F. Kennedy took the oath of office—the economy has continued to expand to record-breaking levels.

"Despite this amazing performance, there are those who today urge a return to the Republican policies in effect *before* Jan. 20, 1961."

The advertisement proceeded to present a purported comparison of the Eisenhower and Kennedy-Johnson Administrations, ending its plea for support of the Democrats by saying:

"The Republican Administration gave America economic stagnation, high unemployment and serious inflation.

"Under the Democratic administrations, America has enjoyed greater prosperity, uninterrupted economic expansion, vastly improved living standards, lower unemployment, more jobs and far less inflation."

(This advertisement, paid for by general union funds, would appear to be in direct violation of the Federal Corrupt Practices Act, which forbids any business corporation or labor union from directly supporting a political party with money from its treasury. While the ad did conclude by admonishing, "Vote your conscience, but be sure to vote," this feigned impartiality could hardly negate the direct support of the entire Democratic Party evident everywhere else in the text.)

With the bulk of COPE's 1966 anti-right campaign centered on the Republican Party, it was felt necessary to take it one step further and train the propaganda guns on the GOP's most prominent individual candidates. Perhaps, following the '66 elections, George Meany would be able to lament the absence of a Goldwater-type GOP leader, but COPE tried its best to create one: in the committee's eyes, Ronald Reagan was the Barry Goldwater of 1966.

The attack on the former movie actor began even before he declared his candidacy for the California governorship and swelled as his campaign progressed. Hardly an issue of the "Memo From COPE" came off the presses without at least one derogatory reference to the Golden State Republican: the May 17, 1965, issue quoted a California Democrat referring to Reagan as the "darling of the right wing"; the June 28, 1965, "Memo" labeled him as a "right-wing TV-movie actor"; the Oct. 4, 1965, issue condemned Reagan for failing to disavow support of Birch Society members; the May 30, 1966, issue spoke of Reagan as a "right-winger and ardent Goldwaterite."

As Reagan had neither the national position nor prominence of a Goldwater, COPE could not very well point to him as an example of "extremist" control of the nationwide Republican structure, so it did the next best thing: Reagan's GOP primary victory, said the June 13, 1966, "Memo," "provided strong evidence that the right wing still holds the reins in the California GOP." This statement must have come as something of a striking revelation to the state's liberal Republican Senator, Tom Kuchel, and to the state GOP chairman at the time, moderate Dr. Gaylord Parkinson.

The anti-Reagan smear campaign culminated (but did not end) in the July 11, 1966, issue of COPE's "Memo," every page of which was devoted to attacking the candidate, his position and his alleged supporters. The four-page diatribe, not-too-subtly headlined "How Reagan Rode Right-Wing Issues to Political Stardom" sought to link Reagan with every "extremist" element imaginable, including the minuscule and impotent National Indignation Convention, the controversial Rev. Billy James Hargis, and, most amazing of all, the notorious anti-Semite Gerald L.K. Smith and his publication, *The Cross and the Flag.*

It seems Smith chose to reprint a Reagan speech, which was part of the public record and could have been reprinted by *anyone.* COPE attempted to link the two by saying, "That Ronald Reagan is singing the songs of the right wing is evident from the way the extremist press and spokesmen pick up his material." (Not a very novel extremist technique, as witness the way the Communist press quickly reprints every anti-Vietnam utterance by such liberals as Senators Frank Church, Ernest Gruening, and George McGovern; are these men—all COPE-backed— "singing the songs" of the Communists?)

After making this statement, COPE pretended to fairness by admitting that Reagan "cannot be held responsible for the way [Smith] uses his words." But then COPE immediately canceled this out by turning around to say "but if they weren't the right words the extremists wouldn't use them."

Another example of COPE's efforts to tie Reagan with those it has already identified as "extremists" is an item in which the committee propagandists point to Reagan's referring to "one of the foremost authorities on communism in the world today." As the "Memo From COPE" notes, Reagan did not identify his "authority" in this particular speech. But just so the union rank-and-file would not wonder too long over who it could be, the COPE analysts arbitrarily and with no foundation in fact claim that Reagan "could be quoting Fred Schwarz [head of the Christian Anti-Communism Crusade] or Birch Society leader Robert Welch . . ." COPE has, of course, constantly attacked both men as "right-wing extremists."

COPE then warns its California membership of a "high-powered, high-priced public relations effort to wrap Reagan in moderation," citing as one proof that "Ronald Reagan has tried to keep Barry Goldwater out of the California gubernatorial campaign . . . [and] tried to shed his image of Goldwaterism." COPE could not be expected to note that

Reagan had decided to accept no campaign assistance from outside the state, and had also turned down speaking offers from former President Eisenhower and former Vice President Nixon.

COPE's "Get-Reagan" efforts were backed to the hilt by other national labor organizations and California AFL-CIO outlets. The Steelworkers' mouthpiece *Steel Labor,* never one to remain stuck in the sand when an "extremist" mirage appears, claimed in September, 1966, that the California State Republican convention "gave actor Ronnie Reagan what he wanted—a platform which will wage a vote drive on white backlash appeal and zero in on what Reagan calls the 'sultans of labor.' The convention's action underscored the charges of many political observers on the West Coast in recent months that Birchers had accomplished a take-over of the California GOP."

The executive secretary of the California AFL-CIO, Thomas L. Pitts, dreamed up a tale—widely repeated before union audiences—that Reagan had met with representatives of the National Association of Manufacturers and "plotted an extremist takeover of California." Reagan's comment was that the Pitts statement "cannot be described as inaccurate—it is a lie."[63]

Pitts' state AFL-CIO council also published a slick eight-page newspaper supplement portraying incumbent Governor Pat Brown as something approaching a saint ("A government that acts—a governor that cares") and criticized Reagan on such vital points as having been "supported by many contributors to the 'right-to-work' campaign in 1958" and having been "a former employe of—and spokesman for—General Electric, a consistent and open antagonist of collective bargaining" (and a company which has had few labor disputes and pays its workers better than the average unionized electrical plants).

Ronald Reagan may have been the chief target of labor's propagandists in 1966, but they did not forget other Republican candidates they felt merited the "right-wing" billing. The Michigan gubernatorial and senatorial races, as has been seen, were awash with heated labor propaganda, with George Romney being labeled "St. George" who was "owned lock, stock and barrel by big business," and Robert Griffin called, among other things, an "economic illiterate."

COPE's effort to elect "Soapy" Williams to the Senate by smearing his opponents began during his primary campaign against Detroit Mayor Jerry Cavanagh. Two days before the voting, Michigan COPE, under the direction of an Auto Workers official, published and had widely distributed a leaflet charging Cavanagh with supporting "the darling of the anti-Negro segregationists," former Rep. Harold M. Ryan. Ryan was attempting a political comeback in a Detroit district and a handful of Cavanagh supporters had endorsed him, printing both names together on a "slate card." But Cavanagh himself had taken no position in the Ryan campaign and sought to have a Circuit Court judge prohibit distribution of the COPE leaflet. The judge admitted that the labor propaganda piece was "an out-and-out appeal to racism," but ruled it was beyond his jurisdiction to prevent its distribution. Finally, candidate Williams himself was forced to condemn COPE's racism by repudiating "the contents of the leaflet as an appeal to prejudice." COPE could afford such reprimands, as its propaganda had done its dirty work and Williams won the primary.[64]

On the individual union level, the United Auto Workers was, as usual, by far the most active labor organization in Michigan in 1966. A special "Labor Slate for Progress" tabloid distributed by the UAW before the primary election even found a way to link Gov. Romney with Barry Goldwater, citing the Governor's endorsement of Ronald Reagan's candidacy ("Goldwater Link Looms In Michigan"). The tabloid took up the rest of its space to support Democratic candidates from governor down to circuit judges. A pre-election issue of the UAW's *Solidarity*[65] newspaper pictured Williams as "a giant of a public servant who'll be a giant of a senator" and gubernatorial candidate Zolton Ferency as a man whose "ideas excite those who listen. His energy sparks new vigor in his volunteer workers. His election would return the state house to the people." (Ferency, a modest and humorously self-depreciating man, probably doubted such a flowery tribute himself; one of his favorite lines during the campaign was to complain that voters were always asking Democrats, "What is a Zolton Ferency?")

Another campaign in which the Auto Workers was a hard-driving propaganda force was the Illinois Senate race featuring incumbent Paul Douglas and liberal Republican Charles Percy; *Solidarity* ran a full-page paean to Douglas, describing him as "the Giant from Illinois . . . a vigorous giant of a man," and the UAW contributed station wagons to the Douglas forces for use in travel and for broadcasting propaganda over portable loudspeakers.

The labor organization which caused the biggest stir with its propaganda in the Illinois race, however, was the Machinists union, which published and distributed what Sen. Percy later characterized as "vicious, unscrupulous and fallacious material, material which they knew full well was false and fallacious . . ." The objects of Percy's wrath were two propaganda items labor had used in his 1964 gubernatorial campaign, which he lost to incumbent Otto Kerner; the items having proved effective once, the Machinists' propagandists obviously saw no need to change the formula and pulled the "vicious, unscrupulous and fallacious" material out of the files for 1966.

One item printed by the Machinists, and made available to all other labor groups, was a handbill asking the poignant question: "Will Percy export your job?" When Percy was president of the Bell & Howell photographic equipment manufacturing company, the handbill charged, he had reduced the company's jobs available in Illinois by opening overseas branches. "An absolute falsehood," was Percy's comment on the propaganda, and he released employment figures from Bell & Howell to "show a steady and sharper increase" in Illinois jobs *after* overseas expansion.[66]

The other piece of anti-Percy labor literature in question wastes no time with sophisticated employment statistics and plays upon one of the union man's pet peeves—a man who crosses a picket line. It also demonstrates to what lengths labor will go to portray the most liberal Republicans as "anti-union reactionaries." This handbill consists of little more than a photograph, taken in 1964, apparently showing Percy crossing a picket line, smiling and shaking hands with one of the pickets.

The alleged "strike" depicted was actually one involving radio-television page boys in New York City and the picket line Percy was shown crossing had been thrown around a Chicago television station where the Republican candidate was scheduled to appear. When first confronted with the photograph, Percy pointed out that it was a New York labor affair, not Chicago's. And, he added, inside the station were union television technical and engineering crews who had obviously crossed the "picket line" too. Said a Chicago *Sun-Times* columnist in commenting on "this reprehensible tactic": "It appeared that the line was there only for Percy, its purpose being to frame him into an incriminating picture to support charges he is 'anti-union'. . . ."[67]

What one nationally syndicated column called the "absolute low" in labor propaganda during the 1966 campaign was an editorial in *The Labor Union*,[68] official organ of the Dayton, Ohio, Building and Construction Trades Council, which concerned the tight congressional race between incumbent Democrat Rodney Love and State Sen. Charles Whalen. The controversial editorial, written by Council head Mike Liskany, was titled "Inflation, Street Riots, Elections?" and constituted an open bid for "white backlash" support of COPE-backed Rep. Love. The editorial first attempted to link Republican Whalen with a local Negro activist, W. S. McIntosh, running as an Independent:

"This writer [i.e. Liskany] has not seen any sign of identification of Candidate Whalen to the Republican Party (or at least the proposed candidate of the Republican Party) identifying his candidacy with the Republican Party. He may be an Independent!

"We have no objection to this, or to any Independent candidate.

However, his purported forays into the West Side with the Independent candidate, W. S. McIntosh, if true, ought to identify him as such."

Although Whalen's candidacy had absolutely no relationship with that of Independent McIntosh, the labor editorialist went on to couple both men through their mutual support of open-housing legislation, an issue Love had not endorsed:

"We have reports that Mr. Whalen purports to be an advocate of Fair Housing along with the Independent candidate McIntosh, who also claims to support this stand. We have no quarrel with this. I simply want to put up to Labor people and the entire community, the voting record in the General Assembly pertaining to Fair Housing, or any other record, and ask that they compare the record of [Whalen and Love]."

Thus, while national COPE was condemning those who opposed open housing legislation as something akin to neo-Fascists, this local labor leader was slyly bidding for anti-Negro votes; moreover, the Ohio labor figure was not challenging open housing on valid legal grounds, as did many of those COPE attacked, but was making a purely racist appeal.

One other example of labor propaganda activity on a congressional level in 1966 demonstrates the continued use (and misuse) of the right-to-work issue. In 1958 the voters of Ohio had rejected a state right-to-work law and most candidates have subsequently treated it as a dead issue as far as the state was concerned. Republican congressional candidate Clarence Miller, opposing incumbent Walter Moeller in Ohio's 10th District, stated in his campaign that he stood by the state voters' decision of '58, but that he would not vote to repeal Section 14(b) in Congress because other states should be able to make their own decisions on these laws.

Labor officials of the 10th District took this simple statement, gave it a good anti-GOP twist, and came up with a full-page advertisement headed: "Do You Favor 'Right-To-Work' Laws? The Republican Candidate for Congress Does." And in the ad's text they carried on the attack, claiming "the Republican candidate for Congress CONTINUES TO SUPPORT legislation which threatens the very existence of labor organizations."[69] The distortion had some effect apparently, even though Republican Miller won. He later commented, "I suspect this [advertisement] did cost us some votes with the laboring element in the District, as we did anticipate doing better in the industrial areas than we did."[70]

As indicated in these last two campaign instances, and others already noted, COPE's propaganda is frequently supplemented by numerous other labor publications. These range from a grass roots newspaper such as Dayton's *The Labor Union,* to the United Auto Workers' *Solidarity.*

In all there are some 225 labor periodicals published regularly in the United States—organs of local and national unions, state labor councils, trade and industrial groups, and others—and every one of them devotes considerable space to political propaganda.

An excellent, thorough study of the political content of union publications was performed by the Bureau of Industrial Relations at the University of Michigan in 1960.[71] This investigation examined 43 "key union periodicals representing major United States and Canadian industry" over the first eight months of 1960 to gauge the percentage of space occupied by clearly political matters (e.g., personalities, issues, elections, etc.).

The result of the study showed that the *average* political content of the 43 publications was 25.84 percent of the total column inches of copy space. (Note that although this was a presidential election year with a high yield of political news, the publications were studied up through August, 1960—before the campaigns began in earnest.) Among other findings by the University of Michigan study:

* "Despite attempts by nearly all of the union newspaper editors to profess political neutrality before the [1960 party] conventions, it was apparent that they were overwhelmingly in support of the Democratic Party.

* "Experience in reading union periodicals teaches the student of unionism that much of what is said in these publications *is designed to achieve an effect,* rather than document the state of thinking of the membership, the editor, or the leadership [emphasis theirs].

* "The *'BOO SHEET,'* a term implying that the greedy industrial bosses must be attacked with fiery stories and cartoons of bloated capitalists, is one of the tactics which go into creating effects through written communications."

A second recent study, conducted along lines similar to the Michigan project but concentrated on one area and one union publication, was undertaken in 1963 by a Minnesota management consultant firm, Henry Teipel Associates.[72] The field of study was Ramsey County (St. Paul), which in those pre-reapportionment days constituted the 4th Congressional District. The district had long been a stronghold for Minnesota's Democrat-Farmer-Labor Party, and Republicans who were proven vote-getters in lower offices were often defeated for Congress by upwards of 40,000 votes; this situation prompted the question the Teipel study was to pursue:

"What is it that is influencing public opinion so strongly in Ramsey County—that the great majority of the public consistently prefer one party's candidates over another's by a sizable margin?"

The answer was not long in coming. The *Union Advocate,* a local

AFL-CIO weekly newspaper was read in an estimated 43 percent of the homes in Ramsey County, a figure second (out of 15 daily or weekly periodicals read in the county) only to the daily *St. Paul Dispatch,* reaching 97 percent of the homes. As the *Dispatch* was reasonably balanced in its presentation of political news, it was deduced that it would be the ardently pro-DFL *Advocate,* found to have between 25 to 30 percent of its space devoted to politics, which would have a partisan impact on public opinion.

To calculate the precise influence of the *Advocate* in political terms, the Teipel study correlated the 1962 vote totals in all Ramsey County precincts, dividing them into postal zones, with the *Union Advocate's* circulation in those zones. On taking these figures to a University of Minnesota statistician, it was discovered: 1) for every 10 percent increase in *Advocate* circulation a 7 percent increase in votes for the DFL could be expected; and, applied to actual practice and allowing for a 12 percent margin of error, 2) some 30,690 votes would be influenced by this publication.

In 1962, the DFL congressional candidate had won by 27,510 votes, or 3,180 votes less than the Teipel's study's mathematical calculation. After ruling out other reasons union members should be voting DFL (meetings, personal contacts), the study reached the conclusion: "The *Union Advocate* is definitely influencing public opinion, and is definitely a heavy factor in winning elections for the DFL in Ramsey County."

Aside from their obvious effectiveness, the local union publications, as with all labor propaganda, including COPE's, have the added benefit of being dirt cheap to mail. In their postal rates, labor organizations fall into the same non-profit, educational category as do religious, scientific, philanthropic, veterans' and other groups. In practical terms, as long as the labor group doing the mailing prepares the content itself—whether a newspaper or an anti-Goldwater pamphlet—the U.S. Post Office considers this "educational" and allows it to be mailed at a third class bulk rate of $1\frac{1}{4}$ cents per pound, while everyone else pays $2\frac{5}{8}$ cents per pound. This inequity and others will be covered in the subsequent section on "COPE's Bankroll."

As concerns the campaign against the "extremists," the union publication proving itself more than capable of supplementing COPE's propaganda is *Steel Labor.* Subsidized by members' dues money (as are all union publications), this monthly, tabloid-size, 20-page periodical makes a regular feature out of alarming against the "danger on the right," picturing the Birch Society, Ku Klux Klan and American Nazi Party as the front ranks of the "rightist army," and all other conservative groups as mere sycophants.

One issue of *Steel Labor* deserving of an Olympic gold medal for journalistic broad jumping in tying the Republican Party in with the "extremists," was the January, 1966, edition. This one issue contained: 1) an article reporting a speech made by Sen. Lee Metcalf (D-Mont.) warning that "rightists are out for blood in the '66 elections"; 2) a somewhat belated "exposé" of the book *None Dare Call It Treason,* terming it an "anti-American book" being promoted by "far-right-wingers in cahoots with the JBS"; and, finally, 3) an article criticizing the Republican Leadership Conference for failing to condemn the Birch Society.

Like COPE, *Steel Labor* employs the time-honored propaganda tactic of guilt-by-association to tie together the Republicans and the "right wing." The fact that a candidate runs under the banner of a political party whose leaders failed to denounce the JBS, with its approximately 75,000 members, is a more important campaign issue for this publication than the cost-of-living increase, the war in Vietnam or a man's qualifications for office. In fact, it is virtually the only issue.

As an extension of *Steel Labor's* diatribe against the far right and Republican Party, in 1967 the Steelworkers published a special four-page issue, reprinting earlier articles, such as those mentioned above, under the title "The Danger of the Far Right." The introduction to the propaganda barrage begins:

"For many Americans, the Goldwater debacle of 1964, widely advertised as a confrontation between the responsible Center of American politics and the Ultra Right which had captured a major party, was a fitting conclusion that the extremists of the Right had been properly dispatched.

"Far from it. The Radical Right flourishes today as vigorously as ever, and phoenix-like, it promises to once more dominate the national convention of one of our great political parties."

Guess which.

Not far behind *Steel Labor* in propaganda volume is the UAW's *Solidarity,* a monthly 16-pager regularly promoting Democrats, demeaning Republicans and carrying the latest pronouncements of President Reuther. *Solidarity* is reinforced in the *UAW* propaganda arsenal by the daily radio broadcasts of Guy Nunn, a vicious business-baiter who won congressional attention following the assassination of John F. Kennedy with his black innuendo that congressmen who opposed the late President's policies were somehow implicated in his death and had no right to eulogize their leader:

"Vulgar sight: Congressmen who feverishly knocked the late President offering empty eulogies. . . . Goldwater belabors rightwing theme there's no hate around, but GOP's Hugh Scott lowers boom on haters. Looking down from gallery in House of Representatives you see feeble old men with enormous power to keep the country on dead center. They shuffle along, deaf to the pleas of the hungry and jobless, cold to the anguish of persecuted minorities—they return year after year like part of the woodwork, but an active, sensitive man in the White House is murdered."[73]

All these individual labor publications and, through them, the union member readership have virtually unlimited access to COPE propaganda materials. Articles may be reprinted and brochures ordered in bulk—all at no charge. In its *How To Win* handbook, COPE encourages the rank-and-file to order propaganda from Washington headquarters and gives suggestions on how it should be distributed.

COPE first reminds its grass roots field troops that "communicating your story to people is essential if your COPE program is to be a success and if your candidates are going to win." And it proceeds to remind them "There's no shortage of printed materials on most issues in which your COPE is interested," suggesting, "It's a good idea to appoint a literature chairman. . . . it's his job to recommend what pieces of literature would be useful, to order them in sufficient quantities, and *to get them distributed where they'll do the most good.*" (COPE's emphasis.)

Other than individual union publications, an important supplement to COPE's propaganda are those of the parent AFL-CIO. As might be expected, the material manufactured and distributed by the federation is primarily concerned with subjects related specifically to trade unionism, but a significant portion of its content is quite definitely political. This may take the same printed form as its political committee's propaganda, or utilize media which COPE itself does not regularly employ.

The AFL-CIO's two periodicals, the 12-page weekly tabloid, *AFL-CIO News,* and the monthly slick magazine, *Federationist,* are both focused on labor news. The magazine features in-depth studies of political issues or personalities with the same leftward slant found in COPE material, but in a restrained manner, refraining from propaganda histrionics.

The reading space in the weekly newspaper is concerned in the main with news of bargaining talks, strikes, labor personalities and the like. The *News'* political content is likely to cover AFL-CIO-endorsed legislation and its congressional progress, and reports on the election activities of both labor and political parties; in this reporting the publication is every bit as anti-right as COPE, as witness a news story on the 1966 election outlook in the West:

"The Republican Party is trying for a comeback in the Upper Rocky Mountain States this year, and the pattern for the November election is GOP conservatives against Democratic liberals. . . . Victory for the Republicans this year would mean that conservative elements had tightened their grip on the party machinery—and conservatives, in the Mountain States, mean a significant proportion of outright John Birch Society members or sympathizers and other rightists."[74]

In such a simple manner, for the *News,* Republicans become conservatives and then turn into Birchites.

Other publications out of the federation's Washington headquarters include those of the union-group departments, such as the Industrial Union Department's periodical, *Agenda.* These, too, deal primarily with reports in their exclusive fields of interest, but still find some space to devote to political propagandizing.

A form widely used by the AFL-CIO in promoting its viewpoint is the motion picture film, with over 250 titles available at Washington headquarters for union locals to rent. These range from such bread-and-butter topics as "Dues and the Union" (17 minutes, $3.00 rental), to entertainment films like W.C. Fields' "Circus Slicker" (10 min., $7.50); the films are produced by the AFL-CIO as well as by such outside concerns as television networks, international unions and government agencies.

In the "films on political education" category are to be found "The Extremists," the anti-right film mentioned earlier in this section, "The Wisconsin Story," an excellent political action film describing the massive register-and-vote campaign waged by COPE in Wisconsin in 1958, and how-to-do-it films covering such subjects as building political coalitions, stimulating interest, working with independent voters.

The purely political propaganda films offered by the AFL-CIO are found scattered throughout its 78-page "Films For Labor" catalogue.[75] They include "One World Or None," which "points out the destructive power of atom bombs," "It's Good Business," a film advertised as an "answer" to supporters of right-to-work laws, and a host of titles on civil rights, economics and other issues. The AFL-CIO also has apparently unlimited access to anti-conservative documentary films produced in recent years by the major TV networks; its titles include the notorious NBC "White Paper" damning the attempts of Newburgh, N.Y. to cut down on welfare spending, and the CBS Reports' documentary, "Case History of a Rumor," a purported "discussion of right wing tactics and propaganda methods."

Another medium the AFL-CIO uses in its propaganda efforts is radio, the two regular broadcasting staples being the Mutual Radio Network's federation-sponsored Labor News Conference and, until mid-1967, the nightly commentary of Edward P. Morgan, on ABC radio. The weekly News Conference seldom concerns itself with practical politics, and usually features an AFL-CIO headquarters official being interviewed by two newsmen on strictly labor and economic matters; Edward P. Morgan, however, was another matter.

One of the blasts COPE most frequently levels at the right wing is its "contamination" of the air waves through the several radio programs to be found featuring "rightists" of varying degrees; COPE not only condemns the politics of these commentators, but urges the rank-and-file to openly harass them by demanding that radio stations give "equal time" for rebuttal. A typical diatribe against these programs is the following, from the June 14, 1965, "Memo From COPE":

"The number of right wing radio and television programs cluttering the airways has increased sharply in the past several months. . . . today, these broadcasts can be heard in every part of the U.S., lambasting pet targets of the extreme right."

COPE could freely make these charges with an earnest straight face, all the while AFL-CIO-sponsored commentator Morgan appeared nightly for thirteen years on prime radio time (7 or 6 p.m., depending on time zone) over the majority of the 123 stations affiliated with the American Broadcasting Company. Furthermore, Morgan's stature as a commentator was enhanced by his concurrent position as a news "analyst" on ABC television, regularly appearing with the network's other "house liberal," Howard K. Smith. On his 15-minute radio program, Morgan most definitely did not act as a consistent "labor mouthpiece," as his topics ranged far and wide, sometimes including criticism of union practices.

But Morgan's collectivist-welfarist principles are confirmed in the nature of the position he assumed after leaving ABC in June, 1967, to become "Senior Correspondent for Investigative Reporting" for the noncommercial Public Broadcasting Laboratory established in large part with government funds; the purpose of the new network was to compete, with the advantage of federal finances, with already-established commercial networks. This anti-business, pro-government control bias—a position firmly supported by the AFL-CIO—was also evident in Morgan's federation-sponsored radio broadcasts whenever he broached political issues.

In the early months of 1967, for example, Morgan joined the rapidly growing labor chorus against Gov. Ronald Reagan, and his attempts to improve the economic and educational institutions in California through better administration and realistic financing. When the University of California Regents, with Reagan's assent, fired university president Clark Kerr, Morgan opined that Reagan had dealt a "crushing blow" to the university, blaming the governor's action on pressure from state "right-wing extremist" elements:

"California has more than its share, perhaps, of right-wing extremists. They are, by and large, at war with society. A few would like to repeal the 20th Century. Several are rich, some are powerful. Many are convinced that the university system seethes with radicalism and that the

Berkeley campus is the center of original sin. Even a couple of regents themselves espouse this passionate thinking."[76] (Gov. Reagan is, as everyone knows, a member of the regents.)

When Reagan a short time later offered his opinion that officials at the state universities, notably those at Berkeley, should not negotiate with radical students over their anarchistic either/or demands, commentator Morgan complained that this sentiment gave him "an acute case of mental indigestion," and offered that "Gov. Reagan's reasoning . . . underlin[es] his own lack of comprehension of the educational world . . ."[77]

Whether the source is the rich baritone of Edward P. Morgan on ABC radio or a crude hatchet-job in a small union newspaper in Dayton, Ohio, the staple of labor's political propaganda is everywhere identical: words. And the purpose of the words, as is obvious in their quotation and as was properly noted in the University of Michigan study on the political content of labor periodicals, is the creation of an effect. And the effect desired for 1968 will be the same the COPE propagandists have sought to create since the early 'sixties: to make the "right wing" a rank-and-file anathema and to make this synonomous with the Republican Party, its policies and its candidates.

Certain developments in the 1966 elections, notably the victory of Ronald Reagan in California by over one million votes, might have appeared to warrant reassessment by COPE of its propaganda strategy. At the end of September, 1966, the columnists Evans and Novak reported on the Democrat-labor scheme of portraying Reagan as a captive of the John Birch Society, revealing that "with some six weeks to go in the campaign the Birch issue indeed is dead. . . . The impact has been zero. Polls taken by both camps show Californians—particularly the 60 percent of the state's population that lives in Los Angeles, Orange and San Diego counties in Southern California—couldn't care less about the John Birch Society or right-wing extremism issue."[78]

A surprising confirmation of the Evans-Novak analysis came from the far-left *Ramparts* magazine. After describing how Governor Pat Brown had three full-time employes doing nothing but researching Reagan's "right-wing connections" for a 29-page report, the *Ramparts* editors belittled the endeavor saying, "The 'connections' were nebulous, as most newspapers immediately noticed," adding that "to claim, as the Democratic 'dossier' does, that Reagan 'uses his considerable platform talents as a magnet to build up neo-Fascist organizations' is gross exaggeration."[79]

But, in truth, COPE and its propagandizing allies could not afford to pay such reports much heed. They had chosen their target and had to stick with it; they had created the monster and it had to be fed.

The propaganda assault for the 1968 presidential-year elections began with the very first "Memo From COPE" to be published after the '66 elections: "The U.S. House," it stated two months before the 1967 House session even convened, "fell into the grip once more of a Dixie-crat-Republican coalition whose war cry in the face of progressive legislative proposals is, and has always been, 'They Shall Not Pass.' "

Even the victories of avowed Republican liberals could not sway COPE from its scatter-shot attack on the GOP:

"While there is consolation in the fact that many GOP winners aren't mossbacks—Hatfield, Percy, Brooke—many others are, and their victories increase right wing political strength."[80]

As the time approached for Congress to meet in January, 1967, the attack increased. "Collective bargaining and the right of free trade unions to operate in our society are expected to face serious tests in the incoming 90th Congress," wrote COPE. "Traditional anti-labor groups already are hard at work laying the groundwork for legislation, viewing 1967 as the most promising year in two decades for restricting the trade union movement."[81]

This warning turned out to be a major theme in COPE's propaganda leading up to 1968, even though no "restricting" legislation passed through Congress. Later in 1967 an issue of the "Memo" tried to revive the old "corporate-conspiracy-against-labor" theme as it told of how "congressional conservatives and major elements of the business community have launched a twin thrust at labor's throat."

Under the bold, black headline "They're Going For the Jugular," COPE described the "thrust" and the two business powers behind it, the U.S. Chamber of Commerce and the National Association of Manufacturers (which it even managed to link with the John Birch Society). When the screaming and invective were brushed aside, however, all the evil plot amounted to was a series of bills introduced in Congress aimed at curbing some of the more outrageous union practices; none of the bills ever passed and some had even been defeated at the time COPE wrote of them. The message was not that there was any danger in this specific legislation, but that the rank-and-file had better back COPE-supported candidates in 1968 or its "jugular" would later be cut:

"Deny the conservatives a political victory in 1968 and their whole strategy crumbles. Give them a political victory in 1968 and their success is assured. . . . Going for the anti-labor forces are all the weapons, all the money and all the political savvy they can muster. . . . Lined up with it will be right-wing political action groups. . . . In 1968 the best bet to preserve your union and your security against the attack is COPE. Give to COPE. Work with COPE in your union and your community. Make 1968 a 'COPE year.' "[82]

By broadening the scope of its propaganda attacks, COPE was able to link the familiar "rightist" and "business" targets together with the conservative bloc in Congress; the alleged aim of this dastardly triumverate was to put the skids to organized labor. This line was reinforced in later issues of "Memo From COPE." The November 27 issue said the "root" of the anti-labor attack "is the fact that weakened unions will diminish the bargaining power of workers." A December "Memo" reprinted the resolution on political action passed by the '67 AFL-CIO convention, a call to arms warning union members of the ominous threat facing them; purportedly reviewing the first session of the 90th Congress, the resolution observed:

"Hand-in-hand with the halt in advance of social welfare programs has come an ominous build-up in Congress of sentiment for restrictive new legislation aimed at weakening labor unions.

"The build-up is planned and coordinated. It is being cultivated in Congress by conservative Republicans and Dixiecrats. It is spearheaded in the public forum by the giant business associations, the U.S. Chamber of Commerce and the National Association of Manufacturers."[83]

The strategy behind this new wrinkle in COPE's propaganda soon became clear. Labor leaders knew that there was already some dissatisfaction with President Johnson and the Great Society among the rank-and-file and they realized this could well increase during the '68 campaign. So, rather than try to calm workers' unrest over such controversial issues as Vietnam, race relations, taxes and inflation, COPE sought to divert their attention by manufacturing a more "immediate" danger: Republican political victories, for the White House or in Congress, would aid the rightist-business-Congress plot to clamp legislative restrictions on organized labor.

"We are urging each international union to set up a special task force so that each member will fully understand this danger," revealed COPE director Al Barkan.[84] Supplementing these task forces in the propaganda assault will be another unique COPE feature for 1968: weekend seminars for local union leaders will be held in the ten largest states; the purpose of the COPE-conducted seminars will be to "minimize" the impact of controversial issues by providing local leaders with information to answer rank-and-file questions and to warn them of the plot to "cut their jugular."

And, as for COPE's regular field operations, the anti-labor conspiracy is being used as the rallying cry to '68 political action. "This threat to the well-being of the trade union movement is entirely political in nature," read the AFL-CIO convention's political resolution: "If conservatives make political gains in 1968, their program inevitably will be on the front burners in Congress in 1969. A political threat demands a political response. An unprecedented threat to the labor movement demands an unprecedented response from the labor movement."

It was apparent that this was the theme COPE was to play over and over in '68, right up to Election Day morn. If the rank-and-file was not buying propaganda telling why they should support labor-backed candidates, COPE figured it could scare them into this support by conjuring up evil images of what would happen if the opposition was victorious. The negative propaganda approach to politics has been a very successful one for COPE, as Barry Goldwater can attest, and in 1968 COPE is placing all its chips on this particular use of the English language.

The words never stop. They reach out and envelop the rank-and-file union member, turning his attention in the direction COPE wants, and then point out the supposed evils threatening his existence. Slowly, the words have insinuated their way toward their target, creating an effect, imprinting an indelible belief in the Republican Party as original sin.

COPE's propaganda is the one most vital weapon in its arsenal, and that capable of the most profound result. It is a conditioning force, and is—must be—constantly at work reinforcing all that has gone before, solidifying the effect. The propaganda goes on and on, and it casts its shadow over all the other activities in the COPE campaign.

# PART FIVE:
## Operations, Strategies and Assorted Nuts 'n' Bolts

If you draw a straight line, placing at one end the point where a voter registers and at the other the point where he casts his ballot, and then shade the entire line with a gray film to represent propaganda, you will have the basic structure of the COPE campaign. It would not be complete, however, unless all along the line were scattered a series of dots representing an assortment of other operations, strategies, projects, and tasks, the number and diversity of which precludes their classification under a single heading.

These varied activities include COPE's assistance to freshmen Democratic congressmen, setting up a coffee hour, and the work done by union wives. Individually, these sundry facets of the COPE operation function as indispensable parts of the whole; perhaps they do not get as much attention as other, previously mentioned projects, but their cumulative role is of major importance.

The simplest way to describe these activities is in the approximate order of their appearance in the COPE campaign:

* The first listing under such a priority would have to be COPE's activity reserved for those odd-numbered years when no national elections take place. Most communities across the nation reserve these years

for electing city and county officials, from the proverbial dog-catcher to mayor—offices many voters consider unimportant and not worth voting on.

COPE does not see matters this way. It not only considers these elections—and the offices to be voted on—important in their own right, but sees the municipal campaigns as a perfect opportunity for rank-and-filers to keep their political muscles in trim, even though they may be a bit tired from the last outing. "Maybe you've just caught your breath from the 1966 elections," said a "Memo From COPE" in February, 1967, "or maybe you're already agonizing over 1968. But don't forget: There is plenty of action for election buffs in 1967. . . . Wherever you live, there's probably at least an important local election going on."[85]

In some areas, COPE pointed out, there were more than local offices at stake. Two states—Kentucky and Mississippi—were to elect governors, four others had their state legislatures up for grabs, and five metropolitan areas—Baltimore, Boston, Chicago, Cleveland, and Philadelphia —were electing a mayor in 1967. Any group involved in political action to the degree that COPE is would be expected to show interest in such important campaigns as governorships and mayoralties, no matter the year; it is COPE's involvement in races for the "minor" posts that may come as a surprise to many politically conscious citizens.

In the very early spring of odd-numbered years national COPE sends out a thick document, prepared by its research staff, listing approximately 1,000 elections to take place that year in cities of over 10,000 population; also included are any state or county campaigns, plus referendum or constitutional amendment issues on the ballots.

From Alamogordo, New Mexico, to Zanesville, Ohio, COPE lists the offices to be voted on, the final filing date for candidates, the date of the primary election (if one is provided for), the date of the general election and a notation on whether or not the office at stake is partisan. In a memorandum accompanying the document, and directed to the attention of state, county, and city COPE directors, national chieftain Al Barkan spells out the reasons why these "unimportant" contests warrant COPE's concentration:

"City elections this year are important in themselves, because the officials elected are closely involved with local problems of immediate and direct concern to the voters. They are equally important because of their potential effect on state and national elections in 1968.

"The 1967 elections afford a splendid opportunity to maintain and improve existing COPE machinery, to train new recruits, and to provide additional activities for those who did such a good job in the COPE program in 1966.

"We hope that in 1967 you will regard the elections in your area, not only in the light of their own very real significance, but as an opportunity to broaden all aspects of our political education program."

The decision for COPE to charge full-force into odd-year city elections was made jointly by the AFL-CIO Executive Council and COPE Administrative Committee at a meeting in Florida, February 24, 1965. One principal cause for the new policy was organized labor's fear of seeing the gains of 1964 wiped out in the congressional elections of '66; continued political activity in 1965, the COPE bigwigs reasoned, would improve chances for liberal success in the following year's national contests. If this reasoning didn't exactly bear full fruit in 1966, this should not discount the importance of COPE's role in the municipal elections.

Another consideration in the February, 1965, decision was the practical effect such activity would have on COPE's overall strategy. Through participation in odd-year campaigns, more voters could be registered, the status of voters already registered could be easily maintained, and precinct organizations could be kept active during the two-year wait between national elections. Also, new union members could be inducted into labor's political operations, experimental propaganda tactics could be tried out, and weak spots in the COPE grass roots organization could be strengthened.

A third reason for an odd-year campaign, and perhaps the most important over the long run, is the value of municipal elections in practical and psychological terms. Writing on this aspect soon after the Council's 1965 decision, COPE director Barkan explained:

"Local elections are significant in their own right. From highways to health care, from urban renewal to mass transportation, from taxes to education, the actions of elected local and state officials determine whether or not a community and its citizens get the progress and services they require.

"Many . . . federal programs require local initiative to get the gears meshing. Community or state officials either can take advantage of, or spurn, assistance offered by the federal government. What they decide to do—in urban renewal, education, health, highway and dozens of other federal programs—has a visible impact on the lives of the citizens they represent.

"The stress on elected officials emphasizes the point that decisions and acts of individuals can be judged by the voters who can re-elect them or replace them if they fail to meet the public interest."[86]

Of course, every politically aware citizen, Democrat or Republican, is conscious of the power vested in the local government. The difference is that COPE takes the time to explain the relevance of this power to the rank-and-file, using it as an added inducement to participate in municipal campaigns.

The psychological benefits of odd-year political activity are as important as the practical results. Put simply, a sweeping victory by liberal Democrats in a vital city campaign will provide much of the atmosphere and momentum necessary to carry the same area for a liberal Democrat congressional, senate, gubernatorial, or even presidential candidate the next year.

COPE's Al Barkan explained that this philosophy was one of the reasons for the committee's mammoth 1967 effort to re-elect Democratic Mayor James Tate in Philadelphia that odd-year. "On Philadelphia," one of the city's newspapers paraphrased Barkan as saying, "hinges the outcome of the 1968 Presidential election in Pennsylvania. On Pennsylvania hinges the East . . . and so on."[87]

Though this may be a shorthand summation of what actually does take place in the political version of the "domino theory," the psychological impact of local elections cannot be understated. It is obviously far easier for COPE to elect a liberal national officeholder in an area already having a liberal local government, than in a Republican stronghold.

* Another COPE effort in grass roots governments is a project called simply—and deceptively—"Programs of Progress." In concept, the "programs" are intended to move state governments to the left, through local COPEs politicking for liberal candidates and lobbying for liberal legislation; the hoped-for result, other than a more friendly state government, is a solidly liberal local base from which pro-labor national candidates can be easily elected.

The psychology behind the "Programs of Progress" has been summed up by COPE's first national director, James McDevitt, in these terms:

"If we become stronger at the local and state levels, we will become stronger at the congressional level. If we elect liberals to the state house and state legislatures, it is inconceivable that we would elect reactionaries to Congress."[88]

In other words, while other political "action" organizations concentrate almost exclusively on national elections and offices, COPE lays out carefully detailed plans to virtually take over state governments, using this liberal base to elect more "friendly" congressmen, senators, and presidents.

The nucleus of what was later to be known as the "Programs of Progress" was formed in Louisiana shortly after the state legislature enacted a right-to-work law in 1954. Bayou State organized labor had spent hundreds of thousands of dollars in a last-ditch effort to stop this legislation, only to fail drastically. The lesson state labor leaders learned from this defeat was that it would be far more effective for labor to put its time and money into a long-range campaign to elect men committed to labor's legislative platform than try to lobby and win over legislators with no such commitment; they promptly set about putting this lesson into action.

The Louisiana state AFL and CIO combined forces and resources to form a Joint Committee (this was a year before the national merger) to direct a statewide drive for labor's legislative and elective goals. Political action committees were established in local unions and central bodies across the state; an intensive voter registration campaign was mounted, which in two years raised the percentage of registered union members from 20 to 50 percent; and "target" districts were selected where labor concluded a "friend" could be elected.

A national AFL-CIO report on the Louisiana project's choice of target districts reveals a great deal about the reasoning behind the selection—reasons that still pertain to COPE's choice of targets under its "Marginal District Project":

"The third step was to select the legislative districts in the state where union membership figures related to past election statistics showed that labor had the best chances to win. These selected districts became the 'targets' for 1956. However, it was obvious that if labor were to win *all* these industrial 'target' districts, we would still lack a pro-labor majority in the legislature. Election of a number of friendly legislators from rural districts, where there was little or no union membership, was necessary to provide a pro-labor majority. Study of past election statistics revealed which of the anti-labor rural legislators would be easiest to defeat. Candidates were then sought against these incumbents. When candidates were found in these rural districts, the Joint State Committee made substantial financial contributions to their campaigns in return for commitments to vote for repeal of 'right-to-work' and certain other legislation. . . ."

As has been seen, this strategy of pouring outside labor money into campaigns in sparsely populated rural states has become a regular COPE practice. The idea did not originate with the Louisiana project, but this was the first time a coordinated, well-organized effort in this direction was shown effective at the lowest level of elective office.

The first results of the Louisiana effort showed themselves in the 1956 elections and were nothing short of miraculous, considering the state's Deep South complexion. The final tally showed a governor, lieutenant-governor, 22 out of 29 state senators, and 51 of 101 state representatives all committed to repeal of the state's two-year-old right-to-work law and to other labor-backed legislation.

And the new pro-labor officials wasted no time in making good on their promises. Shortly after the 1956 legislative session convened, Louisiana became the first state in the nation to repeal a right-to-work law. Soon after this signal victory—on an issue labor had been overwhelmingly defeated on only two years before—other legislation pushed by the Louisiana AFL and CIO came into law: workmen's and unemployment compensation benefits were increased, a proposed general sales tax increase was killed and a tax on business substituted, and—in an effort to get more working union members to the polls—primary election day was shifted from Tuesday to Saturday.

From this solid liberal grass roots base, Louisiana labor was able in subsequent years to have some influence on the ideological makeup of the state's congressional representation. According to COPE's 1966 voting records, the Louisiana delegation in Congress—eight representatives and two senators—had an average rating of 46 percent; considered in a national context, this figure might appear anemic in the eyes of most labor leaders, but it is the highest COPE average for any Southern state delegation.

The task of changing the Democratic parties in Southern states from a conservative to a liberal cast is not an easy one, and the strategists behind the Programs of Progress realize this. Walter Reuther's reported master plan for "political realignment" of the national Democratic Party —through the gradual attrition of conservative members—is a long-range project, and the programs are but one tactic. As the ten-year results of the Louisiana experiment indicate, however, the labor forces have made progress.

After COPE was created and developed into an imposing force in national elections, its leaders began turning their attention toward constructing the liberal grass roots atmosphere necessary for increased pro-labor victories. The rudimentary machinery for national success had been put into motion and the COPE high command sought to extend the impact of their operations by formulating a program, based on that used in Louisiana, to secure a liberal Democratic Party in the Deep South.

"Some day," said COPE director James McDevitt in 1963, "we hope to eliminate the conservative coalition in Congress by reducing the combined voting strength of southern Democrats and Republicans.

"You are going to see a general party realignment in the South. Voters will force the change. They will drive reactionary elements who have controlled election machinery into the Republican Party, which more nearly represents their views."[89]

Taking the basic operational outline provided by the Louisiana project, national COPE streamlined, perfected and put the plan on paper for implementation in other states. Initially, it was thought the plan would be limited to the South, but state labor organizations in other sections soon discovered they could use it just as easily—and effectively. As of mid-1967 there were a total of twelve states fully participating in the Programs of Progress (including Louisiana, Alabama, Mississippi, Tennessee, North Carolina, Colorado, Delaware, Oregon and Texas), and eighteen other states were using parts of it.

The programs are financed by the state's union members through special assessments which are separate from dues payments and other levies imposed by their state AFL-CIO. In Louisiana, for example, unionized workers are charged 20 cents a month to support the "program"; Arkansas' union members pay $1.50 per year, while most other state AFL-CIOs employing a program charge only an additional $1. In a state like Louisiana, this relatively small per capita tax can add up to $130,000 per year for spending on this one project alone.

The programs differ from state to state mostly in the legislative goals they seek; in Mississippi the Number One goal is creation of a state department of labor, while in Tennessee the first concern is repeal of the state right-to-work law. Otherwise, the programs are virtually identical and, in fact, the wording used in their promotional literature is exactly the same—giving rise to the suspicion that national COPE, not the individual state's AFL-CIO, is the real perpetrator of the programs.

The Programs of Progress pamphlet published by the Tennessee AFL-CIO begins:

"Underway is Big Business' massive drive to win control of Congress in 1962. Recent surveys reveal over 200 of the largest corporations, General Motors, United States Steel, Gulf Oil and General Electric and other corporate giants, have trained thousands of executives and management personnel to lead their titanic political offensive."

Two years later the North Carolina AFL-CIO distributed a pamphlet promoting its "program," which began:

"Underway is Big Business' massive drive to win control of Congress and the Presidency in 1964. Recent surveys reveal over 200 of the largest corporations, General Motors, United States Steel, Gulf Oil, General Electric and other corporate giants have trained thousands of executives and management personnel to lead their titanic political offensive."

Lest one think state AFL-CIO propagandists had absolutely no originality—otherwise a reasonable deduction—it would be wise to note how the anti-Big Business diatribes are applied to each state. The Tennessee pamphlet goes on to say:

"At the state level the Tennessee Manufacturers Association, Tennessee Business Men's Association and other Vested Interest Groups are planning and working to elect their candidate as Governor in 1962, and to control the Legislature."

And two years later the North Carolina pamphleteers filled in the proper blanks for their state:

"At the state level the Chambers of Commerce, the State Merchants Association, the Cotton Manufacturers and other Vested Interest Groups are planning and working to elect their candidate as Governor and to control the Legislature."

After the propaganda outbursts and the detailing of the legislative goals—which usually consist of between 15 and 20 points and always conclude with a directive "to oppose vigorously any legislation detrimental to the interest and welfare of the people of (fill-in-the-blank)" —the program outline gets down to the business of how this legislation can be enacted. Included here are instructions on electing "friendly" candidates from rural districts, mobilizing union members' support of candidates, and making financial contributions where they will do the most good.

An important part of most programs is the suggested plan for "development of public support" for the legislative proposals. As most programs are found in Southern states, where voter enthusiasm for labor's liberal goals could not be said to be riotous, a good deal of "public selling" is essential. Commented the 142-page "Programs of Progress for Arkansas" on this subject: "A carefully planned, extensive and adequately financed *Public Relations Program* is necessary to develop widespread and effective support for the proposals in our Legislative Program."

This particular program outline then proceeded to devote a full twelve pages exclusively to public relations. It was also announced that $50,-000 had been budgeted to "adequately finance" the PR campaign.

The Programs of Progress are probably the most thoroughly planned of all labor's political operations. Where else could an activist find a carefully detailed, finely designed plan to take over a state government? It is not inconceivable that such an outline exists for a national program—viewing COPE's repeated success, it often seems that way. What the program plans reveal most of all, however, is the absolutely cold, detached, methodical manner with which labor's political strategists can go about devising a plan directed at controlling the future of thousands of individuals.

And if it would appear that many of these Programs of Progress have not been a smashing success—considering the political complexion of such states as Alabama and Mississippi—it must be remembered that they were instituted on a long-range basis. As the politicians who stay up late Election Night, refusing to claim victory or concede defeat, are fond of proclaiming, "All the returns ain't in yet."

* The most important single strategy COPE employs for selected congressional elections is called the Marginal District Project. This opera-

tion, so important it has been labeled "make-or-break" by COPE officials, is the brainchild of the committee's deputy director, Joe Rourke, a skilled political pro who came to COPE from the Brotherhood of Electrical Workers in 1963. After only two applications in national elections, Rourke's innovation has proved to be one of organized labor's most effective campaign tactics.

The strategy of the project is of elementary simplicty. A "marginal" district is a congressional seat won in the previous election by 55 percent or less of the total vote. If the winner of this race was "pro-labor" according to COPE's ratings, the labor political machine will be out to get him re-elected. If the winner was a conservative, or, as COPE prefers to call him, "anti-labor," then he will be marked for concentrated opposition by the COPE forces, national and local.

A "Confidential Report" from the COPE research department, dated November, 1964, provided a broad history and revealing analysis of the Marginal District Project:[90]

"COPE started early in 1963 to select and give special attention to those districts where tight elections could be expected [in 1964]. Working from a basic list of districts won in 1962 with 55 percent or less of the total vote, special attention was given to selected congressional districts in terms of manpower and financing from COPE and individual international unions. Many internationals gave more help than ever before, and their assistance was more effectively used and coordinated . . .

"The marginal district project . . . concentrated in two major areas:

"1. Raising money for more than routine contributions.

"2. Encouraging international unions to release full-time employes for assignment in specific areas where they were requested."

Elaborating on these two steps, the report commented on the financing aspect:

"By directing funds toward those districts most in need and by spreading contributions over all close districts, these funds were more sensibly apportioned than ever before. There was infrequent repetition of the wasteful accumulation of funds by those candidates who are best at raising money but are not necessarily most in need or most deserving."

And on the subject of providing paid (from union treasuries) manpower to marginal district candidates, the report noted with optimism that "a healthy start has been made in persuading international unions to release personnel for political activity on a sound basis."

A good glimpse of how the Marginal District Project is taken from paper and put into action by COPE leaders was provided in a *Washington Evening Star* article in August, 1964.[91] Reporting on a meeting of COPE's Operations Committee held at a Chicago hotel, the writer said,

"COPE director Al Barkan will distribute a list of the marginal races then discuss all or most of them, indicating how much financial and personnel assistance his group can supply each particular candidate."

Noting that COPE's average donation to an important congressional race is two to three thousand dollars, the *Star* reporter said that in marginal districts "when more assistance is thought needed to complement COPE aid, the international union with the largest membership in the district under discussion will be asked to contribute, with other unions participating if they want."

With the financial arrangements completed, the report continued, the individual unions will outline their own political action programs for the marginal districts, indicating which races they will concentrate on. In this manner, overlapping or duplication of effort by other unions (or COPE) is avoided, and national COPE can effectively coordinate political strategy in all the nation's marginal districts. The meeting over, everyone leaves to go to work.

1964 was the first year the Marginal District Project was attempted, being applied to 89 congressional districts. The COPE-backed candidates won in 61 of these races, for a 69 percent successful batting average. Such was the first-year effectiveness of the project.

As 1966 dawned, COPE again prepared to rely heavily on the Marginal District Project to preserve friendly legislators in districts where close contests could be expected. In addition to concentrating on marginal districts, in 1966 COPE also put special stress on re-electing pro-labor congressmen who scored more than marginal 1964 victories in districts previously "solidly" Republican.

In all, there were 59 incumbent liberal Democrats—46 of them freshmen—who received the benefits of the marginal district strategy in 1966. The importance of these 59 representatives was dramatized several times during the campaign in the "Memo From COPE," with one issue exhorting:

"On COPE's unofficial list of 11 key votes on major legislation in 1965, these 59 congressmen cast a total of 585 right votes, only 40 wrong votes—less than one wrong vote per person—Not one piece of progressive legislation would have made it [without them]. . . .

"In the cold figures of political arithmetic, it's clear that a successful 1966 election—from labor's point of view—hinges primarily on the outcome in the marginal and switch districts of 1964. Many other districts, of course, are important, but these are make-or-break. They include some of the brightest, most imaginative and most liberal members of Congress—the big hitters."

Referring to the re-election of these heavy-hitting congressmen as "labor's toughest political test ever," COPE began its '66 Marginal

District Project by calling 13 area conferences between January 7 and March 21, 1966. These conferences were attended by delegates from local unions and city and state COPE councils in every section of the U.S., and discussions centered on how to send liberal Democrats back to Washington.

Later in the summer, experienced labor politicos from several major international unions were brought to Washington, given thorough briefing instructions on the marginal district to which they were to be assigned, and were sent out into the field. Reporting on this massive deployment, the *Wall Street Journal* revealed in September:

"Half a hundred representatives of various unions have been allocated to individual Congressmen, mostly Democrats, to aid their re-election efforts. Besides helping get out the vote, these operatives are tending to such campaign 'nuts and bolts' as getting literature printed and distributed, recordings made and meetings set up. A week-long training session in Washington preceded their deployment. It's the first time such an operation has begun so early and been so thoroughly organized."[92]

The score racked up by the Marginal District Project in 1966 was not the resounding success the '64 pilot program witnessed. Of the 59 congressional seats receiving extra special attention from COPE, liberal Democrats were retained in 29, for a fraction under a 50 percent "victory batting average." What is important to note, however, is that several of the winning candidates—notably Irwin (Conn.), Evans (Col.), Vigorito (Pa.), Helstoski (N.J.) and Hanley (N.Y.)—were re-elected in districts with a high percentage of Republican voter registration and probably would not have made it back to Washington (after most won initially in the Johnson landslide) without COPE's meticulous attention.

Secondly, and equally important, some marginal congressmen, although defeated in 1966, still managed to rack up a higher percentage of the total vote than the liberal Democrat candidate had received in the last off-year election, 1962. Chief among these were Gale Schisler in Illinois' 19th District (47.6 percent), Weston Vivian in Michigan's 2nd (48.9 percent) and Nieman Craley in the 19th District of Pennsylvania (48.5 percent). It is virtually certain that COPE will attempt to regain these districts in 1968.

Any analysis of the 1966 edition of the Marginal District Project will show that it was not a numerical success, but in terms of strategic value the project had visible potency. More than anything else, 1966 proved the Marginal District Project is eminently worthwhile and capable of having an imposing effect on close congressional contests.

It appears that as COPE prepares for 1968, the Marginal District

Project will assuredly be continued and its operations will not be tampered with to any significant degree. In the '68 presidential-year contests the project will concentrate its manpower and financial aid on two general types of congressional districts: 1) those held by liberal Democrats who were first elected in 1964 and re-elected in 1966 with 55 percent or less of the total vote; 2) those held by Republicans elected in 1966 from districts held previously by a Democrat, even those that just went liberal in '64. These rules are by no means ironclad and there will be variations.

* It is not only the marginal district candidates who get COPE assistance in the form of a trained labor advisor. The customary practice is for a union representative from within the candidate's district to act as his labor "liaison." But in contests of special concern—for the House or Senate—COPE will not hesitate to send in a strategist from outside to give a hand.

The 1966 elections saw something truly unique in this field, as AFL-CIO President Meany personally assigned teams of federation vice presidents (and Executive Council members) to guide the campaigns of two liberal Democrats, one being attached to Senator Paul Douglas' race in Illinois, the other attempting to aid Pat Brown in defeating Ronald Reagan. Meany met with the California task force in early July, hammered out the strategy to pursue in the Golden State, and sent the five executives on their way for the duration; for his part, candidate Brown named former Under Secretary of Labor John Henning as his overall labor coordinator and "contact" with the Washington delegation.

The Illinois task force—which included Roy Siemiller, a Chicago resident and head of the huge Machinists' union with some 100,000 members in the state, and Steelworkers' chieftain I. W. Abel—was instructed by Meany to set up a full-time statewide organization staffed by experienced campaign workers on leave from their union positions. Meany himself went to Chicago August 23, 1966, to discuss the Douglas-Percy race and urge state labor leaders to lend all assistance possible in the tight campaign.

The advisory contributions given by organized labor to deserving candidates do not normally reach the prestigious scale of the Douglas and Brown task forces, but their functions are similar. Basically, the union representatives coordinate the activities of all unions in the district, or state, into one campaign force; they also are expected to raise extra funds when needed, maintain amicable working relations with the regular Democratic Party structure, and see that everyone does his assigned job.

The role of the COPE representative is an influential one, and if he is effective—as most must be—it can mean the difference between a concerted labor political effort, and a lackadaisical campaign—or the difference between winning and losing for the candidate. Conversely, should the presence of an "outside" union advisor on a candidate's staff become public knowledge, it could be disastrous for the pro-labor office-seeker; not many voters like to think that a man seeking to represent them is dependent upon a single special interest group and its representative (especially someone from far away) for his election.

The best example of how discovery of an outside union representative's running of a campaign can work to the benefit of the opposition is provided by Sen. Barry Goldwater's 1958 re-election contest. The story is recalled with relish by Stephen Shadegg, Goldwater's campaign manager, in his fine book, *How To Win An Election,* and deserves to be related in full.[93]

In 1958, Arizona was one of those lightly populated and traditionally conservative states where COPE believed it could build a slick campaign organization around a small number of hard-working union members and, by importing money and manpower from outside the state, win a "bargain basement" victory. Labor had an added inducement in trying to capture the '58 Senate race for the Democrats because Republican Goldwater, a member of the Senate Labor and Public Welfare Committee, had proved to be a very vocal critic of union practices and officialdom and, in fact, was running his re-election race as much against Walter Reuther as against his opponent, ex-senator Ernest McFarland.

It was in May, 1958, that Shadegg, Goldwater and their staff first learned that organized labor was preparing a full-scale "blitz" of the campaign. The COPE regional director, they discovered, had moved from his West Coast home and headquarters to set up shop in Tucson, meeting and talking with labor leaders and COPE-backed Democratic candidates. But, rather than plant the spotlight on this intruder immediately, Goldwater's research team went to work compiling a thick file on his background and Arizona activities.

"Had we exposed the presence of the out-of-state union official when we first discovered him," Shadegg explains, "the exposure would have been ignored by many of the Indifferent [voters] who were not interested in politics in May. The effect would have been forgotten by November."

As the months went by, the union official's file grew in size and explosiveness of content: it was discovered he had an arrest record in California, and an official police "mug shot" was obtained; a list of his political contacts was compiled; photographs of visiting politicos taken; and a thorough day-by-day account of his movements duly recorded in the Goldwater headquarters.

After persuading inquiring reporters not to "break" the story too early—by explaining that they would have a complete information dossier on the COPE operative in due time—Shadegg was able to call a press conference and release the data two weeks before the election. "The story," he candidly states, "was a real shocker."

The cause of the "shock," Shadegg contends, was not that the COPE representative was doing anything illegal, as anyone can participate in an election campaign, or even that he was a labor official. The reasons for the strong public reaction, and a larger vote for Goldwater as a result, went far deeper: ". . . in this case the union boss had moved with great secrecy. Democrat officials in Arizona had constantly denied they were receiving any help from organized labor and a number of opposition spokesmen had emphatically denied the charge that out-of-state political experts had been sent to Arizona by the unions to assist the Democrat candidates . . .

"We had said that out-of-state labor bosses would project themselves into the Arizona political contest to defeat Goldwater. The newspapers printed the truth of that prediction and the union aspect became almost incidental—the obvious resentment was against an 'outsider' trying to tell the people of Arizona how to vote."

Because of the shroud of secrecy COPE wraps around the strategists it sends into states or congressional districts, it is not easy for the opposition to uncover these men and trail their actions as thoroughly as did the Goldwater team. But in many campaigns they are there, nevertheless, and once the presence of an "outside" COPE representative is documented and skillfully revealed to the press, the 1958 Arizona incident displays how the opposition benefits.

\* Aside from the money and manpower fruits of the Marginal District Project, COPE has several other means of assisting incumbent liberal congressmen—especially freshmen—it wants re-elected. The 1964 crop of first-term Democrat liberals spurred COPE, in close cooperation with the party's national committee, into providing an extensive array of services for the newcomers.

They were given "education courses" by labor representatives, covering a broad range of legislative and social issues; union money was provided to cover expenses of newsletters, staff help, and the all-important weekend trips back to the congressional district; COPE and AFL-CIO organizations in a freshman's district were ordered by national headquarters to "talk up" the incumbent, tell non-union people what a great job he was doing, and build his image as a "doer."

This last undertaking is probably COPE's most effective weapon in aiding an incumbent in the pre-campaign days. On a national level it can never match the boost a Democratic Administration can give party incumbents (in the form of government projects for his district, passage of pet legislation, consulations with top-level officials, etc.), so COPE puts its stress on the level where it has unmatched power, the grass roots. Flying a freshmen liberal representative home, providing him with an audience, and later talking around in the community about his speech and activities in Washington, is COPE's way of helping out—and it is probably every bit as effective as the Democratic National Committee's providing the same congressman with a radio tape announcing a new post office for the district.

    * Up until now one might have more or less assumed that COPE's operations and activities were in the hands of men, cigar-chomping bricklayers or barrel-chested steelworkers who took the lead from national headquarters and put plans into action. This assumption should be laid to rest. In fact, COPE considers women such a vital link in its structure that it has a separate national division, the Women's Activities Department (WAD, and the women are known as "WADs"), to coordinate the political efforts of female union members and wives of the rank-and-filers; the national office is divided into two sections, with one WAD chairman for states east of the Mississippi and one for those to the west.

    In one bubbly recruitment brochure, published by national WAD, all sorts of platitudes are offered as reasons for joining the local WAD: "We're proud to be WADs . . . We believe that political action and political education are just about as important to the welfare of our family and friends as anything . . . Do you want to know something? Politics can be fun . . . You know, one of the best things about being a COPE WAD is the sense of belonging you get, the feeling that you're among good people trying to do something useful for your families and your community. Let's put it this way: the warm feeling that you're among friends."[94]

    For all this warmth and cheery idealism, there is another—a more starkly realistic side—to WAD's campaign role. "WAD is an integral and essential part of the COPE structure," says a national COPE WAD leadership manual ("available for leadership only"),[95] "indeed, it is an officially designated subcommittee of COPE. COPE's bylaws are WAD's bylaws, and COPE officers are ex-officio officers of WAD . . . While this Manual will be helpful as well to State WAD directors [as to local leaders], they are expected to receive direction from the National COPE office."

    In outlining the duties of local WAD leaders, COPE "lays down the law" in even harsher terms:

    "If you are a WAD chairman, one thing you must never forget: As a WAD Chairman, you are *appointed* by the COPE Chairman in your jurisdiction—county or central labor council—and as an appointee, to be effective, you must work in harmony with all responsible union officials. You must have their confidence and trust.

"You cannot—you *must* not—become involved in any factional differences. . . . You are therefore advised to resign from any trade union elective position whose activities could diminish your usefulness as WAD Chairman. . . . *Your sole office should be as chairman of WAD.*" (All emphasis COPE's.)

To make absolutely sure the WAD local chairman knows her subservient position in the chain of command, COPE stresses "two important rules [which] should always be heeded"; they are:

"1—The WAD is completely under the direction of COPE. Remember, the COPE chairman, with approval of the [local AFL-CIO executive] Committee, names the WAD chairman, outlines WAD's duties, and approves or vetoes its plans. WAD operates under the COPE constitution and bylaws. It is, in fact, a subcommittee of COPE.

"2—All WAD programs must be approved by the local COPE Chairman. A WAD works with COPE as part of its team. The WAD keeps the Committee advised at all times of what it is doing and what it is planning to do. The WAD executive board should meet with the local COPE officers at least once a month to discuss programs and problems."

With the WAD chairman set in her place, COPE outlines her duties. It begins by stating that she "has as her responsibility helping to establish an effective WAD program in her jurisdiction and to help train and guide volunteers."

What COPE terms "a first order of business" for the local WAD leader, something to be done even before volunteers are recruited, is to "set up and begin to equip a workroom." This could be any sort of room, as long as it is large enough to comfortably hold the essential ingredients: tables, chairs, typewriters, telephones, cabinets, political maps, city and county directories, and shelves for propaganda material. As "WAD does not have its own treasury," COPE advises, expenses for the workroom and other activities "should be financed by the appropriate CLU," or central labor union council of the AFL-CIO in the particular area.

To oversee the day-to-day operation of the workroom, COPE proposes a novel arrangement called "Chairman of the Day." "The 'Chairman of the Day,'" says the COPE WAD leadership manual, "should be appointed by the WAD chairman to direct the workroom for a stated period of time . . . say one day or an evening every week. This gives others a chance to learn all the routines of the workroom, increases their value and involvement, and, importantly, relieves the WAD chairman of the need to be present all day, every day."

Next COPE describes "the single most important job of COPE-

WAD," registering voters, and "the most important activity of WADs," uncovering union members and their families who are not registered and getting them enrolled. Essentially, WAD's role in the COPE voter registration drive is to perform most of the tasks outlined in the section on registration; this includes such vital elements as preparing the central card file, telephoning unregistered rank-and-filers, following up the calls with personal visits, and a variety of incidentals.

To assure that the efforts of volunteer WAD workers are duly recorded and rewarded, COPE suggests the local WAD chairmen keep a "Book of Hours," a full day-by-day account of hours worked by women volunteers. COPE then reveals the type of rewards handed out to the most dedicated workers:

"National COPE will award a pin and scroll to women who have contributed 100 voluntary hours or more to the WAD program. You will be asked to give National COPE the exact record of hours worked and type of work done in each case. Your state organization awards 500-hour pins for volunteers contributing 500 hours, and National COPE now offers 1000-hour and 5000-hour awards as well. Wallet-sized Registration Cards now are available as awards to men who contribute 100 hours to WAD activities."

An item of interest concerning WAD participation in the registration drive, is the importance placed on soliciting absentee ballots—votes cast by qualified voters who happen to be unable to appear at the polls on Election Day. "Some elections have been swung on the strength of absentee ballots," COPE notes, advising that the "WAD chairman should assign members to make a thorough study of state voting laws regulating absentee voting."

This study completed, COPE next suggests an approach: "Through telephoning or visiting union homes during your registration campaign, you will be able to build a list of probable absentees. Mail them information regarding the absentee ballot in time for them to apply for a ballot, receive it, fill it out, and return it so it will be counted."

The closing message COPE gives grass roots WAD chairmen is the old familiar theme stressing the year-round effort, and the fact that the next election campaign begins the second the polls closed for the last campaign:

"As soon as possible after election day, your COPE-WAD should hold a meeting to discuss the outcome and your role in it. At the meeting, include everybody who worked in the campaign.

"A thorough memorandum should be prepared based on the discussion at the meeting and should be forwarded to National COPE. This will be valuable background material for the next election . . .

"And don't forget, use the meeting to plan for the next campaign. The sooner you start, the better. A letdown can be disastrous to your WAD organization. The point is, *never let interest die;* keep it at a high level."

In its *How To Win* handbook, COPE supplements the leadership manual's directives to the WAD chairmen with suggested activities and plans-of-action for the women volunteers. Among the proposed undertakings of the local WADs are: canvassing selected election districts in behalf of COPE candidates; recruiting new workers for precinct action; distributing literature in public places; conducting neighborhood meetings where "friendly" candidates appear.

One important WAD operation is the far-ranging telephone campaign, a strategy put to use in registering voters, recruiting volunteers, propagandizing and getting out the vote. "The best results from telephone campaigns," COPE observes, "are achieved when the callers are centered in the same place, such as a union hall or WAD workroom where telephone banks have been installed to be used for a prescribed period of time by the WADs."

An imaginative, effective activity WAD workers perform is organizing "neighborhood house parties," a COPE-instigated variation on the standard campaign kaffeeklatch at which candidates meet briefly with housewives.

If the candidate's schedule is especially cramped and the main purpose for the house parties is for him to meet as many as possible, writes COPE, the parties should be arranged to provide for the maximum number during a single afternoon, adding: "This means strict adherence to a schedule and arranging the meetings along a route which involves as little time as possible driving from one to the next." With proper planning and figuring 15 minutes driving time between parties, COPE estimates that a quick-footed, hot-handed candidate could attend up to six such gatherings in one afternoon.

Although the chief function of these parties is for the candidate, or his representative, to meet the voters, COPE points out a side benefit:

"In the course of each party, try to find volunteers to give still other parties. But guard against the tendency of the same group of women to attend all house parties. The whole point is: *New faces at each party!"*

\* The last item to be included in this collection of miscellaneous COPE campaign activities would probably be best listed under the heading "Nuts & Bolts." These are seemingly small campaign tasks which nevertheless must be performed if maximum results are expected; they range from preparation for an election race to campaign gimmickery, and can best be summarized by quoting from their description in *How To Win:*

*Preparation: Knowing the Community and its Leaders*

The best way to orient yourself about your area—whether it's a precinct, a ward or a Congressional District—is to get a map. . . . Now, try to get all the vital statistics you can.

Probably the best data to begin with is a detailed precinct-by-precinct breakdown of the results of the last several elections.

If you don't have the newspaper clippings handy, your Board of Elections can supply the figures for the asking. Then get all the other statistical information you can about your community. You'll want to know:

—What the voting habits are in various sections of the community.

—What ethnic groups (German-American, Polish-American, etc.) live in the community, and where they are concentrated.

—What the predominant occupations, incomes and interests are in the various sections of your community.

—Much of this information is available near at hand: In newspaper files, for example, or in the public library. . . .

Once you have begun to gather information—on your area, on the opinion makers, on the political leaders—be sure to record it. Start file cards of the names, addresses and functions of the key people and note your observations about them on your cards. This file of names will be tremendously useful.

*Communications*

Getting Professional Help: If you plan a substantial publicity and advertising campaign—to put across your registration drive, a candidate, some specific issue—it might be well to consult a local advertising or public relations agency. . . .

If there's no advertising or public relations agency in your town—or if you feel you want to do the job yourself—look for professional help within the AFL-CIO family.

Person to Person talks: The cheapest—and still the most effective —means of communications yet invented is the simple talk between two persons.

The personal talk has many advantages—for you can see the person to whom you're talking and you know his reactions immediately. In word-of-mouth campaigns, the talker is able to adjust his language and trim his argument to the individual voter.

Speeches: No need to make a speech about why speeches are important—and anyway, it would be difficult to leave politics speechless. . . . here are some simple suggestions:

—If you plan to say something the whole community should know about, be sure to invite the press, radio and TV, and supply them with advance copies of the speech along with a brief news story summarizing the main points.

—Your speech and your speaker must be awfully good to hold the attention of an audience for more than 30 minutes. *Make that the outside limit.*

—Stick to one or two main points or themes and develop them fully.

—Take the offensive—be positive about fighting for your program.

—Don't dwell too much on the past—instead talk about the future.

—Know your audience and what they are interested in.

Placards, Stickers, Posters & Buttons: On candidate posters, be sure to make the picture of the candidate relatively large—people like to know what the man looks like.

The main thing, of course, is to have the name as large as you can—it has to be so familiar that people reach for it automatically when they see it on the ballot.

And if there's an overriding issue which appeals to a lot of people in your area, give your audience the *reason* why they should vote for your man: For Better Schools Vote for Joe Doe.

*Campaign Tactics*

Form a Campaign Committee: Once you've endorsed a candidate, you'll want to take a careful look at the various groups and segments of the population who might be expected to support him.

As early as possible, contact these groups and ask representatives of each to join in forming a campaign committee. . . .

The campaign committee's first and foremost task is to make a thorough survey of the lay of the land. You'll want to find out how well your candidate is known, how he can best appeal to the various groups, what their voting habits are, what kind of campaign is needed. Once you have a rough overall plan, your committee should appoint the various subcommittee chairmen you'll need for special assignments. These should include: Research, Publicity, Speaker's Bureau, Fund-Raising.

Campaign Strategy: A political campaign usually passes through three stages:

—The *introductory stage,* in which you introduce your candidate and his ideas to your members and the public.

—The *competitive stage,* in which you explain why the candidate is better than the opposition.

—The *reminder* stage, in which you presumably have told everybody about your candidate and his program and in which you now concentrate on a rising crescendo of reminders right up to the minute voters enter the polling place.

This planning is largely determined by a cool assessment of the strengths and weaknesses of your candidate. If he's little known, for instance, the job of getting him around, of introducing him, looms far larger than with a man well-known in his area. . . . Your evaluation of the candidate's assets and liabilities must be sober and completely unsentimental. . . .

Campaign Headquarters: Open at least one campaign headquarters in every city ward or rural county. . . . If at all possible pick a centrally located headquarters with an impressive, neat, cheerful appearance.

A vacant store or office on the main street—one which everybody can see—is usually preferable to a suite on the top floor of a crowded hotel. . . .

Campaign Devices: Here are some of the gimmicks some winners feel helped carry the day for them:

—Coffee-break on wheels. [A Congresswoman] campaigned from a three-room trailer, touring the district block-by-block. Her crews rang doorbells and invited voters into the parked trailer for fruit juice or coffee—and a visit with the candidate. She followed this schedule 14 to 18 hours a day, five days a week—and on Saturdays brought the trailer to supermarkets so she could meet still more constituents.

—Loudspeaker car. One successful campaigner made effective use of a sound-equipped car to tour his urban district. At pre-arranged stops, a non-political musical movie was shown to attract passersby— then the candidate spoke for five minutes. . . .

—Commuters. A Chicago Democrat unseated a three-term Republican with a pre-dawn campaign which saw him at one or another of the stops of the Rock Island or El Trains each day from 6:45 to 8:00 A.M.

—Triangular Car Racks. One midwestern candidate was hurting for funds—but had lots of enthusiastic backers. Some 50 to 75 of his supporters agreed to mount triangular racks (several feet high) atop their cars. The three-sided racks bore signs in luminous paint boosting his candidacy. Even at night, parked outside their owners' homes, the cars continued to attract attention.

This seemingly staggering array of campaign operations, strategies and assorted nuts & bolts should be placed in some general perspective. Unlike the registration and propaganda campaigns, these miscellaneous items are not applied to every COPE campaign throughout the country under the direction of national headquarters. These are selective activities, found either in areas where COPE is strong or where labor is putting on an extra special campaign effort.

Even the Women's Activities Department is not represented in every unionized area, simply because COPE is not well-organized or else the coordinated, semi-independent feminine effort is not needed; the Marginal District Project is restricted to "squeaker" or swing districts, and the suggestions contained in *How To Win* are by no means required practices for local COPEs.

Despite the selective, non-standardized nature of these sundry items, each is found frequently enough to warrant description, attention, and observation by non-labor candidates. Their role in the COPE campaign is fairly precise, acting as they do as supplements to the larger registration and propaganda projects. These are the small arms backing up the heavy artillery in COPE's well-stocked political arsenal.

## PART SIX: *COPE's Bankroll*

Politics has its myths, and mythology has its relevance to practical politics.

Consider Pandora, the original woman, a beautiful creature with a wily nature created by Zeus through Hephaestus to complicate the life of Prometheus and his race of men because of their presumptuous acts toward the gods. Before sending her to earth, the gods gave Pandora a box into which each had placed a different injurious effect, and warned her never to open it.

The gods underestimated the character of their creation, for Pandora had been imbued with an indomitable curiosity. When she reached the home of Epimetheus, the brother of Prometheus who had been *told* never to accept gifts from Zeus, Pandora could not resist taking a peek inside the box. She opened it a crack and out flew all the pent-up sorrows—envy, spite, revenge, mischief and the rest; quickly Pandora closed the lid, but it was too late—only "hope" remained in the box, a hoarded feeling to nurture man as the escaped sorrows pounded him from the atmosphere.

Today, when one delves into the subject of political financing a similar result occurs: peek beneath the surface and out fly wild charges, hidden spending, distorted reports, unfair laws and unreported finances; only truth remains locked inside, sustaining us until the day when everything is equal and campaign funding can be a straightforward business.

COPE is probably no better or no worse than any other political organization when it comes to indulgence in fiscal chicanery. Virtually every individual, independent group and political party tries to get away with as much as it can under the federal law governing campaign finances; only the unlucky few get caught. "There, but for the grace of Dodd, go I," was an oft-repeated refrain on Capitol Hill during the censure proceedings against the Connecticut Senator in 1967.

However! Because of certain factors, including the very structure of organized labor, COPE is able to get away with a little bit more, and to make these advantages pay larger dividends.

Labor is governed by the same law that regulates all political spending, the Federal Corrupt Practices Act, a piece of legislation written into law in 1925 and, despite subsequent amendments, creaking with age. The law is imprecise, overly vague and offers more loopholes than a pair of high-button shoes. In its regulations of spending by candidates for office, it clamps down on the individual office-seekers themselves, but says nothing about the various ad hoc committees a candidate may establish to do his spending for him—an escape hatch which now allows only the wealthiest of candidates to have a chance at higher offices.

In its governing of spending and solicitations by independent political groups such as COPE, the law begins with legal definitions. A "political committee" is any group of individuals which "makes expenditures for the purpose of influencing or attempting to influence the election of candidates or presidential and vice presidential electors" in two or more states of the union, or if the group in question is a part of a national organization. Contributions are defined as "anything of value," and include contracts or agreements, even if not legally enforceable. And "Expenditures" are said to include "a payment, distribution, loan, advance, deposit, or gift, of money, or anything of value, and includes a contract, promise, or agreement, whether or not legally enforceable, to make an expenditure."

The Corrupt Practices Act requires all political committees to make periodic reports (five in national election years, four otherwise) of contributions and expenditures, to be filed with the Clerk of the House of Representatives; these reports remain on file for two years, and may be viewed at the Clerk's office (in the Longworth House Office Building on Capitol Hill) by any interested persons.

These reports must include: name and address of all persons making contributions of $100 or more; total of all other contributions; detail on all expenditures of $10 or more; total of all other expenditures; total sum of aggregate contributions and expenditures for calendar year.

Getting down to the specifics of contributions and expenditures by business and labor, the Corrupt Practices Act declares:

"It is unlawful for any national bank, or any corporation organized by authority of any law of Congress, to make a contribution or expenditure in connection with any election to any political office, or in connection with any primary election or political convention or caucus held to select candidates for any political office, or for any corporation whatever, or any labor organization to make a contribution or expenditure in connection with any election at which Presidential and Vice Presidential electors or a Senator or Representative in, or a Delegate or Resident Commissioner to Congress are to be voted for, or in connection with any primary election or political convention or caucus held to select candidates for any of the foregoing offices, or for any candidate, political committee, or other person to accept or receive any contribution prohibited by this section."

So there will be no confusion in comprehending this section, the act defines a "labor organization" as "any organization of any kind, or any agency or employee representation committee or plan, in which employees participate and which exists for the purpose, in whole or in part, of dealing with employers concerning grievances, labor disputes, wages, rates of pay, hours of employment, or conditions of work."

Stripped to the bone of the right vs. wrong issue, the Corrupt Practices Act makes it unlawful for a "labor organization" to contribute or spend money in election of Presidents, representatives and senators. This means it cannot make contributions or expenditures from its treasury, just as banks and corporations are similarly prohibited from dipping into the till.[96]

What *is* lawful, on the other hand, is for labor organizations to make contributions and expenditures for political purposes from voluntary funds. These funds must be raised independent of regular dues payments and their transaction must be reported to the Clerk of the House. All other labor political spending "in connection with any" national election is illegal. That's what the law says.

And COPE, of course, obeys the law. It files thorough, detailed reports of its political contributions right when the Corrupt Practices Act tells it to, listing all the money it has received from "voluntary" contributions and all its political spending, including direct gifts to candidates. But there the honest truth ends and the fiscal ambiguity begins.

What COPE reports and spends under the heading of "political" finances is only the bare minimum. All other expenditures come under the heading of "educational" expenses, and these are paid for directly out of the union member's pocket. COPE may plunk down $500,000 annually for a voter registration drive concentrating almost exclusively on Democratic voters, and this is an "educational" expense not covered by the Corrupt Practices Act; it may pay the salary of a field representative working on the campaign staff of Democrat "X", and this too is educational; it may print brochures, voting records, periodicals, flyers and handbills, all plumping for the Democrats, but these are all classified as educational and are paid for by union money.

In all, one expert on campaign financing, Prof. Alexander Heard of the University of North Carolina, estimates that "campaign contributions from union treasuries may be made under at least thirteen different headings." According to Prof. Heard, whose work entitled *The Costs of Democracy*[97] is the "bible" on the subject of political spending, the thirteen possible categories are:

-donations to political groups
-spending by a political department
-spending by a citizenship program
-education and information spending
-communications
-public service activities
-public relations and publicity
-research
-legislative lobbying

-legal expenses
-officers' expense accounts
-general administrative and office costs
-staff salaries

The simple reason for COPE's latitude under the heading of "education" expenses is that Congress and the Internal Revenue Service long ago decided labor organizations were non-profit groups and should therefore be exempt from taxation. Specifically, according to the office of the Secretary of the Treasury, "the exempt status granted to labor organizations was first conferred upon them by the Congress in the Revenue Act of 1909 and has been continued up to the present date.

"The provision dealing with the denial of the exempt status with respect to certain charitable organizations if such organizations engage in substantial propaganda activities or otherwise attempt to influence legislation or to participate in any political campaign on behalf of any candidate for a public office, which was enacted by the Congress in 1934, was not made applicable to labor organizations."

The pertinent section of the Internal Revenue Service Code regarding this exemption reads:

"The term 'qualified nonprofit organization' as used in subsection (a) and (b) of this section means religious, educational, scientific, philanthropic, agricultural, labor, veterans, or fraternal organizations or associations not organized for profit and none of the net income of which inures to the benefit of any private stockholder or individual."[98]

What this verbiage means in practical application is that organized labor can do almost anything involving politics. But as long as whatever is being done originates with the organization itself, it will be considered educational, not political. It can print thousands of pamphlets backing Democratic candidates, or use the many other outlets listed by Prof. Heard, for political purposes, and the law will view them as "educational" projects if they are prepared by the labor group in question and are, at least theoretically, prepared for the benefit of the membership.

Of course, the tax exemption stipulation rules that COPE, and other labor organizations, cannot print or mail literature furnished to them by a party or candidate, just as they cannot put a party official on the payroll (unless he is also a union member) or make contributions directly to candidates out of educational funds (something done out of the "voluntary fund," to be discussed shortly). But, considering the partisan bias of COPE's literature and other so-called educational activities, there is no need or danger of its violating this provision.

The educational funds COPE uses in promoting its partisan views do not originate with the committee, but with the parent AFL-CIO. The federation spends on the average of between $10 and $12 million per year, some for legitimate labor purposes (organizing drives, legal costs, routine publicity), but far more for activities that have at least an indirect influence on practical political developments.

Out of the annual AFL-CIO budget comes the financing for radio broadcasts, the *AFL-CIO News,* the headquarters committees (COPE included) and departments, and sizable contributions to non-labor organizations. These funds pay for the services of George Meany and the guy who sweeps up at night, for political propaganda and strike bulletins, for computers and paperclips; they allow the AFL-CIO to roll smoothly and solvently along, and COPE, heavily funded by the federation's bankroll, tags right behind.

The latest detailed AFL-CIO financial report covered the fiscal year July 1, 1966 - June 30, 1967, during which the federation reported spending $10.3 million in general funds and $2 million out of its "special purposes fund." These reports are filed bi-annually at the AFL-CIO conventions in the form of a "Report of the AFL-CIO Executive Council,"[99] and contain detailed tables of federation receipts and expenditures.

A sampling of AFL-CIO general fund expenditures during fiscal '67 should include:

*$425,403.90 for executive office salaries; $27,883.34 for executive travel expenses;

*A total of $770,576.83 spent by the Public Relations Department, including $520,066 for radio programs (including, at that time, commentator Ed Morgan), $21,835 for television, $22,051 for taped recordings, and $15,500 for films and projectors;

*Expenditure of $544,861.31 by the Publications Department covering $191,160 for the *AFL-CIO News* (the report lists elsewhere $57,577 received from subscriptions to the *News*), $182,127 for the *Federationist,* and $22,103 for other printing costs;

*A sum of $294,107.99 spent by the federation's congressional lobbying arm, the Legislative Department, including $234,765 in salaries, $26,674 for travel, $6,990 for printing, and $14,571 for pamphlets;

*A $126,019 figure reported being spent by the Civil Rights Committee, in which $2,122 for printing and $92,809 in salaries are included.

And then there is the expenditure list for the Committee on Political Education, with the electioneering arm of the AFL-CIO having the highest budget in the federations headquarters—$897,141.36 for fiscal year 1967. One item on which COPE outranks even the lofty executive office is salaries, with $430,333.24 going for this item alone in fiscal '67; if this figure is divided by 25—the average number of employees (secretaries included) COPE claims having on its full-time headquarters staff—the result is more than $17,000, an average salary indicating that either COPE's personnel are well-paid or, more probably, it has more workers in the field than it cares to admit.

After salaries, the other expenses COPE lists for fiscal 1967 are:

—$132,429.73 for travel expenses;

—$117,847.04 for printing;

—$66,025.10 for pamphlets;

—$8,656.66 for mailing and postage;

—$2,771.13 for supplies;

—$13,813.17 for telephone and telegraph;

—$4,373.77 for subscriptions (presumably to newspapers and periodicals);

—$22,033.02 for field office upkeep;

—$96,773.49 in matching funds given state COPEs for political activities;

—$2,085 for miscellaneous items.

(As the fiscal year reported here—July 1966 through June 1967— covered the most active portion of the '66 congressional election campaign, it may be safely assumed that these COPE expenditures are fairly typical of a major campaign year. For the other fiscal year reported on at the 1967 AFL-CIO convention—July 1, 1965-June 30, 1966— COPE reported expenses of only $699,425.72, with the largest reductions over fiscal 1965 found in the categories of travel, printing, pamphlets; interestingly, salaries and field office maintenance were roughly equal in this off-year period to fiscal '67.)

These are the basic expenses COPE incurs during a year's operation, moneys covering its salaried personnel, propaganda, communications, office budget, and lesser assorted items. Not included here are contributions made from COPE's voluntary fund, including donations to candidates, or the money for its voter registration drive, an item paid for out of the AFL-CIO's Special Purposes Fund and by other labor sources.

In 1966, AFL-CIO secretary-treasurer William Schnitzler, the man controlling the purse-strings, reported that the federation contributed $375,000 out of the Special Purposes Fund for that year's COPE registration project. Additionally, in '66 COPE received $650,000 by way of the 5-cent levy on all AFL-CIO union members (mentioned in registration section) and $125,000 from the Industrial Union Department. This adds up to $1,150,000—the amount given to COPE for voter registration alone in 1966.[100]

Other items on the AFL-CIO list of Special Fund expenditures for fiscal years 1966 and '67 indicate the degree to which it financially supports the liberal-labor coalition. In the field of civil rights alone, the federation listed these contributions:

* $48,000 to the A. Philip Randolph Institute, a socio-economic-oriented civil rights group headed by activist intellectual Bayard Rustin (the AFL-CIO gives the Institute a regular $2,000 per month stipend);

* $20,000 to the National Urban League, a "moderate" rights group;

* $5,000 to the Southern Regional Council, an education and research organization devoted to analyzing integration problems in the South;

* $10,000 to the Leadership Conference on Civil Rights, a coalition of national leaders working for anti-discrimination legislation.

Other items on the special funds agenda demonstrating the federation's backing of liberal organizations are:

* $36,000 to the National Council of Senior Citizens, a Democratic Party front-group set up to lobby for a Medicare bill;

* $15,000 to the League for Industrial Democracy, a leftist education-oriented group headed by socialist thinker Michael Harrington;

* $20,000 to the National Advisory Committee on Farm Labor, a group lobbying for federal agricultural projects;

* $5,000 to the American Association for the United Nations, a predominantly liberal organization dedicated to spreading the U.N. Gospel throughout the land;

* $20,000 to the Institute for American Democracy, Inc., a pro-Democrat "front" group established to disseminate propaganda attempting to link Republicans with far-right extremist factions.

How funds are raised for these so-called educational expenditures—general and special purposes—creates the most controversy concerning labor's finances. Quite simply, they come from the worker's pocketbook. Just as labor's tax-exempt *spending* benefit comes courtesy of governmental rulings, its greatest benefit in *raising* money is provided by Congress in the form of compulsory union laws.

The Railway Labor Act decrees that any individual in a job related to railroad operations (clerks, conductors, porters, maintenance men, firemen, etc., etc.) must join one of the several railway unions; under the Taft-Hartley Act, every worker must join the union if his is a union shop, unless his state has passed a "right-to-work" law, allowing him to join only if he wants to. In the most elementary terms this means: a man who wishes to continue working in a union shop must join a union; to keep his union membership, hence his job, he must pay dues; the dues money he pays to his local—and, through it, to his international union, and state and national AFL-CIO—may be used for "educational" purposes which, in direct effect, support political candidates and parties to which he may be opposed; if he objects to this use of his dues he may quit his union . . . and lose his job. Most workers, needless to say, remain in the union, keep quiet, and watch their dues money being freely spent for political purposes.

No other organization in the country—political or otherwise—enjoys such a position. None has the benefit of a federal law ordering, in effect, all citizens under the organization's jurisdiction to join it, or lose their jobs, and no other non-religious organization of 14.3 million members enjoys a tax-exemption. These benefits, coupled with the enforced unity organized labor instils among the rank-and-file, give the AFL-CIO and its Committee on Political Education an incredible advantage when it comes to political financing.

One defense COPE usually offers to this charge is that other, supposedly "anti-labor," organizations have semi-compulsory membership and have more money at their disposal. One group frequently cited is the American Medical Association, which does its politicking through the American Medical Political Action Committee (AMPAC).

First of all, there is no federal law under which a doctor *must* join the AMA in order to practice. And if he does not choose to do so, it is unlikely that he will be accused of being a "scab," be blacklisted in his profession, or have his life threatened, as has happened to some workers who have bucked a union. Also, there is some disparity in numbers, with the AMA reporting a 1965 membership of 206,000, roughly 13.3 million less than the AFL-CIO reported at the same time. And, even though a doctor may make more than an auto worker (which will not be the case if Walter Reuther ever has his way), AMPAC reported spending $402,052 in 1964—a rather puny figure compared to COPE's political outlay of $941,947.

COPE wisely does not compare itself to the National Chamber of Commerce in political operations, as the Chamber makes no contributions and endorses no candidates. Besides AMPAC, the other organization COPE points to as representing business—or "anti-labor"—interests in politics is the Business-Industry Political Action Committee (BIPAC), often accused of being the electioneering arm of the National Association of Manufacturers (NAM). True, BIPAC was organized with the assistance of the NAM, but members of the manufacturers' association are not required to join or contribute to the political committee nor is dues money paid the NAM funneled into BIPAC; this vital difference from COPE is reflected in BIPAC's spending for 1964: $203,283.

A second defense of its spending offered by COPE is that, in every national election year a handful of wealthy individuals contributes more to political campaigns than does all of labor; a typical statement, echoed in subsequent years, reads:

"As can be seen, the political contributions of a mere dozen families of means exceeded the total direct political expenditures by workers during the 1956 campaign . . . When it is considered that 12 families in the United States are capable of bringing to bear in an election campaign well over half as much money as organized labor, which represents 16 million workingmen and their families, some idea may be grasped of the magnitude of the task faced by workers in presenting their views to the public and in seeking the election of persons sympathetic to their interests."[101]

(Still another example of labor's "persecution complex" form of anti-business propaganda: they're bigger than we are, so we have to fight dirty. Of course the large share of the 12 families' money went to Republicans.)

Notice here that the writer referred to labor's "direct political expenditures"—those it had to report—and this is an important distinction. These funds represent a fraction of what organized labor spends on influencing politics—in 1956 or any other year—with the rest coming out of the "education" treasury. Needless to say, neither the 12 wealthiest families in the country nor AMPAC nor BIPAC has a tax-exempt educational slush fund from which it can pay for field organizers, thousands of pieces of biased propaganda, voter registration drives, or those many other "educational" operations COPE relies on.

Also very important, although not directly related to finances, is that neither the 12 wealthy families, the AMA, AMPAC, BIPAC, nor any other organization, has the "captive audience" labor has in its membership. The rank-and-file can be approached through the shop, union meetings, or in their homes, and—because of the very nature of the union structure—are constantly "open game" for COPE organizers and propagandists. The primary function of a labor union is to act as the "protector" of the worker; unions were created to protect the member's job, his salary, and get him richer job benefits, but—as is only too clear—the sheltering arm of organized labor has since reached much further. Now the union also protects the worker's political interests, and if you don't like it, buddy, well then you just ain't a good union man and you're trying to start trouble and maybe you just better move on out of this here shop. That's the way it works.

Then there is the important distinction of manpower resources. Even in the unlikely event the AMA could get all its 200,000-odd doctor-members out pounding the pavement and ringing doorbells for AMPAC candidates, this would be a far cry from COPE's field troop force; as BIPAC is an independent organization, not directly tied to any other and without an "automatic constituency," its position is even weaker. Perhaps COPE would argue that the financial contributions of the 12 wealthy families equal the money *and* manpower assistance labor has available from 14.3 million members?

Other than "captive audiences," compulsory membership (in most areas), and tax-exemption, COPE also profits from the structure of organized labor through having funds available for its use virtually all the time. Rival political action groups must launch expensive fund-raising drives, or wait until a campaign heats up, before their war chests are filled; all COPE must do when it is short of cash is call upon the AFL-CIO, international unions, and its own treasury, at any time of day or night, and its needs are met. True, COPE may receive more contributions from workers during a national election year, but the funds for its vital "educational" projects are constant, with little yearly fluctuation.

The funds used for the quasi-political educational expenditures come from the treasuries of the AFL-CIO and its member unions. The regular channel for raising these moneys goes like this: the member pays his dues (usually monthly) to his local union; the local pays a set amount to the international union; the international is assessed a set amount by the national AFL-CIO; the AFL-CIO assessments are then used to finance all federation operations. (State AFL-CIO councils are financed by a separate assessment on all union members in the particular state.)

The figures involved in this transaction are, for the most part, among the best kept secrets in the world. But, some indication of the huge amounts involved can be glimpsed in the national AFL-CIO's regular assessment of affiliate unions of seven cents per member per month. In fiscal year 1967 this head-tax totaled up to an AFL-CIO per capita income of $11,679,772.17.

What this means to an individual union is revealed in the international United Auto Workers 1966 financial report.[102] According to secretary-treasurer Emil Mazey, the one-million-member UAW took in close to $57.8 million in dues in '66, of which it sent $916,709 to the national AFL-CIO and still owed the federation, at year's end, another $92,388. (The UAW also paid out $315,075 to the AFL-CIO's Industrial Union Department.)

Out of the AFL-CIO treasury accrued through assessments of unions, come the expenses for COPE's headquarters operations and the registration drive, as enumerated in the Executive Council's bi-annual reports to the AFL-CIO conventions. This figure—in fiscal 1967 it was $897,141 for headquarters budget and $375,000 for the registration project—are the prime source of COPE's income for its own "educational" activities.

On the state level matters are a bit different. The first resource for state COPE funds is national COPE, which returns a percentage of the money raised from union members in a particular state to the state's committee on political education. (The reasons for doing this, rather than having national keep all the money, will be gone into shortly.) Additional funds are then raised by a direct levy on state union members, going to pay for executive salaries, printing of propaganda, odd-year election campaigns, and other local action projects. (The proposed by-laws national COPE provides for state committees advise this per capita tax on all members in the state.)

The amount of this head tax varies widely from state to state and is continually being altered. The Pennsylvania AFL-CIO, for example, raised the per capita tax for its COPE operations from four cents to seven cents per member per month in 1964; with both the presidential contest and an important Senate race looming in 1968, the Keystone State's head tax could rise again.

In Texas, the state AFL-CIO assesses each Lone Star State union member thirteen cents per month, with nine cents earmarked for the federation's "general fund," one cent for public relations and education, and the remaining three cents going for political education. Again, this assessment could be raised at any time the state AFL-CIO executive board (with the approval of convention delegates) decides to do so.

States with an especially active COPE operation will, obviously, have a higher assessment than others. Michigan's hyper-active AFL-CIO, for instance, orders each state union member to cough up six cents a month for political operations; in 1966, one wire service reporter estimated, this head tax tallied up to approximately $500,000.

In states where a particularly intense campaign is being waged, the per capita taxes are not enough for COPE and an additional assessment is levied. Ronald Reagan's 1966 challenge to incumbent Governor Pat Brown frightened California's AFL-CIO leaders to the degree that every state rank-and-filer was asked to add one dollar to the Brown war chest.

(Individual unions also contributed to the Brown treasury from their own coffers, donations that caused, in one notable case, acute embarrassment. When Local 12 of the Operating Engineers Union in California contributed $50,000 to the Brown campaign, one member filed a suit to bar the transaction; his argument was that he lived in Nevada and he claimed the local had not received the consent of its 2,500 Nevada members before donating their dues money to a California candidate.)

The logical question to arise out of any discussion of labor's educational spending and resources, is: why do union members consent to having their hard-earned dues money used for projects bordering on the overt political? The member pays his monthly dues (out of which comes the state and national AFL-CIO assessments) often because he must in order to keep his job. But it is one thing to pay dues so that the union can bargain for a raise in the member's salary, better job conditions, fringe benefits, etc., and quite another when his union—and his federation—use this money in promoting partisan political candidates and positions to which the members have not consented.

Under the democratic system, membership in any organization is a trust, and doubly so when members are virtually compelled under the law to join. Just as the federal government exercises a trust in spending mandatory income-tax dollars, so must a labor union in union shop areas display utmost caution and concern in the spending of members' dues moneys. It is true, on the other hand, that labor has long been involved in political affairs, and that union members are well aware that a portion of their dues is being spent for political, or quasi-political, purposes.

When a worker joins a union he may be aware of these facts, but he is by no means consenting to them: where the union shop law is in effect, he is joining the union because he wants to work in his chosen occupation at his chosen location. The question is then asked: while a worker may not be consenting to all operations of his union, is not the purpose of union shop laws to protect the unions' security as a bargaining agent —in effect, bar "free riders" who might enjoy union-procured job benefits without actually paying for them; and is not a vital bulwark of this bargaining position the advocacy of, and opposition to candidates and proposed laws affecting not only labor issues, but indirectly related economic and social issues? The union member is also a citizen, the argument runs, and broader economic and social issues have a direct bearing on his standing as a wage-earner and spender, hence the active interest by the union in such issues—even though the members are not consulted on them nor their consent asked.

For the most part, these are precisely the issues dealt with in the celebrated Street Case, in which six Georgia workers (there were more at the beginning, but some dropped out along the extended legal way) filed suit to halt their unions, the AFL-CIO and COPE, from spending their dues on frankly political causes to which these members were opposed.

The basic issue in the case was whether unions affected by union shop contracts, such as those in the railway industry and in states without a right-to-work law, should be authorized, in the words of the appellees brief filed with the U.S. Supreme Court in 1959, to "force minority employees to *accept* and *pay for* political and ideological representation by unions whose views are repugnant to and opposed by such minority employees?"[103]

Continuing, the lawyers for the union member appellees declared their clients "are forced to supply funds for political candidates and ideologies to which they are opposed. To express their individual preferences and beliefs, and to support their own choices, they are compelled to pay twice, while other members can satisfy their political allegiances by the single union contribution. The practical effect is to penalize plaintiffs for their beliefs."

Stating the issue at stake in the most basic terms, the attorneys told the Supreme Court:

"The use of dues taken forcibly from minority employees to support beliefs and candidates which they wish to oppose deprives the minority of their constitutional rights to freedom of speech and press.

"Whether or not the First Amendment freedoms are entitled to a preferred position," the plaintiffs' argument went on, "these individual appellees have a right to express their own political views and cannot be compelled by agents forced upon them by governmental action to accept and pay for political representation by their political foes—collective representatives with such great power, resources and amplification that they can and do submerge and suppress the views of minority employee groups."

And the labor defendants in the Street Case—which included several unions in addition to the AFL-CIO and COPE—made no secret during the litigation of either their "great power," their "resources," or their "amplification." In the case's Stipulation of Facts, that portion of the legal literature which *all* parties agreed was "true, accurate and correct," several striking admissions were listed with the approval and consent of the union defendants. Among these:

* "The periodic dues, fees and assessments which [member] plaintiffs, intervening plaintiffs and the class they represent, have been, are, and will be required to pay under the terms of the union shop agreement hereinabove referred to, have been, are being, and will be used in substantial part for purposes other than the negotiation, maintenance, and administration of agreements concerning rates of pay, rules and working conditions, or wages, hours, terms and other conditions of employment, or the handling of disputes related to the above, but to support ideological and political doctrines and candidates which plaintiffs, intervening plaintiffs, and the class represented by them, were, are, and will be opposed to and not willing to support voluntarily.

* "The funds expended by the labor union defendants for political activities as set forth in this Stipulation of Facts are substantial, and the proportionate amounts of the periodic dues, fees and assessments which are being paid, or which will be required to be paid, by the plaintiffs and intervening plaintiffs and the class they represent are also substantial, and the amounts of such dues which are and will be used ultimately for political purposes are also substantial.

* "The money which has been, is being, and will be paid by plaintiffs, intervening plaintiffs and the class they represent as dues, fees, and assessments has been, is being and will be used in substantial part to support candidates for the offices of President, Vice President, U.S. Senators and Congressmen and their campaigns as described elsewhere in this Stipulation of Facts, and for direct contributions to candidates for various State and local offices, as described elsewhere . . .

*  "In numerous instances substantial amounts of general dues money are spent in State and local elections by various local lodges of some of the defendant labor unions and said sums of money are taken from the general dues funds of the local lodge treasuries. Said money is used for direct contributions to candidates for public office in State and local elections and in paid advertisements soliciting support for such candidates and for sundry other purposes directly connected with the political campaigns of such candidates, to all of which plaintiffs, intervening plaintiffs and the class they represent are opposed.

*  "The political activities mentioned in this Stipulation of Facts do not involve and are unnecessary to the negotiation, maintenance and administration of agreements concerning rates of pay, rules and working conditions, or wages, hours, terms and other conditions of employment, or the handling of disputes relating to the above."

What these five stipulated facts add up to is an admission by the labor defendants (including, remember, COPE) that: 1) the unions are spending dues money for political purposes to which the dues-payers may be opposed; 2) the amount of dues money spent for political purposes is "substantial"; 3) this dues money spent for political purposes includes financial support of candidates for national office and direct contributions to candidates for state and local office; 4) on the state and local level, "some" individual union locals use dues money for direct contributions to candidates, paid advertisements and other distinctly political purposes; and 5) none of these political expenses from the dues treasuries has anything to do with bargaining, wages, negotiations, or any other plant-oriented activity.

These startling admissions, particularly the last, should put the lie to any subsequent protests from labor leaders, to the effect that all their political activities are justifiable in that they have a bearing on the status of workingmen, and that labor's protection of the union-member-as-worker is indistinguishable from that of the member-as-citizen. As to what does and what does not properly constitute an issue deserving labor's political support, Justice William Douglas was later to say in his opinion concurring with the Supreme Court majority in the Street Case:

"It may be said that the election of a Franklin D. Roosevelt rather than a Calvin Coolidge might be the best possible way to serve the cause of collective bargaining. But even such a selective use of union funds for political purposes subordinates the individual's First Amendment rights to the views of the majority. I do not see how that can be done, even though the objector retains his rights to campaign, to speak, to vote as he chooses."

(The Corrupt Practices Act, it should be noted, had no bearing in this court case; the plaintiffs were arguing strictly on the constitutional grounds that use of union dues for political purposes under the union shop law was a deprivation of individual rights guaranteed in the Constitution.)

One strong line of attack used by the union members' attorneys was that these dissident employees "are forced to purchase subscriptions to the union's publications which bombard them with political and ideological propaganda." These rank-and-filers, they went on, are required to pay out of their dues money for a subscription to their union's official publication; therefore, "the required subscription to these periodicals is, we submit, a direct violation of the individual appellees' First Amendment rights, and is an 'exaction of dues, initiation fees, or assessments' which 'is used as a cover for forcing ideological conformity.' "

The argument put forth by the unions' attorneys in refuting this allegation stated that "obviously using funds to pay for . . . publications does not impose conformity. It leaves each of the employees, equally with each member of the public generally, free to make up his own mind, indeed, free to . . . read or not to . . . read." (To which the workers' attorneys replied: "The important thing to remember is that appellants and their affiliates do not rely on coercing a particular individual employee. We are dealing here with enormous numbers of people and a mass response is the objective.")

Otherwise, the essence of the labor union and AFL-CIO defendants' rebuttal to the questions raised in the Street Case was contained in a statement in their brief, saying:

"The right or power of a union to make political expenditures is neither derived from nor regulated by statute or other governmental authority . . . The appellant unions here do not rely on federal law authorizing union political activities or expenditures, because there is no such law. They rely only on the right of a private organization to run its own affairs in the best interests of its membership, absent any properly applicable governmental controls."

Also, the defendants' brief proclaimed, "An employee has no constitutional right to work for a specific employer without having his dues used in part for political or legislative purposes with which he disagrees." (If a chief of state practiced this philosophy he would be properly branded a tyrant.)

The action of the U.S. Supreme Court on these weighty issues was not to rule on the constitutional questions involved, but to quibble with the decision made by the Georgia State Supreme Court. Rather than deal with the substantive issues at hand, the much-vaunted liberal court of Chief Justice Earl Warren avoided substance, sent the case back to the state courts, and provided organized labor with a gigantic loophole through which it could escape, its shady financial dealings intact.

Beyond allowing organized labor to continue its financial business-as-usual, the Supreme Court's action (or, more properly, lack of action) served to deprive union members everywhere of legal grounds with which to challenge their union's use of their dues. The solicitor general of the United States, entering an intervenor's brief on behalf of the federal government, openly acknowledged the interest of government officials in the constitutional issues raised by the Street Case and urged the Court *not to rule* on these issues. Chief Justice Warren and four other justices acceded to this position and remanded the case to the Georgia courts.

In upholding the rights of the individual union members, the Supreme Court of Georgia had affirmed:

"One who is compelled to contribute the fruits of his labor to support or promote political or economic programs or support candidates for public office is just as much deprived of his freedom of speech as if he were compelled to give his vocal support to doctrines he opposes . . . There is a common saying, that 'Money talks—sometimes louder than the spoken word.' In the case at bar, the personal convictions of the plaintiffs on political and economic issues are being combatted by the use of their financial contributions to foster programs and ideologies which they oppose."

Furthermore, the state court, ruling that the plaintiff union members' dues money was being spent for political purposes "not reasonably necessary to collective bargaining or to maintaining . . . said union defendants as effective bargaining agents," forbade the unions from collecting further dues moneys for political purposes. The defendants, the Georgia court decreed, "are perpetually enjoined from enforcing the said union shop agreements . . . and from discharging petitioners, or any member of the class they represent, for refusing to become or remain members of, or pay periodic dues, fees or assessments to, any of the labor union defendants, provided, however, that said defendants may at any time petition the court to dissolve said injunction upon showing that they no longer are engaging in the improper and unlawful [political] activities described above."

Enter the Supreme Court—hand-in-hand with "interested" government officials. During the prolonged delay in his submission of the federal government's brief on the case, the solicitor general explained to the Supreme Court that part of the reason for the wait was "this case involves questions of constitutional law of broad application. Both the Department of Labor and the Department of Commerce, as well as other agencies of the Government, are concerned with the questions involved."

At another point in the litigation, the chief legal spokesman for the government acknowledged that "the issues involved in this proceeding have been the subject of meetings and consultation among various agencies of the Federal Government, and various views have been expressed as to the position which the United States should take as intervenor . . . ."

The position finally taken by the government was to urge the court to avoid all controversy and get rid of the case as quickly as possible, so no one would be embarrassed. In his brief to the Supreme Court, the solicitor general admitted in several places the constitutional implications of the Street Case:

". . . the issues raised by the parties are of great constitutional importance . . ."; ". . . the case presents a spectrum of constitutional problems"; "the disputed political and legislative expenditures cover a broad spectrum of activities, and at least some of them raise delicate constitutional issues."

And then, speaking for the government, the solicitor general's equivocating brief stated: "In our view, the Court need not and should not determine the constitutionality or legality of the various expenditures and activities which appellees challenge."

The attorneys for the union member appellees were completely taken aback by this reverse logic. "We can only regret," they wrote in their final brief to the court, "that the solicitor general, in the determination of basic constitutional issues, has preferred the advice of high officials of the Executive branch, rather than the teachings of [Justices] Marshall, Holmes, Brandeis, Cardozo, Hughes and the others now departed and still living whose exertions in this citadel will be remembered in the history of Freedom." In summation, the brief pointed out that "the solicitor general evidently believes that some of the expenditures under attack are unconstitutional," and urged the Supreme Court to rule on this basic issue.

The Court would not be moved by the appellees' arguments. In a negation of the very purpose of its being, the Supreme Court avoided confrontation with the constitutional issues in the Street Case, preferring placation of organized labor.

The means used by the court to get around the constitutional question was to claim that the section of the Railway Labor Act authorizing union shops did not provide for the unions to use dues money for political purposes. "One looks in vain," wrote Justice Brennan for the majority, "for any suggestion that Congress also meant in #2, Eleventh [the union shop provision of the act] to provide the unions with a means for forcing employees, over their objection, to support political causes which they oppose. . . .

"[Use of dues] to support candidates for public office, and advance political programs, is not a use which helps defray the expenses of the negotiation or administration of collective agreements, or the expenses entailed in the adjustment of grievances and disputes. In other words, it is a use which falls clearly outside the reasons advanced by the unions and accepted by Congress why authority to make union shop agreements was justified."

While this judgment did act to destroy the union appellants' contention that organized labor had "the right of a private organization to run its own affairs in the best interests of its membership," it also served as an escape from a constitutional ruling. For, if the Court could rule that Congress had not intended dues money to be used for political purposes, there could be no question of whether such subsequent use by the unions was in accord with constitutional provisions and guaranteed rights; as the court realized, one cannot rule on something if one refuses to acknowledge its existence.

The dissenting justices on the Court, as will be seen, said that this majority contention was patently absurd. When the union shop amendment to the Railway Labor Act was passed in 1951 every member of Congress had to be fully aware that a portion of the dues money collected under this provision would be used for politics; these men were not innocents, they had seen the AFL and CIO in action, spending millions of treasury dollars in politics.

No mention of political spending was made in the amendment simply because everyone understood such spending was practiced and there were not enough congressmen around at the time to vote through a law forbidding it; as these expenditures could not be barred, there was hardly any need to *guarantee* them. It was, therefore, up to the Supreme Court to decide whether the practice was a violation of the freedoms guaranteed in the Bill of Rights; it chose not to.

Having successfully avoided its responsibility as the highest constitutional adjudicator in the land, the Supreme Court proceeded to find fault with the state court's decision as a justification for remanding the case. After deciding that what must have been an incredibly naive Congress had not been aware that railway unions would spend union dues money for political purposes, the Supreme Court suggested the lower courts order the union appellants to return to the member appellees the portion of their dues which were used for politics.

However, the Court also ruled that the Georgia Supreme Court's injunction forbidding the unions to assess any further dues for political purposes was not justified. "There is no attempt to prove the existence of a class of workers who had specifically objected to the exaction of dues for political purposes," the court claimed. "Thus we think that only those who have identified themselves as opposed to political uses of their funds are entitled to relief in this action."

In other words, if a member wants to try and stop his dues from going into Democratic coffers he has to go up to his union boss and demand that portion returned to him—and then he might as well start looking for a new job. Needless to say, this is not a notably common practice among the rank-and-file.

The concurring opinion entered by Justice William Douglas is worth mentioning, if only for its contorted judicial reasoning. Agreeing with almost everything stated by the dissenting justices, nevertheless, Douglas writes, "There is the practical problem of mustering five Justices for a judgment in this case"; hence, he helped provide the majority and suggested relief for the union member appellees. It sounded as if Justice Douglas was in a hurry to get home to dinner.

In his blistering dissent from the court majority's decision, Justice Hugo Black took the opinion to task first and foremost for its avoidance of constitutional issues through gross misinterpretation of congressional intent in the Railway Labor Act. "Neither [union shop section] 2, Eleventh nor any other part of the Act contains any implication or even a hint that Congress wanted to limit the purposes for which a contracting union's dues should or could be spent," Black argues, continuing:

"All the parties to this litigation have agreed from its beginning, and still agree, that there is no such limitation in the Act. The Court nevertheless, in order to avoid constitutional questions, interprets the Act itself as barring use of dues for political purposes . . . In fact, I think the Court is actually rewriting [section] 2, Eleventh to make it mean exactly what Congress refused to make it mean. The very legislative history relied on by the Court appears to me to prove that its interpretation of [section] 2, Eleventh is without justification. For that history shows that Congress with its eyes wide open passed that section, knowing that its broad language would permit the use of union dues to advocate causes, doctrines, laws, candidates and parties, whether individual members objected or not. Under such circumstances I think Congress has a right to a determination of the constitutionality of the statute it passed, rather than to have the Court rewrite the statute in the name of avoiding decision of constitutional questions."

Summing up his sweeping argument in defense of the union members, Justice Black admits, "There is, of course, no constitutional reason why a union or other private group may not spend its funds for political or ideological causes if its members voluntarily join it and can voluntarily get out of it." However, the Justice goes on, "A different situation arises when a federal law steps in and authorizes such a group to carry on activities at the expense of persons who do not choose to be members of the group as well as those who do.

"Such a law, even though validly passed by Congress, cannot be used in a way that abridges the specifically defined freedoms of the First Amendment. And whether there is such abridgment depends not only on how the law is written but also on how it works."

But Black's arguments went unheeded. The Supreme Court sent the case back to the Georgia Supreme Court which sent it back to the point of origin, the superior court in Macon, Ga. The instructions were for the lower court to determine what portions of the dues money paid by the appellee members had been used for "legitimate" bargaining purposes and what was expended for politics. When the superior court ordered the unions to bring in all records of all moneys received and disbursed since 1953, in order to determine the nature of the expenditures, the unions panicked and said they were willing to pay the appellees back *all* funds they had paid over the years and would excuse them from paying any dues in the future.

The court agreed to this situation, as did the union members involved; their case had been in the courts for eight years by that time, and they had no desire to start all over again. "So we won more than we sought," said one person close to the Street Case, "but we did not have the pleasure of getting all the gory details on the inner workings of the unions in their misuse of the dues and assessments."

A case similar to the Street litigation was brought before the Supreme Court in 1963, and again the highest judiciary in the land refused to rule on constitutional issues. That decision said unions under the jurisdiction of union shop laws could not use members' dues for political purposes against their will; the unions, the Court said, must disclose political expenditures and what percentage of their spending is political. As we have seen, unions have a way of slickly disguising political spending under the "educational" label, so it is hard to see just what this Court decision accomplished.

The main practical impact of the Court's body of opinion on the unions' use of members' dues, however, is its discouraging effect on the rank-and-file. Before having the portion of his dues spent on politicking returned, the member must demonstrate his opposition to this practice, must get his union to divulge the percentage spent on politics, and, in some cases, must get a court order for its return. This is, to say the least, a long, tedious and costly proposition, and one not likely to endear the member to his shop steward, union president or even fellow workers.

But, thanks to an equivocating Supreme Court majority, the worker in a union shop has no other recourse. Meanwhile, labor unions can continue to use their members' dues money with virtual impunity. The Court might have saved itself a great deal of trouble, and principle vs. expediency soul-searching, by quoting Thomas Jefferson, who, as usual, summed up the whole issue long ago:

". . . to compel a man to furnish contributions of money for the propagation of opinions which he disbelieves is sinful and tyrannical."

The collection and disbursal of funds for "educational" purposes constitutes only half of the COPE financial operation. Transactions under the "educational" heading may represent COPE's largest—and most important—monetary operations, but there are some necessary expenditures which, however much the Corrupt Practices Act is twisted, simply cannot be included in this category. These, then, must fall under the "political" heading, funds given for specifically—and undeniably—political purposes and within the jurisdiction of the federal law.

Essentially, COPE's expenditures of a distinctly "political" calibre are—either directly or, indirectly through a state COPE—for the immediate benefit of candidates; also included are such lesser items as postage for non-educational mailings and printing costs for strictly partisan material. And the money spent under the "political" heading is raised through "voluntary" contributions to COPE, as the law insists they cannot come from union dues treasuries.

Although there may be room to question—at least semantically—just how "voluntary" these donations may be in some cases, their collection cannot be legally enforced. But, even if one momentarily grants that the contributions are voluntary, this still does not erase all the ambiguities COPE practices in its political finances—thanks again to the weakness of the Corrupt Practices Act.

It might seem, after COPE has been able to disguise so much under "educational" spending, that everything would be reasonably honest and above-board when it came to political finances and reports on these to the Clerk of the House of Representatives. Such is not always to be found, however. In fact, some of the items on COPE's reports of political expenses would provide good material for a mystery-spy novel.

Take, for example, COPE's contributions in 1964 to groups like the Western Development Committee and the Inter-Regional Civic Association. Now, on the surface these may sound like innocent-enough groups, maybe concerned with conservation or something of the sort; in truth, they were mere "front" groups set up to raise money for the conservation of certain liberal senators who were in danger of extinction in 1964. Thanks to some sharp investigative reporting by Walter Pincus of the *Washington Evening Star,* the public was enlightened as to the real intent of a variety of groups such as these two.[104]

"Special committees, established here in Washington, provide a means for labor organizations and others to contribute to Senate candidates without publicity," wrote Pincus in August, 1964.

"Thanks to an interpretation of federal law, the District of Columbia is not considered a State and therefore the transfer of campaign funds from a Washington-based committee to a state campaign organization is not viewed as an interstate transaction . . .

"The special Washington committees came to light during a study of campaign fund reports filed by labor organizations with the House clerk.

Among those listed and the Senators they reportedly have helped this year are:

"The Western Development Council, reportedly on behalf of Senator McGee, Democrat of Wyoming;

"The Inter-Regional Civic Association, reportedly on behalf of Senator Moss, Democrat of Utah;

"The D.C. Western Development Committee, reportedly for Senator Burdick, Democrat of North Dakota;

"The D.C. Committee for Good Government, reportedly for Senator Proxmire, Democrat of Wisconsin;

"The D.C. Minnesota Committee, reportedly for Senator McCarthy, Democrat of Minnesota."

The writer was forced to use the word "reportedly" in his story simply because no one who had contributed money to these "committees" (including COPE) would reveal the nature of the recipients and no addresses were listed in the Washington telephone directory for any of the committees. However, one 1964 report filed by the Democratic National Committee listed a contribution to the Inter-Regional Civic Association and gave as its address a downtown office building, housing, as Pincus wrote, "a number of law offices, any one of which could be operating" the Association.

The *Evening Star* reporter dropped the matter at this point, but further checking revealed that one of the law firms in the building had as a partner Keith Seigmiller, an attorney who had once been prominent in Utah politics and was considered an intimate of the state's junior senator, Frank Moss, the "reported" recipient of funds from the Inter-Regional Civic Association. When confronted with this string of evidence, an aide to Sen. Moss would only comment:

"The subject of campaign finances is very touchy; because of the Corrupt Practices Law, there are some things I cannot say. Keith Seigmiller is from Utah, he is close friend of Sen. Moss and has consistently supported him, along with other Utahans living in Washington."

Whatever the exact nature and identity of this mysterious Association, COPE gave it a total of $10,000 in 1964 (plus another $500 to Sen. Moss, its "reported" beneficiary). Of the other "front" committees listed in the Pincus story, COPE contributed a total of $10,000 to the Western Development Council (and $500 to Sen. Gale McGee); $500 to the D.C. Western Committee (none to Sen. Eugene Burdick); and $2,500 to the National Committee for Good Government (but none to its alleged beneficiary, Sen. William Proxmire).

A second device COPE employs in its political financial operations is to report huge chunks of money as going only to a state COPE organization, rather than to individual candidates. For example, in its reports to the House Clerk for 1966, COPE noted a contribution of $22,000 on June 20 to the Iowa AFL-CIO COPE. The committee's national headquarters claims it does this because it is policy to return half of the voluntary dollars raised in a state back to the state's COPE. Whether or not this system is used to the precise figure, or if more is given to states with the closest election contests, is difficult to assess; what reports of incoming voluntary contributions COPE does make available are listed only by union, not by state.

Noble as this COPE policy may sound, there are other reasons, of a more practical nature, for disbursing labor campaign funds in this manner. For one thing, there is no way of knowing exactly which candidates benefited from the COPE money and to what amount.

National COPE may give a state committee—such as Iowa COPE—a recorded amount, with the mutual understanding that a portion of this total is to go to Candidate X. Thus, Mr. X gets the money from the state COPE just as he would if national had sent it directly to him, but now COPE need not report having given the funds to X and the candidate need not report having received it. In private, off-the-record conversations, many congressmen will acknowledge having been the beneficiaries of labor financial largesse via their state COPE, but for the public record they remain mum. This is one way in which national COPE helps keep its "friends" from being labeled "labor captives."

Other than direct donations to liberal candidates, state COPEs can use the funds from national in a number of ways—all equally beneficial to the candidate. They can print literature, pay precinct workers, buy billboard space, rent sound trucks, purchase radio and TV time, and spend the money on a host of other political items intended to help the pro-labor office-seeker get elected.

In fact, national COPE prefers to see the funds it passes on to state committees spent as largely as possible by the local COPEs themselves, rather than given to candidates directly. The reasoning behind this is simple: by keeping a tight rein on its political bankroll—spending the money itself, on *labor* political projects—COPE is able, first, to use the funds where it feels they will do the most good, and, second, to make the candidate's campaign subservient to—and, in many instances, dependent upon—organized labor's campaign.

By holding back on its donations, labor is able to gain concessions from candidates, able to make its money pay off with something more than "just" a liberal victory. Anxious to get his hands on the withheld labor loot, a candidate might promise to name union representatives to important patronage positions, or to vote for specific legislation, or to back other labor candidates in crucial primary elections. Money, of course, speaks in many tongues, but perhaps in none more fluently than the politician's.

(In some instances, disputes between labor organizations and candidates have arisen over the control of this money, such as that which developed in Rep. James Hanley's 1966 campaign as described earlier. When a candidate absolutely refuses to accept any labor financial assistance unless he can have complete control over its expenditure, the labor group will usually find that a victory is more important than holding on to its funds and taking a chance on defeat.)

The total sum national COPE contributed to individual state committees during 1966 amounted to roughly two-thirds of all COPE's political expenditures for that year. In its report filed with the Clerk of the House January 19, 1967, national COPE reported having spent $906,165.53 for political purposes during 1966; tabulation of the sums donated to state COPEs over the year add up to $654,750. Following is a state-by-state breakdown, listing the amounts national COPE contributed to individual state AFL-CIO committees on political education during 1966:

| | |
|---|---|
| Alabama — $9,000 | Montana — $15,000 |
| Alaska — $12,500 | Nebraska — $9,000 |
| Arizona — $7,000 | Nevada — $10,000 |
| Arkansas — $6,000 | New Hampshire — 0 |
| California — $41,000 | New Jersey — 0 |
| Colorado — $16,500 | New Mexico — $12,700 |
| Connecticut — $29,000 | New York — $39,500 |
| Delaware — $14,500 | North Carolina — $8,000 |
| Florida — $4,000 | North Dakota — $6,500 |
| Georgia — $3,500 | Ohio — $28,500 |
| Hawaii — $4,000 | Oklahoma — $15,500 |
| Idaho — $14,500 | Oregon — $10,500 |
| Illinois — $20,750 | Pennsylvania — $34,500 |
| Indiana — $12,000 | Rhode Island — $9,000 |
| Iowa — $29,000 | South Carolina — $6,000 |
| Kansas — $11,000 | South Dakota — 0 |
| Kentucky — $5,000 | Tennessee — $20,000 |
| Louisiana — $20,000 | Texas — $13,000 |
| Maine — $8,000 | Utah — $6,000 |
| Maryland — $3,000 | Vermont — 0 |
| Massachusetts — $21,000 | Virginia — $19,750 |
| Michigan — $22,000 | Washington — $19,750 |
| Minnesota — $17,000 | West Virginia — $17,300 |
| Mississippi — 0 | Wisconsin — $13,500 |
| Missouri — $9,500 | Wyoming — $16,000 |

The remaining expenditures COPE reported for 1966 cover a broad range of political items. $3,000 was paid to the polling firm of Oliver Quayle and Associates, $250 worth of tickets were purchased for a fundraising film premier sponsored by the ultra-liberal Democratic Study Group, $2,500 was donated to another liberal front group called the Democrats for Progress Committee, and other scattered amounts went for printing, travel expenses, postage and telegrams.

One interesting item on COPE's list of contributions is a total of $53,500 to the local COPE in Cook County, Ill. This sum, separate from that given the Illinois state COPE, was undoubtedly prompted by Sen. Paul Douglas' sagging efforts in Chicago during his campaign against Chuck Percy; by giving these funds to the Chicago (Cook County) COPE, rather than the state organization, national probably reasoned it would be better—and more quickly—able to assist the Douglas cause.

A handful of individual candidates were also reported to have received COPE contributions in 1966, either in the form of direct donations or tickets purchased for testimonial dinners. These aspirants, however, were undoubtedly but a fraction of the number of liberal Democrats COPE aided; the rest got labor dollars through their state COPEs.

The one state in which COPE directly contributed to candidates instead of the state committee, was New Jersey; while the state COPE did not receive a cent from national, eight of New Jersey's 15 congressional seekers received direct COPE donations. This is but one more commentary on the fragmented status of New Jersey's AFL-CIO, and national COPE's disgust with the situation. As noted previously, the only Republican candidate in the nation COPE reported giving funds to in 1966 was New Jersey Sen. Clifford Case, who had not been endorsed by the state COPE.

The funds national COPE ladled out in 1966 to state committees, candidates, and for miscellaneous items which could not escape being classified "political," were raised, as in all years, through supposedly voluntary contributions. The law declares funds spent in this manner cannot come from dues treasuries, and because of this COPE places great propaganda stress on voluntary contributions. But these contributions are not purely voluntary, and in some instances the law is quietly flouted.

COPE assigns each international AFL-CIO union affiliate a quota in "voluntary contributions": 25 cents for each member. Ostensibly the unions are then to go out and raise this amount by urging members to kick in a dollar apiece for COPE, hoping that at least one-quarter of them will do so and the quota will be met. Not all of the unions do meet their goal, however, as in 1965 COPE reported only 39 internationals having "achieved 100 percent of quota in the COPE Dollar Drive."[105] (And even then, spokesmen at national COPE will anonymously acknowledge, all of these donations are not from voluntary sources and "there are ways" for the unions to juggle figures and disguise money taken from dues treasuries, but submitted as "voluntary.")

Yet, these facts and figures on income are only those which COPE chooses to report. If unions can find a way to hide dues money sent to national COPE as "voluntary," could not COPE just as easily find a way to disguise this money's receipt and eventual expenditure in the political field? COPE annually reports having spent close to $1 million for political purposes, and usually lists an income (from "voluntary" sources) of a few thousand dollars less, regularly showing a deficit.

The balance is presumably made up by the parent AFL-CIO, the source of COPE's educational and administrative expenses. The $1.5 to $1.8 million total which, on the average, is reported spent on all COPE activities (political, educational and administrative) often appears woefully inadequate for financing a political operation as wide-ranging and active as is the Committee on Political Education.

If every AFL-CIO affiliate fulfilled its quota of "voluntary" dollars (whether through actual solicitation from members or juggling the books), sending COPE "two bits a head," this would total up to an annual sum of $3.25 million. COPE reports receiving an average of some $2.5 million less than this figure. If COPE is receiving and disbursing the difference, this is very well hidden and undetectable; it remains an intriguing mystery for all those who observe COPE in action.

In any event, neither the voluntary contributions nor the quotas assigned individual unions are compulsory, in the sense that the AFL-CIO's seven cents per-member-per-month tax on affiliates is mandatory. If an affiliate does not cough up its monthly head tax to the federation, President Meany can yank its charter and have it booted out of the AFL-CIO; if a union is reluctant to contribute its 25 cents per-member-per-year to COPE, only the parties involved are aware of the penalties that await.

Interestingly enough, in its periodic financial reports COPE does not list a single one of these union contributions, because they are supposedly composed of "voluntary donations" from members in the sum of one dollar apiece; the law does not require the reporting of any contribution under $100. Thus, the United Auto Workers' financial reports for 1964 list contributions to COPE totaling $75,000—its quota for the year; yet, at the same time, COPE did not report any contribution from the UAW. That's the way the law works.

A glimpse of how things work on the grass roots level is provided by

COPE's *How To Win* manual. There may be means by which international unions can cover up moneys taken from treasuries, disguising them as "voluntary" contributions, but this does not keep most AFL-CIO affiliates, under COPE's prodding, from conducting a "Give A Buck To COPE" campaign. In an effort to get more workers to cough up a donation to COPE, a large section of the committee's electioneering handbook is devoted to "How To Conduct A COPE Dollar Drive."

"Politics costs money," COPE begins, "money to educate members to the need for political action" and "money to take the issues and candidates before the public." And after some "poor-mouthing" over the political spending of Big Business ("Big Business regularly pours millions of dollars into politics to try to elect its favorite conservative candidates"), COPE gets down to the basic "dos and don'ts" for local leaders to follow when conducting the Dollar Drive:

—DO plan all steps of your Dollar Drive carefully in advance.

—DON'T get started before you have appointed collectors in every department and section of your shop.

—DO appoint one collector for each 10 or 20 members. These are the only ones he or she is to contact.

—DON'T burden one collector with so many people he gets discouraged before he even starts, or can't easily find the time to approach all of them personally.

—DO train your collectors so that they are prepared to answer *all* questions about COPE.

—DON'T embarrass your collector and lose contributions because he isn't quite sure how COPE money is used.

[NB: COPE doesn't explain in *How To Win* precisely how this money *is* used, however.]

—DO approach people positively, appealing simply and directly to them as good citizens and good trade unionists.

—DON'T give people an easy way out by asking them half-heartedly or by annoying them with high-pressure sales tactics.

—DO continue your drive until you are satisfied every member is well informed about COPE and has been asked personally for his or her contribution.

—DON'T announce the end of the drive before your collectors and your publicity committee have had a chance to do their very best.

—DO coordinate your Dollar Drive with the specific period, if any, announced by National COPE. . . .

—DON'T launch your fund drive on the heels of another drain on the pocketbooks of your members.

—DO set up a system of reporting and follow-through, so that your drive collectors know that you are interested and involved in the campaign at every step of the way.

—DON'T just send your collectors off with a pep talk and then leave them to shift for themselves.

Next *How To Win* provides an outline on setting up and carrying out the COPE Dollar Drive:

> The first order of business in a successful COPE Dollar Drive is the appointment of a local union COPE fund-raising chairman . . . The Chairman, with the aid of the [union's] officers and COPE, should divide the membership into small, manageable units. . . .
>
> From within these small units, the persons who will conduct the Dollar Drive should be selected. Each should be given a list of 10 to 20 members—fewer, if possible—within his department or section to contact during the COPE Dollar Drive. . . .
>
> The local union president should send letters to the membership announcing the start of the COPE Dollar Drive and asking each member to make his contribution. Collection days should be those on which members are most likely to have money—*pay days*. . . . you can help your drive along by putting up COPE Dollar Drive posters wherever you can—around the shop, the canteen, union halls. . . .
>
> It's always effective to promote a little competition between the various departments and sections of your shop. Set up a chart on which you enter the daily or weekly box score of totals collected in each department. Display the chart on a large poster in a prominent place where everybody can see it, and publish it in your union newspaper.
>
> It will show your members which department is out in front—and which one is lagging behind—and will thus inspire the laggards into greater activity. . . .
>
> As the drive nears its end, the COPE fund-raising chairman should issue a statement of how far the local union has come and how far it is from the goal of 100 percent success. The members should be reminded that they have only so many more days to go. And they should be given a last-minute persuasive appeal to do their part. . . . This might also be the time for the president of the local union to send a personal letter to all members who have failed to contribute up to that time. . . .

If one thing is obvious from this list of instructions it is that, although these contributions may be voluntary in strictly literal terms, COPE advises the use of every subtle form of coercion imaginable. It urges the local COPE fund-raisers to play upon the union member's "loyalty" to his union and the "solidarity" he should feel toward his fellow members, with the unwritten implication being that if a member does not contribute his dollar (or, in COPE's words, is a "laggard") he is somehow knifing his Brothers in the back.

The key to the dollar drive is personal contact, and COPE describes it as "a concentrated effort to make *every* member of your local understand why his or her money is so urgently needed." *How To Win* suggests that there be one collector for only every ten to twenty members ("fewer, if possible") and that they should be approached as "good trade unionists." If they don't contribute, apparently, they are "bad" unionists. Collectors are advised to make their contacts on pay days, when the member is flush. And often collections are made right in the shop, just after the worker has received his pay envelope.

And to reinforce possible guilt feelings in the non-contributors, COPE suggests the union post a list of everyone who has kicked in, and to print the list in the union newspaper. This, it says, is to "inspire the laggards."

Finally, for those reluctant fellows who have yet to contribute as the drive draws to a close, COPE suggests "a last-minute persuasive appeal to *do their part*" (emphasis added) and, failing this, a personal letter from the union president. As every rank-and-filer knows full well, the president of his local union has considerable power over his welfare: the president can have the worker placed on the nighttime "graveyard shift," can have him shifted to a less desirable position, or can perhaps make him lose his job entirely. There are ways, as COPE is aware, to force people to do things voluntarily.

To buttress collection efforts COPE suggests a variety of fund-raising gimmicks (raffles, dances, picnics, etc.), provides several effective propaganda pieces, and prepares collectors with ready answers to any difficult foreseeable questions they may encounter. For example, if a Republican member asks the collector why COPE appears to contribute mostly to Democrats, the money-seeker is advised to reply that "COPE is interested in the program and platform rather than individual party affiliation. It endorses and helps Republicans as well as Democrats when they stand for the legislation the AFL-CIO believes in."[106]

Whatever the gimmick, argument, method or system used to collect these voluntary dollars, COPE's most revealing directive to collectors is when it advises in *How To Win:* "Don't give people an easy way out . . ."

In the COPE financial scheme of things the worker never has an easy way out. If he does not chuck in his buck for COPE, he is still underwriting labor's political activities. His union bosses take a portion out of each pay check as dues and assessments, part for themselves and part for the AFL-CIO, to pay the bills at COPE.

It may be only a small percentage that is taken out, but relative amounts are not the issue. The point in contention is, as was stated in the Street Case, that when the workers do not approve these politics, "The use of dues taken forcibly from minority employees to support beliefs and candidates which they wish to oppose deprives the minority of their constitutional rights to freedom of speech and press."

What happens to this money when it leaves the worker and finds its way to COPE is a mystery wrapped in a heavy cloak of compulsive secrecy. COPE may, as is reported by itself and the AFL-CIO, spend only $1.5 million in one year, or it may spend almost three times that amount. The specifics of COPE's financial operations infrequently see the light of day.

If labor's ability to collect dues money through compulsory union shop laws would seem an abridgment of constitutional freedoms, this is a matter for the Supreme Court—when it summons up the courage—to finally decide. If COPE is able, under the archaic Corrupt Practices Act, safely to maneuver, it is then up to Congress to write a better law.

COPE, admittedly, takes full advantage of the inadequate federal campaign spending law and uses every gimmick it can devise to further cloud its spending activities. And then, although COPE may not be alone among political action groups practicing fiscal dexterity, it certainly could teach the rest a trick or two.

# PART SEVEN: *Getting Out the Labor Vote*

With the financing, registering, propagandizing, planning, and doing all done, the final piece of action for volunteers in the COPE campaign is the get-out-the-vote drive on Election Day. This is not the end of the line for COPE workers or their leaders, for the activities continue the day after elections with a "Wednesday Morning Quarterback" session, and then preparation for the next round of elections— national, state and local—begins in earnest.

As far as one particular campaign is concerned, however, the effort to get every potential pro-labor vote to the polls on Election Day is the culmination of all that has gone before, the day when the extra bit of energy is expended by volunteers to make sure their previous efforts are not wasted. Here is where the extensive activities of the COPE campaign will pay off with a liberal victory, or else will signal a return to the proverbial drawing-board.

Election outcomes often have been, are now, and will be, "decided" long before the actual voting; everyone seems to know "for sure" what the result will be, and the optimistic candidate has his victory statement neatly typed and double-folded in his inside coat pocket. The fact that many a candidate has slunk home to bed Election Night with his statement unfolded, virginal, with his "for sure" supporters muttering of "vote stealing," has never stopped the same little drama from being enacted over and over again on hundreds of election nights in a hundred different communities.

Overconfidence is one luxury COPE has never felt it could afford. Every poll, every report, every barroom analyst, may tell the labor politicos how great a margin their man will win by, but if those workers are not manning the polls and bringing in the voters Election Day, heads will roll the next morning. As should be only too obvious by now, COPE leaves nothing to chance; no detail is untended and no order left unenforced. Above and beyond all, the Committee on Political Education is not an organization prone to indifference.

This attentiveness is as visible in COPE's get-out-the-vote project as in any other. Here again, as with registration, propaganda distribution, nuts & bolts and the rest, is found the careful planning and meticulous execution.

This drive is most closely related to the registration project, as the two have similar organizational structures, use many of the same tools and tactics, and, in frequent instances, the same personnel. The key to this relationship is found in a directive from one COPE manual:

"When the registration drive is over, the emphasis—organizationally and operationally—should be shifted *immediately* to the Get Out The Vote Compaign." [Emphasis: COPE][107]

The same central card file compiled during the registration drive will be used later for a pre-election voter canvass and used again on Election Day to be sure potential pro-labor voters get to the polls; often, when it comes time for Election Day checking, COPE workers will be assigned the same voters they registered, so already-established contacts will make getting out the labor voters all the easier. And other tactics of the registration drive will be similarly converted, including providing baby-sitters while mothers vote, widespread telephoning to tardy voters, and driving voters to the polls.

The likely result is that where COPE has executed an extensive, well-organized registration drive, there will be a correspondingly effective operation on Election Day. (Of course, there can be either one without the other—we are not dealing with ironclad situations.) Typically, COPE's 1958 Wisconsin operation, whose successful registration aspect was described earlier, saw one union hall full of workers manning 60 telephones and making some 25,800 phone calls to voters between 9 a.m. and 7 p.m. on Election Day.

And in Sen. Estes Kefauver's 1960 Tennessee primary, also mentioned in the registration section, Chattanooga COPE workers made 15,000 phone calls on the voting day. In Knoxville, 96 women volunteers (under WAD auspices) placed 16,000 calls to voters, while the men pitched in as drivers, poll-watchers and all-round handymen. The end product was, in the words of one high-ranking state AFL-CIO official, "by far the best job labor has ever done in Tennessee."[108]

Predictably, COPE itself provides the best outline and description of the get-out-the-vote project in its own *How To Win* manual. Beginning with a reminder ("all your efforts before and during the campaign stand or fall on your ability to get out the vote on Election Day"), followed up with an admonition ("so get set early to flush out the biggest vote ever seen in your community"), COPE tells its field troops to "sit down—right now" to organize the Election Day operation. Then the handbook for success offers suggested guidelines—from Headquarters through Summing Up—for running this all-important project:

### HEADQUARTERS
Open an Election Day headquarters in every precinct, if possible—ideally, it should be near the polling place . . . you'll need several telephones and sufficient space to accommodate your telephone committee, some drivers, and several other volunteers for odd jobs that always come up unexpectedly.

### VOLUNTEERS
Enlist as many volunteers as you can.

Divide your volunteers according to the following assignments:

Checkers; telephoners; messengers; drivers; baby sitters; poll watchers; literature distributors; crews for your sound truck.

There's no need to have all your workers [twenty is about the minimum needed] congregate at headquarters—in fact, that can make for a lot of confusion.

Drivers and baby sitters, for example, might stand by at home, and the telephone committee can call them when they're needed.

If you list them according to the block or area in which they live, you can call the one nearest to the address where he or she is needed—thus saving precious time.

### LAST CANVASS
During the week before the election, have all your volunteers make one last swing through the precinct, ringing the door bell of every voter registered in your candidate's party and every independent voter.

The purpose of this last-minute canvass is:

—To find out, if possible, how the person will vote.

—To remind the voter to ballot early, and to give instructions on the location of the polling place, the hours it's open, and any local rules regarding time off from work to vote.

—To find out if the voter needs help (transportation, baby sitting, etc.). . . .

### ASSIGNMENTS
On Election Day morning, every baby sitter and driver should have his or her list of assignments and should proceed to carry them out.

As soon as the assignments are completed, they should call the telephone committee to report for further duties which develop in the course of the day.

### MAN THE POLLS
Have a full shift of checkers at the polling place as soon as it opens.

Have two checkers for each table, so they can take turns and so each table is covered for the entire time the polls are open.

Where they won't allow you to work inside the polling place, the job of checking off the voters is, of course, more difficult.

If weather permits, you can, of course, set up your checker just outside the polling place.

PHONE CALLS

The names of those who haven't yet voted are turned over periodically to your telephone committee.

These people should then be called again and reminded to vote.

ASSISTANCE

If the telephone committee locates someone who may need a driver or baby sitter, it will dispatch one at a time convenient to the voter. . . .

If [housewives] have small children or if the weather is bad, they often decide not to bother.

That's where your baby sitters and drivers can often be decisive in bringing out the necessary margin for winning a precinct.

LITERATURE

Throughout the day, see that your literature is distributed in front of the polling place.

If weather permits, you should set up a table with all your literature as close to the entrance of the polling place as your local law permits. . . .

Sample ballots are probably the most valuable kind of literature you can hand out on Election Day, since many people will take them into the voting booth, if the law permits.

POLL WATCHERS

The poll watcher's job is to check on the other poll watchers, on individual voters, on fraud, and on possible illegal activities on the part of election officials and outsiders.

They're especially concerned with the right of individuals to vote, and frequently serve a useful purpose uncovering individuals who have no legal right to vote in a given precinct or at a certain polling place. . . .

The most important thing for any poll watcher is to *know the law*— for ignorance could cost your side the election.

REMINDERS

It's always a good idea to run a sound truck through the streets on Election Day, reminding people to vote [and] cautioning them to vote early. . . .

SUMMING UP

It sounds like a lot of work—and it is.

But it's the most important job your COPE can do.

Election Day is the time when all your previous work—building a precinct organization, registering voters, running the campaign, etc.— will really tell.

Make it all pay; bring it all into play by getting out the vote.

And remember: Every vote counts—and counts heavily.

A vital role in the get-out-the-vote drive is played by the female volunteers of the Women's Activities Department. The WAD workers may serve as drivers, precinct workers, poll watchers, telephoners, baby sitters, and general odd-jobbers.

"Each of your members," COPE tells WAD chairmen in the department's leadership manual, "should have a specific election-day assignment and should know what her responsibility will be well in advance of voting day."

The men who run COPE, always ones to make the most practical use of any situation, have realized that the Election Day task WAD volunteers can undertake with the most authority is that of telephoning voters. For this purpose, COPE provides in *How To Win* a detailed set of telephone campaign instructions for both the WAD chairman and the phoners themselves, and these can be easily adapted by any other political action group; first, the suggested procedure for the chairman:

1. Try to have everyone in the hall no later than 9:00 A.M. From 9 to 9:30 instruct the telephoners. Go over with them the instructions for telephoners printed below. Have mimeographed copies of the instructions available.

2. Start the telephoning promptly and continue until calls, including re-calls, have been made.

3. Emphasize that the number of calls made is what counts—so keep the speech short, but polite.

4. Start the re-calls at approximately 3:00 in the afternoon.

5. Stop your calling at approximately 7 P.M. even though you have not completed calling all the numbers on your list.

6. Have at each telephone: Cards or precinct sheets containing the numbers to be called; rubber bands; sharpened red pencils; sharpened plain pencils; small note pads; ash trays.

7. Have in the workroom a list of the polling places and a few extra telephone directories, the telephone number of the Registrar of Voters, the telephone number of the telephone repair man, and telephone number of the person in charge of transportation and babysitting. . . .

8. Be sure food and drink are available and that there are clean dressing rooms handy to the hall.

9. Be sure to keep a careful record of:
   A. Number of telephones in use;
   B. Number of hours each person telephoned;
   C. Number of persons calling;
   D. Number of calls made.

Next comes COPE's proposed list of telephoning instructions for the WAD chairman to reprint and hand out to the volunteers making the calls:

1. Do not argue. Do not be drawn into a discussion of candidates. Be brief but courteous. Remember that it's too late to change anyone's mind on election day. Your call is to get out the vote. Your success is in the *number* of calls made.

2. If no one answers after about 6 rings, hang up and go on to the next number. Don't waste time waiting for someone to answer.

3. In answer to "Where do I vote?" give the address of the polling place listed at the top of each precinct sheet.

4. If anyone needs help to get to the polls, write down the name, the *address,* time they want to go to the polls, and telephone number. (It is important to double-check the address. Sometimes people take old telephone numbers with them when they move to new addresses.) Give this information to *the telephone bank chairman.* She will take over from there.

5. If asked "Can I vote?" do *not* attempt to answer. Instead, take name and telephone number—say, "Someone will call you back in a few minutes." Write the name, telephone number and the question asked on a pad provided and give the information to the Telephone Bank Chairman. Then go on to the next number. (The Telephone Chairman will refer same to an expert seated at one of the extra telephones who will make the return call.)

6. Do not leave messages with children.

7. Put a red mark after each *unanswered* call. This will signify that a recall is to be made later in the day.

8. If your telephone gets out of order, tell the *Chairman of the Telephone Bank* at once.

9. If there is a wrong number response, or if your person has moved, give the trouble-number to *Chairman of the Telephone Bank* and go on with your calling.

10. If by accident any of these numbers you have should be a toll call, *don't* call it.

11. Whenever you leave the telephone station, even for a few minutes, be sure to draw a line under the last name you called, and put your initials there. This will prevent anyone from duplicating calls you have already made.

12. Remember, put a smile and good cheer into your voice!

If this array of operations is put in full working order on Election Day, it is hard to see how COPE could ever blame any subsequent defeat on labor indifference. One could say that COPE does everything but cast all the ballots itself; but, if election laws permit voters to carry COPE's "sample ballot" into the booths (or up to the box) with them, COPE is, in effect, doing just that!

However, it is necessary to point out that the effectiveness of COPE's efforts in getting out the pro-labor votes is a relative matter. Unless COPE has successfully performed all its other campaign functions, has "sold" its issues and candidates, the Election Day drive will have little force; if it has done well in the preliminary rounds, on the other hand, comes the final round on a November day . . . watch out!

Furthermore, in a lackluster campaign, with colorless candidates (on both sides) and no overriding emotional issues, COPE's coordinated efforts on Election Day can make all the difference in the (political) world. Frequently, backers of a tired incumbent candidate, having thought they had lulled the voters to sleep during the campaign, have been shocked to find that COPE came along and woke up enough of them on Election Day to grab away a "sure victory."

But, no matter how relative, COPE's suggested actions for Election Day *are* there, they *are* used, and used, more often than not, very effectively. If they are fruitless last-ditch efforts in a poorly run COPE campaign, the same strategy has provided the difference between victory and defeat in hundreds of others. As with the voter registration project, the drive to get-out-the-labor-vote leaves no potential vote unturned.

And COPE is only too aware that voters—more so, even, than money, manpower or propaganda—win elections. COPE makes its campaigns pay off with liberal victories, not because it *realizes* this basic fact of political life, but because it *practices* it.

## PART EIGHT: *The Morning After*

If the basic ingredients of a political campaign are what that master of verbal *haute cuisine* characterized in another context as "blood, sweat and tears," the antics of Election Night are something else again. Perhaps there are some tears, but, generally speaking, the liquid most in sight is somewhat less saline.

The victors imbibe in joyful celebration, the beaten in joyless consolation. And then, home—perhaps the line is not so straight, but the goal is reached and the sleep of both victor and loser is deep. Morning comes late the next day, and politics—ugh!—is the least desirable topic of conversation for awhile.

Here again, of course, COPE is a little bit different. It's not that labor's political activists don't freely partake of the Election Night festivities, or that COPE lobbies for temperance laws on the side, but, dammit, there's work to be done!

"There's a special pleasure that comes the day after election," informs COPE's *How To Win,* "when you pick up the morning paper and see in cold print the report of a victory you helped fashion. And there's a special determination to do better the next time, if you lose.

"There's just one thing: Win, or lose, *you now must get to work on the next campaign.*"

The italics are COPE's and one can almost visualize them as a huge arm, reaching all the way from Washington to shake the slumbering labor politico from his warm bed, rousing him from what is probably a well-earned respite from political activity, handing him his lunch pail and sending him out to get to work on the next job. "Yes," says COPE, "the time to begin political organization for an election is on the day after the last election."

In the final chapter of *How To Win,* COPE describes this persistent effort as the very essence of the labor political machine: "COPE committees in the local union, city, county, Congressional District and state are continuing organizations. They're not just in business for a single campaign."

"The election just completed," continues COPE, "provides a good yardstick to measure the job you must do next time. Its vote figures will show you some of the progress you've made—but they'll also chart the course for the campaigns ahead."

The best procedure to follow, the committee suggests, is for COPE leaders to set up a "Wednesday Morning Quarterback" session to go over the past election and plan for the next. Among the things to be done in this session, *How To Win* includes the following:

The first thing to do—that Wednesday morning—is to remember the volunteers who worked so hard in the past few months, and especially on Election Day . . . a note of appreciation, or a nice party for all of them—or both—will keep them in the right mood.

The next important job is to take a close, hard look at the election returns in each precinct . . .

Whether they spelled victory or defeat, study these figures carefully. Compare them with the results of the previous elections—and the one before that. What do these figures tell? . . . Ask yourself:

—Was the appeal of a particular issue not as strong as you thought?

—Should the candidate have spent more time in a particular precinct?

—Did the literature go over well?

—Did you do enough to reach the minority groups and other potential allies?

—Would the results have been different if you had a more intensive registration campaign?

—Of the potential voters, how many actually voted?

—Where was the greatest gain in the percentage of people who voted?

—Where was the turnout still relatively poor?

—How did you do in precincts with a heavy population of AFL-CIO members?

You'll do well to review it all. Compare effort with result; see what you can learn about which techniques seem to have worked best.

With the day-after-election "quarterbacking" session adjourned, the scope of the discussions of the past campaign is broadened to include state COPE leaders. In this manner, an overall view of COPE's efforts in a particular campaign is secured and any defective parts in the machine can be examined with an eye toward necessary repairs.

COPE writes that "within a week after Election Day—with all the details of the campaign fresh in everyone's mind—local union, city and state COPEs should sit down and discuss the outcome. Then prepare a memorandum based on the discussion. It will help you to remember at the next election—or it will help your successor, who can benefit from your experiences."

Although *How To Win* does not mention it, copies of the suggested memorandum are also sent to national COPE. From these hundreds of reports—from local, city and state COPEs—and others submitted from the committee's field directors, the national leaders cull all pertinent information that will help improve the labor machine. These memos provide the basic information for national COPE's own "confidential reports," the documents written shortly after every major campaign for the benefit of the AFL-CIO Executive Council and committee personnel.

Most important, however, the field reports filed after each election allow national COPE to maintain an essentially national organization. Power in COPE is not diffused and decentralized as it must needs be in the political parties, with their autonomous state organizations; rather, in labor politics the effort is coordinated from the top.

The national leaders digest the wealth of information from the field and see what has to be done to increase effectiveness. The advice, suggestions and needed repairs evolving from this analysis are then disseminated back to the grass roots. With this material and their own analyses in hand, the local COPE leaders are told to "dive right into planning for the future."

"Your comprehensive analysis of the results of the last election," says *How To Win,* "are bound to be a blueprint for the next one.

"That's the way to develop a constantly improved program for political action. And . . . the sooner you get started, the better."

And the next COPE campaign is underway.

## CHAPTER EIGHT

# COPE's Allies

IN its campaigns and other forms of politicking, COPE, like man, is not an island. It is very difficult for any political action organization, let alone one representing a "special interest" bloc, to win completely on its own. No one group is able to have success and influence without the assistance of other associations, member organizations, and groups representing overlapping interests. COPE, as with the rest, needs and depends upon its allies.

The most seemingly natural ally for the AFL-CIO's Committee on Political Education would be the Democratic Party, as COPE spends most of its time, energy and money on the same causes. This would be, and generally is, true except that the national Democratic structure, as an entity, has grown woefully weak and ineffectual in the mid-sixties. In 1964 Lyndon Johnson ran a campaign virtually independent from the Democratic Party's regular organization, and the party's candidates got by simply through grabbing onto LBJ's coattails; during the 1966 congressional election campaign, the Democratic National Committee furnished little assistance—advice, manpower or money—to its candidates, and the results showed the effect of this inertia.

Because of this lack of party activity, in 1966 COPE *was,* in some cases, a virtual island of pro-Democrat electioneering. Federation president George Meany dutifully noted this in his summary of the 1966 results: "We found ourselves working alone for the first time in many areas."

There were signs after the '66 experience that the Democratic National Committee was making attempts to reinvigorate its operations, a move that included re-establishing close ties with COPE. But the National Committee is in business to win elections, and would be expected to draw on the support of any group who shared common goals—such as COPE; if the party hierarchy becomes more active, obviously COPE will benefit.

But, in many areas of practical politics, the Democratic national leaders need not worry about increasing their action tempo, for they—unlike their GOP counterparts—have a wide range of virtual "front" groups who have all but supplanted the regular party structure. These organizations are "fronts" in that their services directly benefit the Democratic cause, yet they maintain leadership and financial resources independent of the party's national hierarchy. And these groups are the allies from whom COPE draws its most significant support.

Ideologically, these varied organizations represent the liberal "vanguard" of the Democratic Party. As a nationwide structure theoretically servicing all Democratic elements—Southern and Northern, alike—the party's National Committee cannot freely function as a philosophical pacesetter, even though its leaders may be predominantly liberal. Thus, to codify and promote the party's left-of-center segments, the several "fronts" have been established, relatively independent of the regular organization, to serve as the vanguard. Some of these are integrated into the party structure; others, completely autonomous, regularly align themselves with liberal Democratic wing, maintaining close liaison with the Democratic National Committee while doing so.

COPE represents an organizational arm of this vanguard; in areas where it is well-run and experienced, it has either replaced the regular Democratic Party organization or serves as a powerful supplement. The Americans for Democratic Action is the best-known group providing research, position papers and policy statements to serve the liberal Democratic element; other policy groups, of a more specialized nature, include the National Farmers Union and the National Council of Senior Citizens.

On Capitol Hill there is the Democratic Study Group, composed of liberal party members in the House, set up to lobby for new legislation; also, there are the DSG's fund-raising arm, Democrats for Sound Government (also DSG) and the National Committee for an Effective Congress, two organizations that probably have more power and influence in helping to elect liberal Democratic congressmen than do the party's own Senate and House campaign committees.

Among the groups outside the party aiding the Democratic liberal cause are Group Research, Inc., an anti-conservative investigative agency, the League of Women Voters, most important in its voter registration and propaganda efforts, and select civil rights organizations, helpful in registration, propaganda and pressuring. And all of the above-mentioned groups are active in some form or another in congressional lobbying; drawing upon their special interests and individualized contacts, they represent an imposing array of pressures that can be placed on congressmen.

These, then, are the major components of the liberal Democrats' vanguard, and those with whom COPE has the closest alliance. Again, these organizations are more than mere appendages of the Democratic National Committee; they represent interests and points-of-view above and beyond those that can be simply classified "Democrat." These elements are promoting only the party's liberal wing and its goals. Many of those listed have interlocking directorates, with familiar names popping up on various boards of directors, and a handful of wealthy individuals in the liberal community are found to be giving hefty contributions to several of these organizations. This, however, is not "conspiracy," but convenience.

The alliances which COPE establishes with these groups, and some others not mentioned, vary widely on the local level. Depending on the current political climate, and the candidates and issues involved, COPE will solidify its alliances as the campaign approaches. Sometimes COPE will find itself opposing an old ally, as in Philadelphia's 1967 mayoralty campaign, when COPE made an all-out effort for incumbent mayor James Tate while its otherwise-friend, the Americans for Democratic Action, backed Tate's opponent, Republican Arlen Specter.

Traditionally, however, COPE's local alliances have remained constant. Michigan labor is still aligned with the same reform Democrat, minority group and ADA elements which helped it to take over the Democratic Party in the late 'forties; the most powerful segments of New York City labor are still a driving force behind the Liberal Party, created by union "progressives" in 1944. Over such extended periods of time there will of course be some shifting, some coming-and-going, but the main ingredients remain to build a solid political influence bloc.

What does vary considerably are COPE's alliances from state to state, a factor controlled principally by the comparative strength and membership of the other liberal vanguard groups. In Ohio, for example, COPE's strongest associates are other union organizations, the railway brotherhoods and the independent United Mine Workers. In Colorado, COPE has teamed up with the National Farmers Union, Negro and Spanish-American minority representatives and liberal intellectuals. And in 1965 it was reported that several groups in Iowa were being coordinated by the Democratic National Committee in trying to re-elect liberal congressmen; the alliance reportedly contained COPE, the National Association of Rural Electric Co-operatives, the National Education Association, the Co-operative League of the U.S.A., the National Association of Land Grant Colleges, the National Council of Senior Citizens, and the National Farmers Union.[1]

The composition of these state coalitions vary solely because the liberal organizations vary in their strength and influence; the ADA, for instance, is not powerful in Iowa, just as the Farmers Union has little impact in Ohio. On a national level, the matter is a bit more simple; here COPE's alliances are more solidified and lasting.

It should be noted, however, that even nationally, differences of opinion and position arise between COPE and its buddies. One notable instance was the National Farmers Union stand against one-man, one-vote state legislative reapportionment and advocacy of a constitutional amendment permitting one body of a state legislature to be apportioned on some basis other than population, a position completely at odds with the AFL-CIO. Also, the ADA differs with the AFL-CIO on most foreign policy matters; the federation continues to take a firm anti-Communist position on such matters as recognition of Red China and the war in Vietnam.

Despite these occasional differences, COPE's alliances are retained; on the whole, the organizations within this coalition agree more than they disagree, and the men and goals they are promoting are virtually identical. COPE's major national allies, those it is found supporting and drawing upon the most, are: the Americans for Democratic Action, National Farmers Union, Group Research, Inc., National Committee for An Effective Congress, the Democratic Study Group, the National Council of Senior Citizens, and certain civil rights organizations.

On matters of national policy or political action, these allies will normally be found in agreement and will give each other vital assistance; on the local level, while disputes may arise, wherever one of these groups is strong and active they will be found on COPE's side a majority of the time. A brief description of each of the COPE allies follows.

## The Americans for Democratic Action (ADA)

In his inaugural address to the 1967 Americans for Democratic Action convention, newly elected president John Kenneth Galbraith told his audience that "the ADA in the past has had its political base in a rough coalition between unattached liberals and liberal trade unionists." And, effused the noted economist-writer, "so I trust it will continue to be."

A month before Galbraith's remarks, Walter J. Burke, secretary-treasurer of the United Steelworkers of America, had said to a Pittsburgh ADA gathering (of which he was chairman) that the liberal-labor coalition should be maintained and "what we need is a proliferation of the ADA philosophy and to keep the emphasis of government on people."

Such reciprocal sentiments between liberal intellectuals and liberal union leaders have been the hallmark of the ADA's progress over the years, and a principal reason for its success and influence. The scholar-thinkers curtsy, the labor activists bow; together, the liaison has had a solid impact on the course of American politics.

The audiences which Burke and Galbraith addressed were both commemorating the 20th anniversary of the Americans for Democratic Action, covering two decades that saw the organization grow to become a leading liberal force in the nation. When the ADA was founded in early 1947 the liberal-left was not a popular political bloc in America; many ADA proposals seemed simply outrageous at the time and the future could not have looked overly bright.

But, all that changed. "The ADA resolutions of the 1950's have become the laws and government programs of the 1960's," Vice President Hubert Humphrey, an ADA founder, told the 1966 national convention; "the ADA has not only dreamed great dreams, it has helped them become realities." With characteristic exuberance, Humphrey was stating an obvious fact: the ADA had developed "clout."

The organizational roots of the Americans for Democratic Action lie in the tortuous maze of factionalism that pervaded the far left in the 'thirties and early 'forties. Its immediate predecessor was the Union for Democratic Action (UDA), a conglomerate organization which had, in turn, been formed by activist liberals who had bolted Norman Thomas' Socialist Party in dispute over his isolationist wartime policies.

The UDA's lifespan was brief, confused, and torn by internal disputes —traits that did not help it to be overly effective. On the one hand, the UDA was viewed with skepticism by many liberals because it made some effort to exclude known Communists from its ranks, an unpopular position on the Left in those post-Hitler Pact days of the United Front and "Good Ol' Joe"; conversely, radical leftists—including some Communists—had gained sufficient control of the UDA by 1947 that the organization was advocating a third party effort in the 1948 presidential elections and preparing to endorse the Progressive Party candidacy of Henry Wallace.

There was still sufficient opposition within the UDA to this destructive third party move and additional concern over the degree of Communist infiltration to prompt the reorganization of the UDA in order to win broader support in the liberal community. With this aim in mind, in January, 1947, some 400 liberals from the fields of politics, religion, education, and labor gathered in Washington's Willard Hotel to found the Americans for Democratic Action. In criticizing the previous efforts of some liberals to drum up support for the Wallace candidacy, the meeting's presiding officer, Reinhold Niebuhr, theologian and former chairman of the UDA, set the course for the new ADA by reminding his audience that "all our efforts, all our ingenuity must be thrown into the struggle to establish liberal control of the Democratic Party."[2]

Among those who applauded Niebuhr's "New Direction" line were ADA founders Philip Murray, head of the CIO, and his eventual successor, UAW firebrand Walter Reuther; they were but two of the ADA's early backers from the labor ranks.

As with so many exuberant, infant political activist organizations, the ADA tasted early success, if only to see it evaporate a short time later. In the 1948 elections, after brief flirtations with possible alternative Democratic presidential candidates (chiefly Supreme Court Justice William O. Douglas—Reuther's first choice—and the then-unaligned head of NATO, Gen. Dwight D. Eisenhower), the ADA threw its support behind Harry Truman, a man previously regarded by many liberals as a totally unworthy heir to the mantle of F.D.R.

Three years later the ADA's power in the Democratic Party was enhanced by the nomination of ADA founder Adlai Stevenson as the party's presidential candidate, and his appointment of former ADA national chairman Wendall Wyatt as his campaign manager and of Arthur Schlesinger, Jr., the "intellectual conscience" of the ADA, as his head speech writer. Unfortunately for the Democrats, Stevenson and the ADA, this was the wrong time and place for the organization to assert control of the party. The Korean War, the discovery of Communists in high government positions, and other facets of the Cold War had turned the American public sharply against the radical left and anything that smacked of Moscow.

By 1953 the organization's popularity had diminished to the point that the Democratic national chairman, when asked in an interview if ADA support would "help or hurt a candidate," was quick to reply: "I think we can get along without it all right."[3]

The decline was precipitous and in 1956, when Stevenson was again selected to carry the Democratic banner against Ike, he took care not to appoint a single ADAer to his staff, although the group's official support —for what it was then worth—continued undiminished. The major gains made by liberal Democrats in the 1958 congressional elections raised hopes somewhat, but it was not until the election of John F. Kennedy and Lyndon Johnson in 1960 that the ADA was rescued from political oblivion and thrust again into a position of power in the Democratic Party.

The effect the ADA has had on the course of the government has been profound. Bill after bill, act after act, policy after policy, adopted by the Kennedy-Johnson Administrations have reflected the programs proposed by the Americans for Democratic Action: unbalanced budgets, one-man, one-vote reapportionment, *détente* with Moscow, the Nuclear Test Ban Treaty, the War on Poverty, medicare, federal aid to education, massive urban renewal—the ADA's influence has been deep and, no doubt, lasting.

The transition of so many ADA dreams into solid realities has not, however, caused any slackening in the organization's drive for new programs instituting new government regulation and control. Labor patriarch Samuel Gompers chose as his motto the one word "More!"—the same could be adopted by ADA.

As can be seen in the traditions of the labor movement and in the ideological complexion of its leaders, past and present, liberal thought has not been alien to many important segments of the AFL and CIO. The links between labor and the ADA have been forged through similarity of policy positions, financial contributions from AFL-CIO unions to the ADA, and the active participation of labor figures in the Americans for Democratic Action.

The personnel ties between the ADA and the AFL-CIO were formed at the very beginning of the liberal organization in 1947. One of the earliest supporters of the ADA and a principal booster for its influence in the rest of the liberal community was the president of the CIO, Philip Murray; Murray had not supported the old Union for Democratic Action in the early 'forties because, at first, it excluded Communists and the CIO chieftain's own far-left advisors opposed this policy; and when Communism in the CIO later became an increasing problem, Murray boycotted the UDA because it, too, was rapidly turning into a Red "front."

When the UDA decided to reorganize as a more "moderate" liberal force, Phil Murray gave the new organization his full backing, in effect the stamp of approval from the Labor Left. Joining the CIO head as leaders of the young ADA were Walter Reuther, then second man in the CIO and head of the UAW; Gus Scholle, leader of the Michigan CIO and later of the state's AFL-CIO; David Dubinsky, the now-retired president of the Ladies' Garment Workers; Jim Carey, later to lead the International Union of Electrical Workers; Al Hayes, at the time vice president of the Machinists, later the union's president, and Andrew Biemiller, then a U.S. congressman from Wisconsin and now the AFL-CIO Legislative Department head.

The interlocking personnel connections have continued over the years, with numerous labor leaders moving in and out of the ADA hierarchy. Reuther and Dubinsky have stayed on as ADA officials, both now holding the rank of vice chairman. Through 1967, I.W. Abel, the fiery Steelworkers head, served as an ADA vice chairman.

Listed as members of the ADA's National Board in 1967 were Joseph Beirne, president of the Communications Workers of America, Charles Cogen, head of the American Federation of Teachers, Ralph

Helstein, chief of the Packinghouse Workers, Louis Stuhlberg, Dubinsky's successor as ILGWU leader, John Chupka, secretary-treasurer of the Textile Workers of America, Walter L. Mitchell, president of the Chemical Workers Union, Jacob Clayman, administrative director of the AFL-CIO's Industrial Union Department (headed by Walter Reuther), Leon Despres, general counsel to the United Transport Service Employees Union, Victor Reuther, an international vice president of the UAW, and Paul Schrade, head of the UAW's Western Regional Conference. Paul L. Phillips, head of the United Paperworkers and Papermakers, retired from the ADA National Board in 1967, and Jack Conway, director of the Industrial Union Department and an official of Walter Reuther's Citizens Crusade on Poverty, moved up from the ADA board to become chairman of its executive committee in 1967.

Of those AFL-CIO leaders mentioned as also holding executive positions in the ADA, five—Abel, Phillips, Helstein, Stuhlberg and Beirne—were members of the federation's 28-man Executive Council in 1967; of the others, Dubinsky had retired from the Council in 1966, Walter Reuther had quit it the same year and John Chupka's boss—William Pollack, president of the Textile Workers—had been named to the Executive Council to replace Reuther.

Other prominent ADA leaders in '67 frequently associated or allied with the AFL-CIO and COPE included: James Patton, retired head of the National Farmers Union (an ADA vice chairman), and Bayard Rustin, the civil rights activist-intellectual who heads the labor-supported A. Philip Randolph Institute (an ADA National Board member).

The financial bonds between labor and the ADA are equally close, with unions making contributions to the pro-Democrat organization directly out of dues funds. These ties also date back to the ADA's first days, with labor virtually "floating" the organization in its infant stages; two unions, the ILGWU and the United Auto Workers, alone gave ADA a total of $34,000 in the one year of 1948.

In 1966 labor did not give quite this much, as the ADA has curtailed its spending over the intervening years; the proliferation of activist liberal groups—as ADA was originally—during the 'fifties and 'sixties has allowed ADA to concentrate more on dissemination of written propaganda materials, thus cutting down on its spending and activism. But contributions from international unions still constituted a significant portion of ADA's receipts in '66, with the ILGWU and UAW again leading the way, donating $3,000 apiece; the International Union of Electrical Workers (IUE) tossed in $1,000.

The ADA's total expenditures for 1966 were $47,164.25, most of which went for printing costs, salaries and office maintenance. This attests to ADA's not being a big spender as political organizations go, preferring apparently to urge such activity upon the federal government only.

On the question of political policy ties between ADA and organized labor, a frequently embarrassing and sometimes inflammatory paradox arises. In the field of domestic U.S. policy there are virtually no discrepancies at all, and the annual "platforms" of the ADA are all but interchangable with those of the AFL-CIO; on matters such as civil rights, federal budgetary policies, aid-to-education, medicare, poverty, social security, urban programs, and others down the line, the two organizations are in agreement.

ADA also supports such AFL-CIO pet projects as repeal of 14(b), a higher minimum wage, increased workmen's compensation benefits, organizing rights for farm workers, and a stronger National Labor Relations Board. The ADA's backing for this special-interest labor legislation may be motivated to some extent by conviction, but the AFL-CIO's continued boosting of the ADA and politicking for liberal Democratic candidates also plays a big part. This can be seen in the paean to labor contained in the ADA's statement to the House Education and Labor Committee in support of right-to-work repeal:

"Repeal of section 14(b) of the National Labor Relations Act must be viewed within the context of the American labor movement's solid and unique contribution to American democracy. Before collective bargaining became the normal pattern of labor-management relations, American labor industrialization was literally one of jungle warfare. Under collective bargaining, unions insisted that grievance and arbitration machinery be introduced to keep the labor peace. Grievance and arbitration procedures rationalized efficiency and at the same time adequately protected the rights and dignities of workers from petty tyranny in the ranks of some management hierarchs. In a real sense the American labor movement, through collective bargaining, contributed to the tremendous productive capacity of the American economy. The American labor movement was able to show the American workers that they could share in the economy's reward by expanding production."

Such hymns of praise are not to be found, however, when the two organizations begin comparing foreign policy positions. Similarities between the ADA and the AFL-CIO stop, quite literally, at the water's edge.

In mid-February, 1968, the over-the-water differences between the ADA and AFL-CIO took a dramatic new turn. The ADA National Board, in protest over LBJ's Vietnam policy, endorsed the presidential primary bid of Sen. Eugene McCarthy. Promptly, three of the union leaders in the ADA hierarchy—Abel, Beirne and Stuhlberg—resigned and withdrew the support of their unions.

The long-term implications of this rift in the liberal-labor alliance will not be evident until the war is over. It is significant, however, that the ADA in 1968 backed a liberal Democratic presidential candidate, not a third party "renegade"; its major difference with labor was over choice of a candidate, based on his foreign policy stand, not over party preference. It is entirely possible that after a time liberal labor and the ADA will be firmly reunited and begin again to work smoothly together.

The firm anti-Communism of president George Meany and other leaders of the old American Federation of Labor that has contributed to a similarly strong stand by the AFL-CIO, is absent in the ranks of the Americans for Democratic Action. Originally established as a "non-Communist" organization, the ADA has since taken pains to demonstrate that it is not "anti-Communist," having continually opposed subversion laws, the House Committee on Un-American Activities and loyalty oaths. Perhaps the most accurate description of the ADA's stance on this subject has been provided by political analyst James Burnham, who has singled out the ADA as "the perfect example of 'anti-anti-Communism.' "

The discrepancy in this ideological attitude has led the ADA and AFL-CIO to take opposite sides on virtually every major foreign issue dealing with Communist nations or U.S. national defense. Some examples:

ADA: "ADA supports diplomatic recognition of the People's Republic of China and its accreditation to all organs of the United Nations."

AFL-CIO: "The AFL-CIO is firmly opposed to recognition of the Peiping regime and its admission to the United Nations."

ADA: "A peaceful, stable Europe, without national nuclear deterrents, is important to the interest of the United States. Such a Europe can be assured only under conditions of an East-West *détente* and disarmament."

AFL-CIO: "The perils of a false détente are extremely grave. The AFL-CIO, therefore, urges that a strong American military presence in Europe is indispensable to the defense of that continent and to our national security."

ADA: "A relaxation of trade and of long-term credit restrictions must be adopted so that economic exchanges with Eastern Europe can rapidly increase."

AFL-CIO: "American labor holds that helping the Communist dictatorship overcome the difficulties and hardships which its totalitarian policies have brought about will not serve the cause of peace and freedom anywhere or induce these tyrannical regimes to evolve into democracies."

ADA: "In order to bring about the situation whereby the Cuban government will lose its economic dependence on the Soviet Union and the political strings that are attached to that dependence, ADA urges a resumption of trade in non-strategic goods with Cuba."

AFL-CIO: "Moscow is today more active than ever in financing and fomenting Communist subversion and in training terrorist squads skilled in arson, sabotage, kidnapping, murder and wanton destruction of public and private property as we have seen in Venezuela. This drive, directed from Cuba, is directed against our country."

ADA: "We believe that it is neither necessary nor desirable for the U.S. to seek total military victory [in Vietnam]. America's interest in Vietnam is peripheral and what interest we do have is to allow the Vietnamese to determine their own destiny, an aim that cannot be accomplished by force of American or North Vietnamese guns. It can only be accomplished by a compromise settlement that will allow all South Vietnamese, including the Viet Cong, to participate in the reshaping of their own society."

AFL-CIO: "The nature of the war in Vietnam becomes clearer from day to day. The Communists are waging a war of conquest, a war for the annexation of South Vietnam by Ho Chi Minh's regime. This war is not an isolated or local conflict. It is an integral phase of the Communist drive for dominating the world . . . Our convention pledges unstinting support by the AFL-CIO of all measures the Administration might deem necessary to halt Communist aggression and secure a just and lasting peace."

It is such conflicting positions on foreign policy matters that has led ADA leaders to occasional verbal sniping at the AFL-CIO. Despite the AFL-CIO's unanimity with the ADA on domestic matters, the sanctimonious non-unionist spokesmen for the liberal organization cannot resist taking pot shots at the labor federation.

The crux of the attitude of these ADAers was summed up by John Kenneth Galbraith in his inaugural address at the group's 1967 convention:

". . . we must also be aware that large sections of the labor movement are no pillar of liberal strength. On the contrary the leadership is aged, contented and deeply somnambulent. And on important issues of foreign policy its position is well to the rear of Gerald Ford [House GOP minority leader] . . ."

What ADA leaders such as Galbraith forget, however, was quickly pointed out by labor columnist John Herling. It is a factor which directly involves the current liberal-labor coalition and COPE's role in liberal politics. Wrote Herling soon after the Galbraith statement:

"First of all, tho every sector of the labor movement may not please [Galbraith], he ought to know that nearly its total political muscle has been used to support liberal programs, in Truman's day, in Kennedy's administration and today under LBJ. While one does not denigrate the importance of the contribution of non-labor intellectuals, it is the organizations like AFL-CIO's COPE that have often given verbal liberalism a local habitation and a home. . . .

"On the practical political level—and I am convinced Mr. Galbraith is fond of winners—it is the trade unions, at the local as well as on the national level, that in their untutored, even somnambulent way, carried out the registration drives, turned out the voters and manned the polls. Labor has proved itself the durable part of the labor-liberal establishment. It may be slower to act, but it is less apt to quit."[4]

The ADA has always been quick to accept the financial support of unions and the COPE organizational backing of its favorite liberal candidates. Perhaps George Meany and the rest of the Executive Council members not active in ADA can forgive liberals of Galbraith's stripe for their doctrinaire rantings; after all, Meany & Co. might realize, no "intellectual" can remain a member in good standing of the liberal community if he does not periodically damn anti-Communists. Lack of any public rebuttals to Galbraith indicate that Meany may have accepted this fact, but to the general public the ADA president's allegations still appear absurdly hypocritical.

Labor in Michigan joined with ADA elements and other liberal reformers in 1947-48 to throw out the Democratic Old Guard and institute the new party regime under "Soapy" Williams. In New York State organized labor has provided the practical organizational support for the ADA's favorite political retreat, the Liberal Party. And each of the Democratic congressmen listed as ADA officials in 1967—including its outgoing president, Rep. Don Edwards (D-Calif.)—have been helped into office by the sizable support of COPE.

The AFL-CIO and its Committee on Political Education form an essential and vital link in the liberal-labor coalition, but their own allies sometimes are reluctant to acknowledge this.

For its part, ADA lends an intellectual leaven to the liberal-labor coalition. To "progressive" unionists such as Reuther, Helstein and Jack Conway, ADA represents an entrée into the academic world, gracing them with its aura of respectability; in the minds of the imagemakers and media, then, these unionists become—accurately or no—intellectual-activists through merest association.

On the more practical level of political campaigning, though it is an active force in but a few cities, ADA is helpful to COPE in fund-raising, research, and in getting support from the non-labor liberal community. With its blanket membership covering liberals all across the board, including those from other left-of-center organizations, ADA—nationally and locally—represents a liberal clearinghouse and meeting spot—in other words, an ideal place for labor politicos to come (as members themselves) in seeking support for programs and candidates.

Although statements by its "anti-anti-Communist" leaders, notably Galbraith, may on occasion cloud the picture, the alliance between ADA and organized labor is a solid one. The AFL-CIO's material contributions to the coupling—money, cooperating personnel, support for liberal candidates—tend to obscure the practical, if not the ideological, importance of the squabblings over foreign policy.

The ADA and AFL-CIO find themselves in the late 'sixties to be the largest and most prestigious liberal organizations acting as a "buffer" between the left-middle and the New Left militants. And this new role will call for increasingly closer cooperation and alliance between the two.

## Democratic Study Group (DSG)

During the 89th Congress, the Democratic Study Group (DSG) was probably the most influential single force within the House of Representatives. A fellow-liberal organization, the National Committee for an Effective Congress, went so far as to exult in a fund-raising letter that "the 89th Congress became the DSG Congress." After the 1966 elections beefed up the GOP congressional delegation, DSG's power was dissipated somewhat, although it kept up its activities-as-before and salvaged several liberal House victories.

The Democratic Study Group's membership is limited exclusively to members of Congress and, as such, its numerical effectiveness is entirely dependent upon election results. Recognizing this, in addition to advancing the liberal cause in Congress, DSG also raises money, prepares research, furnishes speakers and otherwise assists liberal Democratic candidates for Congress who are potential members of the Group.

This is where COPE comes in. The AFL-CIO unions and COPE almost uniformly support and assist the same non-incumbent candidates as does DSG; they also campaign for and help DSG members themselves win re-election to the House of Representatives. DSG is, for several reasons, limited in the amount of money it can raise and the extent of electioneering assistance it can provide for candidates; COPE, as the principal "sugar daddy" for campaigning liberal Democrats, is the first one DSG turns to when its own resources start running low.

The large portion of DSG's funds and energies go into preparing lengthy research documents on congressional legislation and important issues, material produced to aid liberal Democrats in Congress and, at election time, liberal House candidates. Labor—the unions and COPE

—do not duplicate this in-depth research and content themselves with fulfilling their role of helping the candidates get elected; once the victorious COPE-backed men get to Washington, DSG takes over.

The Democratic Study Group has its origins in a collection of liberal Democratic House members known as "McCarthy's Mavericks," an informal group brought together by then-Rep. Eugene McCarthy (D-Minn.) in the mid-'fifties. McCarthy (together with another future senator, Lee Metcalf of Montana) had originally convened his "mavericks" to fight for pending conservation legislation, but the group quickly went on to discuss other matters and seek other activities.

Shortly after the 1956 elections McCarthy called his liberal allies together to talk over means of solidifying and strengthening their power in Congress at the start of the second Eisenhower Administration. The result of the discussions was the "Liberal Manifesto," an extensive legislative-action program for House Democrats made public the morning Congress convened in January, 1957. The goals outlined in the "manifesto" were characteristic of those pursued by McCarthy's group, and later DSG, arguing most notably for increased federal spending and participation in domestic affairs.

When the document was first released to the press it contained the signatures of 28 Democratic House members—the nucleus of "McCarthy's Mavericks"—but when it was placed in the *Congressional Record* a short time later the list had swollen to over 80 names. Building on this bloc, McCarthy and his lieutenants organized a tight-knit whip system to round up liberal votes and take "soundings" of members' attitudes toward pending legislation.

From the outset McCarthy chose not to challenge his party's leadership in the House, and his whip system worked hand-in-glove with the regular Democratic structure under Speaker John McCormack (D-Mass.). While this strategy was to hamper the group some ten years in the future, the "Mavericks" nevertheless felt they could never gain liberal concessions from the House party hierarchy if the Democratic leaders viewed them as genuine "renegades," "radicals" or anything but loyal party-liners.

It was in 1958 that the McCarthy group—still with no official name or status—first undertook to help elect more liberal Democrats. After compiling a series of research papers, speech outlines, and material on incumbent Republicans, a letter was mailed out (on the letterhead of then-Rep. Metcalf) to between 90 and 100 liberals running against GOP congressmen. Of the fifty addressees who responded by using the proferred information, 35 were elected in November, 1958, and well over half of them joined the ranks of their benefactor.

After the '58 elections, however, the "Mavericks" were no longer

"McCarthy's." Their founder and leading liberal light had been elected to the Senate (together with Lee Metcalf) and the group immediately suffered from a leadership gap; with no successor to McCarthy provided for, the informal grouping fell into disarray and was able to yield little power. When the so-called "anti-labor" Landrum-Griffin bill whizzed through Congress in 1959, the liberal Democrats—new "Mavericks" and old—complained bitterly about lack of a good leader and their inability to muster united strength when needed.

The overdue stock-taking and reorganization soon occurred behind locked doors on Capitol Hill, and the Democratic Study Group emerged. The new DSG burst forth in late 1959, outlining goals and programs in press statements and hiring a full-time staff and research director, William G. Phillips.

The reorganization proved a great boost for the liberal Democrats, with Phillips putting together an energetic and productive research staff, and with House members, such as Reps. Frank Thompson (D-N.J.) and Chet Holifield (D-Calif.), leading the DSG troops on the floor. During Phillips' tenure, research became the backbone of the DSG effort. The legislative background papers, issue monographs, special reports and election guide—called "DSG Campaign Handbook"—which Phillips' staff produced in quantity were intended both to inform DSG House members and to provide campaign materials for liberals seeking to defeat incumbent Republicans.

(Bill Phillips' talents did not go unrecognized by the Johnson Administration, as it hired him for the staff of the Office of Economic Opportunity and, later, as research aide to the Democratic National Committee.)

With their industrious research team in the wings, the leaders of the revitalized DSG were better able to make their imprint on the floor, and on the course of congressional events. In addition to selecting formal officers and reinstituting the old McCarthy whip system, the new liberal House group also established a virtual "shadow" committee setup; liberal Democrats were named to head DSG committees dealing with such fields as foreign affairs, finance, urban problems, and to follow the activities of the standing House committees dealing with the same topics.

The first major victory of the Democratic Study Group came after the election of John F. Kennedy in 1960, and had the full support of the new Administration. The triumph was in the form of a procedural vote to enlarge the House Rules Committee from thirteen members to fifteen; this committee, then under the chairmanship of conservative Democrat Howard "Judge" Smith of Virginia, approved all legislation prior to its going to the House floor, and the increased membership permitted for a more liberal committee—hence, more liberal legislation on the floor.

But bigger victories were in store for DSG—all it had to do was wait a couple of years. Preparatory to the 1964 elections, a solicitation letter was sent to members of the liberal community over the signature of DSG's "founding father," Sen. Eugene McCarthy; the appeal was a whopping success and DSG was at last able to back up its research assistance to liberal candidates with a hefty war chest.

The liberals aided by DSG were, of course, the same candidates COPE was working to elect. While DSG's research assistance was invaluable, its financial largesse when compared with COPE's was meager (although the new congressmen remembered it when they got to Washington and were "rushed" for DSG membership). Beyond these efforts, then, DSG left the campaigning to COPE, working closely with the committee's strategists to avoid duplication of effort, and waited for the results. In 1964, the results were 60 new members for DSG.

With this burgeoning of the ranks, DSG marched into the 89th Congress full of confidence and reformist ideas. House Speaker McCormack let his leadership lieutenants know that he would back DSG reform efforts. This acquiescence by the Democratic hierarchy signaled the first time that an organized intra-party bloc in Congress had been able to control the House majority party, in effect controlling the whole body.

The first order of business on the DSG agenda was a purge of two Democratic congressmen who had supported Republican Barry Goldwater in 1964, Reps. John Bell Williams (Miss.) and Albert Watson (S.C.). Shortly after Congress convened, the Democratic caucus met and stripped Williams and Watson of their party seniority—an indication that DSG not only had power, but knew how to wield it and enforce party discipline behind its position.

A second DSG target in the early days of the 89th was the old familiar bugaboo, the House Rules Committee. Not satisfied with having "packed" the committee two years previously, this time DSG sought passage of a 21-day rule which would permit Rep. Smith's group to examine legislation only for that duration. The House Democrats obediently went along and approved the revolutionary 21-day ruling.

In the remainder of the 89th Congress DSG was largely responsible for marshalling the needed votes for passage of LBJ's highly touted "Great Society" programs. The band of liberal freshman Democrats which COPE had helped elect to Congress and which DSG had organized into a fighting liberal unit, were responsible for the winning votes on medicare, immigration reform, rent subsidies, social security expansion, war on poverty, aid to education, and a raft of other measures.

DSG, as with COPE and other Democratic "fronts," suffered at the polls in November, 1966. In the opening days of the 90th Congress DSG was unable to ward off the unseating of Rep. Adam Clayton

Powell or to prevent repeal of the 21-day rule for which it had fought so hard in '64.

DSG's difficulties in the 90th Congress were not quite as great as some observers believed. The group did succeed in further weakening the Rules Committee by gaining the appointment of a Rules Reform Subcommittee headed by a DSG stalwart; the ouster of Rep. Powell paved the way for another DSG leader, Rep. Carl Perkins (D-Ky.), to become chairman of the powerful House Education and Labor Committee; and a DSG-led fight against the House Banking and Currency Committee resulted in an alteration of its procedures.

These DSG attacks on standing committees—notably Rules, and Banking and Currency—are not accidental and are part of a concerted liberal drive to undermine the congressional seniority system. By chipping away at the personal power and reputation of conservative committee chairmen and by stripping the chairman's official power, to allow for simple majority rule on committees, DSG is accomplishing almost as much as if the seniority system (giving committee authority to ranking party members) were totally abolished. And as the DSG committee reforms become more widespread, the stabilizing influence and sharply defined procedures the seniority-chairman system guarantees may well be gone from Congress.

In looking forward to the 1968 elections, DSG leaders hope for a return to the glory days of the 89th Congress. Although it managed to salvage some victories and influence in the 90th, DSG must again control a majority of the House Democrats if it is to have its way completely. Its leaders are optimistic.

The largest share of the responsibility for winning the electoral victories necessary for DSG to achieve this power falls on the cooperative shoulders of the Committee on Political Education. The first clear indication that labor was giving its full backing—particularly its financial backing—to DSG was an announcement by AFL-CIO chief Meany that his federation would not support a Democratic fund-raising dinner being given in Washington on May 12, 1967.

The proceeds of this dinner were to go to the Democratic Senate and Congressional Campaign Committees, which would then have contributed the funds to party candidates of all shades, liberal and conservative. DSG had long circumvented these regular party fund dispersal organs, preferring to raise its own money for strictly liberal candidates, and it had urged other liberal organizations to do the same; Meany's unprecedented boycott of the party's testimonial dinner gave evidence that labor was going along with DSG and reserving its largesse for liberal Democrats only.

This action was buttressed throughout 1966 with contributions from several labor organizations direct to DSG. The AFL-CIO's Building and Construction Trades Department gave $500, the International Brotherhood of Electrical Workers a total of $400, the Auto Workers' Committee for Good Government tossed in $250, the Trainmen's Political Action League another $500, and a handful of other groups donated a sum of $3400.

DSG also gets financial support from the liberal-labor coalition in the form of donations by individuals prominent in other organizations along the "front." A representative selection of such persons contributing to DSG in 1966 were: Robert Asher, former ADA Vice Chairman ($100 to DSG); Edward Hollander, current ADA Vice Chairman ($100); Robert Nathan, former ADA chairman, currently ADA Vice Chairman and a member of the NCEC national board ($150); Frank Karelson, ADA National Board member ($250); W. P. Kennedy, NCEC Vice Chairman ($150); and George Pratt, Jr., NCEC board member ($5,000).

Other than these contributions, DSG's financial receipts are shrouded in secrecy. The reports it files with the Clerk of the House are spotty and no one connected with the organization will discuss finances. It does list funds incoming from another Democratic "front," the National Committee for an Effective Congress ($22,500 in 1966) and it is known that DSG assesses each member $50 per year (the DSG congressmen also help out by paying the salaries of DSG staffers out of their tax-paid office allowance). Beyond this the picture dims.

A large portion of the DSG budget is eaten up by the research and writing costs, but there is plenty left over for campaign contributions. These donations, ranging up to $2,700 in 1966, are divided among liberal candidates opposing incumbent Republicans and DSG members facing tough fights.

One interesting item on DSG's list of 1966 expenditures was a total of $4,000 to "Iowa COPE." This listing (no funds were noted as going to Iowa Democratic congressional candidates) indicates nothing more than that COPE was pretty much running the show in Iowa that year.

But this is not an unusual relationship between COPE and DSG. While COPE is running things in the field, giving practical campaign assistance to liberal Democrats, DSG is running things back in Washington. DSG's fortunes may have fluctuated broadly during its brief lifetime, but the 89th Congress demonstrated what it could do when DSG congressmen controlled the House Democratic caucus, and the 90th Congress showed that, even with a reduction in members, DSG could accomplish a great deal. Still, DSG's fortunes stand or fall on the basis of election returns; it is up to COPE, more than anyone else, to get those liberal victories and so build the ranks of the Democratic Study Group.

## The National Committee for an Effective Congress

Joining with COPE in lending financial and campaign support to DSG is the National Committee for an Effective Congress (NCEC), a New York-based outfit that gives more money to DSG than to any other organization. There is, in fact, strong evidence to show that NCEC has been the major benefactor and motivator behind DSG since the House group's inception in 1959.

The office the NCEC Washington branch occupies adjacent to Capitol Hill was previously used by DSG, before it moved into a suite in one of the House office buildings. The office space is owned and rented by a former DSG congressman, Walter H. Moeller of Ohio.

The financial evidence of a strong working bond between the two left-of-center groups is conclusive. During one period in 1964—April 17 through October 10—the Democratic Study Group reported receipts of $39,300, of which $34,500—or 90 percent—came from NCEC; in 1966 the percentage was smaller but nevertheless imposing: NCEC gave $22,500 of the total $58,294 DSG reported having received for the year.

Another item deserving introduction as evidence is the contributions from individuals affiliated with NCEC to the House liberal organization. As noted in the discussion of DSG, these donors have included NCEC board member Robert Nathan, Vice Chairman W.P. Kennedy, and another board member, George Pratt, who gave DSG a whopping $5,000 in 1966; in 1964 Pratt donated $3,800 to DSG and during the period 1964-66 he contributed $4,500 to Americans for Democratic Action.

Finally, there are NCEC's bequeathals to candidates. The list of incumbent Democrats it aided in 1966 is a virtual duplication of the DSG roster, and the non-incumbents were the same DSG (and COPE) were helping most to win. All together, NCEC's contributions to candidates in 1966 totaled $30,625, with amounts ranging from $25 to $4,000, going into Senate as well as House races.

(Interestingly enough, an NCEC fund-solicitation letter mailed after the '66 elections stated that "in the past two congressional campaigns— 1964 and 1966—the total NCEC contributions to candidates' committees were over $700,000." This figure is almost $500,000 above the amount NCEC reported to the Clerk of the House as having been donated to candidates or committees during these two years. Again proving COPE is not the only one engaging in fiscal virtuosities in politics.)

But NCEC has additional concerns to being the power-behind-the-DSG-throne. It has established close and productive ties with organized labor, Americans for Democratic Action, and regular (plus some irregular) Democratic Party campaign groups; in 1967 it even made a start toward boosting liberal Republicans into organizing a counterpart to DSG, and NCEC continues to donate cash—although in disproportionate amounts—to liberal GOP candidates.

From the outset NCEC has read "effective" to mean "liberal," and has gone about raising substantial sums from affluent sympathizers in reaching for its stated goal. It has made good on its vow to the point that Barry Goldwater has felt the need to call NCEC's operations to the attention of his conservative followers.

"Whether we like to admit it or not," he stated, "the Committee for an Effective Congress is a most effective tool . . . to elect . . . a so-called liberal Congress. I do not dispute their right to do so. I only warn the conservative element."[5]

When NCEC came into being in 1948, among its first beneficiaries were the liberal Democratic congressmen aligned with another infant left-of-center group, Americans for Democratic Action; although its scope has subsequently broadened, NCEC continued to maintain a working bond with ADA. Not only have wealthy NCEC confidants—notably George Pratt—donated munificently to ADA, but the two groups have frequently shared official personnel. In 1967, noted liberal author Hans Morgenthau, for example, served as a board member of NCEC while holding down a post as ADA Vice Chairman; other ADA notables having held NCEC official positions include Paul Appleby, Robert Nathan, Michael Straight and Telford Taylor.

NCEC did not remain a "specialized" fund-raising agency for long, however, as its leaders soon devised other means whereby the organization could influence events. In late 1954 it was discovered that NCEC—operating through a secretive *ad hoc* committee—had been a prime behind-the-scenes force in the censure proceedings against Sen. Joseph McCarthy earlier that year.

According to published reports, NCEC quietly hired an ex-government public relations officer, rented a suite of offices across the street from the Senate Office Building and worked closely with members of the Senate seeking condemnation of McCarthy. NCEC used its extensive list of backers in the liberal community to round up support of censure and then privately suggested the draft resolution to be used against McCarthy.

In July, 1954, NCEC came into the open and sent a telegram to every senator urging full backing to the McCarthy censure move; one of the signers of the telegram was Walter Reuther, then head of the Congress of Industrial Organizations, and another was Reinhold Niebuhr, the first chairman of ADA. And, concerning the censure motion itself, one of the senators with whom NCEC worked most closely, Ralph Flanders of Vermont, admitted in the *Congressional Record* that "the specifications in [the] resolutions censuring Sen. McCarthy . . . came from the NCEC." The *Chicago Tribune* later reported that NCEC had spent upwards of $57,000 in its drive to condemn the Wisconsin Republican.[6]

One thing the McCarthy censure campaign taught NCEC was that an innocuous and anonymous *ad hoc* committee, operating behind a veil of secrecy, can often be more effective than if its sponsors had acted on their own, using their own name. NCEC was soon to put this lesson to use in other ways.

Discussing the *ad hoc* committee concept as applied to political campaigning, NCEC chairman Sidney Scheuer told a congressional committee following the 1956 elections that "In the recent campaign, for instance, the National Committee for an Effective Congress initiated the formation of a special committee for a Senate candidate, which . . . not only raised funds on his behalf, but helped to provide personnel for his campaign, buy advertising and television time, etc." "Where it is thought the appeal would be more effective," Scheuer told the panel, "*ad hoc* committees may be formed . . . for the purpose of soliciting on behalf of particular candidates."[7]

It was later disclosed that the "Senate candidate" Scheuer had mentioned was Sen. John Sherman Cooper, with the liberal Kentucky Republican the recipient of a $50,000 clandestine campaign fund controlled by an NCEC affiliate going under the name of "Citizens' Fund for Cooper." The Fund's activities, those outlined by Scheuer, were under the direction of former Cincinnati Mayor Charles P. Taft; closing the circle, the brother of the late Sen. Robert A. Taft was later to head Republicans for Progress, a group promoting so-called "moderate" GOP programs with the help of NCEC's moral and financial support.

NCEC has evidently pursued this form of "undercover" campaign operation, as otherwise mysterious special committees continually pop up at election time reportedly for the benefit of some liberal Democrat or other. The fine hand of NCEC can be seen in such *ad hoc* fund-raising groups as the D.C. Minnesota Committee, allegedly established to aid NCEC favorite (and DSG founder) Sen. Eugene McCarthy in 1964, and which received $2,550 from NCEC that year; or the D.C. Western Development Committee, reported in '64 to have aided Sen. Eugene Burdick (D-N.D.) and recipient of $5,000 of NCEC's money. As has been noted, these committees have also been heavily funded by COPE and other labor factions.

In 1959 NCEC began taking an interest in potentially more powerful, concentrated and durable liberal groups, with its role in establishing and assisting DSG; a few years later NCEC sought to apply the same strategy to the Republican side of the congressional aisle. As of 1968 its efforts to turn the Republicans in Congress to the left had not worked as well as with the Democrats—through DSG—but NCEC will only try harder.

NCEC has long followed a policy, similar to that of COPE, of giving token contributions to GOP candidates in the name of "bi-partisanship." In 1966 NCEC donated to 20 Republicans running for House and Senate seats (as compared with donations to 43 Democrats), but in 1964 this policy slipped a bit and NCEC gave to only one GOP candidate. A rather unorthodox strategy employed by NCEC in contributing to Republicans is to "cover its bets" by also giving to their Democratic opponents, apparently being unable to decide which one would be the more "effective."

Whether or not NCEC is going all out to build the ranks of liberal Republicans in Congress will not be known until the 1968 elections. If it donates large sums to Republicans challenging incumbent conservative Democrats, or if it aids GOP liberals in primary campaigns against conservatives, this will indicate a concerted drive by NCEC to make the House liberal Republicans' "Wednesday Club" over into a carbon copy of DSG.

Otherwise NCEC's goal in the 1968 presidential election will be the re-election of several liberal Democratic Senators facing trouble because of their stand opposing President Johnson's war in Vietnam. Said a 1967 NCEC fund-raising letter concerning these "doves":

"Among Democrats, we find the men of courage in the deepest peril in 1968, including Senators Church, Clark, Fulbright, Gruening, McGovern, Morse and Nelson . . . Every dollar that you give now is worth two dollars given at the crisis of the campaign . . . With your help we can provide the country with a real alternative to resentment, reaction and retreat."

NCEC's doctrinaire liberal foreign policy stance, as indicated by its opposition to the Vietnam war, does not at all deter its cooperation with the AFL-CIO and COPE; as with the ADA, these differing views are tolerated, if not outrightly ignored, by George Meany. All the same, labor's ties with NCEC are not as substantive as with other groups but are of a more supplemental nature, with both having a similar practical goal—election of liberal Democrats—and helping each other out wherever and whenever possible.

Unlike some liberal organizations, NCEC does not depend upon other groups—notably labor—for the bulk of its financial support. Since its inception NCEC has been compiling an extensive list of names (some estimates say it now numbers 50,000) of wealthy liberals in and out of the public spotlight, and these are the prime sources of its income; this list is unique in that the majority of persons contribute only to NCEC and are not prominently connected with a slew of other groups.

Thus, organized labor is not found to be one of its major financial supporters, and, in fact, NCEC has on occasion given money to labor political adjuncts. In 1964 it gave $7,000 to the Auto Workers' politically active Citizens for Good Government, and another $9,294 to Texas COPE.

The contribution to Texas COPE reveals the nature of the working relationship NCEC maintains with organized labor, even though the connections are not always visible. The most important local race in Texas in 1964 was the re-election bid of Democratic Sen. Ralph Yarborough, a liberal maverick who had been frozen out of the regular state party controlled by his arch-foe, Gov. John Connally; the state COPE had been the force behind Yarborough's primary victory against a Connally ally and—in the absence of regular party assistance—it had continued to run the Senator's campaign in the general election.

It would be expected that National COPE contacted all other liberal factions desiring to aid Yarborough, telling them to send their money to Texas COPE, rather than to the candidate (who would have had to report the contributions and be subject to attack for having received "outside left-wing money") or to the state Democratic leadership (who would probably never have given it to Yarborough). As its spending records show, NCEC went along with this arrangement, just as COPE goes along with sending some of its wealth to the *ad hoc* committees of which NCEC is so fond.

COPE's alliance with National Committee for an Effective Congress is, then, based on the same practical political goals and the election of the same liberal candidates. NCEC will join with COPE in the latter's strategy of putting liberals into office in the South and it is not inconceivable that COPE will forgo its hard-nosed Democrat bias and aid NCEC in electing more liberal Republicans. The alliance, in short, is based on a similar purpose.

## The National Farmers Union

One of the best examples indicating the nature of the alliance between organized labor and the National Farmers Union (NFU), the country's third largest farm organization, is an incident described in the *Congressional Quarterly Almanac* for 1965. Analyzing the campaign by labor and Administration forces to repeal section 14(b) of Taft-Hartley, this objective source thus described the congressional strategy:

"To ensure House passage of HR 77 [the repeal bill], members of the Johnson Administration sought to form a farm-labor coalition in which Northern Democrats from industrial areas would vote in favor of the 1965 omnibus farm bill . . . in return for support of Section 14(b) repeal from farm state Democrats. Although many farm state constituents opposed repeal of Section 14(b) and Northern Democratic constituents opposed the farm bill because wheat provisions would cause a rise in the price of bread to the consumer, Administration spokesmen argued that each group could justify taking an unpopular position on one of the measures by pointing out that this stand secured passage of the other.

"Several pressure groups, including the National Farmers Union and the AFL-CIO, worked hard to cement the coalition . . . An analysis of House voting on passage of the two bills shows that the coalition technique was extremely effective. In the voting on [repeal] only three Midwestern and four Western Democrats opposed the bill, whereas only four Midwestern and one Western GOP members voted for it. The farm bill (which passed 221-145) got 51 votes from Eastern Democrats and only two votes from Republican Easterners."

The primary product of the NFU-labor alliance is liberal legislation; the COPE-backed big city Democrats will support farm bills sought by the National Farmers Union, and rural Democrats whom NFU can influence will vote for AFL-CIO-endorsed urban legislation. This "see-saw" coalition was very productive in the 89th Congress and, while many of its members were defeated in 1966, there is always the threat it might rise again.

The alliance, for all its legislative emphasis, does have its broader political aspects. In predominantly rural states, such as Colorado, Idaho, Oklahoma, Iowa, and Kansas, the National Farmers Union has given COPE the extra push needed to secure liberal election victories. NFU itself is not a hyper-active campaign force and its electioneering arm, the Rural Political Education Committee, has had few visible accomplishments (in 1966 it reported spending an infinitesimal $475). But, through continual propagandizing and lobbying for liberal legislation, NFU has molded its membership into a politically conscious and active bloc which has added a political dimension to the labor-NFU coalition.

The strong foundation of the alliance is mutual admiration, a warm sentiment having grown out of decades of seeking common goals and holding common "progressive" ideals; the sentiment can get so warm, in fact, that it begins to melt and turn all mushy:

"The National Farmers Union . . . has had a long and friendly relationship with organized labor . . . The NFU historically has stood shoulder-to-shoulder with organized labor for socially progressive legislation."

*—AFL-CIO News,* April 6, 1963

". . . Farmers Union has had the good sense to join with organized labor and the people of good will to create a people's movement in America."

—NFU President James Patton,
March 14, 1966

"[James Patton is] one of organized labor's staunchest supporters from the farm community."

—*UAW Solidarity*, Jan. 1, 1966

One of the reasons for the particularly close—and warm—ties between the Farmers Union and labor is that they have been fighting side-by-side on the liberal front since the turn of the century. The NFU was born in a Texas[8] cow barn in 1902, some 16 years after Samuel Gompers had officially organized his American Federation of Labor.

In 1940 the Farmers Union received the boost which was to thrust it into a national spotlight and place it in the forefront of the liberal-labor coalition. James G. Patton, the son of a union leader, a product of the cooperative movement and president of the Colorado Farmers Union, was elected to head the National Farmers Union. More than anything or anyone else, it was Patton, a fiery orator and self-proclaimed "hell-raiser," with his glistening white mane and austere black eyepatch, who led the NFU into what national prominence it has enjoyed.

By 1966, Patton apparently decided the NFU had seen enough of its legislative dreams become realities—at least under his leadership—and that it was time to step down. Patton's successor is Tony Dechant, a former New Deal officer who has served in the NFU national headquarters in Denver, Col., since 1943. Though pledging to carry on the Patton legislative legacy, it is possible Dechant may make some changes in NFU's attitude toward practical politics. Following his being named to head the Farmers Union, one observer reported that Dechant "will strive for a closer though informal coalition among farmers, labor unions and possibly small-town businessmen."[9] The shape and nature this alignment might assume in a national political campaign must await the 1968 election race.

The long-standing political ties between the parent NFU and organized labor will continue. Ever since John L. Lewis' Congress of Industrial Organizations began backing NFU's radical farm programs in the late 'thirties and Jim Patton helped raised money for CIO PAC in '44, the bond between the two has become very close.

In fact, there has been only one issue in recent times where the AFL-CIO and the Farmers Union have been found on opposing sides, the one-man, one-vote state legislative reapportionment issue, and even here the NFU's internal debates belied just how deep its alliance with organized labor was. James Patton had taken the same stand on the issue as that of his allies in the ADA and AFL-CIO, endorsing the Supreme Court decision that all state legislatures must apportion the seats of both houses based on population only; the delegates at the '65 NFU convention, fearing a loss of representation in their rural districts, rebuked Patton's stand and passed a statement calling for a Constitutional amendment allowing one house of a state legislature to be apportioned on some other basis.

Of the convention's delegates supporting the Court's ruling, several alluded to the NFU's ties with labor and the fact that by opposing the reapportionment ruling the NFU would be opposing the AFL-CIO; the *New York Times* discovered this wariness when it reported:

"Other speakers said opposition to the 'one man, one vote' principle enunciated by the Supreme Court . . . might alienate friendly Congressmen and labor unions."[10]

Otherwise relations between labor and the NFU have been smooth and have resulted in a string of legislative and political successes. Because of the lack of a significant nationally directed NFU electioneering operation and with most of its Washington activity focused on legislative lobbying, political coalitions combining the Farmers Union and COPE are found on a state-by-state, almost random basis; when an important campaign looms in a state containing sizable amounts of NFU and labor members, a coalition will be formed for the race—in between times it is only the professionals at COPE who keep working.

Iowa, for example, saw a heated Senate race and re-election bids by four freshman liberal Democrats in 1966; a coalition was formed, including COPE and NFU, to aid the Democratic cause. In Colorado, in the same year, a COPE "Memo" reported, labor, NFU and certain minority groups were "brought together" by a senatorial, gubernatorial and four tight House races.[11]

In his congressional testimony supporting repeal of 14(b), then NFU president Patton revealed yet another aspect of the COPE-Farmers Union alliance. Discussing right-to-work ballot campaigns in several states, Patton described his group's energetic role:

"The right-to-work forces didn't do so well. They were unable to get enough signatures on a petition to place the issue on the ballot in Montana. In this state, the Montana Farmers Union allied itself with labor to defeat the issue . . .

"Farmers Union members have helped conduct campaigns against these so-called right-to-work laws in Washington, California, Idaho,

Kansas, and Ohio in 1958. Farmers Union members helped labor union members win six out of seven of these campaigns . . . We fought side by side with our brother workingman of labor against so-called 'right-to-work' in many other states . . ."

(A new twist to the labor-NFU bund turned up in 1964, when Patton reportedly asked AFL-CIO leaders to consider joining with the NFU in organizing a "giant" new farmer-labor food cooperative. Apparently no one was too enthusiastic about the idea, for as of early 1968 no such creation was known to man.)[12]

In all instances and at all levels at which the Farmers Union and AFL-CIO have joined forces it has been primarily because both discovered the other was there, right beside them; they were both opposed to right-to-work laws, both backing liberal Democratic candidates, both promoting new collectivist legislation, both holding the same leftist philosophy of government and action. When two organizations have so much in common, and when their leaders share a warm admiration for each other, close alliances grow up naturally.

The new leadership of the Farmers Union is reportedly seeking closer political ties with labor, so this facet of the alliance may be even more productive. Judging solely by the widespread farmer dissatisfaction with Orville Freeman and the Johnson Administration, any COPE-NFU joint effort in 1968 will be an uphill climb, with whatever Democratic nominee.

However, the Farmers Union's strength has never been based on a mass of members, but on its propaganda, organizing and lobbying skills. Throughout its history the NFU has proved adept at overcoming a comparatively small membership and making its influence felt; if in 1968 it sees the liberal Democratic banner beginning to slip badly in the hinterlands, it will launch a full-scale campaign to swing the farmer back and raise the banner up. And COPE will be there—ready, willing and able to lend a hand.

## National Council of Senior Citizens

The story of the National Council of Senior Citizens is a short and simple one. It was organized in 1961 as a pressure group of elderly persons lobbying for one thing: medical-care-through-Social-Security legislation. The twin forces behind its formation and throughout its existence have been the Democratic National Committee and the AFL-CIO.

Of all the Democrats' "front" groups, the Council is the most blatant —and probably the most reprehensible. Run by shrewd political manipulators and legislative arm-twisters (few of them very elderly), the

NCSC—under the pretense of bipartisanship—has capitalized on the hopes and fears of indigent, struggling retired elderly Americans to achieve partisan political goals.

The idea, impetus and leadership for the NCSC came out of a 1960 campaign committee, Senior Citizens for Kennedy, an organization responsible for lining up thousands of traditionally Republican elderly votes for JFK. In August, 1961, the head of this group, Aime J. Forand, the former Rhode Island Democratic congressman who introduced the original medicare legislation, sent out a letter announcing the formation of the National Council of Senior Citizens for Health Care through Social Security. Although the title was later shortened, the letter marked the birth of this front.

Writing to an estimated 1900 liberal leaders active in labor, welfare work, government and groups dealing with the aged, Forand said:

"The primary purpose of our new Council, as the full name indicates, is to weld senior citizens' organizations and millions of interested individuals from all over the country into one strong and effective voice in Washington. While our immediate goal is to secure legislation providing health care for the aged through Social Security, our hope is that this new organization will eventually provide the framework for a non-partisan progressive council representing the views of older persons on major issues confronting the nation."

Despite Forand's glib assertions, the Council had no intention of being "non-partisan." A whole host of leaders from the Senior Citizens for Kennedy Committee joined with Forand to help organize the new Council, including two labor organizers, Jim O'Brien of the Steelworkers and Chuck O'Dell of UAW, who were among the original founders of the Kennedy group; another transplant was Blue Carstenson, a man who typifies the rapid mobility of personnel among Democratic "front" organizations. Carstenson had been an active field director for the Senior Citizens for Kennedy, became executive director of the National Council of Senior Citizens (while in his early thirties) and, after passage of medicare, left to join the National Farmers Union as head of the NFU Washington office.

This migration from the Kennedy campaign group to the council was no mere coincidence. Commenting on the role of Forand and other "veterans" of the Senior Citizens for Kennedy Committee in establishing NCSC, Walter Pincus wrote in the *Washington Evening Star:*

"Though the basic effort was to enlist support of the thousands of old age clubs across the nation for medicare, there was also the possibility that the senior citizens could be wooed into supporting the Democrats rather than Republicans at election time. . . ."[13]

To make this "possibility" a certainty, the Democratic National

Committee came riding on the scene, its moneybags wide open. In 1962 the committee reportedly gave $5,000 to help get NCSC going; in 1963 it donated $40,000, or one-third of the council's reported budget; in 1964 the Democratic National Committee reported giving the council $25,000 and LBJ's personal fund-raising group, The President's Club, tossed in $14,000.

If the national Democratic Party seemed overly kind to the council, organized labor was proving itself no piker. In fiscal 1962—covering the council's first months in existence—the AFL-CIO reported giving NCSC $9,000 from its euphemistic (and dues-supported) "special purposes fund"; in fiscal year 1963 this figure rose to $22,000, in 1964 shot up to $29,000 and for fiscal year 1965 went back down to $24,000, in fiscal 1966 dropped to $14,000 and in fiscal 1967 jumped up to $22,000.

Organized labor also lent the council a helping hand with personnel. Union organizers were active at both the NCSC's national headquarters in Washington and at the grass roots; in 1964, for example, it was reported that "at least four of 13 council field representatives primarily represent labor unions in their particular cities."

At the opposite end of the NCSC hierarchy, the man who replaced Forand as head of the group in 1963 was John W. Edelman, a former legislative lobbyist for the Textile Workers Union. (Interestingly enough, the TWUA was the same union that spawned Al Barkan, COPE's national director.) But if Edelman was the most prestigious, the most active labor men in the Senior Citizens Council were the aforementioned Chuck O'Dell and Jim O'Brien.

In their respective unions, O'Brien (Steelworkers) and O'Dell (Auto Workers) were in charge of the retirement programs. It is common practice in the AFL-CIO for a union to urge its retiring members to join "Golden Ring" retiree clubs and thus remain active in union affairs; virtually every union has these clubs and the UAW and USW have two of the largest.

When O'Brien and O'Dell began putting together the Senior Citizens for Kennedy, they simply took the willing members of the clubs in their charge and made them elderly Kennedy campaigners; when the NCSC was founded, these two—together with similar organizers of the elderly from the Ladies' Garment Workers and Electrical Workers—simply repeated the process. One sample issue of the council's monthly publication, *Senior Citizens News,* reported that three large Auto Workers locals (one in Danville, Ill., two in Chicago) had paid the annual NCSC dues so all their retired members could join the council. Such rapid, ready-made assimilation from labor to NCSC is one reason the council was able to claim 65,000 members a scant two weeks after Aime Forand sent out his appeal letter.

UAW organizer O'Brien, at least, was known to be fully aware of the political possibilities of a group like NCSC. One issue of the council's newsletter paraphrased an O'Brien speech in which he reportedly said "as with the Negro vote," it is a "challenge" to reach out and help the nation's senior citizens "mature politically."

But O'Brien was far from being alone among members of the labor hierarchy desiring to bring about the "maturation" of the senior citizen's political potential. In brief, political achievement was the Number One aim of the AFL-CIO in supporting the council.

When it was founded, leaders of the NCSC applied for and were granted a tax-exemption under the section of the Internal Revenue Code exempting non-profit, non-partisan organizations "operated exclusively for the promotion of social welfare." Since that time the council has practiced some very partisan and very political methods of promoting social welfare; it has never been registered as a lobby, its leaders say, because the function of the council is to "educate" and "inform" senior citizens.

Its erstwhile "educational" efforts have not prevented the council from describing itself as a "powerful political force" or listing in its literature as one of its activities its having "supported congressmen and senators who supported medicare." Nor did the non-political tax-exempt pledge prevent NCSC president Edelman from saying in 1966:

"If we can bring about the re-election of nearly 60 first-term congressmen who voted for Medicare and send more like them to Washington, we can help the elderly poor out of their poverty."[14]

As every one of the "nearly 60" freshman congressmen who had backed medicare were, conveniently enough, liberal Democrats, it was only natural that the Democratic National Committee would take an interest in the council's affairs. And as the AFL-CIO's Committee on Political Education goes about "informing" and "educating" its members in the same manner the council does, it was only convenient that organized labor support the council.

And so, hand-in-hand the AFL-CIO and NCSC joined with other liberal groups to push through medicare legislation. Then, as with the other deeply indebted COPE allies, the council put its pressure behind repeal of 14(b), with president Edelman saying the measure "is an essential step in the construction of the Great Society"; noting NCSC support of repeal, the *Reader's Digest* commented, "It is hard to imagine how this would benefit those who are retired."[15]

The Council has helped labor out in other political ways. It joined COPE in its anti-conservative propaganda drive by attempting to make senior citizens fearful of "right-wingers." In one 1965 speech council head Edelman was said to have "reported increasing activity by members of the John Birch Society [and] by other right-wing groups . . ." "These conservatives and ultra-conservative organizations," Edelman told his elderly audience, "will turn back the clock on the gains we have made for older people if they ever get a chance."[16]

After the 1966 elections the council used the anti-right theme to prod its members into pressuring Congress for increases in Social Security benefits. "The conservative forces in the Congress of the United States," said president Edelman, "are rallying their traditional opposition to decent increases in Social Security. The older people themselves are going to have to take an active role in this fight—just as they did in the fight for Medicare."

And finally there is NCSC's assistance to labor in actual political campaigns. Although its tax-exempt status *does* rule the council out of formal campaigning as a body, there are many ways it can assist in the election of liberal Democrats. One way is to get audiences of NCSC members aroused with speeches calling for the re-election of unnamed, yet unmistakable, "first-term congressmen who voted for medicare."

Another way would be to give COPE the NCSC mailing list, or otherwise identify the members to labor campaigners; and then, with council leaders smiling on, if COPE wishes to contact these people and urge them to work against the same "conservative forces" the NCSC has been attacking, why, who's to know?

(One of the first campaigns council members are known to have had an influence on was the 1962 Indiana Senate race between incumbent Republican Homer Capehart and Democrat Birch Bayh; it must have been doubly discomforting for Capehart, an elderly 65 at the time, to see his fellow senior citizens working so hard for young—34—whipper-snapper Bayh.)

The National Council of Senior Citizens may have been founded primarily to push for medicare, but in no way was it rendered impotent when Congress approved that legislation in 1965. Even though it lost its most emotional issue "pitch," the Council kept up its membership after medicare and has lobbied in behalf of increased Social Security benefits, increases in the minimum wage, urban programs, and other legislation written by the Democratic Administration.

After all, the Democrats—with a hefty assist from labor—made the NCSC; they funded it, gave it leadership and proposed an emotion-tinged legislative measure with which to arouse the political instincts of elderly persons. With all this work going into the council and with something coming out, in the form of an increasing elderly vote for Democratic candidates, the party's hierarchy is certainly not just going to let it fade into oblivion. The Democratic leaders have got a good quasi-political lobby going for them in NCSC, and they will keep it around.

## Civil Rights Organizations

The relationship between the two "movements"—civil rights and labor—have become, in the late 'sixties, inordinately confusing; because of the rapid flux of the Negro revolt it is impossible to take the whole subject and arrive at precise definitions. Labor leaders are as mystified as the rest of white America at the status and direction of the black power factions, and content themselves with proceeding largely as before.

On one level of the civil rights movement there definitely still exists a firm and powerful alliance with labor. This alliance, found in the Leadership Conference on Civil Rights and in the work of Bayard Rustin and A. Philip Randolph, is basically one of seeking common political and legislative goals; because of the problems involved, the latter has received more attention and has had more influence than the former. The legislative victories this coalition has achieved have led to political success and to a disposal on the part of "moderate" Negro elements to look upon organized labor as a trusted ally.

Beyond this cozy coalition, however, lurk the depths of the "black soul" expressed in militant tones and the corresponding threat of rising white antagonisms, the presence of two huge blocs of Americans—affluent workers and disaffected Negroes—who see little in common, and don't bother to hide it. It is in this realm that labor, for decades the outspoken champion of equal rights, is badgered and reprimanded for its alleged failings.

"The labor movement is all for the civil rights movement," a Washington D.C. rights leader has commented, "but when it comes to getting Negroes into the highly skilled building crafts, labor sings 'The Star-Spangled Banner' in the front of the union hall and 'Dixie' in the back."[17]

This comment indicates the major practical criticism of organized labor in its handling of racial matters, a complaint that skilled crafts' trades unions, notably those in the fields of building and construction, practice racial discrimination in their apprenticeship and hiring policies. A 1966 U.S. Labor Department study, for example, found that in twelve major cities only sixteen Negroes were being trained as electrician apprentices, five were learning the plumbing trade and two were working in sheet-metal unions.

The situation has become serious enough for so responsible a civil rights leader as Whitney Young to remark that "the majority of the 1,500,000 Negroes who hold union cards have tickets to do the hardest, dirtiest and most menial jobs that industry requires." And in early 1966 the federal government got into the act when the Labor Department asked for government legal action against the St. Louis AFL-CIO Building Trades Council; members of some of the council's unions had walked off a job when the employer hired Negro plumbers from an independent union, and the Justice Department prosecuted for violation of the Equal Employment Opportunities Act.

Organized labor's reply to discrimination charges is usually that they cannot find sufficient qualified Negro applicants to fill the skilled jobs, and that many of those who are skilled are not interested in apprenticeships. Accurate as this assessment may or may not be, it still remains that racial discrimination in apprentice training is but another detrimental effect of labor power and monopoly job control: when unions are legally entitled to hold every job on a building project (or in a plant), and can dictate the qualifications to be met to get the jobs, it becomes a simple matter to close the door against Negroes (or Poles, or Episcopalians, or Republicans).

(Union leaders are also fond of pointing out a "paper progress" of sorts by noting that in 1940 the old AFL contained 23 affiliates with color bars in their constitutions, and today no union has such a provision. This is meaningless. In 1964 the New York State Commission for Human Rights ruled that Local 28 of the Sheet Metal Workers International Association, AFL-CIO, had "automatically excluded" Negroes from union jobs ever since 1948 when the union had deleted from its constitution a ruling "that no Negro could ever become a full member.")

Criticism of the AFL-CIO by radical liberals—black and white—goes much further than the discriminatory practices of some unions. When the dominant labor element in the Leadership Conference on Civil Rights refused to endorse a statement condemning Congress' action in unseating Rep. Adam Clayton Powell, with AFL-CIO spokesmen explaining that Powell had sometimes blocked their pet legislative projects, NAACP head Roy Wilkins and other "moderate" civil rights leaders in the Conference began questioning labor's commitment to the cause; when New York City union leaders, including labor council chieftain Harry Van Arsdale, did not campaign for a civilian police review board in 1966, prominent and prolific leftist writer Nat Hentoff wrote that "Van Arsdale's silence on that issue—and he was far from alone among the labor hierarchy—was disgusting."[18]

Summarizing the attitude of many disaffected grass roots Negroes, one of their most articulate spokesmen, Detroit Democratic Rep. John Conyers, explained in one interview:

"The lower class Negro—those earning less than $3000 a year—are not caught in the union's sphere of influence. They have been long overlooked by the unions and they are not impressed by or interested in union politics. These lower class Negroes used to be apathetic to politics, but the civil rights struggle has given them a new voice and a new hope in the political world. It is now a new challenge to labor to harness this new political bloc . . ."

The reactions of the Negroes to these various problems in relating to organized labor have been multifold. In some states Negro leaders have been flirting with the idea of supporting right-to-work laws, others advocate formation of independent trade unions "For Black Only," while still more have abandoned any hope that organized labor will ever help them out. "The Negro remembers," says Rep. Conyers of this latter bloc, "when he was ignored by the unions and is not impressed with any new importance in their eyes—the Negroes believe the unions are too middle class and do not have their real interests at heart."

Talk of Negro activist organizations taking up the right-to-work cause was limited—at least vocally—at first to California. In November, 1966, a spokesman for the National Right to Work Committee was invited to address a meeting of California's influential Negro Leadership Conference; after his presentation, the Conference chairman, physician Dr. Carlton B. Goodlett, told reporters "the benefits of a right-to-work law are certainly worth studying."

"The Negro community," Dr. Goodlett continued, "has heard a lot of pious declarations from union leaders. But the rank and file of organized labor has clearly been voting to perpetuate racial discrimination."[19]

In the tumultuous racial months of 1967 Dr. Goodlett's voice was alone in asking Negroes to consider support of right-to-work. More of them were turning toward the alternative of establishing independent trade unions under the aegis of the Negro American Labor Council (NALC).

The NALC was founded in 1960 by Negroes in the AFL-CIO who sought to end discrimination practices in unions affiliated with their federation. Led by Asa Philip Randolph, son of an itinerant preacher who organized and became president of the Brotherhood of Sleeping Car Porters and is the only Negro sitting on the AFL-CIO Executive Council, the NALC members sought to put pressure on the AFL-CIO unions to end discrimination. By 1967 they viewed this endeavor as a failure and sought a more militant alternative.

"The factual record clearly indicates that twelve years after its merger, the AFL-CIO has been either unwilling or unable to eliminate racist patterns in its major affiliated unions," said NAACP labor secretary Herbert Hill at a NALC organizing session in May, 1967. At the conference Hill was one of the most active in lining up support for independent unions, concentrating on service employees (janitors, laundry workers, orderlies, etc.) and other low-paid workers; "We who struggle against racism," Hill declared, "are in reality fighting for the regeneration of the American labor movement as a vital, militant institution in American society."[20]

The outspoken Hill had plenty of support in his call for bucking the AFL-CIO "establishment" through "Freedom Labor Unions." Representatives of the United Auto Workers and Steelworkers on the Negro American Labor Council agreed with Hill's assessment of racial matters in the AFL-CIO and did not argue against formation of independent unions; Council head Randolph did not publicly go along with the younger NALC militants, but absence of any critical comment was interpreted as a "green light."

The older unionists and many civil rights leaders realize that independent unions may be a dramatic rebuke to the AFL-CIO, but their practical effectiveness is limited; the fields where union discrimination is most prevalent—notably building and construction—are also the fields in which AFL-CIO affiliates have most thoroughly organized, and getting an employer or job contractor to deal with an independent group is a virtual impossibility (the St. Louis episode notwithstanding). Therefore, these skeptics feel, independent unionism is a dubious strategy from the standpoint of both tactics and economics.

On the other hand, passage of right-to-work laws, depriving unions of automatic, blanket control of all jobs in a plant or at a construction site, would permit workers to be chosen by employers solely on the basis of their qualifications. In a right-to-work situation, the onus of discrimination would fall on the employer (who is subject to the federal Equal Employment Opportunity laws), not an oligarchical, dictatorial union; the Negro worker would obviously be far better off in such a situation.

This extended brief of criticisms and alternatives concerning labor racial matters represents, for the AFL-CIO, the darker side of its relations with civil rights organizations. There is a brighter side. Not all Negro leaders expect or insist that organized labor drop everything and take up the cudgel for civil rights; as NAACP leader Roy Wilkins once pointed out:

"It must be understood that all organized bodies have their primary and secondary purposes. The primary purpose of the NAACP is to combat discrimination against Negroes. The primary purpose of labor organizations is to protect the wages, hours, and working conditions of its members. Civil rights activity for them is desirable but must be secondary. Inevitably these differences in emphasis will produce tensions in greater or less degree."[21]

(Wilkins is no apologist for the AFL-CIO. In a speech to the federation's 1967 convention he praised its overall civil rights policy but charged that unnamed "powerful and important unions" were still guilty of "foot-dragging" in helping Negroes find job opportunities.)

Because what Wilkins was attempting to define is understood by many of his fellow Negro leaders there is, amidst the flow of caustic comments from black militants and the threats of "Freedom Unions," a discernible alliance between the labor and civil rights movements. Evidence of the coalition is found in organizations, in legislative lobbying cooperation, and in political action projects.

While the AFL-CIO's own Civil Rights Department is conducting a massive "education" campaign to effect a "liberalization" of members' racial views, the federation's hierarchy is working with civil rights and religious leaders to construct a strong working coalition. The focus of this coalition is the Leadership Conference on Civil Rights, a conglomerate of some 70 groups dominated by organized labor; the Washington director of the Conference is an AFL-CIO headquarters official, Marvin Caplan, its general counsel is noted labor lawyer Joseph Rauh, Jr., and the bulk of the Conference's operating funds come from the AFL-CIO ($10,000 during 1965-66).

The Leadership Conference represents an attempt by the established members of the liberal-labor coalition to speak as one voice on civil rights matters; sometimes the effort fails, as when labor refused to go along with the others in protesting the ouster of Rep. Powell from Congress, but more frequently the alliance has succeeded. If its victories are considered mere palliatives by the black militants, to the rest of the Negro community they represent the major accomplishments of the 'sixties.

The Conference members were the prime movers of public opinion behind the 1964 Civil Rights Bill and, after passage, in getting the Equal Employment Opportunity Commission organized, staffed and operating. A victory with even broader immediate impact was the '65 Voting Rights Act, which assured disfranchised Negroes in several Southern states the right to register and vote, a move that has greatly boosted COPE's strategy to elect more Southern liberals. Otherwise, the labor-dominated Leadership Conference has worked with federal agencies, cabinet-level departments and government officials in pushing the civil rights cause.

A more radical focus of the labor-civil rights alliance is the A. Philip Randolph Institute, a little-known "educational" outfit funded by the AFL-CIO to the tune of some $24,000 annually ($2,000 per month). Although he is not officially connected with this body, the fact that A. Philip Randolph's name was selected for the institute indicates the high standing the federation's executive council member has as a labor spokesman on civil rights matters.

Randolph may occasionally be at odds with the AFL-CIO hierarchy on racial matters (notably the Powell issue, when he accused Congress of "racism") and he may still get rankled over discriminatory practices, but the patriarchal organizer has always maintained that a liberal-labor coalition was the most feasible, practicable course of action toward civil rights progress; when other Negro leaders began questioning the effectiveness of the alliance, he reaffirmed his belief and called on labor to do the same, saying to the 1963 AFL-CIO Convention:

"Let our alliance be strengthened. It is labor's own interest. For the Negro's protest today is but the first rumbling of the 'under class.' As the Negro has taken to the streets, so will the unemployed of all races take to the streets . . . To discuss the civil rights revolution is therefore to write the agenda of labor's unfinished revolution. The labor movement cannot ignore this under class. It cannot degenerate into a mere protective association, insulating the 'haves' from the 'have-nots' in the working class . . ."[22]

Randolph's views on coalition politics are seconded by the man who heads the Institute, Bayard Rustin. A former Communist youth leader who has "moderated" his views to espouse pacifism and socialism, Rustin sometimes finds himself in paradoxical situations: some leftists criticize his stand favoring non-violence and coalitions, with new left activist Staughton Lynd calling him a "labor lieutenant of capitalism"; in another socialist faction are those who praise Rustin's utopian programs and elsewhere vehemently criticize organized labor, without apparently realizing it is the AFL-CIO that is paying Rustin's salary. Through it all, Bayard Rustin, a close confidant of the late Dr. Martin Luther King in the pay of Big Labor, maintains his faith in alliances.

When the Randolph Institute was founded the statement of purpose declared that "the fundamental problems now confronting the Negro community in the areas of jobs, housing and education cannot be solved by the civil rights movement alone. A broad coalition of labor, civil rights, liberal, religious and progressive business groups is required to exert effective weight in the political arena. The most essential component of the coalition is the alliance of Negroes with the labor movement as the largest and strongest force working for democratic social change."

Putting outlines into specific action, Rustin has worked to build a lasting alliance that would form the vehicle behind the utopian socialist programs he devises; an example is this Rustin plan-of-action issued in 1964:

"I want the fight to go beyond segregation and discrimination and want to build allies with labor, with church forces, and the liberals to demand the following five-point program: full employment; national economic planning; to train people within this planning for existing jobs; a federal subsidy for education, which is our most important 'industry' today; and, finally, a $30 billion works program to help absorb the unskilled Negro labor . . ."[23]

More recent Rustin proposals have included a $50 billion federal "Freedom Budget" for Negroes and a plan to pay children from poverty areas to go to school. Upon passage of the 1965 Voting Rights bill, Rustin called together labor and civil rights leaders to begin organizing a "Negro-poor whites-labor-liberal" political coalition to capitalize on the thousands of new voters the bill would create; this particular coalition did not endure for too long, as several Negro elements—notably CORE, SNCC and Dr. King's SCLC—departed when black power and "Hate Whitey" came into vogue.

From out of this flurry of activity—the Leadership Conference's lobbying, Bayard Rustin's proposing—and as a result of the labor-civil rights organizational and leadership *entente,* have come tangible legislative and political success. In the 1963-64 88th Congress there was the Civil Rights Act, in the '65-66 89th Congress there came the Voting Rights Act, and in the '67-68 90th Congress the emphasis was on legislation to regulate the sale and rental of residences, the so-called "open-housing" bills.

The Kraft Poll of AFL-CIO members taken in early 1967 showed union workers disagreed with the federation leaders on only one major issue—open housing—with 43 percent supporting it, 46 in opposition and 11 percent "not sure." Despite this rejection, George Meany testified in favor of the legislation before a Senate subcommittee, explaining that "we have refused to abandon a position because some of our members disagreed with us."[24] The fact that "some" was a majority of those with an opinion on the subject did not faze Mr. Meany.

(The congressional testimony part of the coalition, it should be noted, is not a one-way street, as civil rights spokesmen have testified in behalf of such parochial labor legislation as repeal of 14(b), extending and raising the minimum wage, and amending unemployment compensation laws. And in the AFL-CIO Executive Council report of 1965 it is noted that support of Negro leaders—including Dr. King—has greatly aided some unions in organizing and bargaining campaigns against management.)

George Meany's resolute action on such civil rights matters as open housing must come as something of a surprise to his critics inside of labor and out. Whenever AFL-CIO critics came around to specifics, one of the items they pointed to as indicative of the federation's "complacency" and "inaction" was toleration of racial discrimination by affiliates and lack of initiative on the part of the leadership; certainly Walter Reuther was one of the most vocal of the Meany detractors on this subject, and claimed this AFL-CIO attitude was one reason why his UAW had to "go it alone" in setting up organizations like the Mississippi Voters and Educational League to register Deep South Negro voters.

(Reuther is far from pure concerning racial practices within his own union. A report by the U.S. Equal Employment Opportunities Commission in early 1967 found that only 2.4 percent of the skilled workers in the auto industry were Negroes, a figure lower than that in the Michigan construction industry—another frequent Reuther target for its alleged discrimination. In fact, the report found, approximately one-quarter of the auto industry's unskilled—i.e., lowest paying—male jobs were held by Negroes.)

But George Meany and the AFL-CIO leadership have taken action in the civil rights field and, as Meany says, "We still have a long way to go." After opposing the 1963 March on Washington, Meany gave his blessing to delegations from 17 federation-affiliated unions taking part in the 1965 Selma-to-Montgomery march, and sent a personal emissary to address the demonstrators on the steps of the Alabama capitol at the march finale. More important still, the federation hierarchy has given its Committee on Political Education the "go ahead" to form coalitions in the South to register new voters and elect more liberals to local and national office.

"With heavy Negro registration," observed an AFL-CIO report after passage of the Voting Rights bill, "the possibility of weakening the power of conservative Southern racists in Congress, of electing more liberal congressmen from the South and of creating a better climate for organization in the South becomes a distinct and imminent probability."[25]

Taking its cue from the leadership, COPE began devising strategy to capitalize on the influx of newly eligible voters. "Whatever the registration gains may be," said a 1965 COPE "Memo," "there is no Southern state in which Negroes are likely to become a majority of the electorate, though there are approximately 80 southern counties where this could be the case. Thus, the arithmetic that matters most is that of coalition voting." Applying this hypothesis to a specific case, COPE looked forward to the 1966 re-election possibilities of Sen. John Sparkman (D-Ala.); the "Memo" estimated that the Voting Rights act would add about 250,000 Negro voters to the Alabama rolls, reducing the white-Negro voter ratio from ten-to-one to four-to-one.

In such a case, wrote COPE, "a coalition of Negro voters and white liberals or moderates could be decisive provided Sparkman makes his appeal to them." Sparkman did make this appeal, received campaign help from labor and civil rights factions, and won by 169,120 votes.

And the moral of the story, as COPE saw it, was "that Southern candidates now not only *can* be liberal but in many cases *must* to attract the new liberal coalition that the 1965 Voting Rights Act makes possible."

So with COPE active at the grass roots, the AFL-CIO hierarchy makes its way as best it can in the tangled mass of the civil rights leadership. The federation's leaders know that some house-cleaning is in order before they can be free of discrimination charges and, in another direction, there are indications that AFL-CIO spokesmen will be speaking out with increasing frequency on civil rights matters.

Neither one of these efforts is expected to please the black militants and other activists critical of organized labor, but the AFL-CIO has effected a coalition with civil rights factions that has had significant success. Only the direction of the Negro revolt can tell whether the alliance will continue to be effective and the AFL-CIO watches and waits.

## Group Research, Inc.

Group Research, Inc., came into existence in 1962 with the sole purpose of keeping tabs on conservative (or "right-wing") organizations and individuals. One of its most conspicuous and consistent patrons has been organized labor, particularly COPE. Some people have gone so far as to suggest that labor has been the financial angel behind GRI or, at the least, that relations between the two were—as they say about rumored Hollywood lovers—"extremely close."

Group Research director Wesley McCune disputes this accusatory view. "The only relationship I have with COPE," he has asserted, "is that they buy my material; it is strictly business. They have taken some of my information and rewritten it for their own pamphlets, but I have never worked directly with them."

McCune's reply did not shed quite the proper amount of light on this alliance. Labor not only uses a great deal of GRI-produced information, but union members also help collect the original information, several unions actively promote GRI products, and COPE has a special deal worked out with GRI and its printer so that it can obtain the organization's publications at a bargain-basement rate; and at one point in GRI's short history, Walter Reuther's Industrial Union Department of the AFL-CIO was involved in the direct shipment of Group Research publications to GRI subscribers.

Whatever the extent of labor's role as a booster, Group Research has many other good customers among COPE's allies. The Democratic National Committee has promoted and financed GRI, examples of the group's "research" have turned up in material and speeches out of NCEC, ADA and Farmers Union, and several liberal legislators—most of them COPE's best friends—have used GRI information to belabor the conservative opposition.

Whatever the factors behind the popularity of Group Research, the organization is virtually one-of-a-kind. In its five years of existence, director McCune and his small staff have filled rows of file cabinets with detailed information on every group and publication defined (by GRI) as right-of-center and every individual connected—however remotely—with them. In short, Group Research has accomplished what McCune set out to do: gather and disseminate derogatory material with the intention of having it utilized in stifling and harassing political conservatives.

Group Research, Inc., may not be precisely definable as a one-man operation, but it *is* controlled and dominated by a single individual, Wesley McCune. McCune conceived the idea of GRI and has done an imposing job of implementing this conception in a short period of time.

The man who directs GRI is another example of the type who has been around the liberal front for a long time, moving with ease from one group to another, from one interest bloc to another. In his 52 years Wes McCune has put in time with the National Farmers Union and the Democratic National Committee, serviced labor on the National Labor Relations Board and written a handful of books for liberal activists. Now, with GRI, he services the entire liberal front.

Born (1916) and raised (his father was a banker, realtor and farm implement dealer) in Colorado, McCune attended the state's university as an undergraduate and law student. Graduating from law school in 1939, McCune came east to Washington, working in rapid succession for the National Labor Relations Board and the Department of Agriculture. He finally settled down as an assistant editor in *Newsweek*'s Washington bureau, covering the agriculture, labor, business and legal beats and collecting material for the first of his four books, *The Farm Bloc,* published in 1943.

After serving a wartime stint as a merchant marine officer, McCune shifted to the Capital offices of *Time* and *Life* magazines, covering legal and economic subjects, and in 1947 he went to Kiplinger's *Changing Times* as senior editor. With the 1948 election of Harry Truman, McCune got started on the road which was to lead him deeper into the liberal front and, eventually, to Group Research.

When Truman named Charles F. Brannan as his Secretary of Agriculture, the new farm policy maker selected McCune as his executive assistant and to help devise his controversial "plan." McCune stayed on as long as Brannan did and in 1952, when the Democrats were evicted from all Washington's federal executive offices, Brannan departed to become legal counsel to the National Farmers Union and Wes McCune joined the public affairs staff of the Democratic National Committee. Four years later he followed his old boss Brannan to the NFU's Denver headquarters, where he held the title of public relations director and editor of the *National Union Farmer*.

While working for the Farmers Union and before leaving to set up Group Research, McCune produced his third and fourth books, *Who's Behind Our Farm Policy* (1956) and *Ezra Taft Benson: Man With A Mission* (1958). In his work dealing with President Eisenhower's conservative Secretary of Agriculture, McCune found a novel way to attack Benson, a frequent target of liberal criticism, by concentrating on his standing as a leader in the Mormon church.

Benson, McCune wrote, is "the first clergyman to hold a U.S. cabinet post in 100 years. . . . Because he wears ordinary clothes, as all Mormon clergy do, it has not been realized that his membership in the Cabinet is akin to putting a top official of any other denominational hierarchy in the political administration of power—a Cardinal of the Roman Catholic Church or an Episcopal Bishop, for example." Then McCune darkly noted the "constant injection of religion by Benson into official government activities."[26]

What McCune did not divulge was that the Mormon church is a lay church and its Council of Elders, of which Benson was a member, is nothing more than a lay advisory group; nor was Benson a full-time, paid church official, as is a Cardinal or a Bishop. This was the type of "research" training McCune was later to bring to GRI.

Wes McCune himself is best at describing the gestation and birth of Group Research:

"Actually, I got started on this project back in 1943, when I was doing some work on the farm bloc. Doubleday came to me and asked me to do a book on farm policy [i.e., *The Farm Bloc*] and what the influences were on it. In the course of doing the book I collected a lot of information on the different groups who were influencing and dealing with farm problems; my last chapter dealt with non-farm organizations, such as the Chamber of Commerce, who were active in this field. This is when I began collecting and filing information on the different groups.

"Then in 1956 I did another book, *Who's Behind Our Farm Policy*, in which I did essentially the same thing. I covered non-farm groups active in influencing public policy.

"When the John Birch Society came along and began getting active it really aroused my corpuscles; people who knew of my files and collecting information on different groups started writing me and asking questions about the different right-wing organizations. So, here I was sitting out in Denver with all this information, and I saw a way to put it to use."

At about the same time some others foresaw the political potential of information such as that possessed by Wes McCune—the dynamic Detroit duo of Walter and Victor Reuther. It may be merest coincidence, as McCune contends, that the now-famous anti-conservative "Reuther Memorandum" was delivered to Attorney General Robert Kennedy and widely circulated among liberals a scant 42 days before Group Research was incorporated in the District of Columbia. Nevertheless, the Reuthers' directive did say:

"Private agencies can do much, too, to identify and expose the radical right. Indeed, in the long-run the extent of participation by private agencies in this struggle is more likely to determine its outcome than anything the Government can do. The press, television, church, labor, civic, political, and other groups whose constitutional freedom is directly involved must carry the prime burden in this struggle."

A little over a month later a private agency named Group Research, Inc., was formed "to identify and expose the radical right." And helping it along the way were "the press, television, church, labor, civic, political, and other groups" who felt that a retired candy manufacturer in Belmont, Massachusetts, was seriously threatening their constitutional freedom.

(Joining with Wes McCune as incorporators of GRI were two other liberal front figures: James Heller, an active member and one-time secretary in the Washington, D.C., American Civil Liberties Union chapter; and Daniel Singer, a former secretary-treasurer for two interrelated liberal groups, the Council for Abolishing War and the Lobby for Abolishing War, which gave campaign assistance to so-called "peace" candidates. A board member of both these groups, incidentally, was former McCune employer and Farmers Union president, James Patton.)

Whether or not the Reuthers' conception of something like GRI in their "Memo" was just coincidence, subsequent assistance given the new organization by Walter Reuther and other labor elements was no fantasy. The first indication of such aid was a letter mailed to national labor leaders by Emanuel Muravchik, national field director of the Jewish Labor Committee; in his March, 1962, letter Muravchik asked that union members submit information concerning "activities of the ultra-rightists and their relation to the right-to-workers and anti-labor employers in their localities" for use in "a pamphlet which will trace the ties between anti-labor elements and the Birchers, both by industry and by region."

A short time later GRI subscribers began receiving their materials accompanied by a pink mailing slip reading: "Industrial Union Department, AFL-CIO, 815 16th Street, N.W., Washington, D.C." The note from IUD, which is headed coincidentally enough by the elder Reuther, also solicited information from union members, saying, "Please remember that we would very much appreciate receiving any clippings, publications, or other evidence of activity in your area."

With the IUD sniffing out "evidence" of right-wing activity and the Jewish Labor Committee calling for material tracing "the ties between anti-labor elements and the Birchers," it was no shock that the lengthiest and sauciest report published during Group Research's first year was a 36-page indictment of the National Right to Work Committee. Sure enough, the report tied the committee to the Birch Society.

Since its inception Group Research has had two principal products: lengthy reports, such as that on the Right to Work Committee, which are combined in the GRI Directory-Index; and a four-page bi-monthly newsletter, *Group Research Report*. There is also a "query service" available to GRI subscribers for special requests and urgent questions.

The concise and informative *Report* contains information on the activities of allegedly right-wing groups and individuals, plus financial reports, book reviews and political news involving these elements. Originally available only to full subscriber-clients of the entire Group Research service, the *Report* can now be purchased by non-clients at an annual cost of $25.00.

The main product going to clients only are the GRI in-depth reports, which are bundled together in its loose-leaf *Directory*. The reports, usually concerning right-wing groups, individuals or publications, are extensive and thorough in their attempts to tie one organization (or publication) with a host of others on the right (usually the John Birch Society); the reports are intended for editorial use and many of the subscribers (a list and the number are kept secret) are suspected to be in the press, communications media and other "opinion molding" positions.

The most damning criticism of the investigative organization has come not from the expected so-called right-wing elements it attacks, but from a trio of liberal Republican officeholders. In October, 1965, Sen. Thruston Morton (R-Ky.) delivered a series of broadsides against GRI that were quickly seconded by fellow GOP liberal Sen. Hugh Scott and the then Governor of Oregon, Mark Hatfield (now U.S. Senator).

Morton began his assault by denouncing the Group Research policy of "guilt-by-association," calling its *Directory* "a three-volume blacklist." The Kentuckian, a former assistant secretary of state and a Vietnam "dove," warned that "this list of dangerous extremists who are threatening our country carries the name of General Eisenhower along with that of the hate-mongering Gerald L.K. Smith; it draws no distinction between Bishop Fulton Sheen and the American Nazi leader, George Lincoln Rockwell."

And if GRI did not mean to imply that all those mentioned in its literature were rabid right-wing extremists, Morton suggested, the organization should change its advertising and promotional policy. Alluding to a full-page GRI advertisement running in *Progressive*[27] and other liberal publications, Morton stated that "the ad is topped by pictures of hooded Klansmen; a swastika-adorned Nazi shouting into a microphone; General Edwin Walker, the one-time Birchite candidate for the Democratic gubernatorial nomination in Texas; and the John Birch Society leader, Robert Welch. It is under such a heading that Group Research . . . advertises their wares, and with the accompanying text which speaks of the dangerous extremists who are threatening our country, the brand is clearly placed on all those whose names appear on the list."

This same advertisement was the crux of Morton's second charge against Group Research, its seeming ignorance of left-wing extremists. In the magazine ad GRI had defined itself as "a four-year old private, non-profit organization of professional research people who maintain vigilant watch over the activities of extremists of all shades who threaten American democracy." Part of the GRI "watch," Morton found, must be done with a blindfold on.

After looking in vain for the names of Gus Hall, U.S. Communist Party head, or known supporters of Communist causes, Morton concluded: "When the compilers of this list look to the Left, they obviously lose their sight completely. If we are to accept their own boast that they watch over extremists of all shades, then they see nothing wrong with the extremists of the Left even though they be members of the Communist Party."

Morton also took note of the modesty Group Research demonstrates when it asks subscribers not to mention GRI, but "the original source." Commented Morton, "That suggests some things. It suggests to me that either they are not willing to stand behind their work or they want someone else with a better standing than theirs to peddle it to an unsuspecting public."[28]

The seven-page rebuttal to Morton's remarks prepared by Group Research was most notable for what it did not say. No explanation was given as to why it urged clients not to refer to GRI when quoting its material, nor did Group Research say anything about why it never made mention of extremists on the Left, including admitted Communist Party officials.

(GRI director McCune did say in a later interview[29] that he did not have the time to investigate left-wing groups, adding that, besides, "there is no vacuum of any kind" in doing this, citing the work of the House Un-American Activities Committee and Senate Internal Security Subcommittee. A strange attitude for the director of an organization which claims to "maintain vigilant watch over the activities of extremists of all shades who threaten American democracy.")

What the Group Research defense did do was haggle over Sen. Morton's semantics in charging GRI with practicing "guilt by association" and publishing a "blacklist." Group Research latched onto the one word "blacklist" and attempted to throw the whole dispute into confusion.

GRI's first point was that it "is not capable of blacklisting, even if it wanted to, because it has no power, direct or indirect, to enforce its findings. GRI cannot hire, fire or discriminate against anyone; it has never suggested such treatment; and it knows of no subscriber to its services who is interested in such misuse of its research material."

Moreover, pleaded the defense, "the director of GRI has stated many times that one's feelings against any group or person must never be allowed to take the form of suppressing the expression of opinion. The entire emphasis has been on identification, as opposed to suppression."

Finally, Group Research argued that the "blacklist" is no list at all, "but an *index,* and there is a very big difference." It then noted that the instructions for the *Directory* stressed that "the mention of a person or organization . . . has no editorial significance of itself. . . . The user must draw his own conclusions in each instance."

Without a doubt Group Research is semantically correct in claiming its index is not a "blacklist." By niggling over Morton's unfortunate choice of terms, GRI was able to obscure other important questions about its activities—such as its allegation that its "entire emphasis has been on identification, as opposed to suppression." This is totally absurd and represents another instance of reality intruding upon GRI's remarkable innocence.

First of all, Group Research itself does not practice what it presumes to preach. Do advertisements soliciting GRI subscriptions by using photographs of racists and Nazis, or identifying such responsible groups as the Free Society Association and Americans for Constitutional Action as "directed toward imposing an inflexible thought control on the nation," serve merely as "identification," or is it purposeful slander? GRI director Wes McCune is himself an offender of his own dictum; in a 1963 speech he trumpeted to the Women's National Democratic Club in Washington that the damage done by "extremists at the community level in terms of fear, hate, distrust, violence, smear and suppression . . . is so widespread that it defies ability to keep track of it."[30] This is "identification"?

Despite such abdication from its "identification, not suppression" pledge, Group Research still maintains that once it has warned subscribers that mention in the *Directory* "has no editorial significance of itself," its job is done and it is innocent of any subsequent misuse (even "suppression") by GRI clients. The question is, why would Group Research publish and distribute potentially inflammatory material if it did not intend for it to inflame? Just because GRI cannot "enforce its findings" does not mean it is not responsible for clients using its material to smear, slur and suppress; in fact, GRI would invite just this when it says in the instructions for its material: "The user may draw his own conclusions."

When it comes to drawing conclusions, COPE is one of the best. A survey of COPE's anti-conservative propaganda is itself proof of the degree it relies on Group Research material for its own use; the committee's solicitation for and distribution of Group Research material among union members is also a factor in this alliance.

The first inkling of how COPE intended GRI's material to be used came in a memorandum sent to state and local COPE leaders in March, 1963, informing them that national COPE had "made arrangements to get special material on right-wing organizations and other pressure groups from Group Research, Inc., in Washington, D.C." To encourage union members to use the GRI information, COPE devised a "hidden plot" behind so-called right-wing activity:

"Although the right-wingers talk most about the menace of communism, impeaching Chief Justice Warren, repealing the income tax, 'getting the U.S. out of the U.N. and the U.N. out of the U.S.,' and the alleged 'no-win' foreign policy, at the root of their efforts is determined anti-labor activity and an all-out drive against social welfare legislation. Combatting them at the national and community level is essential for organized labor . . ."

And how were local COPE leaders and workers to use the available GRI material? Advised the national COPE memorandum:

"When you hear that a right-wing speaker is coming to town, check him immediately in the *Directory* and alert friendly groups. Inform your local newspaper by personal visit if possible of the character, background and connections of the speaker . . .

"Armed with the facts about extremist groups, labor union members can take some leadership in combatting them, either by heading them off before they really get started or by limiting the damage they do and helping to dry them up.

"Preventive action is best, of course, but is not easy. The idea is to alert democratic groups to the possibility of trouble and meet with their representatives. Ordinarily it is best not to pass resolutions or take a vote. But there is sometimes an advantage in arranging a meeting at which community leaders actually sign a warning statement, for release to the press, in advance of a right-wing meeting, exposing its nature and intent."

In such easy manner does a group supposedly combating right-wing activities in order to preserve democracy—by not taking any votes—use Group Research's purported "identification" material to suppress and harass. Says the COPE directive about public suppression: "editors and broadcasters should be visited with facts about right-wingers which they presumably do not have at hand. They should be urged to publish such material. In many cases, exposure alone will turn the tide." So much for the innocence of Group Research, Inc.

GRI's complicity in COPE's arrogant use of its material is deepened by the special arrangement the committee has in procuring the bi-weekly GRI *Report* for union members at a cut-rate. When Wes McCune says his "only relationship" with COPE is "strictly business" he is admitting roughly half of the actual situation; what COPE does is go to the printer Group Research uses and buy copies of the *Report* fresh off the presses, and then mail these to grass roots COPE leaders and members. McCune maintains "I never see their money or talk with them, they deal directly with the printer," as his defense against allegations of a close GRI-COPE tie; McCune would make either a bad undercover agent or a bad businessman.

(Individual unions also promote GRI wares among the membership, one worthy example being the International Association of Machinists. "Enclosed is a leaflet explaining the Group Research *Report*," wrote the IAM monthly *Education Bulletin* in October, 1965; "Group Research *Report* provides the facts about far right extremist organizations, their programs and leadership . . . If you are concerned about the growth of extremists' activities and want to know what is going on, you can find out by subscribing to Group Research *Report*. Your lodge [political] Education Committee may want to recommend that the lodge [i.e., local] subscribe to Group Research *Report*."

(In July, 1963, the *Arkansas Union Labor Bulletin* reported that the state AFL-CIO Executive Committee had "voted to subscribe to the reports of Group Research, Inc., on members of the extreme right wing. The subscription will cover copies for about 700 'opinion leaders' in Arkansas to be mailed out by the state AFL-CIO."

(Additionally, evidence of GRI-originated information regularly appears in such labor publications as *Solidarity, Steel Labor,* the Communications Workers' *CWA News* and the *United Rubber Worker*. As Group Research studiously advises its clients not to refer to GRI as a source and instead to cite "original sources," there is no way to prove "beyond a reasonable doubt" that anti-conservative material originates with GRI; but it is safe to assume that these labor publications have neither the staff, expertise nor resources to compile the extensive anti-right-wing material used in their articles completely on their own.)

As for COPE's use of Group Research material in its own publications, one of the first examples was the COPE "Memo" of March 25, 1963, asking, "What Is The Right? . . . And Why Is It Wrong?" It turns out that the right "is dedicated, determined and dangerous. It has money, manpower and militancy." As if that wasn't enough to scare the living daylights out of some ignorant "Memo" reader, he also found "right-wingers basically are 'againsters.' They set out a whole smorgasbord of spites. They fire salvos of propaganda bombarding individuals and institutions they fear and mistrust."

COPE then set out a list of six of "the right wing's priority list of 'againstisms,'" leading off, naturally, with "they are against labor unions." Together with the list, however, COPE inserted this fascinating disclaimer: "[bear] in mind that not all extremist groups advocate the entire list, but some do, and almost all espouse most of it." Conceding that readers could wade through this sentence to begin with, what are they then to believe? That even if a suspect party doesn't believe in *any* of the six, he's still an "extremist"; or that if someone supports one of the "againstisms"—like being "against big government"—he's definitely an extremist, or what? Pity the poor workingman who must depend on COPE for The Word.

Not content with confusion, COPE also sought to spread a little "fear and mistrust" of its own among union members. The "Memo" told its version of the story about a school board member in California who was supposedly forced off the board as a result of a Birch Society campaign of "smear and slander" and "blatant lies and ugly insinuations." Not only was the gentleman booted from the board, writes COPE, but "he died eight months later at 36, leaving a widow and three young children." (This sentence was written in bold face in the "Memo.")

Insinuation? Did someone say something about "ugly insinuations"? Certainly COPE would never use such things; why, on the very next page it is gallantly noted—in a spirit of "fair play," no doubt—that "not all the victims of the right-wingers die."

Subsequent examples of COPE using what is all-but-obviously (*sans* citation) Group Research material have not gone quite so far as to convict the right wing of involuntary manslaughter, but have done quite well in the character assassination department. Such exhibits, all mentioned in examining COPE's "Propaganda Arsenal," include the anti-conservative pamphlets "The Target Is You" and "They're Playing For Keeps," most of it anti-Goldwater and anti-Reagan material, and the absurd "interlocking directorate" chart of imponderable black lines. Also there is the COPE "Memo" of June 12, 1967, devoted to unearthing "right-wing agents, . . . a small, underground force of right-wing propaganda pros . . . at work in 11 western states"; a similar story had appeared in the Group Research *Report* of May 31, 1967.

Outside of organized labor, Group Research's most prestigious client and promoter is the Democratic National Committee. One of the first to publicize this link was Mark Hatfield, governor of Oregon at the time of his 1965 charges against GRI.

What Hatfield had found was that during 1965 the Democratic National Committee had given Group Research two contributions totaling $10,000. GRI director McCune later explained that the money from the DNC was in payment for GRI services during the '64 campaign; DNC chairman John Bailey's only comment on subsidizing GRI was to say its Republican critics were "not familiar either with the organization [they] are talking about or the material it distributes."

Hatfield was not satisfied. Speaking of Group Research's *modus operandi,* he charged "This approach—lumping of the known patriots with the wild-eyed radicals—outdoes McCarthy. It misleads. It smears. It destroys. It defames. It feeds on fear. And to think it is subsidized by one of our Nation's two political parties. I call upon every responsible Democratic leader from Bethesda to precinct committeemen in Oregon to disavow this scurrilous compilation."[31]

Rather than a disavowal, it was later learned that connections between the Democratic hierarchy and Group Research were closer than expected. In August, 1965, top Democratic strategist John Bailey had sent out a letter to party leaders and workers which represented an open solicitation for Group Research. In his "Dear Friend" epistle, DNC chairman Bailey clearly exposed the principal factor in GRI's success and popularity among liberal elements, when he wrote:

"The Democratic National Committee receives a constant flow of mail from Democrats in all parts of the country reporting on activities of the John Birch Society and others of the radical right and asking for our help.

"So far as possible we have tried to provide this help. But to do so we have had to depend heavily on the only national research organization that has systematically kept track of the activities of the radical right and has readily available the information on individuals and organizations that is so essential to combatting their activities.

"This organization is Group Research, Inc., which was established 4 years ago as a private, nonprofit organization. Since then it has rendered invaluable assistance to organizations with right-wing problems—among them the League of Women Voters, the National Education Association, the Parent-Teachers Association of America, the National Council of Churches, and the AFL-CIO.

"Enclosed is a brochure describing this organization, and a sample copy of the newsletter that is its principle [sic] publication. If the radical right is active in your area you may want to give serious consideration to subscribing to the newsletter, and perhaps the other services that are available. It is our experience, and that of others, that you will find them extremely valuable in countering rightwing activities."

(The first to report distribution of the Bailey letter and GRI brochure by the Democratic National Committee was *Chicago Tribune* columnist Willard Edwards.[32] In its defense against Sen. Morton's accusations a few weeks later, Group Research noted "charges" against it by "rightwing spokesmen" in the press, specifically citing "an article by Walter Trohan in the *Chicago Tribune.*" So much for the "research" of Group Research, Inc.)

Making the marriage even sweeter, the Democratic National Committee has promoted GRI materials in its publications and used these materials itself in fighting such pet GRI targets as allegedly right-wing radio and television programs. As for printed catering, the DNC's bi-weekly newspaper *The Democrat* in August, 1965, lauded "the unique work performed by Group Research" and noted GRI's "newsletter is now available for the first time."

The national committee's campaign against "right-wing radio and television programs"— a project participated in by most of GRI's clients and COPE's allies—began in 1964, when all its anti-conservative activities were directed at the ultimate end of defeating Sen. Goldwater. That year a DNC vice chairman sent a letter to radio stations carrying supposedly right-wing programs, saying, "All of these programs have repeatedly attacked the candidates, programs, and policies of the Democratic party. In view of the coming political campaign, I thought you should be aware both of the content of these programs and the claims for time to which these attacks can make you liable." Such a blatantly coercive use of the Federal Communications Commission's "fairness doctrine" by the party in control of the White House (and FCC) prompted a spokesman for one of the stations to call the letter "an attempt to intimidate."[33]

An attack on these programs from another Democratic source in 1965 turned up one more illustration of how Group Research spreads its information around. Sen. Gale McGee (D-Wyo.), who has on occasion placed GRI material in the *Congressional Record* verbatim, took off after the usual rightist radio targets in a Senate speech; McGee's remarks and his GRI-type documentation were quickly reproduced and praised in a column by Drew Pearson. In his remarks McGee compared the broadcasters to Hitler, and Pearson, in typically graphic style, labeled the list a "rollcall of haters."[34]

By far the most farcical GRI outlet to emerge on the national scene was a group (The National Council for Civic Responsibility) formed in 1964 for the express purpose of distributing anti-Goldwater propaganda. When founded, the council's head, a self-styled "modern Republican" named Arthur Larson (also a board member of the National Council of Senior Citizens), disclaimed any such singular purpose; but an issue of the GRI *Report* noted that "Larson said his organization will use the factual material prepared regularly by Group Research, Inc."[35] Later, syndicated columnist Jack Anderson told the whole story behind the mystery group:

"The National Council for Civic Responsibility was formed on too short notice to obtain a tax exemption. So the Democrats quietly arranged with the Public Affairs Institute, a tax-exempt foundation, to take it over. This permitted the council to solicit tax-deductible contributions. The biggest donation, however, was a fat $50,000 check from the Democratic National Committee's 'book fund.' Later, the Democrats handed over another $10,000 in cash."[36]

With this "cover" blown asunder, it was obvious the NCCR had to disband and liberals had to find another means to attack the conservative opposition. The answer was the Institute for American Democracy, formed in 1966 with its purported goal being to "defend the American middleground with an educational program shedding much needed light on the Far Left and Right." (Subsequent mention of far Leftists in IAD publications is about as common as in GRI material.)

The Institute for American Democracy was not fooling anybody. In the very first issue of its regular newsletter, *Homefront,* it said, "We have ready access to the Group Research, Inc., reports and a half-dozen other active files on extremist organizations." And there among the IAD's original sponsoring committee were fifteen men previously members of the National Council of Civic Responsibility, including the NCCR's chairman, Arthur Larson, union leaders Walter Reuther and Jacob Potofsky (both also with the ADA), and James Patton, retired head of the Farmers Union and ADA Vice Chairman.

Confirming the Institute's ties with organized labor were contributions totaling $20,000 from the AFL-CIO (out of the Special Purposes fund) to the IAD between 1965-67.

The chairman of IAD is Dr. Franklin H. Littell, president of small Iowa Wesleyan College, who like Arthur Larson advertises himself as a "moderate Republican"—theoretically to reassure the public that it is not only Democrats who berate conservatives. Dr. Littell wasted no time establishing his own credentials as a "responsible" fighter of extremism.

As he demonstrated in a *Christian Science Monitor* interview, he knows a few slogans himself:

"Dr. Littell is a phrasemaker of blunt terms. The radical Right are not 'kooks,' he charges, 'they are flesh-eaters.' He calls them 'merchants of fear,' peddling 'superhate and super-patriotism,' whose unsophisticated proselytes becomes fanatical 'supersure.' "[37]

The IAD's first projects were, like Littell's vivid phraseology, nothing new among GRI-COPE confidants. It published a pamphlet on right-wing radio broadcasts ("air pollution" it flippantly called them) and implored the Internal Revenue Service to deprive right-wing groups of their tax-exemptions. In the same style that its predecessor NCCR had employed, dashing madly about seeking a tax-exempt "cover," while attacking right-wing groups for having tax-free status, the IAD has mobilized public opinion for IRS action against "extremist" groups while it was enjoying a tax-exemption.

But, as with Group Research and COPE, such little hypocrisies do not faze the IAD a bit. The intention of these groups is to discredit all conservatives, and one effective way of doing so is to lump responsible conservatives together with bona fide extremists, including racists and anti-Semites; or, as Sen. Morton correctly branded it, to practice "guilt-by-association."

This has been the stock-in-trade of Group Research since its inception. GRI director McCune has voiced displeasure with the tactic, but still finds means to justify his using it: "It is a bad practice and I don't like to do it, but you must realize that I deal with a wide range of activities and sometimes goof and maybe unfairly lump several differing groups together. I agree that it is unfair to put a publication like *Common Sense* and one like *Human Events* or *National Review* together under the heading of 'conservative publications,' because 'conservative' is a word I respect. But, I do think that associations are important and a lot can be based upon them."

In many cases associations certainly are important and instructive. Anti-Communist publications and legislators have frequently cited Communist "front" records or associations in documenting a case against such individuals as government security risks, a practice regularly condemned as "witch hunting" by some of Mr. McCune's best clients.

The fact is that Group Research does *not* make it clear when there are absolutely no associations between groups right-of-center, thus leaving an open implication that the associations *do* exist. The issue of the GRI *Report* mailed out by the Democratic National Committee with chairman Bailey's letter is a perfect case in point. It reported the financial growth of the John Birch Society and "other groups at the same end of the political spectrum"; one of these was the American Conservative

Union, which at its founding meeting voted to bar JBS members. But *Report* readers—including many Democratic Party workers seeing the publication for the first time—had no way of knowing this and could not be blamed for subsequently viewing the ACU and JBS as one and the same.

This issue of the *Report,* entitled "Right Wing Gets Deeper Into Politics," went on to mention such reputable conservative individuals and organizations as Sen. Goldwater, Gov. Reagan, Sen. Strom Thurmond, the Young Americans for Freedom and the American Farm Bureau, right along with an assortment of segregationists, anti-Semites, religious fanatics and all-out nuts. No distinction was made, however.

Up to the point that Group Research does not editorialize in its publication, it is exempt from accusations of "smear"; it presents all information in a straightforward, factual manner and advises "the user must draw his own conclusions in each instance." But by not placing the organizations, publications and individuals it mentions—albeit factually —in some sort of perspective on the right, or by not telling the reader the crucial difference between a group like the ACU and the Birch Society, it is performing no "identification" service at all, but leaving the door wide open—all the while feigning innocence—for the wildest accusations or "conclusions" imaginable. And every time the American Conservative Union (or any respectable conservative group so associated with genuine extremists) is accused by GRI clients as being "extremist" or a "Birch-front," Group Research is as much to blame as those making the false charges.

This was the type of propaganda which Group Research had used so effectively in 1964 in heaping discredit, if not always invective, on Sen. Goldwater. And the plan is to do the same again in 1968.

In the eyes of Wes McCune and his Group Research, Inc., the Republican Party is in the grip of conservatives, rightwingers, extremists and other pejorative nouns; 1968, he and his co-workers seem to feel, will be 1964 all over again as far as the GOP is concerned. All of which means that GRI's propaganda in 1968 will be 1964 all over again.

Group Research makes its money by investigating and reporting on the right wing and, luckily for it, COPE and the other liberal front groups have latched onto the anti-right, *ergo* anti-Republican, strategy as their favorite and most effective. It is a foregone conclusion that as the 1968 race heats up, the material produced by GRI will be sure to turn up in the propaganda of COPE, the Democratic National Committee, the Farmers Union, the Senior Citizens Council and most of the rest of the "Allies." It gets around.

## CHAPTER NINE

# How to Cope with COPE

THE only way for a Republican and/or conservative candidate or group to adequately "cope with COPE" would be to set up a parallel organization with all of COPE's advantages and resources.

If the factions COPE regularly opposes could establish an organization which millions of men were required to join, which was financed by tax-exempt money demanded of these men, which could address the men through publications and speakers they could not easily avoid, which could engage in partisan political activities with virtual impunity under the innocuous title of "education" and use organizations originally constructed for another purpose, and which could influence both elections and the actions of candidates once elected, then and only then would COPE's opponents take a step toward equaling the influence of the AFL-CIO and its Committee on Political Education. The most important missing ingredient would be labor's decades of experience in doing all these things.

Barring such an unlikely development, the means by which COPE's natural adversaries may contend with COPE are twofold. One would be the legislative actions Congress could take to restrict some of the more outrageous of labor's political advantages and abuses; the second would include the political methods which candidates and groups could practice to dilute COPE's structural power and win a larger share of the rank-and-file vote.

Talk on Capitol Hill concerning legislation to curb labor abuses usually revolves around political financing; it is not that labor does not have other advantages beyond being able to bankroll a huge war chest; it is just that cash is probably its most reliable lever of influence and that which is easiest to control through legislative action. "Labor's main effectiveness in politics is money," says Rep. Bob Wilson, chairman of the Republican Congressional Campaign Committee. "Labor leaders know how to separate a union man from his money and how to spend it. Take this away from them and they are no better than anybody else."

When the talk gets around to specifics, most of it centers on the Corrupt Practices Act and what should be done to close up some of its more gaping loopholes. Rep. John Ashbrook (R-Ohio), a frequent target of COPE campaigns, thinks "we need to tighten the Corrupt Practices Act to pierce the protective curtain around 'educational' activities by organizations such as COPE, because they are political activities. Expenses for field organizers do not have to be reported, nor such projects as 'get-out-the-vote' drives, because they are claimed to be 'educational.' The law should be rewritten so they would have to report these."

Sen. Charles Percy (R-Ill.) says there is nothing wrong with labor engaging in partisan politics as long as voluntary funds are used. He thinks that something should be done to preserve and protect this voluntary approach. "We all know that what unions call voluntary political funds aren't voluntary," says the Illinois Republican, "but they should be; as long as the money spent by unions in politics is raised fairly and honestly, and voluntary funds are used, it is perfectly alright for them to campaign."

GOP strategist Wilson would like to see more attention paid to enforcing the present Corrupt Practices Law, particularly that section which bars—as with dues funds—unions from contributing "services" to political candidates. "Unions will assign full-time paid personnel to help a political candidate and nothing will be said about it," argues Wilson, "and I think this should be enforced. As it is now, when you complain to the proper authorities in the Justice Department they play politics and won't do anything."

And so it goes, and it is apparent that just about everyone sitting in the House and Senate has a considered opinion on exactly what needs to be done with the Corrupt Practices Act to better police labor's political spending. A few have actually gone so far as to write and introduce legislation. When congressional labor forces mounted their drive to repeal 14(b) in the House during the 89th Congress, then Rep. Robert Griffin proposed an amendment to the repeal bill barring money taken from workers in a union shop being used for anything other than legitimate collective bargaining purposes; in their undying crusade to protect the workingman from the encroachments of freedom, the COPE-influenced congressmen voted repeal and rejected the Griffin amendment by almost identical margins.

In the 90th Congress, labor forces again maneuvered to thwart a regulatory political spending bill which would have gone a long way toward curbing union and business abuses alike. This measure, called the "Election Reform Bill" and introduced by Rep. Robert Ashmore (D-S.C.), would have established a five-man (no more than three from one party) presidential Federal Elections Commission to oversee all political spending.

Ashmore's bill also directed political action committees to spend only voluntary contributions on influencing elections, with the Elections Commission deciding whether or not an action had this intent or if it was genuinely bi-partisan (for which non-voluntary money could be used); "union members could still make voluntary contributions to COPE," explained Ashmore. "It is just that COPE could no longer levy fees or charge unions for money used in political activities." The legislation also demanded complete spending accountings from candidates and, in a much-needed and imaginative regulation, prohibited individuals from contributing more than $5,000 to any one candidate and a committee supporting him, or to two committees "substantially supporting the same candidate[s]."

The Election Reform Bill did not generate great enthusiasm among those erstwhile reformers, the House members supported by COPE. According to Rep. Ashmore, the body examining his bill, the House Administration Committee, "notified COPE at least three times, inviting them to testify and send a representative, but they never sent anyone up to talk with us." It was soon apparent that, rather than a public discussion, COPE preferred to spread the word among its friends in the House to stop the bill's progress; subsequently Rep. Ashmore found it impossible to get enough members of the Administration Committee together to pass the bill onto the floor of the House. "We have not been successful in getting a quorum in the committee to pass on this bill," said a disgruntled Ashmore, "you can draw from this what inferences you like."[1]

One very good reason reform bills like this fail is that they cover several aspects of the political financial problem beside labor, such as candidates' fund-raising and spending. Just as surely as all members of Congress have a personal remedy for the sickly Corrupt Practices Act, most are loath to support any actual meaningful reform if it goes so far as to inhibit their re-election campaigns. When it comes to political spending legislation, few recent congressmen seem anxious to make the next edition of *Profiles in Courage*.

The only answer to this stalemate is for the public to demand honest election laws, and to demand that their representatives and senators get busy writing them. The alternative public response is the one found more often: cynicism, a not very productive attitude. It is, therefore, up to responsible national and local citizens' organizations—including labor—to help mobilize this public demand, or else the stalemate of inaction, perpetuating dishonesty and injustices, will continue.

But organized labor has actually helped maintain the status quo. While AFL-CIO convention resolutions and its platform proposals establish a labor position on a broad spectrum of issues, no mention is made of political spending reform. In light of COPE's repeated attacks on the political outlays of Big Business, this might seem a startling omission; in the light of reality, what it does show is the hypocrisy behind this favorite COPE theme.

For, even in the unlikely possibility that business "fat cats" pump more cash than labor into the political campaigns, the AFL-CIO realizes that any reform legislation would inevitably put a damper on COPE's monetary influence. The situation is embarrassing for labor since it is usually Republican or conservative Democratic congressmen who introduce and promote political spending reform bills. When these are presented in Congress, even though they affect business political action committees as much as labor's, COPE and the AFL-CIO take the recourse—as with the Ashmore proposal—of amassing silent resistance. And the stalemate persists.

It is axiomatic that Congress should pass no spending reform bill before it writes legislation policing its own fiscal activities. But, as concerns labor, there are other means than strictly spending bills to effectively curb some union political abuses. COPE's propaganda would inevitably term any such singular legislation "anti-labor," when all that such legislation would be doing would be to place COPE and other labor electioneering groups on an equal plane with their non-labor competitors.

A first step in this direction would be to take labor political action committees out from under the protective "educational" shield provided by the Internal Revenue Service's tax-exempt rulings. Every national organization involved in direct partisan political activity should be, by law, technically and physically separate from any other organization; labor action committees should be separated from labor federations and labor unions, with their automatic tax-exempt "covers," just as business committees (such as AMPAC and BIPAC) are already autonomous groups.

The labor political committees could still maintain two spending outlets, one for distinctly political purposes and the other for legally defined "non-partisan" activities (including registration, office and salary expenses); labor federations and unions could then contribute to the latter, while the former would be stocked by genuinely voluntary contributions. Moreover, these committees—business and labor alike—would also be required to make full and complete annual reportings of every single receipt and expenditure.

(Labor federations and business associations would both be allowed to continue congressional lobbying, but they should be restricted in their propaganda activities; mention of specific political campaigns in house organs would be outlawed, as would dissemination of political propaganda. As for individuals' contributions to political campaigns—the area in which business has an advantage—these should be limited in amount and in the number of committees contributed to, which were aiding substantially the same candidates.)

Such an arrangement would be a start toward doing away with the duplicity to be found where a labor union can transfer dues funds to COPE under the guise of "voluntary dollars," where the AFL-CIO can pay (again out of dues funds) for COPE field representatives who organize political campaigns, and where COPE is required to report only a fraction of what it spends each year. By having autonomous labor political committees, with full reporting demanded, financial operations would at least be more visible and give the union member a clearer picture of just where his dues money was going.

Barry Goldwater, for one, thinks that the time will soon come when union men themselves will demand that Congress write laws requiring their unions to make a full accounting of the expenditure of dues money. "I have a feeling," says the former presidential candidate, "that union membership is getting a little tired of seeing its funds wasted on so many different and nefarious political programs, and that in the future there will be a calling to account; this will result in a more controlled and restricted activity on the part of leaders of the labor movement in this country in politics."

Any piece of legislation incorporating this arrangement could, of course, be construed to be "anti-labor," but it would definitely not be giving any advantages to already-disadvantaged business political action committees. The legislative aim is to place the focus of campaign spending and activity back where it belongs, with the political parties.

Not to be forgotten in political spending proposals are the union members, whose situation provides another approach to reform legislation. One method would be that proposed by Griffin in his amendment to the repeal bill, barring dues funds collected in a union shop from being used for political activities.

Another possibility would be to emulate the current practice in Great Britain, a method advanced by Justice Felix Frankfurter in his dissent in the Street Case. Under a law dating back to 1913, a British union member may "contract out" from political contributions by informing his union that he does not want his dues money used for political purposes.

Another approved approach toward restricting labor's political advantage is the passage of right-to-work laws, or, on a congressional level, a national right-to-work law permitting only *voluntary* unions, unless an individual state elects to maintain union shops. With the right-to-work situation now more or less at a standoff, and with the pros and cons dutifully deliberated over a period of twenty years, the issue is not one many politicians are going to emphasize in their campaigns. Yet, the National Right to Work Committee, in addition to pushing for individual state laws outlawing the union shop, is waiting for the day when Congress will pass a nationwide voluntary union ruling.

If such a law should ever come to pass, the likely result would be that unions would only intensify their political activities so that they might elect a friendly Congress which would repeal it. On the whole, however, the workingman (as concerns his union's spending of his dues money on political activities) would be markedly better off with such a law. But, for the time being, there are probably more realistic ways for COPE's opponents to contend with organized labor as a political force.

They could, for example, concentrate on practical politics and go after the votes of the union's rank-and-file. Top Republican Party strategists are convinced that a sizable union member vote for GOP candidates is there to be garnered in the right circumstances. This conclusion is based on the evidence the strategists value the highest, the past success of Republicans in getting this vote; mentioned frequently are the 1966 victories of Ronald Reagan, Chuck Percy, Robert Griffin, and in another Michigan example, the '66 victory of Rep. Don Riegle, defeater of an incumbent Democrat who had won in 1964 by some 60,000 votes in Flint, Michigan, the most top-heavy union city in the United States.

There is also additional information buttressing the case for a potential Republican rank-and-file vote, notably polls. The AFL-CIO's own version of the Kraft Poll of its members showed Lyndon Johnson receiving no more than 60 percent of union votes against four top GOP presidential prospects, and as low as 46 percent against one, both figures a dramatic drop from the 70 percent-plus of union votes LBJ corralled in '64. A highly regarded polling by the Communications Workers of America in mid-1967 appeared to bear more bad news for Democrats; it reported that only 22 percent of CWA members backed President Johnson's re-election, with another 22 percent going both to the late Sen. Robert Kennedy and Republican George Romney and 16 percent each to Ronald Reagan and non-contender Barry Goldwater.[2]

Democratic Party chairman John Bailey interpreted such findings to indicate that "when a man works and has good wages, he can be independent of candidates endorsed by union leadership. He can ignore the candidate who has a good union record. And the legislation and issues that once meant bread and butter to him are no longer so vital when he casts his ballot."[3]

Bailey may have been overreacting, perhaps consciously so, in an effort to jolt the lethargic Democratic Party machine into action. It must be remembered that the Kraft and Communications Workers' Polls were taken in early 1967, at a time when Lyndon Johnson was riding low on the public popularity charts. Later in the year, COPE glowingly released the results of a series of informal polls taken at twelve different AFL-CIO union conventions, a survey showing LBJ the favorite of 2473 of the 4502 delegates polled, or 54 percent; Senator Robert Kennedy was the second choice of the delegates, attracting 16.9 percent of their votes, and the highest-ranking Republican was New York's Governor Nelson Rockefeller, receiving only 4.6 percent of the total delegates' votes.

Despite the contrast and conflict in these several pollings (inevitably bringing up the overall question of the reliability of polls), Republicans express guarded optimism over the political situation among the rank-and-file. Two of the most knowledgeable and outspoken GOP strategists on the subject of the labor vote are Rep. Bob Wilson and Sen. George Murphy, chairmen, respectively, of the Congressional and Senate Campaign Committees.

"I believe that the ability of labor to deliver the vote is overestimated," Sen. Murphy begins, explaining that "this development is because the rank-and-file today resent the intent of their bosses to dictate political choices and resent this intrusion on their freedom." Rather than a temporary phenomenon, Murphy believes "this is a trend and will be greater in 1968."

Speaking from personal experience in entertainment industry unions, the California Senator declares, "As a union member for forty years I've always opposed labor going into politics and taking political power. This is improper. It impairs the ability of unions to properly represent union members." Giving an example, Murphy argues, "Don't think for a minute that Walter Reuther would ever jeopardize his friendship with LBJ just to take care of some members' problems that happened to conflict with what LBJ wanted."

Rep. Wilson also feels that "the idea of a labor bloc vote is now fallacious" and that "the labor leaders just can't deliver anymore," but he sees the situation in light of political issues rather than rank-and-file resentment over leaders' practices. "The political philosophy of organized labor no longer deals with the problems of labor," Wilson feels. "Instead it concentrates on social welfare, big government issues that are detrimental to the workingman."

This fervent attachment to standard liberal doctrine has, according to Wilson, led organized labor into a deeper relationship with the Democratic Party. "That labor is still the backbone of the Democratic Party and that the party depends upon it for support," elaborates Wilson, "is demonstrated by the fact that the Democratic Congressional Campaign Committee has only a three-man staff, while we have a staff of 33 on the

Republican side; if labor ever withdrew its support from the Democrats, the whole party structure would collapse and have to be reorganized."

The effects of this bond are mixed, Wilson observes. "Labor's political operation is more streamlined than ever before, but this doesn't necessarily mean it is more effective; it has grown fat and lazy with success. The old emotional appeals aren't working anymore."

Although both Wilson and Murphy express optimism over the present situation, they are quick to add that this is no automatic vote simply waiting for Election Day before going Republican. "In a close race with a large labor vote," says Wilson emphatically, "I think the Republican candidate must make an all-out appeal for the workers' votes; he must use every technique to get this vote. The appeal can't be half-hearted by any means—this is luxury the Republicans simply can't afford."

Or, in the words of Sen. Robert Griffin, "A lot of rank-and-file union members who resent it if their dues are spent for political purposes also resent it if the Republicans don't care enough to come out and seek their vote."[4]

As for what campaign tactics GOP candidates might employ in seeking out union votes, most strategists stress exposure through propaganda and factory gate visits. Bob Wilson also suggests that Republican aspirants form labor committees to endorse them and sponsor advertisements, with members of the committee drawn from independent non-AFL-CIO unions and "dissidents" from unions "affected adversely by national Democratic Administration policy"; Wilson notes as an example that maritime or shipping workers in the export-import field might support a Republican candidate because of their disenchantment with the Democrats' low tariff policies.

Outlining an overall statewide campaign approach, Robert Griffin offers the following suggestions based upon his experience in the 1966 Michigan Senate race:

"A Republican running in a state like Michigan, with large urban and rural areas, has two choices as to how to campaign. You can go through the motions in the urban areas and consolidate your strength in the rural, Republican areas; or you can take your Republican rural strength more-or-less for granted and move into 'the lion's den,' the urban areas, and try to win votes.

"While we took periodic swings through the outstate area in 1966, I concentrated most of my efforts in Detroit (my wife did a lot of campaigning in the outstate area, however); the result of this strategy was that I got 43 percent of the vote in Wayne County, while the usual Republican percentage is around 35 percent."

One thing GOP planners agree on is that it is foolish to try to duplicate COPE's organizational activities, with I. Lee Potter, executive director of Wilson's Congressional Campaign Committee, stating flatly that "Republican campaign workers shouldn't try to counter labor's pro-Democrat political activities."

This goes especially for such COPE projects as recruiting campaign workers and registering voters. If a Republican tries to round up precinct volunteers in labor neighborhoods he will most likely find only resistance (a union member might want to vote Republican, but chances are he will not want to risk the wrath of his Democratic friends and union bosses by openly campaigning for the GOP) and arouse COPE's suspicions; as for registration, Sen. Griffin reveals that in 1966 "we did not register voters in great numbers in Detroit, we concentrated on distributing literature and handshaking—we let COPE do our registering for us."

The indispensable political ingredient called propaganda is one area in which COPE's opponents might borrow a few ideas from the labor committee. A survey of the anti-Republican, anti-conservative publications that stream out of COPE will reveal a definitive style: terse, sparingly written, with the "message" presented in a "gut-style" that aims at the lowest common emotional denominator in seeking a positive response; COPE's propaganda wastes no time with flowery language or involved lengthy explanations of issues or candidates, but goes straight to the point with a string of one-or-two-syllable words. This is a style that has developed over many years of labor political activity and has proved successful; there is no copyright on it.

(An excellent example of propaganda which can dramatically appeal to union members in behalf of GOP candidates was a brochure distributed in '66 by Ronald Reagan's supporters, asking in bold type, "CAN A UNION MAN BE ELECTED GOVERNOR OF CALIFORNIA?" It seems that a union member had never held the governor's chair and, as former president of the Screen Actors Guild, Reagan had a chance to be the first; this pamphlet, outlining Reagan's stand on labor issues, was widely circulated in labor wards and is estimated to have had a great influence in producing a positive answer to the question posed.)

The value of these various tactics notwithstanding, the most effective strategic approach a GOP candidate can employ in campaigning among union members is to develop appealing issues and then go to the workers to expose and explain them. "The Republicans have not done enough missionary work among the blue-collar workers," says Lee Potter, "the Republican candidates have not gone into the communities where these people live and talked about issues."

Potter's boss Bob Wilson echoes this observation, asserting that "it is improbable that *any* Republican can win the endorsement of a labor union unless he wants to sell his soul. The only route for a Republican in getting labor votes is to by-pass the leadership and go straight to the workers."

In doing this, Wilson admits, the GOP candidate "has to play down his Republican label and go after the workers as citizens, not as union members. If the workers are already Republicans, the candidate has their votes; if they're Democrats—as most are—he must approach them as being unbiased, a man who happens to be a Republican and who is interested in the same things the workers are."

The practice of GOP office-seekers going directly to the workers—perhaps playing down, but by no means avoiding, the Republican label —and confronting them with issues is not a common one. The customary Republican action has been for party candidates to either "write off" the labor vote as hopelessly lost or to avoid discussion of important issues (even those concerning labor) when campaigning in working-class wards; aware of the latter practice, Senator Griffin declares, "Republican candidates in seeking votes among laboring people must meet the issues head on, not shy away from them as many GOP candidates have done."

A major factor in this seeming shyness is the fear on the part of many Republicans of appearing in the least bit "anti-labor." If a GOP candidate goes before a union audience or into a workers' neighborhood and espouses a position at odds with the labor leadership, this fearful feeling seems to run, he will then be publicly branded "anti-labor" and will have lost all hope of getting a substantial union vote.

A demonstration of this fear in action crept into the press in May, 1967. Casting about for issues that could carry him—he hoped—to the White House, George Romney launched a trial balloon of sorts when in several speeches he denounced a handful of union leaders (including the Reuther brothers) for their demands for increased wages, which had led directly to higher consumer prices and could lead, ultimately, to inflation. After one Romney speech pursuing this wholly logical line of reasoning, the *Washington Post* quoted a "GOP leader" as moaning, "The last thing the Republican Party needs these days is to look as if it is anti-union." And nothing more was heard from Romney on the subject of union bosses and labor-caused inflation.[5]

The fact that union members are *also* consumers and react as sharply to higher prices as any citizen, and that they do not want inflation no matter who causes it, was lost on this "GOP leader" and others who identify with his fears. They see criticism of any labor figure or any labor policy as an attack on all labor and proceed to interpret this in terms of lost votes.

This plainly need not be the case. While in the House, Bob Griffin was the co-author of what some labor leaders called "the worst piece of anti-labor legislation in the century," yet, during his '66 campaign, he carefully explained how the Landrum-Griffin bill served to protect the rank-and-file worker from abuse and dishonesty on the part of his union bosses; Griffin's campaign was not anti-labor, but anti-labor corruption.

Similarly, Ronald Reagan's major labor issue in his gubernatorial race was a call for a secret ballot in all union policy decisions, a change which would allow the worker safely to express his true beliefs rather than have to face the intimidating experience of raising his hand or voice. Reagan was campaigning against the undue power invested in labor leaders—whom he publicly labeled "the self-anointed sultans of labor"—and his solution was no more radical than providing the worker with the same privacy in voting as is accorded voters in governmental elections.

The Republicans who quiver at the thought of COPE calling them "anti-labor" must realize that workingmen voters are as intelligent as any other variety. As GOP planner Potter says, "The workers are thinking people, they know what is going on, and they will vote for the candidate with the best approach to the issues." If a candidate goes to these voters, openly and honestly discussing the issues and their practical applications, the workers will respond accordingly and not think the GOP aspirant "anti-labor." All that becomes necessary is for the Republican candidate to be sure his position is made absolutely clear, and then distortion becomes either impossible or futile.

Another common misbelief lodged in the heads of some Republican leaders is that a GOP candidate must put on his "liberal image" when he campaigns among the rank-and-file, or, as it is often put, try to "out-Democrat" the opposition. Putting this fallacy to rest, GOP campaign director Potter says, "The Republican candidate doesn't necessarily have to be a liberal or a conservative, as the large union vote received by both Reagan and Romney indicates. The candidate has to get into areas where the workers live, he has to get an audience and exposure and tell the voters what he'll do on the issues."

Campaign Committee Chairman Bob Wilson explains the situation in a different manner:

"With a Republican trying to win the votes of workers, identity is more important than philosophy . . . Of course a conservative will have a hard time meeting the demands of labor leaders, but then so have a lot of liberal Republicans; the point is that any Republican will have a hard time meeting the demands of labor leaders, and they can't win their support unless they compromise their principles. But actually the workers don't care as much about the leaders' demands as they do their own problems, like taxes, high prices and so forth."

Potter used as an example in buttressing his argument the similar success of liberal Romney and conservative Reagan in winning a sizable labor vote; a better example might be to contrast the Reagan success with the apparent failure of another prominent liberal Republican, Mayor John Lindsay of New York City, to win labor support. Even after the youthful mayor settled New York subway workers' and teachers' strikes by awarding the largest contracts in city history, the *New York Times* was able to write in late 1967 of "the personal coolness that pervades relations between Mr. Lindsay and the bulk of the union hierarchy in the city."

The newspaper quoted a labor leader as saying that Lindsay "despises us and it comes through, no matter how friendly he pretends to be." The *Times* then placed this hostility in a political perspective, analyzing:

"New York's Democrats, who had been looking for John V. Lindsay's Achilles Heel ever since he got to City Hall 21 months ago, believe they have found it in his handling of muncipal labor relations."[6]

Such assessment, however, is predicated on the attitude of labor leaders in New York; it is thought that Lindsay got a great many rank-and-file votes in his 1965 election victory (although COPE endorsement was denied him) and the workers may still support him. Whether or not this support materializes when he seeks re-election, the Lindsay Lesson is that a Republican's appeal to the structured demands of the union bosses will most likely not reduce their pro-Democrat bias, or concurrent Republican hostility a bit.

The demands of the workingmen, on the other hand, are much more unstructured; they involve everyday matters that affect millions of citizens, not union members alone. Time was when union men were a tight-knit bunch—"solidarity forever" and one-for-all—but this attitude has passed on with the ghosts of Eugene Debs and Joe Hill. Workers today are affluent, successful citizens caught in the stream of a rapidly flowing society where cataclysmic changes can occur overnight; their politics are founded, more than anywhere else, on the application of day-to-day realities to their societal situation.

Political issues appealing to this situation and founded in the basic philosophy of one party can be as quick changing as the situation itself. They are many and varied, with some cropping up during the course of a campaign and others broad and inclusive enough to be applied over a period of years.

Rep. Wilson believes that "Republican candidates must go over the leaders' heads and appeal to the workers on their other interests, not as union members." Elaborating, the GOP spokesman lists possible issues in this category:

"A Republican could appeal to workers as hunters, by arguing against gun control laws; or as Legionaires, by stressing military preparedness;

another good issue is taxes, because a union man hates taxes as much as the business man; there's also the poverty program, because union men resent poverty workers making as much money as they do; and I don't think Republican candidates should avoid the open housing issue in labor areas, because there is more concern over these laws with home-owning workingmen probably than in any other group."

Senate GOP campaign strategist George Murphy agrees in essence with his House counterpart, albeit with a few new issue-twists. "The best issues a Republican candidate can use in getting union members to vote for him," observes Murphy, "is just to stress the overall lack of performance of the present Democratic Administration. Tell them about the high-cost-of-living, about how LBJ wants to raise taxes, and tell them about how he had mishandled the war in Vietnam and wasn't trying to win."

As for the special interest labor legislation, Murphy thinks that "Republican candidates should by all means talk about labor issues, but only as they affect the general public. Don't be afraid to say that no small group is entitled to special consideration if it would adversely affect the general public."

The experiences of Ronald Reagan and Bob Griffin offer specific labor campaign issues used successfully by GOP candidates. Both these men were able, first, to turn attacks on them by labor leaders to their advantage. In Griffin's case this involved getting opponent "Soapy" Williams to admit that, had he been in the Senate, he would have voted for the labor-denounced Landrum-Griffin bill.

The attack on the aspiring California Governor involved the emotional right-to-work issue and the candidate's stand on it. "Ronald Reagan is for Union Busting Right To Work Laws," trumpeted labor propaganda. Not so, said Reagan's labor backers, and they produced literature from California's 1958 right-to-work referendum campaign to prove it; as an officer of the Screen Actors Guild Reagan had campaigned against a state law, with his union saying right-to-work "can wreck your Guild and rob you of your professional benefits."

During the 1966 campaign Reagan reinforced this position by stating, "Right-to-work laws are too big a gun for the problem we're trying to solve," and then going on to propose alternative measures aimed at protecting the workingman's freedom. This open distortion by labor leaders and the ability of Reagan forces effectively to expose and counter it, were greatly responsible for the wide acceptance the Republican found among union members.

One positive labor proposal made by Griffin with wide appeal to union members concerned the administration by labor leaders of private pension plans for retired workers. Documenting how some unions use devious methods to prevent workers from getting a fair share of a pension plan, Griffin praised the concept of the plans (which are funded by workers and employers) but pointed out the need for close supervision:

"If private pension plans are part of the workers' wages—a saving for his future and security in his old age—they represent a strengthening of individualism and independence in an era of increasing dependence on government . . . there is need for precise language and stricter controls of how pension funds are handled, invested, and dispersed."

Among Griffin's suggestions toward this end was legislation preventing plan administrators from using assets for their own interests, guaranteeing benefits for a worker who changes jobs, requiring full disclosure of all the plan's financial operations and limiting the percentage of pension funds that can be invested in other enterprises.[7]

In the California campaign, Gov. Reagan balanced his opposition to right-to-work laws with a proposal for secret ballots in deciding union policy matters, including strike votes. "A union shop contract should be permitted," said Reagan in one speech, "but it does involve a certain amount of compulsion. Because I accept this degree of compulsion in trying to balance the rights of all involved, I believe there is an obligation to protect the worker who is required to join the union. It can be pretty hard for a member to decide to stand up or raise his hand at a union meeting in opposition to the leadership of the union."[8]

To insure collective bargaining rights, Reagan also proposed the establishment of a state labor-management board to handle all labor disputes. On another labor issue of special concern in California, Reagan backed the efforts of farm workers to organize in a union, with the understood stipulation that these workers would not be able to take any action preventing the harvesting of perishable crops.

Although Ronald Reagan was one Republican candidate who did not support right-to-work as a campaign issue, several proponents of the law used it with some effect in 1966 campaigns where congressmen favoring repeal of 14(b) were defeated. "In every campaign where the public stand of the candidates was explained to the electorate," said the National Right to Work Committee following the elections, "voters overwhelmingly rejected the advocates of compulsory unionism."

Specific races used by the committee to support this contention included the victories of Republican representatives Sam Steiger of Arizona, Sherman Lloyd in Utah, William Henry Harrison in Wyoming, William Scott in Virginia, and the four GOP candidates who defeated Iowa incumbents who had voted for repeal.

"Not only does the elimination of compulsory unionism strike at what we feel is a root cause of major political and economic problems," the Right to Work Committee summarized, "but it *is* an issue which can be presented in terms to which widespread public support can be rallied."[9]

The committee's analysis and documentation offer convincing arguments for the political potential of this issue—in 1966. The House vote on repeal of 14(b) and the Senate filibuster took place amidst great public controversy in 1965 and early '66; they were still in the voters' minds as they listened to the candidates and cast their ballots in November, 1966. Whether or not the issue will "wear" well enough to have impact in 1968 is another question. (But if fear of alienating workingmen is a possible reason for avoiding the right-to-work issue, it must be remembered that in the Kraft Poll of AFL-CIO members only 54 percent said they favored repeal of 14(b).)

If the right-to-work question is not a feasible issue in 1968, there are certainly many others that can be used by COPE opponents in attracting the labor vote. The best are probably those outlined by Rep. Wilson and Sen. Murphy: taxes, cost-of-living, open housing, Vietnam, or, as George Murphy sums it up, the "overall lack of performance" on the part of the Democrats. Indeed, the Republicans are formulating a long and impressive list of criticisms to present to the Democrats in '68, and among them there surely should be plenty to attract a sizable workingman vote for effective GOP candidates.

Meanwhile, however, COPE is not exactly standing still. 1968, the COPE strategists realize, could well be a sweeping "Republican year," with the GOP taking the presidency and a majority in the House of Representatives. With the large share of labor leadership still wedded to the candidates and politics of the Democratic Party's liberal wing, organized labor will go to almost any extreme to prevent this from happening.

At the same time, COPE has demonstrated it is not sure what course to take or what strategy will work, and the result has been increasing signs of desperation. As 1968 approached, it was almost possible to see the symbolic fingers of COPE reaching for the "panic button."

A significant finding of the Kraft Poll concerned the attitude of union members toward legislation endorsed by the AFL-CIO. The results actually released by the federation showed members giving support to a long list of programs (e.g., truth-in-lending, water and air pollution control) that were relatively insignificant yet emotion-tinged (would any union member raise his voice in *favor* of polluting water or air?) and giving support to other issues (e.g., higher minimum wages and improved workmen's compensation) normally expected to receive rank-and-file backing.

Among the results the AFL-CIO chose to make public only one issue was listed—open housing—on which the membership position was contrary to that of the leadership. Yet COPE director Al Barkan could write that the poll showed "some uncertainty and unease among unionists, notably concerning jobs and economic security, some areas of civil rights and Vietnam. . . ."[10] Why weren't the results on these questions made public at the same time as the others? Obviously, COPE was trying to keep something from someone.

Whatever the reasons for the mystery shrouding the Kraft Poll, COPE quickly reacted in a fairly typical and not unexpected manner, as its leaders stepped up the old standby tactics of propaganda and hard-core organizing. Nothing changed appreciably in either COPE's approach to the 1968 elections or in the AFL-CIO's stand on liberal issues.

The first reaction was an attempt to dispel the disillusionment with LBJ which COPE had found among the union membership. Throughout 1967 the bi-weekly "Memo" and other COPE propaganda concentrated as much on promoting Lyndon Johnson as they did on attacking the usual Republican-conservative targets.

When LBJ declined renomination in March, 1968, and AFL-CIO President Meany swung his support to Vice President Hubert Humphrey, COPE tagged obediently behind—although no attempt was made to determine which of the three Democratic presidential candidates was preferred by the 14.3 million AFL-CIO members. The COPE "Memo" issue which carried Meany's endorsement (as a lead article) also contained a front page column full of Humphrey quotes lauding the Great Society.

COPE did not miss a step. It continued propagandizing for the liberal legislation proposed by successive Democratic Administrations and, with Lyndon Johnson out, COPE just inserted the name of Hubert Humphrey and kept going. There was no time to stop and reflect, for a commitment had to be met.

COPE's post-1966 propaganda efforts on behalf of the Democratic Administration reached new levels of urgency. The committee knew it had a job to do in boosting the stock of the Great Society, its creator LBJ and heir apparent HHH, before November, 1968, rolled around; it had to justify to the membership a long line of legislative programs and high-spending activities that have worked to the detriment of union members, and COPE had also to explain away the fact that all this liberal legislation had done precious little to prevent decay of American cities or increased rates of crime.

As 1967 wore on and the '68 campaign year began, a concurrent theme appeared in COPE's propaganda, one which soon came to predominate over the pro-LBJ "line." This was aimed at warning union members of the consequences of a Republican presidential victory, or GOP congressional gains, of the severe "labor-curbing" legislation that would supposedly result once the purported rightist-business-congressional conservative "conspiracy" took power. In effect, COPE was attempting to frighten the rank-and-file into backing labor-approved candidates.

Undoubtedly COPE will continue to plump hard for the Administration legislative program, trying as always to portray liberal Democrats as the personificaion of All That Is Good. Knowing, however, that this positive approach might be risky if left all alone, COPE is "covering itself" by coming up with a suitable—and louder—attack on the opposition; if it cannot sell the Democrats as Shining Virtue, COPE hopes to make them at least the lesser of two evils.

One thing the AFL-CIO members' poll did appear to show was that rank-and-filers were demonstrating increasing signs of intelligence, independence and selectivity in their approach to politics and political issues; few have "gone over" to become loyal Republicans, but there is evidence showing union members now take a good hard look at the issues and candidates before voting, and do not just blindly follow their leaders' instructions. If this assessment is accurate, it would not seem that COPE's desperation propaganda, hauling out the shopworn image of Big Business ogres trying to "cut labor's throat," will have much effect.

What this propaganda does indicate of COPE—and all of the organized labor hierarchy—is that, rather than reconsider its position in light of a moderation in the rank-and-file's liberalism, it will only try to obscure and confuse issues in an attempt to counteract this drift, through propaganda.

One way in which COPE did decide to act positively on the poll was to set up political organizations in the suburbs. The Kraft survey had shown that 50 percent of union members lived in the suburbs, including 75 percent of those in the burgeoning under-30 age bracket. Moreover, the poll indicated the suburbanite workers were more interested in local and neighborhood issues than in the national programs and candidates on which COPE had been concentrating; COPE's erstwhile liberal clichés, it was found, had little appeal to these union voters, who tended to view national issues in light of their own economic security and social standing.

Here the AFL-CIO's reaction was not to re-examine its views in trying to regain the support of this large bloc of members, but to expand COPE's organizing strategy with an eye to the members' interest in local issues. COPE's solution to the problem, in other words, was not substantive, it was tactical.

COPE's advice to local organizers was to take "an issue that is current and is hot in the community"—it could be as small as an unrepaired street light—and throw up an *ad hoc* committee to fight on the issue; once this issue passed from the scene, and COPE had demonstrated it was "on the suburbanites' side," the *ad hoc* organization becomes a permanent COPE political operation. Such an arrangement may be a brilliant organizing tactic, but it remains that for COPE leaders issues that serve the needs of the people are secondary to the greater objective of imposing a COPE apparatus on the neighborhood.[11]

Again, the new-found independence, economic security and local concern of these union men may be going against the labor political operatives. Rep. Bob Wilson thinks so, believing that "the thing that will work against COPE's new move to the suburbs is affluence; the union members in the suburbs just won't go for COPE candidates if the candidates are against their interests."

(From a purely partisan standpoint, Wilson adds that he's "glad to see COPE starting in the suburbs; they will be wasting a lot of money that might be better spent somewhere else. It's a strategic error on their part, but I don't mind that.")

The workingman in the suburbs is more concerned, like the junior executive next door, with his mortgage payments, children's education and whether or not the sewer system is up to par, than he is with the frequently irrelevant (for him) national legislation promoted by the AFL-CIO. COPE, however, cannot afford this view. Organizational force has been its trump card since its founding and COPE is responding to this new situation in the best way it knows how.

A similar COPE response to the Kraft Poll was found in its reaction to the discovery that younger union members were less enthusiastic than their elders in supporting, and working for, labor's political-legislative goals. Here COPE reacted by institutionalizing its "youth arm"; the committee had always encouraged young people to help out in its activities, but in 1968 this random participation was to be organized on the same concentrated scale as COPE's many other operations.

One facet of this "youth brigade" was Teen-COPE, using members' sons and daughters in such routine committee projects as voter registration, propaganda distribution and Election Day telephoning. A more ambitious undertaking was COPE's alliance with the United States Youth Council, an organization which is to supply volunteers from its several member-groups for more sensitive political projects; COPE is counting on the Youth Council campaigners to do the bulk of the politicking for labor candidates in low-income wards of several large cities in "swing" states.

Both these youth-oriented innovations are calculated to stir up the interest of young AFL-CIO members in COPE's activities, and they may succeed. It remains, however, that here again COPE responded to a new situation—disenchantment among young unionists—with an old tactic—organization.

The polls and recent electoral experience have tended to indicate to COPE that the old methods are no longer working the way they are supposed to, and that the Democrats are in trouble. COPE's immediate response was, essentially, more of the same—more propaganda, more organizing; more words, more plans. And, amidst the frantic plotting and frenzied propagandizing, there were signs of COPE becoming a little desperate.

Desperate, perhaps, but not defeated. Despite the cautious skepticism toward COPE's new organizing and propagandizing efforts displayed by Wilson and other GOP spokesmen, it is very possible that the labor politicos will succeed. These tactics are, and have been for decades, their stock-in-trade, and the attempt to positively relate the current personal concerns of union members to the broader liberal issues backed by the AFL-CIO may be accomplished.

More important, despite the confidence shown by Wilson, Murphy and other GOP strategists that Republican candidates can win more rank-and-file votes, there is the real prospect that the Republicans will make no effort to do any such thing. Most of the new programs and strategies emanating from Republican sources seem to emulate the nature of those coming out of COPE: more of the same. No concerted effort has been made by GOP national officials to work out a plan dealing with how candidates can approach rank-and-file voters; there have been no guides offered as to formulating issues, exposing candidates, explaining positions or doing any of the little "nuts-'n'-bolts" things necessary to round up workingmen's votes.

The burden of such activity rests with the Republican National Committee, but here is found only indifference toward the possibility of winning more labor votes. The RNC's library contains few books relevant to the labor political situation, its files on labor are woefully inadequate and out-of-date, its research department makes no attempt to analyze voting trends in labor wards or districts, and staff officials speak of the union rank-and-file in the vaguest generalities and look to the future with bewilderment, mumbling clichés.

As a former GOP leader in a state where labor was frequently a powerful political force, RNC chairman Ray Bliss (from Ohio) would be expected to rectify this situation and pay a little attention to helping Republican candidates make inroads among the union rank-and-file. From what is visible, this has not been the case.

The Republican Senate Campaign Committee operates with a small staff, concentrating on disseminating financial contributions and research material for speeches. Its leaders are aware of the potential union rank-and-file vote for GOP senatorial candidates and do assist in developing issues and approaches to win this vote; because of its material limitations, however, there can be no concerted program in this direction.

The liveliest awareness in the GOP hierarchy is found in the Republican Congressional Campaign Committee, chaired by Bob Wilson and directed by Lee Potter. Their large staff is on top of the labor political situation, cataloguing union contributions to Democratic candidates, preparing research material on issues with rank-and-file appeal, instructing GOP candidates on methods of exposure, analyzing labor voting patterns in marginal congressional districts, and performing several other functions which can help candidates win labor votes and get .elected to Congress. But this industry benefits only House aspirants.

(The National Committee could certainly take a few lessons from its congressional affiliate, but a long-standing, absurd feeling of rivalry on the part of RNC staffers toward the Congressional Campaign Committee has kept them from learning anything.)

Independent of the Republican Party are organizations such as the American Medical Political Action Committee and the Business-Industry Political Action Committee. These are autonomous groups who assist GOP candidates with the same frequency that COPE aids liberal Democrats (although all similarities in operation, resources and expertise start and stop right there). These two groups—and they are the major pro-GOP non-party factions—do not yet have access to the funds or multiple staff skills necessary to combat COPE and, both having been formed since 1960, have not accumulated the experience and savvy that is essential in supplementing party activities and organizing on their own.

Such was the situation of the Republican Party vis-à-vis the rank-and-file union members as the presidential year of 1968 dawned. GOP spokesmen and strategists had many ideas on getting the votes of workingmen, but very little action had followed.

America's unionized workingmen may now be ready to give Republican candidates a full hearing, perhaps vote for them, but it is a vote that must be sought after and fought for. COPE's singular purpose is to pursue the votes of AFL-CIO members on behalf of liberal Democratic candidates, and any effort to counter this drive by Republicans must be equally forceful and single-minded; to rely on a scatter-shot approach, hoping to lure rank-and-file votes along with hundreds of thousands of others with the same blanket appeal, is downright poor politics.

When he first joins a union (in many cases before this) the workingman is subject to a continual broadside of pro-Democrat literature, speeches and man-to-man conversations with his labor leaders; he and his vote are patronized, romanticized, cajoled and catered to, with the result that the union members have provided labor political machines with their muscle and liberal Democrats with their victories.

If union members are now moving away from this position and exercising more independence and selectivity in choice of candidates and attitudes toward issues, it will not be a rapid movement, nor revolutionary in scope. They may vote for one Republican, then revert to the pro-Democrat form on the rest of the ticket; they may agree with Republicans on a stronger stand in Vietnam, yet succumb to liberal clichés on social welfare issues.

In short, for the GOP to win a significant share of these votes will take assiduous politicking and an imaginative, realistic program aimed specifically in this direction. It is by no means guaranteed that COPE has "lost touch" with these voters, that the candidates and issues it promotes have forever lost their attraction, or that the 1966 defeats of labor-backed candidates were anything but a temporary setback.

If, superficially, the old COPE strategies are no longer working as before, the Republican Party has yet to demonstrate it has anything better in mind. Upsetting any near-parity of political power that may exist between the two forces is the mere fact of COPE's experience and test-proven ability in dealing with membership problems that might arise; the GOP, meanwhile, is starting from scratch, and starting late.

COPE can be combated and with effective planning its candidates can be defeated on their home ground, the labor wards. A handful of 1966 races and others scattered in the past have proved this. But the effort must be year-round, day-in-and-day-out, if it is to succeed.

Days after the polls closed in November, 1966, COPE was telling its constituency: "The Time to Start For '68 Is *NOW!*" It has been going ever since, and only when the polls close in November, 1968, will the COPE leaders know what good it has all done.

The AFL-CIO's Committee On Political Education is a continuing organization. It has been in operation full-time since the federation merger in 1955 and, before that date, its progenitors had been continuing since the turn of the century. For COPE, as with all organized labor, there is more at stake in an election than the fortunes of a single candidate: it views the political arena as the place where the fortunes of the labor movement are decided. In many, many ways the voting booth has replaced the bargaining table as the battleground for organized labor, and COPE—as its mightiest warrior—is dedicated to protecting and enlarging upon the fortunes at stake.

At times COPE may have stumbled, but it has risen to fight—and win—again. It is as worthy an opponent as any political candidate, organization or philosophy could ask for. To combat COPE—to cope with it—demands as mighty an effort as it is capable of producing. It can be done.

# Notes

## CHAPTER ONE

[1] James L. McDevitt, July, 1957; quoted in Appellees Brief presented to U.S. Supreme Court, March 16, 1960, in case of International Association of Machinists, *et al.* v. S.B. Street, *et al.*

[2] *Detroit Free Press,* June 2, 1966.

[3] *UAW Solidarity* (official publication of the United Auto Workers, AFL-CIO), November, 1966.

[4] *Washington Post,* November 11, 1966.

[5] *Time,* November 11, 1966.

[6] *Time,* November 25, 1966.

[7] *Washington Post,* February 16, 1967.

[8] Estimates of labor congressional strength from *Nation's Business,* August, 1964. According to the publication, the figures were compiled "from voting records published by union political organizations."

[9] Johnson letter and Meany response reprinted in *AFL-CIO News,* November 28, 1964.

[10] *Time,* November 17, 1967.

[11] *Washington Post,* November 8, 1967.

## CHAPTER TWO

[1] Private correspondence from John O. Davis III, assistant editor, American Institute of Public Opinion, Princeton, N.J., December 3, 1963.

[2] *New York Times,* December 8, 1963.

[3] *Washington Post,* September 6, 1965.

[4] *Wall Street Journal,* March 1, 1967.

[5] *Village Voice* (Greenwich Village, New York City, N.Y.), December 1, 1966.

[6] "What Can The Young Believe?" reprint of Kennedy speech in Philadelphia, February 24, 1967, *New Republic,* March 11, 1967.

[7] Andrew Kopkind, "Repeal of 14(b)—Mildest Filibuster in History," *New Republic,* October 16, 1965.

## CHAPTER THREE

[1] Vaughn Davis Bornet, *Labor Politics In A Democratic Republic* (Washington, D.C.: Spartan Books, 1964), p. 31.

[2] Joseph Gaer, *The First Round: The Story Of The CIO Political Action Committee* (New York: Duell, Sloan and Pearce, 1944), p. XII.

[3] *Newsweek,* September 25, 1944.

[4] This set the tone for the future.

[5] *Union Political Activity Spans 230 Years of U.S. History,* COPE publication no. 106, reprinted from article in *American Federationist,* May, 1960.

[6] Bornet, p. 31.

[7] Bornet, p. 32, from Gompers' annual report in *AFL Proceedings,* 1908.

[8] Bornet, p. 27.

[9] Upton Sinclair, *The League For Industrial Democracy: Forty Years Of Education* (New York: LID, 1945), pp. 15-16, quoted by Philip M. Crane, *The Democrat's Dilemma* (Chicago: Regnery, 1964), p. 106.

[10] Fenner Brockway, *Inside The Left* (London, 1942), p. 229, quoted in Crane, p. 104.

[11] Arthur Schlesinger, Jr., *The Politics Of Upheaval* (Boston: Houghton Mifflin Co., 1960), p. 563.

[12] The ten expelled unions were: United Mine Workers, Amalgamated Clothing Workers, International Ladies' Garment Workers, United Textile Workers, Oilfield, Gaswell, and Refinery Workers, Mine, Mill and Smelter Workers, Flat Glass Workers, Amalgamated Association of Iron, Steel and Tin Workers, United Auto Workers, United Rubber Workers.

[13] *Newsweek*, September 25, 1944.

[14] Schlesinger, p. 593.

[15] Gaer, p. 53.

[16] Gaer, pp. 60-61, from report by Philip Murray to CIO convention, November 1-5, 1943.

[17] Philip Murray, "Labor's Political Aims," *America*, February, 1944, quoted in Gaer, pp. 67-73 (also reprinted by PAC in CIO publication no. 102).

[18] Special Committee on Un-American Activities, *Report On The CIO Political Action Committee* (Washington: U.S. House of Representatives, 1944), quoted from text of Earl Browder speech to 1944 CPUSA convention.

[19] William E. Mullins, "I Object To My Union In Politics," *Reader's Digest*, September, 1944.

[20] Louis Waldman, "Will The CIO Capture The Democratic Party?" *Saturday Evening Post*, August 26, 1944.

[21] Gaer, p. 173.

[22] In the 1937 New York City elections, Sidney Hillman and the Clothing Workers had supported FDR's 1944 GOP opponent, Gov. Thomas E. Dewey, for District Attorney.

[23] *Newsweek*, September 25, 1944.

[24] Gaer, p. 110.

[25] *Newsweek*, November 13, 1944.

[26] *New Republic*, December 4, 1944.

[27] *U.S. News & World Report*, February 24, 1956.

[28] *Ibid.*

[29] *Business Week*, September 24, 1955.

[30] *Business Week*, November 3, 1956.

[31] Anonymous, *Fraternally Yours, James L. McDevitt: The Portrait Of A Man And A Movement* (Harrisburg: Pennsylvania Federation of Labor, AFL-CIO, 1956).

[32] *Business Week*, September 22, 1956.

[33] *Time*, September 10, 1956.

[34] *Ibid.*

CHAPTER FOUR

[1] Lester Velie, *Labor U.S.A.* (New York: Harper & Brothers, 1958), p. 20.

[2] *Time*, March 21, 1955 (Meany cover story).

[3] *Ibid.*

[4] *Ibid.*

[5] Lewis incident reported in *Time* article and Velie, p. 16.

[6] *Time, op. cit.*

[7] *Newsweek,* November 19, 1962.

[8] *Washington Post,* December 10, 1965.

[9] David Saposs, *Communism In American Unions* (New York: McGraw-Hill Co., 1959), p. 202.

[10] *New York World-Telegram & Sun,* March 24, 1964.

[11] *Washington Post,* December 10, 1965.

[12] *Ibid.*

[13] *New York Times,* December 30, 1966.

[14] Harry Bernstein, "Labor's Plump Man Makes Stranger Out of Reuther," reprinted from *Los Angeles Times* in *Washington Post,* February 26, 1967.

[15] *New York Times,* December 8, 1967.

[16] *Washington Post,* December 4, 1967.

[17] *New York Times,* December 10, 1967.

[18] *Ibid.*

[19] Fred J. Cook, *Building the House of Labor: Walter Reuther* (New York: Encyclopaedia Britannica Press, 1963), p. 18.

[20] The Reuther letter was originally printed in *The Challenge,* July, 1934; this was a Socialist youth publication of which May Wolfson (later Mrs. Walter Reuther) was managing editor and Andrew Biemiller (later chief lobbyist for the AFL-CIO) was contributing editor. Fred Cook does not mention the letter anywhere in his friendly biography of Reuther.

[21] Cook, p. 116.

[22] *Ibid.*

[23] Cook, p. 119.

[24] Eldorous L. Dayton, *Walter Reuther: The Autocrat of the Bargaining Table* (New York: Devin-Adair Co., 1958), p. 157.

[25] Dayton, p. 172.

[26] Dayton, p. 173.

[27] Dayton, p. 180, quoted from Wechsler article in *Harper's,* March, 1948.

[28] Dayton, p. 192.

[29] For a good example of liberal criticism of Jay Lovestone, see Dan Kurzman, "Lovestone's Cold War," *New Republic,* June 25, 1966.

[30] Quotes *re* ILO boycott from *Newsweek,* June 27, 1966.

[31] *Washington Post,* June 11, 1966.

[32] *Ibid.,* August 27, 1966.

[33] *Ibid.,* November 15, 1966.

[34] Excerpts from UAW administrative letter published in *New York Times,* December 30, 1966; subsequent quotations of letter from this source.

[35] Thomas W. Braden, "I'm Glad The CIA Is Immoral," *Saturday Evening Post,* May 20, 1967.

[36] *Washington Post,* May 8, 1967.

[37] *Detroit Free Press,* February 17, 1967.

[38] *Newsweek,* January 1, 1968.

[39] *Washington Post,* January 9, 1968.

[40] *US News & World Report,* February 20, 1967.

[41] *New York Times,* December 10, 1967.

[42] *Washington Post,* February 26, 1967.

[43] *Ibid.,* September 25, 1967.

[44] *Ibid.,* February 26, 1967.

[45] Anonymous, *Fraternally Yours, James L. McDevitt: The Portrait Of A Man And A Movement* (Harrisburg: Pennsylvania Federation of Labor, AFL-CIO, 1956).

[46] *Ibid.*

[47] *Ibid.*

[48] *Ibid.*

[49] *Ibid.*

[50] *Ibid.*

[51] *Ibid.*

[52] *Ibid.*

[53] The biography opens with the statement: "The features one notices first in James L. McDevitt . . . are soft grey eyes and a square, decisive chin." The Pennsylvania AFL-CIO also published a biography of the then president of the Steelworkers called *David McDonald: Man Of Steel*. It was so overly flattering that an embarrassed Man of Steel had the books recalled and burned.

[54] *Fraternally Yours.*

[55] *Ibid.*

[56] *Ibid.*

[57] At a meeting of local union officials in Hartford, Conn., July 19, 1956; quoted in "The Real Aims of Union Leadership," National Association of Manufacturers, April, 1958.

[58] *Fraternally Yours.*

[59] "Unions Push Biggest Political Campaign," *Nation's Business*, August, 1964.

[60] *Ibid.*

[61] Alexander Barkan, "COPE Needs Foot Soldiers To Achieve Election Success," *Seafarer's Log* (publication of Seafarer's Union, AFL-CIO), July 24, 1964.

[62] *Ibid.*

## CHAPTER FIVE

[1] Edward Swayduck, "The Greeks Had A Word For It," reprinted as paid advertisement in *Washington Post,* December 19, 1966.

[2] *Ibid.*

[3] Bates finally submitted his council resignation in September, 1967.

[4] *Sioux Falls Argus-Leader,* May 24, 1959.

## CHAPTER SIX

[1] John A. Grimes, "Labor's Image," *Wall Street Journal,* March 1, 1967.

[2] "Memo From COPE," February 6, 1967.

[3] Grimes, *op. cit.*

[4] "Memo," October 17, 1966.

[5] "Memo," April 17, 1967.

[6] James P. Gannon, "Labor Leaders Alarmed By Diminishing Support Among Rank And File," *Wall Street Journal,* July 6, 1967.

[7] Alexander Barkan, "The Union Member: Profile And Attitudes," *American Federationist,* August, 1967.

[8] Sidney Lens, "Reuther Vs. Meany: Open Break," *Commonweal,* February 17, 1967.

[9] Grimes, *op. cit.*

[10] Lens, *op. cit.*

[11] A.H. Raskin, "Absent Peacemaker in the Meany-Reuther Split," *New York Times,* February 6, 1967.

[12] Raymond Moley, "Political Unions' Woes," *Newsweek,* December 19, 1966.

[13] A.H. Raskin, "Why Labor Doesn't Follow Its Leaders," *New York Times,* January 8, 1967.

[14] Arthur Kornhauser, Harold Sheppard and Albert J. Mayer, *When Labor Votes: A Study Of Auto Workers* (New York: University Books, 1956).

[15] William E. Mullins, "I Object To My Union In Politics," *Reader's Digest,* September, 1944.

[16] Quoted in editorial, *Saturday Evening Post,* December 29, 1956.

[17] All quotes *re* Street case from Appellees Brief filed with U.S. Supreme Court March 16, 1960, by Appellees' attorneys of the law firm Gambrell, Harlan, Russell, Maye and Richardson, Atlanta, Georgia. The author here wishes to express his gratitude to the attorneys for making the extremely useful Street case literature available.

[18] Quotes from this incident from press conference transcript published in *Inside Michigan,* February, 1956, and reprinted in pamphlet, "The Rank And File Speak Out On Political Action," published by Republican State Central Committee of Michigan, Lansing, 1956.

[19] "Bad News For Union Bosses," *Nation's Business,* December, 1965.

[20] "Meet COPE's Oldest Volunteer," *UAW Solidarity,* December, 1966.

[21] Quoted in Street case Appellees brief, *op. cit.,* as written in March, 1956.

[22] "Memo," April 17, 1967.

[23] Alexander Barkan, "We Can Do The Job," *American Federationist,* May, 1958.

[24] All presidential vote statistics, unless otherwise indicated, from *Selected Presidential Returns—1964 Elections,* COPE Research Department publication, March, 1965.

[25] John C. O'Brien, "Political Poll On Reliability," *Philadelphia Inquirer,* October 23, 1962.

[26] "Unions Push Biggest Political Campaign," *Nation's Business,* August, 1964.

## CHAPTER SEVEN

[1] Fay Calkins, *The CIO and the Democratic Party* (Chicago: University of Chicago Press, 1952).

[2] *Washington Post,* March 11, 1965.

[3] *Philadelphia Inquirer,* May 18, 1967.

[4] *Steel Labor,* (publication of United Steelworkers of America, AFL-CIO), July 13, 1963.

[5] *Michigan CIO News,* March 17, 1948, quoted by Calkins, p. 115.

[6] *New York Times,* February 6, 1949, quoted by Calkins, p. 120.

[7] *Detroit News,* September 28, 1950, quoted by Calkins, p. 123.

[8] Calkins, p. 142.

[9] *New York Times,* April 16, 1967.

[10] "Unions Push Biggest Political Campaign," *Nation's Business,* August, 1964.

[11] Calkins, p. 67.

[12] Calkins, p. 66.

[13] *Nation's Business.*

[14] "Labor Turned Out the Vote for 'Keef'," *AFL-CIO News,* August 20, 1960.

[15] "Union Goal for November 8: Every Member A Voter," *U.S. News & World Report,* October 10, 1960.

[16] COPE publication no. 127.

[17] City directories are available from R.L. Polk & Co., Publishers, listed in the telephone book of every city for which a directory is published. Cost varies according to city population. (For a comparison, the Washington, D.C., directory costs $135.)

[18] COPE publication no. 158c.

[19] *Wall Street Journal,* October 11, 1966.

[20] *Ibid.*

[21] *New York Times,* February 6, 1966.

[22] *Washington Post,* February 24, 1966.

[23] *Philadelphia Inquirer,* May 21, 1967.

[24] *Washington Post,* September 8, 1966.

[25] *Congressional Record,* June 4, 1964, p. 12309. Rep. Long did vote for repeal of 14(b) when it came up.

[26] *1966 Congressional Staff Directory,* ed. Charles Brownson (Washington: The Congressional Staff Directory, 1966).

[27] *New York Times,* August 7, 1966.

[28] Private correspondence with author, December 6, 1966.

[29] Raymond Moley, "AFL-CIO COPE in 1962," *Newsweek,* October 22, 1962.

[30] *Nation's Business,* August, 1964.

[31] All information on COPE 1966 endorsements from COPE Research Department document, November, 1966.

[32] "Labor's Love Lost," *Time,* April 1, 1966.

[33] Peter McGavin, executive secretary of AFL-CIO Maritime Trades Department, quoted in *Washington Post,* February 19, 1966.

[34] *Time,* April 1, 1966.

[35] *Washington Evening Star,* April 2, 1966.

[36] *Ibid.,* March 26, 1966.

[37] "Memo from Cope," March 7, 1966.

[38] *Washington Post,* February 22, 1967.

[39] *AFL-CIO News,* September 15, 1962.

[40] *Ibid.,* June 6, 1964.

[41] From a 1956 issue of *Labor,* quoted in Street Case Appellees Brief, filed with U.S. Supreme Court, March 16, 1960.

[42] *Detroit News,* September 28, 1966.

[43] Brock Brower, "Puzzling Front Runner," *Life,* May 5, 1967.

[44] *Wall Street Journal,* July 29, 1960.

[45] *Washington Post,* July 30, 1964.

[46] *New York Times,* May 22, 1966.

[47] "Memo From COPE," December 27, 1965.

[48] Arthur Kornhauser, Harold Sheppard and Albert J. Mayer, *When Labor Votes: A Study Of Auto Workers* (New York: University Books, 1956), p. 118.

[49] Quotation used in COPE's "Programs of Progress" literature (see p. 243).

[50] "The Target Is You," COPE publication no. 130c.

[51] Produced by COPE, 1964.

[52] *Washington Post,* August 11, 1964.

[53] According to *1964 Congressional Quarterly Almanac,* "Goldwater urged that the NATO supreme commander be delegated authority to order the use of tactical nuclear weapons available to American forces in Western Europe." The White House later reluctantly admitted the NATO chief already had this authority.

[54] "They're Playing for Keeps," COPE publication no. 163c.

[55] *Steel Labor,* May, 1967.

[56] *Ibid.,* October, 1966.

[57] "Memo From COPE," November 1, 1965.

[58] "Memo," February 7, 1966.

[59] "Memo," October 4, 1965.

[60] "Memo," April 4, 1966.

[61] "Memo," October 17, 1966.

[62] See *Washington Post,* November 4, 1966.

[63] *New York Times,* August 7, 1966.

[64] *Washington Post,* August 1 and 2, 1966.

[65] *UAW Solidarity,* November, 1966.

[66] *Chicago Sun-Times,* August 24, 1966.

[67] John Dreiske, "A Misleading Picture," *Chicago Sun-Times,* August 17, 1966. See also *The Machinist,* official publication of the IAM, August 4, 1966, for copy of photograph and other anti-Percy material.

[68] October 21, 1966 issue. For related material, see Rowland Evans and

Robert Novak, "Labor and the Democrats," *Washington Post*, December 5, 1966.

[69] *Perry County Press*, November 2, 1966.

[70] Private correspondence with author, December 27, 1966.

[71] Frederick R. Shedd and George S. Odlarne, *Political Content of Labor Union Periodicals* (Ann Arbor: University of Michigan Press, 1960).

[72] Henry Teipel Associates, *A Study of Public Opinion in Ramsey County* (St. Paul, Minn., 1963).

[73] Guy Nunn, "Friday PM Wrapup," reprinted in *Congressional Record*, December 17, 1963, p. A7671, from collection of Nunn radio broadcasts published by UAW, December 16, 1963.

[74] *AFL-CIO News*, October 1, 1966.

[75] AFL-CIO publication no. 22a, as revised May, 1964 (available from AFL-CIO Pamphlet Division, $.25 per copy).

[76] *AFL-CIO News*, January 28, 1967 (the weekly *News* reprinted one Morgan broadcast in each issue).

[77] *Ibid.*, March 18, 1967.

[78] *Washington Post*, September 23, 1966.

[79] "Golly Gee, California is a Strange Place," by the editors, *Ramparts*, October, 1966.

[80] "Memo From COPE," November 14, 1966.

[81] "Memo," January 9, 1967.

[82] "Memo," October 2, 1967.

[83] "Memo," December 25, 1967.

[84] *Wall Street Journal*, December 13, 1967.

[85] "Memo," February 20, 1967.

[86] "Memo," May 3, 1965, reprinted from *American Federationist*, May, 1965.

[87] *Philadelphia Inquirer*, May 21, 1967.

[88] "Unions Open New Attack on Conservatives," *Nation's Business*, March, 1963.

[89] *Ibid.*

[90] Confidential report from COPE Research Department, November, 1964.

[91] Walter Pincus, "Labor Mapping Plan For 1964 Campaign," *Washington Evening Star*, August 3, 1964.

[92] *Wall Street Journal*, September 26, 1966.

[93] Stephen Shadegg, *How To Win An Election: The Art of Political Victory* (New York: Taplinger, 1964), pp. 71-77.

[94] "Meet The WADs," COPE publication no. 115.

[95] "Women's Activities Department Manual," COPE publication no. 58c.

[96] The Taft-Hartley Labor-Management Relations Act of 1947 reinforces this regulation on organized labor's spending, stipulating that union dues not be used for "political" purposes.

[97] Alexander Heard, *The Costs of Democracy* (Chapel Hill: University of North Carolina Press, 1960).

[98] Title 39, U.S. Code, Section 4452(d).

[99] *Report of the Executive Council of the AFL-CIO*, presented at the sixth AFL-CIO convention, San Francisco, December 9, 1965.

[100] *Washington Post*, September 1, 1966.

[101] "Union Political Activity Spans 230 Years of U.S. History," *American Federationist*, May, 1960.

[102] "Emil Mazey Reports," *UAW Solidarity*, June, 1967.

[103] Information *re* Street case taken from following: Appellees Briefs filed with U.S. Supreme Court March 16, 1960 and December 29, 1960, by appellees' attorneys, Gambrell, Harlan, Russell, Moye and Richardson, Atlanta, Ga.; Stipulation of Facts, signed by counsels for defendants and plaintiffs before trial; decision of U.S. Supreme Court, June 19, 1961.

[104] Walter Pincus, "Labor's Hidden Donations," *Washington Evening Star*, August 4, 1964. Pincus later moved to the rival *Washington Post*.

[105] "Memo From COPE," January 24, 1966.

[106] The reply to *that* answer will be found in this book's section on "Choosing a Candidate."

[107] *AFL-CIO COPE Register and Vote Manual,* COPE publication no. 127.

[108] Stanton Smith, coordinator of Tennessee AFL-CIO state and local central bodies, quoted in *AFL-CIO News,* August 20, 1960.


CHAPTER EIGHT


[1] *Des Moines Register,* July 6, 1965.

[2] Clifton Brock, *Americans for Democratic Action* (Washington: Public Affairs Press, 1962), p. 51.

[3] *New York Times,* January 15, 1954.

[4] John Herling, "Man Overboard," *Washington Daily News,* April 11, 1967.

[5] Quoted in NCEC brochure.

[6] NCEC's anti-McCarthy activities first reported in *Chicago Tribune,* July 22, 1954; Senator Flanders' admission appeared in *Congressional Record,* August 2, 1954.

[7] Statement by NCEC Chairman Sidney Scheuer, December 12, 1956, before Senate Special Committee to Investigate Political Activities, Lobbying and Campaign Contributions.

[8] Point, Texas.

[9] *Washington Post,* March 17, 1966.

[10] *New York Times,* March 18, 1965.

[11] "Memo From COPE," April 18, 1966.

[12] *Washington Post,* September 20, 1964.

[13] Walter Pincus, "Democrats Support Group Fighting For Medicare Plan," *Washington Evening Star,* May 1, 1964.

[14] *Senior Citizens News,* June, 1966.

[15] Kenneth O. Gilmore, "Let's Stop Exploiting People Over 65!" *Reader's Digest,* September, 1966.

[16] *Senior Citizens News,* October, 1965.

[17] *Time,* January 28, 1966.

[18] *Village Voice,* November 24, 1966.

[19] *Washington Post,* November 29, 1966.

[20] *Ibid.,* May 29, 1967.

[21] Roy R. Evans, Secretary-Treasurer Texas AFL-CIO, "The Labor Movement's Role," *Texas Observer,* September 1, 1967.

[22] Quoted in *Commentary,* February, 1964.

[23] *New York Times,* May 17, 1964.

[24] *Washington Post,* August 27, 1967.

[25] *Report of the AFL-CIO Executive Council* to the sixth AFL-CIO convention, December, 1965.

[26] Wesley McCune, *Ezra Taft Benson: Man With A Mission* (Washington: Public Affairs Press, 1958), quoted in *Facts For Farmers,* April, 1958.

[27] A copy of the controversial advertisement can be found in *Progressive,* April, 1966.

[28] Text of Morton remarks in *Congressional Record,* October 21, 1965, pp. 26948-26951.

[29] *Los Angeles Times,* October 31, 1965.

[30] *New York Times,* April 23, 1963.

[31] *Ibid.,* October 15, 1965.

[32] *Chicago Tribune,* September 13, 1965.

[33] *Washington Sunday Star,* October 18, 1965.

[34] Drew Pearson, "Right-Wing Radio-TV Probed," *Washington Post*, December 10, 1965.

[35] *GRI Report*, September 30, 1964.

[36] *New York Post*, March 3, 1965.

[37] *Christian Science Monitor*, November 21, 1966.

## CHAPTER NINE

[1] Ashmore's bill remained locked in committee throughout the First Session, 90th Congress, and there was little prospect for passage in the Second Session. Perhaps coincidentally, Rep. Ashmore decided to retire at the end of the 90th Congress.

[2] *New York Times*, August 31, 1967.

[3] *Ibid.*, August 27, 1967.

[4] *Washington Post*, January 31, 1967.

[5] *Ibid.*, May 11, 1967.

[6] *New York Times*, October 8, 1967.

[7] *Detroit News*, October 31, 1966.

[8] *Los Angeles Times*, September 18, 1966.

[9] Hugh Newton, Director of Information, National Right To Work Committee, "The Right To Work: A Political Asset," published by NRTWC, 1967.

[10] Alexander Barkan, "The Union Member: Profile and Attitudes," *American Federationist*, August, 1967.

[11] "New Frontier: Politics in the Suburbs," COPE publication no. 177c.

# Index